Also by Jean Lacouture:

EGYPT IN TRANSITION (*with Simonne Lacouture*)

VIETNAM: BETWEEN THE WARS

DE GAULLE

HO CHI MINH

THE DEMIGODS

NASSER

TRANSLATED FROM THE FRENCH

BY DANIEL HOFSTADTER

NASSER

a biography by

Jean Lacouture

SECKER & WARBURG
LONDON

First published in England 1973 by
Martin Secker & Warburg Limited
14 Carlisle Street, London W1V 6NN

Copyright © 1973 by Alfred A. Knopf, Inc.

Originally published in France as *Nasser*
by Editions du Seuil, Paris
Copyright © 1971 by Jean Lacouture

SBN: 436 24052 1

Contents

CONTENTS

Chronology

1922 Egypt's independence declared.

1924 *April:* The first parliament is elected with Zaghloul's Wafd party in the majority.
  November: The assassination of Sir Lee Stack, British commander-in-chief of the Egyptian army, causes Britain to tighten its grasp on Egypt.

1927 Death of Saad Zaghloul.

1936 Wafdist government of Nahas Pasha arranges for evacuation of Egypt by British with exception of Canal Zone.

1937 Same government obtains an agreement at the Montreux Conference ending the terms which limited Egypt's sovereignty.

1942 British power play against King Farouk in order to set up an anti-Nazi cabinet under Nahas.

1945 Creation of the Arab League, led by Egypt. Gamal Abdel Nasser establishes contacts with future Free Officers.

1946 Violent revolutionary demonstrations in Cairo and Alexandria.

1948 Palestine war between the newly formed state of Israel and the Arab states. Abdel Nasser and his unit surrounded at Fallouga.

1949 Victorious Israel signs Rhodes Armistice with Egypt.

1950 Wafd party dominates Parliament following national elections.

1951 Nahas government denounces treaty of 1936 and launches "the battle of the canal" against the British.

1952 *January:* Cairo burns.
  July 23: A group of officers led by Lt. Col. Nasser seizes army GHQ and imposes upon Farouk the choice of General Naguib as head of the army.
  July 26: Farouk, forced to abdicate, leaves Egypt.
  September: General Naguib becomes president of the Council of the Revolution.

1953 *June:* Republic is proclaimed. Naguib is president both of the republic and of the council. Nasser is vice-president.

1954 *February–March:* Conflict between Naguib and Nasser. Following a month of political struggle Naguib remains as president of the republic while Nasser becomes president of the council.
  July: Initialing of the preliminary Anglo-Egyptian agreement. British to evacuate the Canal Zone in 20 months.

October: Signing of the Anglo-Egyptian treaty.

November: Wide-scale repression of the terrorist group Muslim Brethren following an attempt on Nasser's life. Naguib, implicated in the crisis, is ousted and placed under house arrest.

1955 *February:* Signing of the Baghdad pact. In Gaza, murderous Israeli commando raid. First meeting between Nasser and Tito.

April: Colonel Nasser represents Egypt at Afro-Asian Conference at Bandung. Leftist groups decide to support the military regime.

September: Ratification of arms contract with Czechoslovakia.

1956 *January:* Independence of the Sudan.

February: Signing of an agreement of intent between the International Bank and Egypt concerning the Aswan High Dam.

June: Nasser elected president of the republic by 99.9% of votes cast.

July 18: United States retracts loan for Aswan.

July 26: Nasser announces in Alexandria that the Canal Company will be nationalized, "in order that the canal be made to pay for the dam."

October 29: Israeli Army enters the Sinai.

October 30: London and Paris announce that they will intervene "in order to separate the combatants."

November 1–5: U.S. and Soviet pressure to end the intervention.

November 6: Cease-fire in the Suez.

1958 *February 22:* Proclamation of the UAR—union of Syria and Egypt.

July 14: Monarchy is overthrown in Baghdad.

1959 Crisis in Iraqi revolutionary government. Repression of the Left in Egypt.

1960 Nasser visits UN.

1961 *July 23:* Confiscation and nationalization of assets in Egypt.

September 28: Syria withdraws from UAR.

November: Repression of "millionaires" and "reactionaries." Five French diplomats arrested.

1962 *May:* Nasser redefines his "socialism" in the form of a charter and projects "democratic" regime.

September: Overthrow of the monarchy in Yemen.

1963 New but fruitless attempt to unite Syria and Egypt in which Iraq was also to be included. UAR intervenes in support of the republic in Yemen.

1964 *January:* Pan-Arab conference in Cairo on Jordan River water rights.
May: Khrushchev visits Aswan Dam site. Imprisoned Communists set free.

1965 Ben Bella is overthrown in Algiers—setback for Egyptian influence. Nasser seeks in vain to withdraw from Yemen.

1966 Defense pact between Cairo and Damascus.

1967 *April:* Serious incidents between Syria and Israel.
June: Six-Day War. Nasser resigns, but returns in a few hours.
September: Khartoum Conference opts for political solution with Israel. Suicide of Field Marshal Amer.

1968 Popular demonstrations demanding democratization of regime.

1969 *March:* Reform of Nasserist system. "Free elections" of single party officials. Nasser declares war of attrition on Israel. Heavy losses for UAR.

1970 *July:* The *Raïs,* after two trips to U.S.S.R., accepts the Rogers plan for political settlement with Israel.
September 22: Pan-Arab conference in Cairo.
September 27: "Agreement" between Hussein and Arafat.
September 28: Death of Gamal Abdel Nasser.

Introduction

"YOU LIVE, O ABU KHALED!"

We had gathered by the millions on the banks of the Nile, between Rodah and Bulak, to witness the last voyage of Gamal Abdel Nasser, the president of the United Arab Republic. He had died three days earlier at the age of fifty-two; we were waiting for something extraordinary to happen, something in proportion to the man himself, to his public life and to the mighty city which had served for eighteen years as his rostrum and his arena.

There, on the Gezira bank, a murmur arose. The clamor mounted, until the furious march of the military band seemed suddenly to fall silent. An oblong object hovered over the crowd, draped with the national flag, whose white stripe alone was visible—it was Gamal's coffin. The cry became clearer: "You live, O Abu Khaled!"

Then the shaggy wave of onlookers—so adept at bursting through the dikes of the police—took on a maddening rhythm. Vice-President Anwar el-Sadat, Nasser's appointed successor, fainted in the midst of eight chiefs of state whom the crowd had swept into the sanctuary of the building which houses the Council of the Revolution—where we had talked several times to Gamal Abdel Nasser. Mahmud Ryad, the minister of foreign affairs, turned his livid face to the chief of a foreign government and muttered, "We have lost control of the situation. Anything can happen."

Anything—yet this was by no means the worst, this collective suicide of the masses, entranced into a sort of crazed inversion of Nasserism. This people had invented the victory of stone over death: here now was the most powerful product of its imagination. The solemn ceremony had become a vast primitive rite, and the leader's coffin was seized and borne aloft by the crowd. Before being laid in the earth, Gamal Abdel Nasser's body was buried in the living masses of his people, the object of a funerary rapture worthy of the Old Kingdom. Thus must the barge of the god-king have drifted toward the final resting-place of the dead.

A strange reconquest. He who had held Egypt like a familiar prey, to remodel her and impart to her the measure and form of his unchecked, unshared dream, now found himself on the other side of death, himself seized and devoured by his spellbound people. The personification of power, the identification between the leader and the masses, had led to an epic reincarnation. The mandate which they had granted him they now took back along with his mortal remains. The people reclaimed the rights they had given up to their leader a little over fifteen years earlier.

What did this spontaneous rite of possession-depossession mean, beyond the mere exercise of political power? Were these people entreating death, or sudden absence? Over whom were these orphaned people really weeping—over their vanished chieftain, or themselves? Over the emptiness in which he had abandoned them that October 1, 1970, suspended between peace and war, between East and West, between collective liberty and individual constraints, between fury and reason? Was it tenderness or anguish which rent the throats of these unwearying, convulsive mourners? Was this grand, billowing love—like that of June 9, 1967, the evening on which people had entreated the vanquished leader not to resign—the inception of a form of spontaneous democracy, a plebiscite without the rule of law? Or was it a tumultuous reminder, all institutions having been tamed and emasculated, and all forms of social groups annulled by the terrible authority of the *Raïs,* that his sudden absence left a frightening abyss? With innumerable cries the onlookers at least kept up their spirits, like children lost in the woods.

What would Abdel Nasser have felt, had he been able to witness these heartbreaking farewells? What would that great adherent of modernization have thought of this primal ceremony, this, in a sense, pre-Nasserian peasant ritual? Today forty years of industrialization, twenty years of paramilitary discipline, and ten years of a very special short of socialism were ending in a hurricane, a surge of frond-bearing fellahin in *gallabiyas,* a lyrical stream of hyperbole and profuse sentimentality. Did the impetuous crowd, the religious slogans, the funeral rites signify Egypt's return to the chaotic fevers of the past? Where were the responsible elites, the heirs of an authority which, ambiguous as it may have been, was also pretty clever at channeling the ardor of this admirable people toward modernism? Was history itself bidding farewell to Gamal Abdel Nasser?

On the balcony from which we watched the entranced, seething crowd, we could also see the familiar surge of the Nile. Suddenly we remembered something. Was this not the first of October, the time when, frothing with muddy tributaries and laden with the Sudanese earth, the great river threatens to leave its bed? But this year, for the second time, the swells remained an unvarying green. The High Dam had fulfilled its mission, regularizing the course of the river and sifting the ancient grime from its waters (by no means its most salubrious effect). Even after his death, the *Raïs,* the dike-builder, had bequeathed more than anguish and tears. He had left a deeply changed Egypt, an Egypt which now would have to live without him.

For our part we have tried to evoke this figure, whom we came to know through frequent contacts during almost four years as a press correspondent in Cairo (1953–6) as well as through several later meetings. Is this work a biography? A straightforward portrait? The reader will perhaps object to an occasional bias, to the hasty writing, to the failure to remember this or that fact, to the oversimplified descriptions.

In advance, we accept these criticisms. The character of Gamal Abdel Nasser was the object of such contrary and such intense passions, and was itself of such deep, carefully maintained, so deftly masked complexity, that a simple observer, especially a Westerner, could not possibly claim to represent him in his real fullness, nor to gather in so few pages a record which might belong to historians and above all to Nasser's compatriots.

We have simply tried to present the testimony of a direct observation of the career of the *bikbashi,* later the *Raïs,* a chronicle (colored with critical sympathy) of one man who brought to our time the symbol, for some, of bellicose ambition, and, for many others, of hope.

But now we shall let the facts speak for themselves.

PART ONE

A Child of Egypt

1

A Pyramid of Alienations

Enfeebled by the misfortunes and ruses of the longest history in History, wearied by the intrigues and the voracity of the great powers, slumbering in a sort of perpetual exile from herself—so Egypt would have appeared to a superficial observer toward the end of the First World War. Although the October Revolution had already occurred several months earlier, the German and Allied armies were consolidating their strength for what seemed the decisive struggle for world domination; at the same time forces were gathering which would soon explode in the second Chinese revolution, and Japan too was committing to the contest just enough resources to declare her ambitions.

Really, Egypt was triply exiled from history: by the political and diplomatic regime recently imposed upon her; by the system of production and trade in which she had been forcibly confined; and by the fundamentally cosmopolitan ruling class which dominated her economy and her public life.

It was in December 1914 that London, responding to "strategic necessity," had decided to place Egypt (over which the British colors had fluttered since 1882) under a veritable protectorate, and to substitute for the Khedive Abbas Hilmi, regarded as suspicious and recalcitrant, another dynast, Hussein Kamel, himself soon to be replaced by Prince (later King) Fuad, the father of Farouk.

Thirty years of "indirect rule" practiced by Lord Cromer and Field Marshal Kitchener—interrupted, of course, by quite direct interventions—had accustomed the Egyptian people to all the forms of alienation. But this latest manipulation of sovereignty ruthlessly reopened their most ancient wounds.

This became plain in 1915, when the students of the faculty of law decided to boycott classes, believing that "it is impossible to teach law in a land where all rights are violated." The following year, a group of young bourgeois, inspired by the Young Turks and styling themselves the Young Egyptians, tried to assassinate the monarch and later his prime minister. At the same time the censorship of the British general staff smothered any press worthy of the name, including even the prudent *Garida* of Lutfi el-Sayed, the exponent of the modernization of contemporary Egypt.

A second factor making for alienation was the profound integration of Egypt into the world market, not in the role of partner—as would have been the case with a developed power or one in the midst of development—but in the role of simple supplier, utterly dependent and controlled. These were not trade relations but bonds of dependency. The opening of Egypt to the world market had of course paved the way for the passage from a feudal system to a capitalist regime; but internal development, remaining essentially agricultural, was focused, by the foreign protector and by local owners, on the cotton crop, to which absolute priority was granted.

"This priority meant that the economic activity of Egypt was turned not toward internal needs but toward western markets, subject to their fluctuations and crises. Hence this economy was virtually dependent on those monopolies concerned with the finance, commerce, transport and industrial processing of the cotton crop."[1]

[1] Mahmud Hussein *et al.*, *La Lutte des classes en Egypte de 1945 à 1968,* Paris, 1969, p. 22.

But Egyptian dependency was made manifest not only in her reduction to the role of a "cotton farm for Lancashire." It was also the result of the extraordinary range of foreign investments (English, French, Italian, Belgian, and Swiss) which transformed Egypt into a sort of testing ground for modern capitalism. Banks, light industry, insurance companies, trade patterns, not to mention the greatest enterprise in the country, the Suez Canal, all were inspired, controlled, and financed by London, Geneva, or Paris.[2]

The foreign observer might be accused of caricaturing this situation were he not able to cite a reliable source, the Cairo correspondent of the *Times* of London at the end of the century: "One could hardly expect the representative of the Queen to support a project benefiting the Egyptian consumer but risking the ruin of English manufacturers [1899]."

The alienation of the Egyptian nation had even deeper origins on a third level, that of the entrepreneurial class, the merchant bourgeoisie, the "local business elite." In fact there were two networks of trade and enterprise, one branching from the traditional artisan class, the other from manufactured products. The majority of the population was still bound to the former, which was controlled essentially by ethnic Egyptians. But the latter too was growing. Until the revolution of 1919, this class was not Egyptian but Levantine, Greek, and Armenian. It was regarded as "Egyptianized," and its individual members did adopt an Egyptian mode of behavior. But as a group it played the traditional role of relaying exploitation, which characterizes the social class that French Marxists call *la bourgeoisie compradore*.

To suggest the importance of this economic stratum, of the firmness of its roots and of its domination of every more or

---

[2] The French interests were the most developed. They were valued at four billions of *francs-or,* including the Compagnie de Suez, the Crédit Foncier, and the Compagnie Lebon (the gas and electricity distributor).

less modern enterprise at the expense of native Egyptians, we shall cite several features pointed out by Jacques Berque: "Out of a list of contractors of construction materials fifty names long, we find no more than three Middle Eastern names, not to speak of Egyptian ones. . . . Even among exporters of manually collected commodities such as eggs, gum arabic, and sesame, which required direct contact with the fellah, we find only four local names in twenty-five registered at Alexandria. . . . The grocery business went uncontested to the Greeks. . . . Such a subjugation, which affected more than the structure of wealth, production and consumption, demoralized the citizen. Foreign interventionism was suffered beyond the limits of decency."[3]

Far deeper than the level of wealth and production, indeed, we find still another form of alienation: the alienation of culture, values, and language. When, in November 1917, Fuad I mounted the throne, he spoke French with a Corsican accent, but knew only enough Arabic words to chide his domestics.[4] Only those who spoke French or English could apply for positions in Cairo or Alexandria. What serious literary review could be published in anything but French? What theatrical event worthy of "society" could be held besides Italian opera, the Covent Garden Ballet, or the Comédie-Française? What library would be frequented by the right

[3] Jacques Berque, *L'Egypte, impérialisme et révolution*, Paris, 1967, p. 304. It must not be forgotten however that less than one per cent of the inhabitants of Egypt until 1930 dressed in European-style clothes. The hunched tailors who ironed with foot-operated irons and specialized in vests, caftans, *gallabiyas* and *beggas*, etc., were Egyptian. Moreover, Damiette has been for five centuries the center of hand-tooled leather—shoes, *babouches,* and so on—for the whole Mideast. They spoke of Kurdi leather (from the Kurds, arrived at the time of the Crusaders) the way Europeans speak of Cordova leather.

[4] In fact, Fuad spoke rather less than he croaked. During the *première* of *La Petite Chocolatière,* his cousin the prince Seif el-Din had dispatched a bullet into his vocal cords.

people which did not offer first and foremost Renan, Wilde, Loti, or D'Annunzio? But the triple alienation suffered by the Egyptian people was already broken and rendered problematical by the fits and fevers of the war. In imposing the protectorate of 1914, London had affronted Egypt too cruelly not to disturb her apparent slumber. Each gesture, each new start, each evolution of this epoch ran counter to the status quo.

Thus, the British general staff began the drafting of men (the old corvée) and provisions, raising from 1914 on, in this "protected" but neutral country, a "labor corps" of 117,000 men, of whom a part, an army without guns, accompanied the army of Kitchener on the Somme front, while a camel corps participated in Allenby's campaigns against the Ottomans. The requisitions of grain and cotton made possible the most cynical profiteering, and Egypt was occupied by an expeditionary force from the various horizons of the Empire estimated in 1918 at nearly 300,000 men.

Hence the sudden redistribution of wealth and the social and moral perturbation described as follows by the best British historian of this period, George Young: "The wealth of the country was doubled during the war, the cotton boom yielding revenues of £1000 per feddan.... Illiterate fellahs made fortunes. British gold suddenly irrigated and enriched an irresponsible class, and distinctions began to blur among the ruling class of Turco-Circassians, the middle class of Copto-Syrians, and the Arabo-Nubian peasantry, yielding eventually to a new, westernized class structure of entrepreneurs, bourgeois, and proletarians."[5]

Another cause of anxiety, also linked to the necessities of the English war effort, but more specific, was the decision of the British administration of Khartoum to institute systematic irrigation of the Sudanese Gezira, a cotton-rich area situated

---

[5] Several variations would be made on Young's formulation.

between the two Niles. This measure appeared to the Egyptians as a deadly menace, touching the very source of their life. A great cry was heard in the land: "They will divert the Nile!" Nothing could have more brutally forced the country to take a stand against the occupier. The "full belly policy," of which Lord Cromer, like his French rivals of the day, had bragged, was finished. Exploitation and confiscation showed their real face.

In four years, from 1914 to 1918, the British presence had sunk from the role of a dauntless and rather competent organizer of a stunned population to that of a cynical exploiter and myopic policeman of a nation still in rags but, even so, hungry for its rights.

Already the colonial structure, weighed down by the war, was riddled and cracked. The Egypt of 1918 was no longer reducible to imperial discipline, primarily because the economic troubles of the war had warped and eroded the colonial pact. But also the schools created by Mohammed Ali and Ismail, and later by foreign missions and British specialists such as the counselor Dunlop, and lastly by Saad Zaghloul, the Minister of Public Education at the beginning of the century, had created a middle class of functionaries, doctors, teachers, and lawyers, ready to take public responsibility, both political and technical, for the country. Finally, Egypt's position at the crossroads of the world rendered her more susceptible than any other nation to Wilsonian ideas, and to the rumors and repercussions of the great Oriental resurrection initiated by the Japanese troops of 1904, the Turkish reformers of 1908, and the Chinese intellectuals of 1911.

The way of revolution was nonetheless not open to Egypt—that is to say, genuine revolution, restoring independence to the state, sovereignty to the people, dignity to the individual, and basic rights and the opportunity for a decent life to the working man.

In 1919, a broad and generous uprising reopened to Egypt the gates of history, broke her internal exile, and gave her an appetite for struggle. The accomplishment and meaning of the "Wafd," the delegation led by Saad Zaghloul—who was forthwith elevated to national leadership in the face of the British occupier and subsequent manipulator—was the resurrection of the idea of the nation, and the advancement of the middle class already awakened some forty years earlier by the revolt of Arabi and Sami el-Baroudi (frustrated officers and anxious bourgeois who heralded and prefigured the uprising of 1952, which they inspired even more directly than the Wafd did).

It was not, however, this decisive collapse of the predatory forces of cultural exploitation and domination which cut Egypt off from the outside world with its own interest and values. Greater efforts would be required to wrench Egyptian society from the old system of multiple passivity, of interwoven forms of submission and complex resignation, which had knitted the course of its life, tying it to the monotonous flow of the river and its seasons, burying it beneath a pyramid of hierarchies, taboos, frustrations, and abdications to which, all too often, it had simply acquiesced.

2

The Force of Circumstance

Between two high, tawny cliffs spreads the valley of the Nile, the immobile sarcophagus of a land in perpetual resurrection. The level verdure stretches out serenely: cotton fields, onion gardens, trembling stands of palm trees—a gentle plain ablaze with sunlight, cross-hatched by canals, and majestically bisected by the royal river. Here and there, sublime stones jut out, proud in their resistance to the centuries and the sandstorms; consumed by time, vain with the profile of Osiris or Hathor, they display the greatest glory of any monument in history. Here an amazing continuity slumbers, disdainful of the militant, of the true believer, of death itself. Even the sorrows and the raggedness seem to defy both order and insurrection. The weight of eternity transfixes all things. What could anyone accomplish here that would seem worthwhile, that could find some hold on eternity?

Consider first the geography. Excepting the fate of certain Greek isles, of certain Swiss cantons perhaps, or certain Andean republics isolated by their altitude, rarely has history circumscribed a collective destiny in a more authoritarian manner. Here the master's eye is everywhere. There are no *jebels* for a *fellagha,* no coverts for irregular troops. The country is too open and limited for any guerrilla campaign to be waged for long; obedience is inscribed in its physical profile. The landscape prohibits revolt and consolidates power.

Only the hostile desert could afford escape or resistance. A local chieftain, rising up against the tax collector, could perhaps stage a brief insurrection; but soon he would be under the fire of a flotilla or a column dispatched from Cairo to restore public order. True, after the revolt of 1882, the nationalist journalist Abdallah Nadim succeeded for years in maintaining an underground right in front of the British. But his rather tardy notoriety comes precisely from the uniqueness of his adventure.

Listen to Ibn Khaldun: "There are lands . . . where uprisings are so rare that the sovereign never worries. Such a land is Egypt. Here one finds but one master and his obedient subjects."[1] And in a minor key, here is another expression of this docility—the proposal made about 1940 by the distinguished actor-playwright Naguib el-Rihani: "Just allow me to wear in the street the general's uniform from my last play, and to utter in the gardens of Cairo the speech which I delivered, and all Egypt will be mine!"

Another determining factor, and a very destructive one to national will power, was the demographic pressure. When medicine and hygiene began to progress markedly under colonial rule, and since the cultivation of cotton called for an abundant laboring class (and preferably a juvenile one, the care of the plant being perfectly adjusted to the height and agility of children), an astonishing demographic push soon took place. From 1882 to 1918, the Egyptian population grew from less than six million to more than twelve million souls. The phenomenon had something atmospheric about it, something inevitable. What else could one do but accept the little "gifts of God" while putting them to the best possible economic use? Inasmuch as the cotton boom paralleled the

[1] Yves Lacoste, trans., *Ibn Khaldoun: Nassance de l'histoire—passé du Tiers-Monde,* Paris, 1966, I, p. 338.

birth boom, a sort of tacit benediction seemed to link the two phenomena as coefficients.

The people of the Nile speak often of heaven—not in terror, but with acceptance. They do not see themselves as sinful: they are satisfied with their conduct before god. This unshakable optimism derives as much from the ancient Pharaonic period as from Islam. Pharoah's subjects had no other ambition than to let a fine day slip by (*ihr irou nefer*). They simply thanked the god-king for giving them the right and the means. Similarly, it is in confidence and serenity that the Muslim faithful prepare for the moment of final reunion with Allah. Anguish is not their forte.

Though the Jew or Christian may be haunted by sin or by anger from on high, the Nilotic Muslim is assured by his faith of his own eternal glory, and that all success—familial, economic, patriotic—is his true right and the foretaste of divine benediction. It is a world of robust optimism in which tribulation hardly matters and in which success comforts, a world which is obsessed above all by the problem of continuity, of fidelity in faith—in one word, of stability.

Even supposing that an outside element might come to trouble this serenity and induce the stooped Egyptian people to modify its destiny by direct action, would it still have the physical energy to accomplish the deed? Malnutrition in Egypt is, as we shall see, unlike the famines of India or the food shortages familiar in China. A sort of vital equilibrium has been established between this people and its patiently domesticated land. But this equilibrium is far below the level which assures man the control of his body and his spirit. It is easy, on a full belly, to condemn resignation, but more difficult to reject it when one works twelve hours a day at an average of $84°$ F, nourished only by a bit of biscuit and white cheese, or an onion perhaps, and some black tea.

To all these predetermined factors, to all these objective

fetters on the will to live and the freedom to build, must be added a prejudice profoundly rooted in the Egyptian popular consciousness: that every decision is taken elsewhere, in Cairo or perhaps still farther away, by the holder—native or foreign —of the real political, technical, and economic power.

In the eyes of the Egyptian peasant, what could be the role of his own will or liberty when such a flawlessly rigorous system presides over his subsistence and his life? One could fault—for being too forced and overgeometrical—the thesis of Wittfogel on "hydraulic despotism," or rule founded on the control of the water, which supposedly characterizes the Egyptian mode of production. The behavior of the master-hydraulician in the rural society of the Nile Valley has evolved profoundly, from the organized annual floodings (from the earliest times to the nineteenth century) to so-called "perennial" irrigation (since the time of the construction of the great dams in the era of Mohammed Ali) and the total domestication of the river course achieved since 1969 by the Aswan High Dam. This thesis cannot explain both the Pharoah and the khedives, both Farouk and Gamal Abdel Nasser. But a continuity persists which every Egyptian revolution must grasp as its starting point.

Such was the era, such was the earth, which gave birth in successive waves to the first attempts to modernize the Egyptian nation: first in 1919, with the appeal of a national leader of high stature and immense generosity, Saad Zaghloul, whose efforts were broken by the forces of foreign domination; and then, from 1952 on, under the impulse of another leader equally infused with nationalist passion, better armed than Saad for merciless combat with the great powers, but too passionately absorbed by the national and personal aspects of the struggle for emancipation, and too distrustful of the masses to realize the revolutionary project of which he was the incarnation: Gamal Abdel Nasser.

Saad Zaghloul had not yet launched his movement in early 1918, when Gamal Abdel Nasser was born. But the twenty years which formed the personality and political strategy of the man of July 1952 were greatly influenced by the earlier battles of Saad and the style which Saad had imparted to Egyptian public life, so that one is obliged to dwell for a moment upon this "father of the people" whose immense statue, raised by Mokhtar beside the Kasr el-Nil bridge, presided over the funeral of Nasser on October 1, 1970.

Saad Zaghloul exemplified the archetypal Egyptian peasant in his strongest points and his richest virtues: a powerful girth, a massive head, natural eloquence, good nature, generosity, stubbornness. The son of a well-to-do farmer, he studied first at the Koranic University, went on to law, and made himself known as a prestigious magistrate. Noticed by Cromer, he agreed to become the minister of public instruction, before eventually rejecting this creative complicity.

In 1918, he appeared as the natural spokesman for the nation when, on the very eve of the European armistice, he presented himself to the British High Commissioner, Sir Reginald Wingate, and demanded the abrogation of the protectorate and the emancipation of Egypt. He was shown the door. For three months, he kindled public opinion, held meetings, and even telegraphed Paris, where the peace conference was being prepared. The ninth of March, he was deported to Malta with three of his companions. Yet soon London was forced to admit that the Egyptian nation had come alive once more. The inflammation of the populace was so intense, so coherent, so clearly unanimous that Saad was freed and able to reach Paris to represent his people at the peace conference.

This uprising in the spring of 1919 was not a revolution

properly speaking, for only a political order was in question—interpreted and symbolized by a man and his party. But one cannot overlook Saadian Egypt's acquisition of the treaty of independence of February 22, 1922, which, for all its ambiguity, inaugurated a new era for the colonial peoples of two continents, and was hailed accordingly. Nor can one underestimate for that matter the long-term social consequences of the quasi-revolution of 1919. For in effect it launched the progressive substitution of a native bourgeoisie—the social offspring of Saad—for the class of "Egyptianized" cosmopolitans whose long predominance we have already mentioned.

Just because the regime of 1952 and its leader rendered such slight homage to the precursors of 1919[2]—while idealizing the failed revolts of 1881 led by Arabi Pasha, that vulgar prototype and ill-fated model of Gamal Abdel Nasser—there is no reason to minimize this quite typically Egyptian movement. The founder of the Wafd was often betrayed by his own men and never enjoyed—with perhaps three or four exceptions—the noble posterity which he deserved. But one should not forget that the Wafd expressed in its true richness that it was, in the deepest sense, the *delegate* of the Egyptian people. To define it is to describe Egypt itself: generosity, brio, gaiety, barechested forthrightness, the contradictions and mythomania of millions of electors. The Wafd expressed that oddly spongy, warm, and discontinuous quality which is Egypt's alone.

To observe that the Wafd, after the death of Saad Zaghloul, was first tolerated and then infiltrated by the local feudal clans as well as by foreign imperialism does not authorize one to deny it all revolutionary value. It was at the very least the executive agency behind the measures which redrew, before

---

[2] In the preamble of the "charter" of 1962, Nasser harshly criticized the leaders of 1919 for having been unable either to deal with social problems or thwart the "ruses of imperialism."

the regime of 1952, the face of modern Egypt: its severance from juridical and judiciary colonization by the treaties of 1922 and 1936 and the Convention of Montreux; its spiritual reunification by the collaboration, at the highest echelons of the party, of Copt and Muslim leaders; the development of education under the aegis of Taha Hussein, beginning in 1950; and the elaboration of legislation, even if rather spottily applied, to govern modern labor conditions.

A disconcerting mixture of nationalist fervor, agrarian conservatism, social progressivism and extortionary cynicism, the Wafd put an indelible stamp on the rebirth of the Egyptian nation into the modern world. Although admirable before 1936, and still thoroughly impregnated with the example of Saad, it declined thereafter, enfeebled and compromised. But the fezzes of the opportunists, the insolent paunches, the decorations for servility, were not enough to annul the services rendered, the replacement of religious communities by the ideal of one national community, the demonstration to the eyes of the world that public opinion can exist and even triumph in the East—and, above all, the release of the Egyptian people from its long apathy.

Such were the forces gathering when a petty official's son was born, who, thirty-four years later, would resume the struggle in the name of the Egyptian people. The leaders of the proto-revolution of 1919 had already failed, having expressed Egypt's needs without actually throwing into combat the deep forces which she had harbored since 1920. This was because the heirs of Saad were too enfeoffed to the landowning class to dare to question the agrarian order and the condition of the peasantry. For Nasser this precedent would be rich with lessons.

Egypt could never be changed by the action of urban elites alone, could never be liberated by the mere liberation of the intelligentsia, the middle-level officials, or the modernizing businessmen. It was necessary to get at the roots, by tearing off the peasants' feudal yoke, by wresting the nation from the system of imperialist trade, and by linking the national struggle with those of other emerging peoples.

Such were the mood, the circumstance, the precursors, and the objective.

3

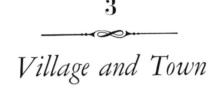

Village and Town

Alexandria: is it really part of Egypt or already the Mediterranean world, already Europe? Alexandria, at the end of the First World War, was a city of almost half a million people. In the midst of the last century, under the direction of the viceroy Mohammed Ali, and later the khedives, the city had recovered a part of its ancient splendor and had been suddenly enriched by the economic activity aroused by the war and the British occupation.

Who here would recognize the Egypt of the Nile and its peasants? One Alexandrian in three could not speak Arabic. Beneath the palms of the Corniche, on the terrace of Moharram with its cafés, in front of the Hotel Cecil, and all the way to the waterfront, you spoke Greek if you were a merchant, Armenian if you were an artisan, Italian if you fancied yourself an *artiste,* English if you had a stake in the government, and French if you were rich or wished to be thought so. A fine book by E. M. Forster evokes, with a mingling of wonder and compassion, the Alexandria of the turn of the century, that "Alexandria *ad* Aegyptum" which seemed moored to the African earth like a vessel straining to stand out to sea.

True, on the beach of Sidi-Bishr, a wealthy foreigner could no longer permit himself, as he could on the eve of the 1881 uprising, the luxury of thrashing an Egyptian constable who had approached to remind him of some rule of decorum or of public order. But in the post office, what European traveler would actually bother to fall in line to pick up a postal order? And from the Mohammed Ali Square to the customs house, one could see very few Egyptians not engaged in servile tasks. Clea, Justine, Mountolive, Balthazar, the protagonists of Durrell's *Alexandria Quartet,* define and delimit a furiously cosmopolitan society, at once scintillating and blasé, of all places in the world the least likely in appearance to serve as the cradle for a revolutionary enterprise. But in appearance only.

It is here that a minor postal employee called Abdel Nasser Hussein arrived to settle in early 1915. He had come from far away, this postman, from a little village in Upper Egypt near Assiout, six hundred kilometers from the sea, four hundred kilometers from Cairo. The name of the village was Beni-Morr. Abdel Nasser Hussein was born there in 1888, to a family of fellahs, or more properly of small land-proprietors, who cultivated a patch of ground of about five feddans (a little more than five acres, considered sufficient for the subsistence of a moderate-sized family).

The father, Hussein Sultan, was a petty notable. Thanks to the influence which he wielded, the village, deprived of a school up to that time, saw itself granted, toward the turn of the century, a little class in Koranic studies. It was here that Abdel Nasser Hussein received his first lessons. Yet when he reached five, Beni-Morr still had no primary school. His father sent him to the nearest town, Assiout, which comprised at that time thirty thousand inhabitants; the Coptic community had founded one of the many Christian schools of Upper Egypt which admitted Muslim children as well. It was here that the youngster obtained the diploma which opened to him the avenue of public administration, the fond hope of all the peasants' sons of the Nile Valley.

By what circuitous route or turn of fortune, thanks to whose protection, was the young Abdel Nasser Hussein, employed in the postal administration, sent to Alexandria, then the central seat of the communication services, and the dream of every employee? A thorough inquiry might perhaps lead to savory discoveries about the administrative mechanisms and shifting influences in the Egypt of the Protectorate. The fact is that the newly arrived functionary was assigned to the postmastership of the suburb of Bacos. Of course Bacos was by no means an elegant neighborhood. But nonetheless for a young man leaving the adobe lanes of Beni-Morr and the harsh rabble of Assiout, that universe of dust, familial hierarchies, and penury, the avenues of Bacos must have had considerable charm. For two piasters you could sit in the tram alongside a veiled gentlewoman, and maybe even get a glimpse of the sea.

Early in 1917, the young postal clerk married the daughter of an Alexandria coal merchant, Mohammed Hammad. A good marriage. Hammad, himself an immigrant from Upper Egypt, had been successful. He was one of those rare Egyptians who were paving the way toward a modern economic system. Already he was almost an "entrepreneur." The little postman, a peasant's son, in fact found access, in marrying Mohammed's daughter Fahima, to another social stratum. He remained linked to the small landowning middle class but was also a member of the civil servant class. Yet from that time on he would depend mainly on the urban petty bourgeoisie. His in-laws would help him to resolve many of his subsistence problems (in Alexandria he earned eight pounds a month, which would perhaps correspond today to about $40) and assure his son an education beyond the economic status of his family.

Gamal,[1] the oldest son of Abdel Nasser Hussein and Fahima Hammad, was born on January 16, 1918, in the Bacos postal clerk's little house—a simple cube of brick and plaster in a charmless little courtyard—where comparative ease reigned. But do not picture him growing up under the picturesque palms of Alexandria, facing the Mediterranean, mingling in its pomp and cosmopolitan froth. His childhood was that of a typical official's son, shuffled from post to post and from school to school. Gamal was three years old when his father was reassigned to Assiout. He was seven when the postal clerk was sent to a little village near Suez, Khail el-Arbein, before being attached to Khatatba, then to Damhanour, one of the larger towns of the delta, then once again to Alexandria and finally to Cairo.

It was at the Assiout elementary school, at the age of six, that the postman's son began his primary studies, which he pursued further at the school set up at Khatatba by the railway administration. At the age of seven he was sent to his uncle Khalil in Cairo by his father, by now weary of searching, from village post office to village post office, the means of ensuring his son's education.

His early childhood, after the departure from Alexandria, during the period of his schooling in Assiout, was nonetheless spent in Beni-Morr, the old family village. This experience marked him deeply. Later, he would often use the expression, "my village," especially to evoke the strength of family structure, the warmth of cooperation, and the harshness of economic and social constraints.

Situated at the edge of the canal, which is rather wide at

[1] The word means "beauty." The hard "g" is Egyptian. In other Arab countries they say "Djemal."

this spot, Beni-Morr is the dreariest of Egyptian villages, a shapeless heap of brick and clay, of drab gray huts clumsily fashioned, with their unkempt locks of hay on the veranda, and the smell of manure everywhere. Here the gamoussas, rust-colored water buffaloes with the long horns of the goddess Hathor, emerge from the canal, dripping with mud more viscous than honey. Here a peasant wrapped in his *gallabiya,* tumbling in gray-striped folds, passes by, straddling a donkey. There strides a woman shrouded in black, her brown face bare and shriveled by strain: if she is not carrying a faggot, then she is balancing a pan or an earthenware pot (*balas*). There a gang of urchins gallops about between the Koranic school and the cotton fields, hunting the parasites nested beneath the leaves. Beni-Morr: a village like so many others.

But Beni-Morr is also a village of the Saïd, a middling valley of the Nile, where men are whole-hearted, firm and rugged, and do not gladly suffer any infringement of their rights.[2] The dark skin of the people of the Saïd bespeaks the African continent and its hot blood. Here also the Christian population, routed and driven back in the eighth century by the Arab and Muslim conqueror, stood fast in a kind of underground resistance and put down roots in the slime. It still often composes the majority of the population. In Beni-Morr, as in nearby Assiout, Christians make up a third of the inhabitants, a fact which did not fail to affect Abdel Nasser's ideas about interreligious relations.

[2] A curious remark from Ahmed Aboul Fath's book, *L'Affaire Nasser,* Paris, 1961: "A world-wide survey conducted several years ago to determine the densest centers of criminality showed that this record was held by the city of Chicago, followed immediately by the Abnub district in which Beni-Morr is located. . . . The latter village is notorious not for commonplace crimes, but solely for donkey-thievery. . . ." We might add in passing that donkeys are the most essential production tools in all of Egyptian agriculture—Mahmud Azmi suggested that the statue of an ass be placed in every Egyptian village square!

This village of the Saïd is a veritable microcosm of Egyptian rural society at the end of the first quarter of this century —a society marked by three phenomena which determined its structures, its mode of production and trade, and its style of life. These were, in chronological order: the seizure of the entirety of the arable land by Mohammed Ali, who converted it into an enormous state farm; the installation of "perennial" irrigation, assuring an almost complete control of the course of the Nile; and lastly the prodigious development of cotton cultivation which from 1880 on drastically modified the countryside and the life of Egypt.

Hence the triple character of rural life: it was thoroughly hierarchized, controlled, and dominated by the masters of the land and the hydraulic engineers; it was consecrated to perpetual labor, with overpopulation requiring intensive production despite the maximum yield assured by irrigation; and it was dominated by speculative monocultures. These factors helped dramatize the social climate, to turn the fellah's life into a concentrationary system, an eternal regime of forced labor.

But even more stringent was the agrarian structure in which this cotton-based production developed. In his *Egypte nassérienne,*[3] Hassan Riad distinguishes thus the fundamental categories of Egyptian village society in the twentieth century:

(1) the "landless," too poor and ill-equipped to own a single feddan: they hire themselves out as agricultural laborers, and make up the Egyptian sub-proletariat;

(2) the "poor peasants," exploiting dwarf-holdings of one feddan or less (under one acre) which are insufficient to ensure them full employment and elementary subsistence;

[3] Paris, 1964, pp. 20–5.

(3) the "intermediary strata" exploiting one to five feddans, a plot large enough to assure the full employment of the family and its subsistence, but not afford-
ing recourse to an exterior labor force. Two types of
cultivators must be distinguished here: the small proprietors, and the small tenants who lease parcels of
greater domains;

(4) the "rich peasants" who exploit, either as owners or as
lessees, domains of five to twenty feddans: such was the
position of Saad Zaghloul's father, Zaghloul Ibrahim,
who was also the *omdeh,* or village chieftain;

(5) the "rural capitalists," who exploit or direct the exploitation of properties exceeding twenty feddans;

(6) the "aristocrats," or latifundiaries, whose political influence—at the time which we are discussing, i.e., before the Second World War—often reflected their
economic preponderance, and who, more and more,
became absentee landlords.

In this manner, feudalism (a notion which, by the way,
would require certain qualifications as far as Egypt goes)
seemed to ripen into what one might term a rural capitalism.

One category concerns us particularly here: that of the
"intermediate stratum," often described in Marxist terms as
"the small freeholders." For it was to this class that the family
of the young Gamal belonged, and whose aspirations, if not
whose interests, he would interpret for the rest of his life.
This class was largely dominated and exploited by others, yet
still on the way toward liberation, or at least toward reloca-
tion in the cities by means of the civil service—in essence
toward modern technology and the universe of knowledge.

On this point, an exemplary "family saga" of Egyptian
society in the first half of the century is formed by the careers
of the grandfather Hussein Sultan, free peasant, the father
Abdel Nasser Hussein, nomadic civil servant, and Gamal him-

self, military officer risen to head of state. This saga begins in
the land, passes through the state, and leads to political
power.

At the heart of Gamal Abdel Nasser's career were two
fundamental elements: the peasant family of Beni-Morr fast-
ened to its cotton-bearing patch of mud, maize, favas, and
onions; and the great heritage of state power of which
ancient Egypt is a model for the world. Let us not forget that
the masterpiece of Egyptian sculpture is neither a goddess, an
emperor, nor a condottiere, but a thickset, surefooted *sheikh
el-balad,* village headman, with the staff of authority in his
hand.

Another word on the human landscape which engendered
Gamal Abdel Nasser—the extended family. His father had
five brothers: an elder one, who practiced a bit of commerce
at the village level to ease his family burdens, and four
younger brothers: Khalil, whom we shall meet again in Cairo,
and Adel, Attia, and Taha, who remained attached to the
plot at Beni-Morr. Gamal's maternal grandfather, the coal
merchant Mohammed Hammad, was hospitable to him, especially after the death of his mother, Sett Fahima, and the re-
marriage of Abdel Nasser Hussein.

It was a family, in short, like so many others: heavy,
tyrannical, caviling, at times mendacious, but strong in its
solidarity. Gamal was to observe this well, beginning with his
first steps as a conscious child, and later as a schoolboy and as
a responsible young man.

4

A School Called "Renaissance"

Gamal was seven years old when he arrived in Cairo to stay with his uncle Khalil, a petty official in the service of the Wagfs (national Muslim institutes of mortmain). His father, tossed from village to village, from Khatatba to Khail el-Arbein, had decided, at the price of separation, that Gamal should continue to pursue his studies in the big city. And Khalil owed it to his brother to welcome the child: it was thanks to the postal clerk that he himself had been able to study in Alexandria, far from the lamentable Koranic school of Beni-Morr. He was not rich, this uncle Khalil; to the five or so pounds a month which the administration allotted him he added the meager profits from a land-lot brokerage. But with the help of money orders from the postal clerk he was able to enroll Gamal at the el-Nahassin school.

The school was in the neighborhood of Khan Khalil, the commercial center of Cairo, in the shadow of the great Islamic university Al-Azhar. Also within sight were the tomb of the Sultan Qalaun, Bab el-Nasr—the gate of victory —and the exquisite fountain of Abderrahman in the very heart of Cairo. Religious devotion and business mingled intriguingly with history and the struggle for daily subsistence. This was the quarter of the cauldron-makers and coppersmiths —half alchemists, half successors to the old fire-worshiping cults. What better school to study the Egypt of the *medina,* of city life—after years in the village and field—than this quarter of deepest Cairo, of flames and blackened stones: swarming, passionate, buzzing with prayers and altercations. Gamal was to spend three years at the el-Nahassin school, three years marked by a great sorrow.

He was eight years old when, arriving for a vacation at Khatatba, he learned that his mother, Sett Fahima, with whom he had not corresponded in one year, had died in Alexandria two months previously. Gamal was to remain deeply wounded by this disappearance. It was one of the most frequent subjects in his conversations with his friends, who were struck by his precocious gravity. Things became even worse when less than two years after the death of Fahima his father remarried. He would never really forgive the postal clerk for having begun a new life so fast; and never again would he re-establish a real family life with his father and his three brothers at home.

Gamal was eleven years old in 1929, when Abdel Nasser Hussein summoned him back home; he had just been re-assigned to Alexandria, where there would be no more problems in educating his son. The boy enrolled in the school of Ras el-Tin near the royal summer palace. It was here that he would hear the first echoes of political struggle, receive the first blows of a police blackjack, and form the first features of what one might already rather boldly call his political consciousness.

Political consciousness at thirteen? The British historian George Young has very correctly remarked that "in the Orient, adolescents are more quick to take political action than men." (This observation seems less picturesque to us since the Parisian May of 1968. Thirty years earlier, Egyptian schoolboys were toppling ministers and braving the blows of Russell Pasha's cops.)

In 1933 the postal administration recalled Abdel Nasser

Hussein to Cairo. He had been appointed postmaster of the residential section of Koronfish, situated between Ezbekieh, whose gardens had delighted General Bonaparte, and Abassieh, the future birthplace of Nasser's *coup d'état.* Gamal was fifteen. The postal clerk and his family moved into the *cul-de-sac* of Khamis el-Ads (*ads:* lentils, and by extension any dried vegetables, an odor characteristic of petty officials—Hussein did his marketing there on Thursdays). The house, situated beside a Karaite synagogue (a sect so heavily influenced by Islam that services could be held in a mosque provided that Hebrew was used), belonged to a Jewish family, the Shamuels. The young Gamal seems to have gotten along well with these landlords with whom at times he even took meals, as the ritual dietary laws of the two communities are quite similar.[1]

Here, between his father's post office and the synagogue, the young man spent five decisive years, 1933 to 1938. In Alexandria he had "tasted" political action for the first time. In Cairo, he would study, militate, struggle, be arrested, and eventually begin law school before choosing the military profession, not as a caste, but as a means to action.

For two years Gamal Abdel Nasser continued to attend the courses of the *En Nahda* school. The name means "renaissance" and is closely linked to the history of the modern Arab world: under this catchword were grouped those Syrian, Egyptian, and Palestinian intellectuals who had launched, sixty years earlier, a movement of political and cultural resurrection against the Ottoman overlord. For Gamal too it was no empty expression. He was not a model pupil, and only with difficulty did he pass the final examination of his secondary studies—which was called, because of the French

---

[1] "Visit the Christian, but dine only with the Jew," goes an Egyptian proverb.

educational inspectors, the baccalaureate, though it is actually closer to the French *brevet supérieur* (*kafa'a*).

But at this time the youngster made the first ties of his political career—in particular with a young man seven or eight years older than himself, Hassan el-Bakury, who was later to be one of his cabinet ministers and a go-between with the "Muslim Brethren." And he read passionately, providing himself with enough intellectual baggage to merit the title of "advanced autodidact"—if by autodidact is understood a man whose learning owes more to his own will power than to his cultural milieu.

In his very useful biography,[2] Georges Vaucher examines the results of an ingenious survey which he conducted among Gamal's old fellow-students and teachers, examining primarily the books and authors which impressed the young man. First, there was Mustafa Kamel, the figurehead of the Egyptian nationalist movement of the end of the nineteenth century, who inspired the "National party" (*Watani*), which, even more than the Wafd, was to become the cultural cradle of Gamal Abdel Nasser; Ahmed Shawki, the national poet; and above all Tewfik el-Hakim. To open today his *Spirit Recaptured,* one of the first (and least impressive) novels by the author of the *Diary of a Country Prosecutor,* is almost to read an evocation of the youth of Gamal.

But the postal clerk's son also tackled foreign authors. An article has been rediscovered which was originally written in 1934 by this "high-school junior" for the *En Nahda* school magazine. The article is devoted to Voltaire. Since the author of *Candide* was hardly one of the *Raïs*'s mentors, this little document entitled "The Man of Liberty" is especially curious:

> Although the revolution against tradition was already strong in the eighteenth century, few *philosophes* were

2 *Gamal Abdel Nasser et son équipe,* 2 vols., Paris, 1959.

among its leaders. Yet it was Voltaire and Rousseau who forged the most mighty and most murderous weapons. . . . Those who followed them were to dedicate their lives to the great revolution of 1789. . . . Voltaire struggled hard to survive as a free-thinker.

About the level of a solid young French *lycéen* of the same age. Yet what a pity, certain unkind readers will say, that Gamal did not hang on to this ardent attachment to free thought!

One year later Gamal the journalist had become Gamal the actor. The *En Nahda* school was having its annual cele-bration, honored that year by the presence of the (Wafdist) minister of public education, Naguib el-Hilali—the very same man whom Nasser and his fellows were to expel from the office of premier on July 23, 1952. The program featured a performance of *Julius Caesar*. Gamal played the role of Cae-sar, which the program, drawn up for the occasion, presented as a popular hero, liberator of the masses, and "conqueror of Great Britain," who was assassinated as if by accident. Georges Vaucher tells us that the honest postman Abdel Nas-ser Hussein, seeing his eldest son fall beneath the dagger of Brutus, almost sprang up to the rescue. Tragedies were rarely played in Beni-Morr.

But the young Gamal had other preoccupations besides Voltaire and Shakespeare. In 1935, at the age of seventeen, he finished the period of his secondary studies. He was a tall lad, athletically built, taciturn but given to sudden fits of pas-sionate eloquence. He was sick with Egypt's sickness, sick with the fevers which agitated his country. Egypt was then being goaded by the rod of Ismail Sedky, the only right-wing statesman strong enough to oppose Zaghloul's heirs; yet Egypt was still hungry for rights, independence, public freedoms, and elementary social justice.

The creation of the Axis and the expansion of Mussolini's ambitions gave an international and more dramatic character to the Egyptian problem. Would London choose to strengthen its grip, the better to control this strategic crossroads; or to conciliate Egypt by substituting for the occupation an association based on independence? The Foreign Office opted for the second alternative. But the leaders of the Tory party preferred to wheel and deal. Nobody in London seemed conscious of the necessary price to appease Egypt's rancor and to slake her thirst for liberty. As for Cairo's feeble governments of that period, they were simply not of the stature to force the hand of a Stanley Baldwin, a Samuel Hoare, or a Ramsay Mac-Donald.

Gamal was treading water. How could he act? Whom could he summon? Whom could he follow or lead? His school-fellow Hassan el-Nashar has recalled in the review *Akher Sa'a* (July 1958) one of the young man's characteristic attempts to approach those in responsible positions:

> We had decided to make contact with the leader of a political party. We obtained an appointment for March 12, 1935. He was a highly placed person, a minister. When we arrived, he had just left his office. Gamal rushed over and intercepted him in front of his elevator, saying: "We have formed a group of high-school students and we wish to know your advice on the best way to save our country." The minister counseled him to contact the university students. One month later, we went to find these people. But what were they discussing? Politics? The national struggle? No. Nothing serious at all: how to fill the positions on the executive student council; who would be president, secretary, and so on. What, organize youth against corruption, against imperialism? Unthinkable. We decided to work only with secondary school students.[3]

[3] Vaucher, *Gamal Abdel Nasser et son équipe*, I, p. 71.

A law student, Abdelaziz el-Shurbagi, was the closest thing to a political leader at the university; Gamal went to see him. A lawyer today, he has pictured the interview in these terms, as reported by Georges Vaucher:

> He had not yet formed his political ideas, his program. He was overwhelmed in the agitated world of politics. He went here and there, visiting the centers of political parties with the hope of finding one which would answer to his nationalist aspirations. The popularity of the Wafd's practical organization seemed remarkable to him; the entire nation assembled around a leader[4]—that was real power. But he was more attracted by the principles and program of Misr el-Fatat. The ideal party, which would contain all the elements necessary for the realization of the national aspirations, did not exist.

Here then is our young patriot, "overwhelmed in the agitated world of politics," in quest of a leader, a lesson, a program, a noble adventure. The Wafd already appeared to him as a legacy from the past, immolated in its own institutions, gagged by its own eloquence, paralyzed by its own governmental ambitions. The National party suited his aspirations better. He admired its young leaders, Fathi Redman and Nunedin Tanaf, who were to become cabinet ministers in 1952. But the party was weak. As for *Misr el-Fatat,* it was a fascist-inclined organization lately created by a lawyer, Ahmed Hussein, a murky, vehement figure whom we shall glimpse again here and there. He was a ruthless troublemaker, an intriguer, a heady adventurer and wily extremist, forever ready to plead "not guilty" after egging his unsuspecting legions on to the worst misdeeds. *Misr el-Fatat* means "Young Egypt." Ahmed Hussein went so far as to deck out

[4] At that time, Mustafa Nahas.

his partisans in green shirts:[5] he did not try to conceal his sympathies, and would quote Goebbels or Ciano at the drop of a hat.

Gamal was seduced by these excesses; but did he allow himself to be utterly possessed by them? This cannot be proved. Occasionally he would march with the "Green Shirts," fight at their side, and take part in their meetings. But nobody, with the exception of Ahmed Aboul Fath,[6] has held that he was actually a member of this alarming phalanx.

No portrait of the Gamal of 1935 could be stronger or clearer than that which he himself draws in a letter to his friend Hassan el-Nashar, dated September 2, 1935:

God has said: "we must prepare, and muster all our forces against them [the British].

But where is this force which we must muster? Today the situation is critical; Egypt is at an impasse, perhaps even in the throes of death. . . . There are in Egypt men of dignity, who will not let themselves die like animals. But where is the burning nationalism of 1919? Where are the men ready to sacrifice themselves for the sacred earth of the fatherland? Where is he who could rebuild this land, that the weak and humiliated Egyptians may arise again and live free and independent?

Mustafa Kamel has said, "To live in despair is not to live at all!" Yet right now we are in utter despair. We are retreating, my friend, we are going backward, fifty years backward. We have returned to the time of Cromer. . . . But in Cromer's day, someone came along who could throw him off the saddle. . . . Today who can stand up, who can fight back? They say that the Egyptian is cowardly, that he flinches at the slightest sound. He only needs a leader who will lead him to battle. Then this Egyptian will be-

[5] It is true that the Wafd, at one time, had been "Blue Shirts."
[6] Ahmed Aboul Fath, L'Affaire Nasser, Paris, 1961, p. 205.

come a thunderbolt which will make the edifice of persecution tremble. . . .

Mustafa Kamel has said, "Even if my heart moves from my left side to my right, even if the pyramids move, even if the current of the Nile changes direction, I will never change my principles." Everything which has happened up to now is a long introduction to a greater and more important task. Several times we have said that we would work together, to wake the nation out of its sleep, to arouse the forces hidden deep inside the people. But alas, up to now nothing, no, nothing, has yet been accomplished.

My friend, I await you at my house, September 4, 1935, at four o'clock in the afternoon, to discuss this matter. I hope you will not miss this appointment. Gamal.

The whole creature is already there, with his mixture of mad exaltation, searing conviction, and bureaucratic precision. "I await you at four o'clock to discuss this matter. . . ." Decidedly, a punctilious Carbonaro is born, in whose brain the fatherland burns insensibly—as in von Salomon's hero. The enemy had best keep an eye on this lyrical organizer. A single incident would serve to warn the British.

It was not long in coming. On November 10, 1935, Sir Samuel Hoare declared in the House of Commons that London was opposed to the re-establishment of the Egyptian constitution. What, London intervening in this matter, which concerned only the people of Egypt! The day after, all Cairo was in the streets—all Cairo, that is, below the age of twenty. Gamal directed a column of outraged high school students. On the thirteenth, the agitation became organized. On the Rodah bridge, two of his comrades were killed. In the vicinity of Saad Zaghloul's old mansion, now "the house of the people," the young Abdel Nasser faced a platoon of British soldiers. A bullet gashed his forehead. He was conducted, bloody-faced, to the nearby offices of the newspaper

Al Gihad (the Holy War), whose issue of the following day (November 14, 1935) mentioned among the demonstration's casualties the names of the former war minister, the Wafdist General Hamdi Saif el-Nasr, and several students—one of whom was a certain Gamal Abdel Nasser.

The British decided to ease the strain, and less than a month later King Fuad announced the re-establishment of the constitution of 1923. The tension was dissipated, and with it the energy displayed in those November days. Twenty years later, in his *Philosophy of the Revolution,* Abdel Nasser bitterly revealed: "I placed myself at the head of the *En Nahda* student demonstrations, crying with all my strength: 'Long live complete independence!' But our enthusiastic clamors were lost in the general indifference."

It was not the last time Gamal was to feel solitude. In the succeeding months a new Wafdist cabinet negotiated with London an evacuation treaty which satisfied the greater part of the country, although not the intransigents to whom he belonged. The latter could not accept having to pay for the departure of the English soldiers and a perpetual treaty of alliance inserting Egypt in Great Britain's strategic system.

While the country drowsed on in what seemed to him a cowardly compromise, the young Gamal witnessed the doors of his own school close against him. Police reports designated him as a dangerous agitator. Frightened, the school's director begged him to absent himself and refused to allow him to take the examination for his baccalaureate; that year he attended school only forty-five days. A protest movement took shape among the students; once again the director gave in, but this time in favor of the postman's son. And Gamal took his examination.

Now what? Political action called him. But how could he pursue it? And within what framework? Where would he find the most efficacious means? He began to dream of a career in the law, the way of the bar and the world of the judiciary—from which the noblest Egyptians had, in fact, come: Zaghloul, Nahas, Wissa Wassef, Ahmed Maher. He enrolled, in October 1936, in the faculty of law at Cairo, although not without also preparing for the entrance examination of the police academy. But he seems not to have evinced much juridical cleverness. Moreover, the law faculty revealed itself to be a rather timorous milieu, hostile, in any case, to all forms of direct action. The angry young men of his brand were regarded as blundering fools, and remained isolated. Seven months later, he quit.

Why not try to join the army then? Wasn't this what he was really seeking, the lever with which to topple Mustafa Kamel's pyramid? Ahmed Hussein's "greenshirts" certainly knew how to fill the streets; what if the khaki shirts were to get started—wouldn't they know how to stay in the streets, to seize and occupy them?

PART TWO

Toward Power

5

Cadets on the Sidelines
of War

Gamal Abdel Nasser had fought against the treaty of 1936 first because it legalized and prolonged the English military presence in the Suez Canal Zone, but above all because it was the fruit of a transaction with the occupier: Egypt, according to his kind of nationalism, could wrench herself away from the old humiliations only in the most blinding clarity and trenchant defiance.

Yet in fact this "merchants' treaty" would eventually open to him, albeit through a detour, the road to power: first, by clearing the Egyptian horizon—the alien forces being billeted from now on in the Canal Zone—second, by thus allowing free play to political forces, and third, by shattering the ban preventing the sons of poor families from applying to the military academy. Now, with Egypt as its ally, London could no longer oppose an expanded Egyptian army open to young men of lowly origin. The decree of the Nahas government doing away with class discrimination was no sooner published than hundreds of young men, the sons of petty bourgeois and rich peasants, presented themselves as candidates. Rumor had it that only fifty would be examined. And, moreover, admission to the entrance examination required the passing of a preliminary interview to determine the candidates' characters.

Gamal was summoned before a commission composed of high officers. The president of the commission requested his name. "Gamal Abdel Nasser Hussein." "What does your father do?" "He is a postal employee." "Where do you come from?" "Beni-Morr, in the province of Assiout." "Are your people peasants?" "Yes." "No one in your family has ever been an officer?" "No." "Why do you want to become an officer?" "To serve my country." "Do you own property?" "No, I am a man of the people." "Did anyone recommend you?" "No." "Did you take place in the demonstrations of November 1935?" "Yes." The dialogue was terminated forthwith. Poor men's sons could indeed enter the army, but outraged patriots, no.

In his biography Georges Vaucher mentions Gamal's petition to have this veto lifted. The young man demanded an audience with the undersecretary of state for war, General Ibrahim Khairy Pasha, who was to preside at the next session of the commission, in which forty-four candidates for the academy were to be admitted. The general agreed to receive Gamal, was utterly charmed by him, and lifted the restriction.

In March 1937, Gamal became part of the "second wave" of poor boys who were joining—and who were later to transform or at least to proletarize—Farouk's army. All of a sudden he was a cadet, a student officer. He was now nineteen.

Let us not idealize our protagonist nor the environment in which the next phase of his career was to enfold. If Gamal Abdel Nasser, a young man full of vital energy, sap, and ill-contained power, had chosen the profession of arms, it was to be sure primarily out of patriotism and realistic good sense. But more down-to-earth reasons were in force too. His meager success at law school? Not likely: this would be to confuse cause and effect, to confuse lack of success with the absence of any genuine interest. A more probable explanation is this: that the abolition of the old "capitulations" which followed close upon the treaty of 1936, and which freed the Egyptian judicial system from foreign tutelage, had recently wreaked severe economic havoc. Now foreign investors, both those in Egypt and those based overseas, tended to shrink back suspiciously. Hence the Egyptian petty bourgeoisie now encountered an economic recession which obstructed the once beckoning path toward business success.

So, if a young Egyptian, thrown back on a career in government, chose that of army officer, it was probably largely because it seemed to offer status improvement at a reduced price. Study at the military academy cost a bit less than study at law school, and however the army might be ridiculed, it did remain the major instrument of power. Gamal acted by doing what Stendhal called "choosing the red" (by the same token, Gamal's childhood friend Hassan el-Bakury chose "the black" and became an influential sheikh). Nonetheless, these nationalistic Julien Sorels were certainly not cut out to become good conformist officers.

And what an army! "It's nothing to brag about," one of its chiefs, Marshal Aziz el-Masri, confessed at the time. "But consider this: It's the English who built it for us, and of course they had no interest in its becoming dangerous."[1] Russell Pasha remarks ironically in his memoirs that rank was measured around the waist: a thin general was either an imbecile, a sick man, or a genius. In 1937 the Egyptian royal army looked like a jigsaw puzzle of parade units, quasi-police forces, and cavalry squadrons for polo-loving pashas' sons.

Hence the importance, at least on the political level, of the injection of new blood in 1937–39 by the promotion of the

[1] One of his peers, General Fuad Sadek, was to say ten years later: "There are only two good officers in the Egyptian army: Abdel Moneim Ryad and Hafez Ismail. . . ." (The first, after becoming general chief-of-staff, was killed on the Suez Canal in 1969. The second, the ambassador to Paris in early 1970, was shortly recalled by Nasser to serve as head of the secret intelligence service.)

ambitious sons of the landed petty bourgeoisie—dominated as they were by feelings of social frustration—out of a state of economic penury and national alienation.

It was on March 17, 1937, that Gamal Abdel Nasser, this postal worker's son and grandson of a fellah of Beni-Morr and a coal merchant of Alexandria, this passionate Saïdi with broad shoulders and burned complexion, this militant nationalist once shot before the "house of the people," entered the military academy of Abassieh on the periphery of Cairo, not far from the suburb of Koronfish where his father worked and his family lived.

The course of military study lasted in theory for three years. But the reformation of the Egyptian army, decided by the Wafdist government with somewhat tardy encouragement by the British, required the accelerated training of military cadres. Nasser spent only seventeen months at the Abassieh Academy before receiving his first commission. Quite rapidly the discipline of the orderly and studious life, as well as his taste for his new studies, channeled his militant fever.

In this austere framework where he could satisfy his double thirst—for authority and for education—Gamal became a "good pupil" whom the instructors held up as an example. His violence matured into ravenous self-application. Before six months had passed, he was promoted to corporal and head of a study group. Among the recruits placed under his guidance he noticed a thin lad, also from the Saïd, who loved to laugh and to dream out loud: his name was Abdel Hakim Amer and he was to remain for over thirty years a privileged friend. (Their companions gave the two young men special nicknames: Abdel Hakim Amer was "Robinson," on account of his passion for travel stories, Gamal Abdel Nasser was "Jimmy." Why "Jimmy"? We shall encounter this Anglo-Saxon name once again in a situation which may throw some light upon it.)

Georges Vaucher was able to examine the loan registry of the school library, and hence to find out which books were borrowed by the cadet Abdel Nasser in 1937 and 1938. The research is enlightening. Keeping to English works alone, which at that time constituted the core of the library, he noted with special interest that Gamal had borrowed the following: *Bonaparte, Governor of Egypt* by Charles Roux; *Lawrence* by Robert Graves; *The River War* by Winston Churchill; *Gordon* by John Buchan; *Foch* and *The History of the War of 1914–1918* by Liddell Hart; Ludwig's *Napoleon;* Robertson's *Soldiers and Statesmen;* Jarvis's *Yesterday and Today in Sinai;* and Wavell's *Palestine Campaign.* Gamal revealed an obvious passion for the role of the hero, the exceptional man (though it is also true of course that the English and French historical schools of the day were smitten with the same passion).

On July 1, 1938, the cadet Gamal Abdel Nasser Hussein took the final examination of the school, achieving an average of 14 points out of 20, corresponding approximately to 13 in military history, 17 in mathematics, 19 in administration. Curiously enough, this skilled practitioner obtained only a 14 in a, for him, absolutely essential subject: civil administration. In that domain he was to make significant progress.

First assignment: Mankabad, in Upper Egypt.

"Yesterday I began my work in Mankabad," wrote Second Lieutenant Abdel Nasser to his friend Hassan el-Nashar, the favorite recipient for his youthful confidences. "It's a beautiful country. The atmosphere is poetic and excites the imagination: a landscape of desert, of farmland, of ponds and canals. In the north, tilled fields, and in the south, a mountain range which runs east–west, gripped by the desert as by a pair of strong hands. I have the pleasure of announcing to you that my character has stayed solid. Gamal at Mankabad is the same Gamal whom you have known for so long, and who searches in his imagination for reason to hope. But his hopes vanish like clouds."

As we can see, the social matrix of the Military Academy and subsequent entry into garrison life had not yet remodeled the passionate young man of 1935. The romantic dreams of adolescence had not been swept away, nor nationalist nostalgia tamed. Moreover this first garrison at Mankabad was not far from Assiout and Beni-Morr, permitting Second Lieutenant Gamal Abdel Nasser to revisit his original village and see with new, though experienced eyes, the misery of peasant life.

As luck would have it this first assignment drew him into association with two companions who were to play major roles in his life: an infantry second lieutenant, Zakaria Abdel Megid Mohieddin, whom he chose as his successor in 1967; and a second lieutenant in the signal corps, Mohammed Anwar el-Sadat, who would become his official political heir in 1970. The three young men rapidly established friendly ties. As often happens, this friendship was based on a common resistance to a higher power: that of the caste of superior officers. Here is what Anwar el-Sadat recounts in *Revolt on the Nile:*[2] "Our officers thought only of humiliating us, while prodigally displaying their respect for the English. The worst of all was the commander of the sector, a general called Mahmud Seif, who thought he was the red Sultan Abdel Hamid."

But the young men found some compensation: "One evening in the winter of 1938 we climbed the Jebel Sherif to have dinner together: lentils, chestnuts and sugar cane. Gamal said: 'Let us make this meeting into an historic reunion. Let us take a vow to stay faithful to the friendship which unites us. This unity will permit us to triumph over all obstacles.' It was my first real encounter with Gamal. Up to then, I had

[2] London, 1957.

not found him too friendly: he was too taciturn for my taste. . . ."

Extrapolating a bit, Anwar el-Sadat has made this evening into a sort of "Mankabad oath," the true founding, according to him, of the 1952 movement. It was beginning at their stay in Mankabad, he claims, that the three friends "started to recruit adherents" and to "form cells of protesters."[3] Having lived in a typhoon, how could anyone not take himself for its epicenter? The congenial Anwar has given in to this temptation. In any case, he attributed to Gamal an analysis of the situation which made the English responsible for every evil. It was a bit simplistic, but it would hardly change.

Several weeks after the lentil supper at Mankabad, Second Lieutenant Nasser asked to be transferred to the Sudan, where Cairo was sharing its responsibilities with London, though not without revindicating sole sovereignty over the area. For that time, the idea of going to the Sudan was unusual. The Egyptian younger generation was now less interested in this far-off country than it had been fifteen years earlier, when the English *Sirdar* (commander-in-chief) of the army, Sir Lee Stack, had provoked the expulsion of the Egyptian forces from the upper valley and made of the Sudan a sort of Alsace-Lorraine—especially in the eyes of the leaders of the Watani party which had inspired men like Nasser. In any case one can perceive in this initiative a concern to explore directly the diverse aspects of the national dossier, to learn through experience what the Sudan really was like, that land of Gordon and the Mahdi, where Winston Churchill had taken part in the "river war."

After a brief stop in Alexandria, he found himself on the Khartoum train. Soon the grave Second Lieutenant Nasser noticed a person beside him who had just been hoisted into the

[3] *Ibid.*

railway carriage by his servants with a flood of kowtows and flatteries. "I am a member of the Senate," he announced. "I'm known as a big talker and a josher. I'm the only one who opposed the treaty of 1936." "And," recounts Nasser, "he began to tell me his life story. Each time I tried to slip a word in, he would blurt out 'Wait, wait . . .' and continue even more vehemently. At last I managed to ask him where he was getting off: 'Thank the Lord,' he said, 'for having sent you a companion to keep you company as far as Beni Suef.' "[4] This charming letter to his confidant Hassan el-Nashar reveals that the dour *Barrèsian* fellow could exhibit, in occasional gusts, a sharp sense of caricature. This oscillation occasionally reminds one of de Gaulle as a Saint-Cyrien around 1910.

What was the real reason for his request for reassignment to Khartoum? There Gamal could be reunited with his comrade of Abassieh, Abdel Hakim Amer, the likable "Robinson." Their sympathy grew firmer, quickened by the narrow-minded stupidity of their superior officers, who were even worse than those of Mankabad. Their rebellious attitude eventually caused them to be sent for three months to Jebel Awlia, an industrial center where important projects for the mastery of the Nile were under construction. But on May 1, 1940, while, elsewhere, the course of history was accelerating, Gamal was named a lieutenant and charged with the responsibilities of an adjutant, or administrative officer, of the first battalion at Atbara, later at Khartoum. He was bored to tears, and his morale reflected it: "Since I am the only one in this place to believe in conscience and loyalty, I am persecuted, for punishment here is reserved for the conscientious. Do you remember our plans for reform, which we hoped to put into effect within ten years? Now I think it will take a thousand

---

[4] About three hundred kilometers from Cairo.

years. . . ." (Another letter to Hassan el-Nashar, August 1941)

At the end of the year 1941, six months before the opening of the Russian front, and at the very moment when the United States was forced by Pearl Harbor to enter the war, Lieutenant Nasser returned to Egypt. He arrived in the midst of a great debate: he was assigned to the El-Alamein base at the very moment when Rommel was intensifying his march across Libya, toward Egypt. Was Rommel the great liberator? Many Egyptian officers thought so, and behaved accordingly. Among them was Anwar el-Sadat, who, back from Mankabad, threw himself into the anti-British clandestine movement, contacting one by one the pro-Axis groups masterminded by the Germanophile Marshal Aziz el-Masri, and the organization of the "Muslim Brethren."

Sadat even organized, in one of those floating villas moored to the banks of the Nile and called *dahabiehs,* a rendezvous for the reception of information about British military activities, for the benefit of Rommel's general staff. Along with the aging Aziz el-Masri, some of his colleagues unsuccessfully attempted to reach the front lines of the Africa Corps: among them were Hassan Ibrahim, Hussein Zulficar Sabri (Ali's brother), and Abdel Moneim Abdel Rauf, all future companions of Gamal Abdel Nasser. In Cairo and Alexandria crowds gathered chanting slogans in favor of Rommel (and of Mussolini, too, whose name, whether by some typically Egyptian foible or by sheer naïveté, the street urchins deformed into "Musa Nili," the Moses of the Nile!).

At El-Alamein, Gamal stayed aloof from this agitation, which he liked all the less for having recently met a figure who for years would serve as a model: Commander Wagih Khalil. The equipoise of this officer seems, under the circumstances, to have guided the younger lieutenant's conduct. But a decisive event was about to take place in Cairo, which would tear the isolated officers of El-Alamein away from their phlegmatic meditation.

On February 4, 1942, the British High Commissioner, Lord Lampson, cutting short the king's timid but growing pro-Axis sympathy—Farouk had just sacked a pro-Western premier, Hussein Sirry—had the royal palace surrounded by General Claude Auchinleck's protection and imposed on the sovereign a Wafdist cabinet under Nahas Pasha. (The successors of Zaghloul were almost the only politicians who both believed in a community of interest between Egypt and the democracies and could also capture a majority of the citizens. No Westerner or Russian should forget the Wafd's services to the struggle against the Axis. Yet, from an Egyptian point of view, its prestige suffered considerably on account of this policy.)

In the whole country, and in the army especially, it was as if the state, in the person of the king, had been slapped. A still unknown general, Mohammed Naguib, wrote immediately to Farouk: "Since the army has not been afforded the possibility of defending Your Majesty, I am ashamed to wear my uniform. I request therefore the authorization to resign from the Egyptian Army."[5] The sovereign refused his resignation; but the name of Naguib was to circulate around the country and among the troops, and to prepare the events of tomorrow.

As for Gamal, his reaction was more political, one might even say more dialectical: "I am ashamed that our army has not reacted against this attack. If it had dared, the English would have retreated like pansies (*khawalates*).[6] But I am happy that our officers, who up to this time have thought only

[5] Naguib, *Egypt's Destiny,* London, 1955.
[6] This letter to Hassan el-Nashar has been published with an alteration of the word *khawalates* to read "bullies."

of enjoying themselves, are starting to speak of revenge. This shock has put the soul back into more than one corpse. They have learned what dignity is, and that they must be ready to defend it. It's a cruel lesson, but a lesson nonetheless."

For this reason February 1942 must be considered a doubly important date: the army, animated so far by essentially corporate if not conservative ambitions, awoke to national consciousness; and the Wafd was ruined as the incarnation of the national aspirations. Even to a man like Nasser, whose wider and wider divergence from the older party we have witnessed, the Wafd had previously remained at least the true heir of Zaghloul. But no longer, after that February 4.

September 9, 1942, on the eve of the battle of El-Alamein (October 19), in which the British forces definitively repulsed Rommel from Egypt, Gamal Abdel Nasser was promoted to captain (*yuzbashi*). Odd, this career advancement for an officer on the sidelines of the war, an officer who witnessed the war without taking part in it. How did he feel? Did the cause of Egypt seem to him essentially outside this contest?

Six months later he was named an instructor at the Abassieh Military Academy, which he had left five years earlier, and had to begin to prepare for the general staff examination. A few months later he was to meet a girl of Iranian origin, Tahia Kazem, through the interposition of Abdel Hakim Amer, a friend of her brother, a Cairene rug merchant.[7] He would marry her. She was to give him a peaceful family life, and five children.

Was he becoming bourgeois, this old hothead of the *En Nahda* school? What had happened to the Gamal of that flaming letter to Hassan el-Nashar? Perhaps there were fewer

7 The shop is still there, on Kasr el-Nil Street, near the Midan el-Tahrir.

flames, but the fire smoldered under the coals. He read a lot: Clausewitz, Liddell Hart, *Modern Egypt* by Lord Cromer, *Egypt Since Cromer* by Lord Lloyd, *Suez and Panama* by Siegfried. Classic, almost banal, reading matter. Less banal, however, were the contacts which the instructor-captain made with a growing number of young people, some in the military, some not, but all possessed by two passions: the will to emancipate Egypt, and fury against social injustice.

The war was over: the victory of the Western democracies was by no means regarded as such in Egypt, despite the Wafd's gesture. Nahas in any case had been fired by Farouk in September 1944—and since the danger had passed, London did not bother to support him. So the king called in Ahmed Maher, the brother of the old fox Aly Maher, whom we shall meet again. The new premier was brilliant, eloquent, even reputed to be an ardent nationalist. He thought himself strong enough to deal with the West, to obtain from Churchill the evacuation of Egyptian territory. But the very day he declared war on the Axis, February 15, 1945, he was assassinated during a session of Parliament.

6

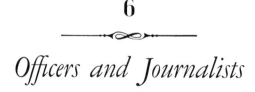

Officers and Journalists

Strange were the country, the society, and the climate uncovered by the wave of war in its ebb. We have spoken above of the upheavals caused in Egypt by the First World War.

The second multiplied them tenfold. From 1939 to 1945, the destiny and the mentality of Egyptian society were to be utterly transformed. First, the war profits: from 1940 to 1943, bank deposits climbed from forty-five to one hundred twenty million pounds. During the same period the number of millionaires in pounds went from fifty to four hundred. The suspension of imports from Europe gave a strong push to local industry: the Misr spinning and weaving company, which payed 11 per cent dividends in 1938, was shelling out twice that amount four years later. In 1943 the sugar refineries were netting profits of 1,350,000 pounds.[1]

Ali el-Shamsi Pasha, the president of the National Bank, drew attention in his annual report of 1942 to the prosperity due to the influx of foreign capital following upon Great Britain's cotton purchases and the expenses of the Allied armies. "The profits of industrial companies have doubled since the opening of the war," he added. When the war ended, Egypt had a credit balance of almost 500 million pounds,[2] composed of provisions, indemnities, and war damages.

Naturally this enrichment of the state and of the privileged class was in large measure paid for by those who were economically weak—newly impoverished by inflation and rising prices (which had passed in four years from index 131 to index 353). At first the peasantry had managed to eke some gain out of the cotton booms: but these were rapidly keyed down, as cotton acreage was reduced to allow a production increase in cereals required by shortages in the cities (whose interests, once again, took precedence over those of the countryside). From this measure the fellahin suffered so greatly that the Wafdist cabinet exempted an extraordinary number of peasant families from taxation in 1942—over one million,

[1] Approximately 150 million *francs lourds.*
[2] Approximately 6 billion *francs lourds.*

in fact. A member of parliament declared at that time to the newspaper *Al-Misri:* "On the eve of the French Revolution, the people of Paris cried, 'We want bread!' The people of Cairo have just done the same, by attacking convoys of wheat. The situation of this country may be termed revolutionary."[3]

This prognostication was to be borne out as doubly astute: the brisk industrial push stimulated by the war was brutally stopped in the aftermath of hostilities, as most enterprises were not competitive (or not so deemed by their owners). The massive disbanding of "war labor" threw into the street in 1945 a horde of unemployed estimated at over 300,000, only adding to the more considerable bulk of the traditionally unemployed. An alarming mass of workers camped in the outskirts of the great cities, an urgent reminder of both national priorities and inacceptable inequalities.

Egypt came out of the war rich and ambitious. But the Egyptian people were divided and frustrated—especially prior to the social legislation of 1945–6. The local capitalism tended to follow a monopolistic pattern, general proletarization deepened, and a frenetic movement toward the cities destroyed the older town-country balance. The king, once popular, remained forever branded by the humiliation of February 1942, which had also marked the Wafd with the stain of infamy. The foreign occupation, which had mobilized on Egyptian soil more than one and a half million soldiers of all nations, had liberalized social customs and provoked, in reaction, a wave of xenophobic puritanism which would become a new but essential source of public energy in the years to come.

But the Egypt of 1945 was by no means solely a feverish and diseased body. It was also a country which had just played a major strategic role, which disposed of considerable inter-

[3] Claude Estier, *L'Egypte en révolution,* Paris, 1965, p. 83.

national credit,[4] and which appeared, if not as the leader, at least as the center of the movement for Arab unity, which had just gained new strength through the foundation of the Arab League. London and Washington were themselves learning to play, and not unsuitably, the Arab game, which they had already confused in their eyes with the problem of supplying the West with oil.

No, the war did not only dislocate the social body of Egypt, it also exacerbated all its tendencies both positive and negative, and most notably its revolutionary tendencies: Stalingrad echoed longer among the Egyptian masses than El-Alamein.

Everything conspired—the prosperity as well as the misery, never before so strongly wedded—to bring the Egypt of 1945–6 to a furious boil. A spirit even less passionately in search of national renewal than Gamal Abdel Nasser would have taken the hint. Gamal himself trembled with hope, and perhaps with apprehension. We shall return later to this feeling of ambivalence, so basic to the double personality of the postman's son. In his personality the agitator of 1935 struggled with—but also strengthened—the dour general staff officer of Abassieh. Whether it was the summit of state power, the mood of youth, or the condition of the workers and above all the peasants to which he turned his attention, he saw only sources of trouble, feverish agitation, reasons for fear and hope.

The head of the government, Nokrashi Pasha, an honest, patriotic man, but limited in outlook and fundamentally conservative, had just received a humiliating rebuff from Sir Miles Lampson, now Lord Killearn. An envoy of Nokrashi had requested the evacuation of Egyptian territory, and Lampson had retorted that it was out of the question until further orders had been received. Several weeks later, in January

---

[4] The national debt was reduced 95 per cent for the first time since Ismail.

1945, an Egyptian politician notoriously in collusion with the English, Amir Osman Pasha, was assassinated by a band of conspirators directed by Tewfik Hussein, and in which some role was played (he was later sentenced for "indirect participation") by one of the earliest companions of Abdel Nasser, Anwar el-Sadat.

Two centers nourished the growing fever: the university and the press. The role of the students in this period of Egyptian history recalls that of their predecessors in Czarist Russia at the end of the nineteenth century. In his excellent essay on *The Young Intellectuals of Egypt in the Aftermath of the Second World War,*[5] Raoul Makarius discovered no less than seventeen mass student demonstrations in the course of the year 1946—six of which involved the death of several young people. And he draws attention to the fact that every change of government—if not of political orientation—came at that time from this sort of pressure.

As for the press, it was in a state of continual, intense, buzzing excitement. The number of publications tripled in three years. The number of journalists grew from 1,200 to 8,200 between the prewar and the postwar period. Many of these papers lasted only a few months—sometimes only weeks. But they kept up an intellectual ferment which Egypt had never before known and would never see again, at least in this form.

The newspapers proliferated, extensions of the action, or rather the propaganda, of the two current types of revolutionary or extremist organizations: those which styled themselves Marxist—notably the EMNL (Egyptian Movement of National Liberation) founded four years earlier by Henri Curiel —and those inspired by Muslim fundamentalism—the "Muslim Brethren" and the *Shabab Muhammed* (Youth for the

[5] Paris, 1960; The Hague, 1960.

Prophet). It was in the second rather than in the first current that the "socialist party" directed by Ahmed Hussein should be placed: for it was nothing more than the reappearance of the old *Misr el-Fatat* (Young Egypt) which had bewitched Abdel Nasser back in the days when fascism was still respectable.

It is to the Left alone, however, that we must attribute the responsibility for the great revolutionary days which marked the year 1946—which just missed being the year of Egypt's real revolution. On February 9 the students launched a powerful anti-British demonstration: the moment they crossed the Nile, the police prefect Selim Zaki opened the Abbas bridge, where they had congregated en masse: twenty demonstrators under twenty years old were drowned.

Twelve days later, in response to an appeal of the "worker-student committees," tens of thousands of demonstrators converged on Ismailia Square, where they clashed with the British forces massed before the barracks of Kasr el-Nil. Machine guns opened fire: three dead and twelve wounded were counted. This day, March 21, has since been celebrated in many countries as an anniversary of "victory over imperialism." But the "worker-student committees" had frightened the Crown, Ismail Sedky, and the British too thoroughly not to pay a heavy price. From now on they were prepared to countenance any intrigue and any alliance to smash this popular front.

Gamal had also taken stock of this new movement. He was tempted to dissipate his energies in it. What was this Marxism, he wondered, in whose name so many men were risking their lives? It was during this period, and to answer this question, that Nasser met two men who were to have a big influence on him and who would serve as intermediaries between the revolution and the general staff officer of Abassieh: the

magistrate Ahmed Fuad and Lieutenant Khaled Mohieddin.
The first was a young deputy prosecutor who had joined from
its inception the EMNL of Curiel. He was an intellectual of
calm demeanor whose gravity recalled that of Captain Abdel
Nasser.

As for Khaled, he was the cousin of the Zakaria Mohieddin
who was one of the "conspirators" of Mankabad, one of Gamal's very first companions. He was a young cavalry officer
with rosy cheeks and a timid smile who read Marx and Bevan
and frequented assiduously the little groups which gravitated
around the EMNL. The magistrate in a sense initiated Abdel
Nasser into the elements of Marxism, though with no great
success, as we shall see. The cavalry officer did however vividly demonstrate to him that one can be close to communism
and passionately attached to the national interest. The future
leader would retain the latter lesson best.

Gamal extended his contacts with the Marxist sympathizers
of the 1945–6 period to other types of organizations: the
"Muslim Brethren" through the agency of Anwar el-Sadat and
Abdel Moneim; Abdel Rauf, the aviator who had tried in
1942 to reach Rommel's forces; the "socialist party," in which
he had kept several friends; and the Wafd, whose left wing
was now headed by several talented young men, among whom
were the lawyer Aziz Fahmi, the writer Mohammed Mandur,
and also a journalist, Ahmed Aboul Fath, the editor-in-chief
of *Al-Misri,* the biggest daily in Cairo. Aboul Fath was the
brother-in-law of an officer with close ties to Gamal, Saroit
Okasha. The journalist and the captain later became allies and
even friends. Because of this friendship their rupture in 1954
would seem all the more explosive.

Would it be correct, in evoking these contacts, relations,
and liaisons, to push the date of the creation of the *Dhobat el-
Ahrar* (Free Officers)—the armature of the great Nasserian
enterprise—all the way back to 1945–6? This is the thesis

which we adopted in a preceding work,[6] but a close examination of texts and attitudes has suggested a certain amount of rethinking. It is also the thesis of several of the Free Officers, one of them Anwar el-Sadat, whose good faith is not suspect, but who is animated by a certain concern for anteriority and historical "legitimacy." It is rather rash to place, as they do, the beginning of the enterprise either in 1938 (Mankabad) or in 1942 (the reaction against the British coup de force) or in 1945.

But it was at this time that a half-dozen officers from twenty-five to thirty years old began to meet regularly, sometimes at Gamal's or Abdel Hakim Amer's, sometimes at Saroit Okasha's, Khaled Mohieddin's, or Ahmed Fuad's: one day Salah Salem would appear, with the drawn features of an angry samurai; another day it would be the robust aviator Abdellatif Boghdadi, who in 1942 had followed General Naguib in tendering his resignation to the king; and yet another day it might be Kamaleddin Hussein, a young and somewhat doltish artillery officer who hardly concealed his sympathies for the Muslim Brotherhood.

Every once in a while Anwar el-Sadat would turn up, always agitated, always proposing some lightning action: the dynamiting of the British Embassy or the liquidation of a traitor. He had established what one would call today an organizational chart of the conspiracy, branching into five committees, one of which specialized in terrorism. The only thing missing was the organization itself. The fiery Anwar in his fever for action even tried to associate his friends, with Gamal at their head, with an activist group directed by Captain Mustafa Kamel Sedky, the fourth husband of the illustrious belly dancer Tahia Carioca. A waste of energy: Gamal stayed out.

For the *Dhobat el-Ahrar* to ripen, it still had to undergo a

6 Jean and Simonne Lacouture, *L'Egypte en mouvement,* Paris, 1956–1962.

cruel test and the transformation of confusion into indignation: for these young men, this role was played by the Palestine war.

To speak of an organization, a committee, or a plot in the period prior to 1948 is probably incorrect. What did exist was a group of comrades (a *Bruderschaft*) united by friendship, or complicity in anger, a group of officers whose ringleader or prime instigator seems to have been Captain Abdel Nasser. These soldiers shared a will to transform Egypt, and were able to free themselves from corporatist habits, and from all professional exclusivism: the magistrate Ahmed Fuad and the journalist Ahmed Aboul Fath were among the comrades whose advice they solicited. Hence theirs was no little barracks cabal, but the preparation or rough draft of a whole political movement.

There was no ideological cohesion in all this, as we have seen. Some sought inspiration from the Muslim Brethren, others from the Communists, still others from the "socialist" and neo-fascist extremists of Ahmed Hussein. So far there were only conventicles, experimentation, groping. But one key figure was forging himself, working out within himself a synthesis between the adolescent agitator and the painstaking general staff officer. This key personality began to gather around himself a team. Perhaps this team was conspirational rather than revolutionary. Yet to pass from conspiracy to revolution often requires no more than the intervention of objective conditions which may transform a technical plot into a larger movement.

Soon the silent rebel would encounter the thrust of real revolution.

7

Adventure in Palestine

The Palestinian drama did not burst like an unexpected storm on Gamal Abdel Nasser and his companions. According to his *Philosophy of the Revolution,* he participated in demonstrations every November against the Balfour Declaration—Britain's 1917 promise to create a "Jewish national home" in Palestine. And he had read the works of Allenby and Wavell on Palestine, as well as the excellent history of *The Arab Awakening* by Georges Antonius.[1]

On November 29, 1947, the United Nations voted its approval of a partition plan which allotted the Zionists a large sector of Palestinian territory. This excited acute anger among the nationalistic youth of Egypt—although a majority of the Marxists approved the Soviet Union's vote in favor of partition. Captain Nasser was not responsive to their point of view. Instead he even visited the Grand Mufti of Jerusalem, Amin el-Husseini, to offer him the services of a group of volunteers, namely, himself and his friends. But the Cairo government, already in the throes of preparing its own intervention, hamstrung his initiatives: Gamal's offer was turned down.

Was Gamal able to analyze the situation in greater depth once his first wave of anger had subsided? Could he already smell out the aura of collusion, tricksterism, and mendacity

[1] London, 1935.

which hovered over everything, even in the midst of a genuinely tragic situation, the partial exile of the Arab people of
Palestine? Could he unravel the hidden intentions of the king
and his counselors, themselves more or less manipulated by
the British will to channel Egyptian bad blood into something
other than the occupied Canal Zone? Farouk and his clique
needed above all to find an escape valve for the alarming popular pressure built up in February 1946: and if possible, a
way to show up the Egyptian Communists, who called themselves patriots and yet stayed aloof from the outrage over Palestine. Too, certain Levantine advisers, whose Syrian or
Lebanese origin was held against them by the people, saw a
fine opportunity to "go native" in sharing the indignation and
the cause of the people of the Nile Valley.

Nothing suggests that Gamal Abdel Nasser was aware of all
this before the eventual debacle had unmasked the guilty parties. Although he did mention, in his account of the Palestine
war,[2] that the shadow of war provided a pretext for the royal
police to sniff out the malcontents—if not the conspirators—
within the army, he seems to have joined the adventure wholeheartedly, at once stung by injustice and enraptured by the
thought of the action ahead. And he was all the more delighted since the army officer whom he then admired the most,
Colonel Ahmed Abdel Aziz, had already managed to leave for
Palestine as a volunteer. Gamal burned to join him.

On May 15, at dawn, the first detachments of the Egyptian army crossed the Palestine border. On the sixteenth,
Gamal Abdel Nasser, who had just been made the commanding officer of an outfit and his captain friends Abdel Hakim
Amer and Zakaria Mohieddin moved up in a column toward

[2] Published in March 1955—on the eve of Bandung—in the review
Akher Sa'a (which reproduced a series of three war documents presented by
Abdel Nasser for the benefit of the armed forces).

the front. But here are Gamal's own words—full of verve and, it seems, of sincerity—which tellingly re-create the mood of this pathetic tragedy:

On May sixteenth I left my home to enter the campaign. Tumbling downstairs, I repeated over and over to myself: "We are leaving for war, for war, for war!" . . . Our apprehensions began when we arrived at El-Arish, one of the main bases behind front lines and still blacked out. We did not even know the whereabouts of the unit we were to join, and no one was there to show us. We headed for the HQ, expecting to find a beehive bursting with activity: it was deserted. It was like a forgotten house in a region abandoned by everyone.

At last we found a young staff officer. This unfortunate young man was terribly worried—he was desperate for his dinner. We invited him to share what we had left, and soon we were united in laughter. But the rise and fall of our voices, resounding under the vault of the desert, left a strange echo within me.

As a commanding officer Nasser was assigned to the Sixth Battalion. It was stationed at Rafah, and had already sustained a costly defeat while attempting to take the nearby kibbutz of Dangur. The outfit was soon transferred to Gaza, where it received the orders to take another enemy position, Deir Snid. "Our soldiers, unprotected by armor and in full daylight, were dashed against solid fortifications," wrote Gamal. "When one wave fell, another would replace it. My heart was embittered to see naked infantry fighting against fortified positions and coming back to huddle like rats over a crust of bread and cheese. . . . The night of May 20 was one of the saddest of my life. I visited the camp hospital, whose beds were strewn with the wounded and mutilated soldiers of

Deir Snid. Yes, it is true that nothing could stop our soldiers in their march toward death. But were we sending our soldiers into battle, or into a slaughterhouse?"

(It is difficult to know when this was written. It was published in March 1955, in the wake of the Israeli raid on Gaza, at a moment when Nasser as head of state wanted to impart a sort of martial spirit to the nation, and a certain confidence to the army. It is a curious text, in any case; more than a mere indictment of the current high command, it rings very true at times, and contains some very moving passages.)

It is worth the trouble to continue our reading of Gamal the historian. We see him run into "a soldier who was taking down his tent for the second time that day, in obedience to a succession of orders and counter-orders, and loudly chanting 'Shame! shame!' All the while he was modulating the words in his dialect, a naïve but heartbreaking expression of everybody's feelings." Several days later, he was indignant to receive the order to march toward Fallouga and Beit-Gabrin, "while the Cairo newspapers had published the itinerary in advance. . . ." Was this a "political war," he wondered, distraught. Everything happened as though the Egyptian high command was concerned only with occupying as much territory as possible with the sole aim of dazzling public opinion and foreign observers, without thought of lives or of the dispersion of forces suffered by the units involved. "How I despised those rookie generals, relaxing in their armchairs, totally unaware of what a battlefield is like, totally unaware of the sufferings of the combatants, and content to place an idle finger on the map and order that such-and-such a position be taken."

The first truce intervened. Nasser, chief-of-staff of the Sixth Battalion, had pitched camp at Ashdod in Palestine. One day he asked a simple soldier: "Tell me, what are we doing here?"

The answer: "Maneuvers, *effendim* (Sir)." "What maneuvers?" "The Rebiki maneuvers." (Rebiki is a village between Cairo and Suez.) Gamal was thunderstruck by the soldier's pathetic ignorance. And yet when Gamal himself became the master, twenty years later, he would hear many more stories of the same ilk.

The truce was broken July 8. Two days later, Captain Nasser blatantly decided to ignore an extravagant order. The commander of the sector had without notification "withdrawn the troops which covered us. A real spirit of revolt roared within me." On July 12 Gamal was wounded in the chest by a bullet. "I tried to stop the hemorrhage with my handkerchief, while at the same time a strange sensation invaded my soul. I felt no fear, no pain. I merely felt full of regrets." Removed to the nearby hospital of Magdal, he was immediately operated on. Around him were "bloodstained clothes, and the groans which the wounded were trying to stifle. I thought about war, and how I hated it. I told myself that if ever I reached a position of responsibility I would reflect a thousand times before sending our soldiers to war."

The second armistice imposed by the UN, from the end of July to the beginning of October 1948, enabled the Haganah to strengthen its forces and to better its positions—no one, in fact, actually respected the official cessation of combat. On October 4 began the battle of the Negev, from which the Israeli forces had decided to dislodge the Egyptian army. The Sixth Battalion, that commanded by Abdel Nasser (back at the front after a convalescent leave in Cairo during August) was ordered to defend the sector at Beit-Gabrin and Erak el-Manshia, an important communications link between the Bethlehem-Hebron zone and the coastal zone of Gaza—the two principal strongpoints of the Egyptian army.

The Sixth Battalion was ordered to take the village of Mehrez from which it had recently been dislodged. Soon, however, this operation was entrusted instead to the First Battalion, commanded by Zakaria Mohieddin. Gamal offered to cover his friend during the mission, and moved up toward Mehrez. "The fires of hell were raging there. I admit that, for the first time in my life, I was afraid. I thought of my family. I had no idea what would happen to me. Happily this state of mind left me at the end of three minutes, and I regained my composure. I was invaded by that feeling of indifference which is the soldier's trump card."

A happy turn of phrase, but even less so than the passage which follows: "I had officiously offered to join the attack. All I was really required to do was fall back. On the way back I ran into Zakaria. I wished him good luck." Here comedy has caught up with drama. Good luck, Zakaria, the fire's a bit heavy. The warrior thinks only of surviving. But the writer has the sense of the simple truth.

So began the battle of Fallouga, opening with an Egyptian setback, also a personal setback for Nasser: the fall, on October 18, of Erak Sueidan, the crossroads between the two positions which he had to hold, Erak el-Manshia and Fallouga. The unit protecting his western flank was the Ninth Battalion. "Unluckily," he writes, "the commanding officer was on leave. The second was killed by a mortar shell. The third had driven off in a car all the way to Ismailia. . . ." Opposite, General Yigal Allon commanded the attack in person. On October 20 the route to Hebron was also cut; the two Egyptian units were sealed off from their bases and encircled at Fallouga.

This time, however, they were well commanded, by a great devil of a colonel of Sudanese origin, Sayed Taha, nicknamed "the black panther" (it is he who was called "the tiger of Fallouga," and not Gamal Abdel Nasser, as legend had it once his renown made him seem worth flattering). At Taha's side, Captain Nasser found several of his friends, Abdel Hakim Amer, Zakaria Mohieddin, Salah Salem, Saroit Ikasha. One could almost say that here the *Dhobat el-Ahrar,* or Society of Free Officers, was born.

From the story of Fallouga, a trial firmly withstood by all, Gamal Abdel Nasser was able to construct, not without eloquence, the central myth of the Egyptian drama: "Our hearts remained close to our dear homeland, left to the mercy of monsters. We were suffering the consequences of their ambitions, their schemes, their whims—right there under fire and without provisions. My heart went out to dear Egypt. I asked myself then: is not our homeland another Fallouga, a much bigger Fallouga? This is only the reflection of what is happening in Egypt. Is not our homeland also besieged by an enemy, left prey to ambitious and greedy men?"

If Gamal knew how to make a symbol of Fallouga, the siege of Fallouga made of Nasser an officer whose reputation began to grow beyond the circle of the faithful. His companions-in-arms have recounted how, when the Israeli advance guard had begun to infiltrate the pocket of Erak el-Manshia, he telephoned to Mohieddin, the chief-of-staff of the nearest regiment, to bombard his own sector at the risk of being hit himself. The operation was successful: Abdel Nasser counterattacked and was able to re-establish contact with the rest of the besieged forces. In this way at least two Egyptian regiments were able to hold their ground and to await the armistice and the honorable exit which their gallantry had earned them, a gallantry which was recognized and saluted by the Israeli military chiefs.

Beyond this professional "recognition," the battle of Fallouga brought Gamal Abdel Nasser another type of rather unexpected contact. During the June armistice the commander of the Sixth Battalion had been designated by Colonel Taha to make contact with a representative of the enemy army. The officer designated by Yigal Allon was called Yeruham Cohen. He was also a captain. The two men left interesting accounts of these encounters. Gamal's constitutes a section of the *Philosophy of the Revolution.* Not without dignity, he pays tribute to his adversary, noting that he viewed him primarily as one of the Zionist fighters who had wrested their independence from Britain before depriving the Arabs of their lands. If he questioned him avidly on the methods of the Haganah and the Stern gang, it was not in an altogether disinterested fashion. For his part, Yeruham Cohen also captures this aspect of his interlocutor.[3]

The battles in Palestine had many more effects on Egypt and Gamal Abdel Nasser. They brought into the limelight the name of a general who had already attracted the attention of his peers by his gesture of 1942: Mohammed Naguib. He had been wounded three times—and the last time so grievously that he was given up for dead on the battlefield. He was the direct sponsor of Abdel Hakim Amer, then an officer in his general staff; and he was very close to the brilliant Colonel Ahmed Shawki, the commanding officer of the best regiment in the army, the Thirteenth Infantry. Before long Naguib became a major figure in the eyes of the younger officers.

If in this absurd conflict he discovered a candidate for the leadership of his future coup, Gamal also lost the two men who until then had inspired him the most: Colonel Wagih Khalil, who had been his superior at El-Alamein, in 1941–2; and Colonel Ahmed Abdel Aziz, head of the volunteers who had left for Palestine before the declaration of war, who died in August 1948, hit by fire from Egyptian lines. The day before, during a meeting in the tent of Kamaleddin Hussein, a young officer of Nasser's group, he had said in the presence of Salah Salem, another "Gamalist": "The real struggle is

[3] See Part Six of this book, "Confronting Israel."

elsewhere. Do not forget this—the real struggle is in Egypt."

But a defeat is a defeat. These Egyptian troops had fought valiantly, and their honest commanders had "saved the honor" of the unhappy army. Men like Gamal Abdel Nasser had no need of Abdel Aziz's speeches: the army had done what it could. It was the entire state which had cracked. In the palace, the general-staff, the political parties, the governmental institutions—all was evasion, frivolity, subterfuge, and connivance. Even an organization like the Muslim Brethren, whose combative exaltation he had admired, thought only of using the conflict as a means to seize power. The Communists as a whole had disassociated themselves from the common cause, quarreling among themselves as to its correct interpretation. For the moment Gamal had no use for such attitudes. He rejected them totally.

The Captain Abdel Nasser who returned from the war was now thoroughly disillusioned. No one had survived the disaster untarnished. He might continue to hunt for allies, but no longer for a mentor, a champion, a natural leader. One thinks of de Gaulle at the end of May 1940.

The somber mood of the army, the rancor which it had accumulated, the rumors about "defective arms" supposedly delivered with the complicity of the king or his entourage (which would not have lost in the transaction)—all this was public and notorious by the time the veterans of Fallouga returned to their barracks. Abdel Nasser's quarters were in Ismailia. It was there that he learned, on March 23, 1949, that the Syrian, Colonel Hosni Zaim, had just seized power in Damascus. It was the first *Putsch* in a long series. Gamal seems not to have viewed the Syrian coup as a model, but he gave it serious attention.

One month later, Captain Nasser, on leave in Cairo, was summoned by his commander-in-chief, who took him at once to the office of the premier, Ibrahim Abdel Hadi. Abdel Hadi was the successor of Nokrashi Pasha, assassinated in late December by a member of the secret society of Muslim Brethren (whose leader, Hassan el-Banna, was to fall several weeks later to the gunshots of the king's agents). What did the head of state want from this unknown officer?

Abdel Hadi, who interrogated Nasser in the presence of the secret police chief, Ibrahim Talaat, accused him of having formed a secret society of officers to prepare for a clandestine struggle. He demanded the surrender of the names of the officers linked with the Muslim Brethren. The war and the police repression following the murder of Nokrashi had revealed Anwar el-Sadat's contacts with the Brethren, as well as the sympathy of certain officers, like Kamaleddin Hussein, for Hassan el-Banna's partisans. But the police were interested in the Brethren rather than in the officers themselves. Hence, Nasser was soon out of danger—at the very moment when the police should have had their eyes on him.

It was then that he really began in earnest the first phase of the great conspiracy: the formation of the *Dhobat el-Ahrar,* the committee of the Free Officers.

8

Give Me a Dozen Resolute Men

There are at least ten versions of the founding of the clandestine group that helped Nasser overthrow Farouk and to seize the machinery of state. We have kept our distance from

Anwar el-Sadat's version. Sadat, without playing down Gamal's role, obviously tends to spotlight his own, with an expressive enthusiasm in which imagination wins out over simple authenticity.

The version we shall give is based largely on information from Saroit Okasha; first because he was very close to Nasser; but also because no special ideological tendency informs his account; and no personal ambition seems to impel him to aggrandize his own or anyone else's role; and lastly because he is an intellectual, trying to extract the meaning out of every event without compromising his own honesty.

It was at the end of the summer of 1949, after spending several weeks of inactivity to discourage the police investigations which followed his visit to the premier, that Gamal Abdel Nasser once again convened his comrades. They no longer met at his home, but preferably at that of Abdel Hakim Amer, who had come to be recognized as his lieutenant. Gamal defined five goals which, he felt, would have to be realized within six years. Hence the target year of the conspiracy was 1954.

First goal: the construction of a general staff of Free Officers, concentrated enough to keep a secret and act as one body, but also numerous enough to radiate throughout the entire army. At the end of November 1949, an initial executive committee was formed. It comprised Gamal Abdel Nasser, Abdel Hakim Amer, Salah Salem, Gamal Salem, Abdellatif Boghdadi, Khaled Mohieddin, Kamaleddin Hussein, Hassan Ibrahim, and Abdel Moneim Abdel Rauf. Abdel Rauf had close ties with the Muslim Brethren, and was for this reason excluded from the group two years later. On the other hand, the committee soon picked up Nasser's two earliest companions, Anwar el-Sadat and Zakaria Mohieddin, and later on, Hussein Shafei, Yussef Saddiq, and Abdel Moneim Amin. Neither Saroit Okasha nor Ali Sabri, nor his brother Hussein

Zulficar, nor Ahmed Shawki were ever members, despite the services which they rendered and the role they were to play later on.

A few words about these men: it is not they who changed the face of Egypt—Egypt changed by itself. But these men will return so often in the course of this narrative that it seems appropriate to situate them more precisely. From the social point of view, they were all, like Gamal, the sons of lower-middle-class families with the exception perhaps of the Mohieddins and Abdel Moneim Amin, who were from the middle class. (As for the Sabri brothers, they came from a frankly aristocratic family related to the queen but through a ruined branch. This origin was perhaps one of the reasons for their being excluded, as were for similar reasons Saroit Okasha and Ahmed Shawki).

Two of these "founders," Abdel Moneim Amin and Yussef Saddiq, were dropped from the group as soon as the coup was over: the first because of a stance judged too pro-Western, the second for his unbroken membership in a Marxist organization, the MDLN (formerly EMNL).

None of these men had stature comparable to Nasser's. Gamal Salem had intellectual gifts comparable to those of his leader, but his bad health, capricious character, crudely technocratic conceptions, and perhaps his abuse of hashish, kept him a marginal figure. Zakaria Mohieddin was a remarkable organizer, gifted with clear and balanced judgment; his cousin Khaled was a man of the people and had a good sense of political culture; Abdellatif Boghdadi was a robust manager; Abdel Hakim Amer had high animal spirits, charm, a fine staff officer's technique, and plenty of good sense. But had it not been for Nasser the team would have risked getting trapped by internal polemics, surprise raids, or even re-adherence to the regime.

The second task was propaganda. From before the time of

the Palestine war, the left-wing elements of the rudimentary new group had published and distributed several tracts. As of November 1949, this became perhaps the principal activity of the *Dhobat el-Ahrar*. In 1950, these tracts were turned into a unique organ bearing the title *Voice of the Free Officers*. The first issue, drawn up like most of the others by Khaled Mohieddin and distributed in late November 1949, was entitled "The Army Gives a Warning." It described the "defective" state of the arms issued to the troops during the Palestine war. Exceptional boldness? No. At the same time, a member of parliament, Mustafa Marei, denounced in the Senate the corruption of the king's entourage, while the weekly *Rose el-Youssef* spoke of the arms affair with as much frankness as the officers' tracts (which frankness, by the way, landed the *Rose*'s director, Ihsan Abdel Kouddous, in jail).

The same newspapers also published several highly acid circulars signed "The Unknown Soldier." Only the director knew that the author was General Naguib. But the officers had another and even more important tribune: *Al-Misri,* the big Wafdist daily, whose editor-in-chief was Ahmed Aboul Fath. Aboul Fath was the brother-in-law of Saroit Okasha, through whom he had become friendly with Abdel Nasser. It was at Gamal's insistence that *Al-Misri* boldly published an announcement of the murder of an officer, Abdel Kader Taha, whose wife the king had allegedly coveted. The principal responsibility for the crime was imputed to General Hussein Sirry Amer, the *bête noire* of the Free Officers. And so the conspirators began to move out their pawns.

They were lucky to have a head start in realizing the third point of their program, information and subversion. One of them, Salah Salem, was in effect a member of the cabinet of General Haydar, the minister of war, while Anwar el-Sadat was close to Dr. Yussef Rashad, one of the king's physicians. When Abdel Hakim Amer was in his turn attached to the staff of General Naguib, then director of the infantry, Captain Nasser could feel satisfied that he disposed of excellent listening posts and footholds of subversion.

The fourth goal on the program was liaison with other subversive organizations. With the Muslim Brethren structural ties existed, if only because of the mediation of Abdel Rauf. But we have seen that, since his troubling interview with Premier Abdel Hadi, Gamal Abdel Nasser preferred to keep his distance from the Brethren. For this reason Abdel Rauf was excluded from the group in 1951, while the other sympathizers of the great fraternity, Anwar el-Sadat, Kamaleddin Hussein, and Hussein el-Shafei, were invited to curb their ardent devotion.

On the Communist side, permanent ties also existed. True, Khaled Mohieddin was not actually registered in the MDLN. But Yussef Saddiq was, and also Captain Ahmed Hamrush who maintained a liaison with the Free Officers, in company with the magistrate Ahmed Fuad. In a highly interesting but rather hostile book about his former friend,[1] Ahmed Aboul Fath insists that Gamal had a membership card in the party under the pseudonym of "Maurice." Those militants of the MDLN which we have been able to interview have all firmly denied it. Nonetheless Abdel Nasser often met with the authorities of the MDLN—but never their principal theoretician, Henri Curiel, who, arrested during the 1948 war and later exiled, had moved to Italy and later France. (Certain persons claim that the founder of the MDLN never ceased to fascinate Gamal.)

The officers also had no scarcity of connections with the socialists of Ahmed Hussein. Hussein's sympathizers were later to become the most compromising members of the organization. But the fascist lawyer himself avoided young

[1] *L'Affaire Nasser*, Paris, 1962.

fellows like the plague, although he had helped to train them. They seriously threatened to pull the rug out from under his feet: did they not have the same clientele and apparently parallel aims to those of the former Green Shirts?

The contacts of the Free Officers were not limited to aboveground parties and organizations: societies and conspiracies were teeming then, above all in the army. There was, for example, the group headed by the petulant Captain Mustafa Kamel Sedky, a declared revolutionary. For a clandestine movement, this group was much discussed; Sedky, so it was said, was actually being used by the king's secret police (unless this member of Farouk's "iron guard" were to betray his own employers). The labyrinth was hopelessly confusing. Yet Gamal was able to find his way, astutely avoiding this seductive swashbuckler who, surrounded by women, reminds one of a Florentine chronicle of the quattrocento—not unlike other protagonists in the political life of Cairo in 1950. . . .

In the midst of this pestiferous swamp a passage suddenly appeared, leading straight to the fifth goal of Gamal Abdel Nasser's program: action. In 1950 the king resigned himself to the holding of free elections. Was this an attempt to regain a sort of factitious popularity? Or perhaps to beguile his old enemies of the Wafd into the quagmire in which he himself was already stuck? For in the Egypt of 1950, free elections automatically signaled the success and return to power of the old party. Its recent bad behavior had not yet entirely discouraged its clientele, and it still preserved in its leader, Mustafa Nahas, the ideal medium of "Egyptianism."

Like the king, the Wafd wanted to regain its ascendency over the masses at any price. And this entailed outbidding its most nationalistic rivals. In no time the Wafd, architect of the treaty of 1936 which young extremists like Gamal had so violently decried, began to stand, in London's eyes, for the abrogation of the treaty. In fact, on October 8, 1951, the Cairo parliament did unanimously approve the treaty's abrogation, thus turning the British contingent stationed in the Suez Canal Zone into an illegal occupier, and a justifiable target for patriotic vengeance. This was tantamount to a declaration of guerrilla war against the British forces of the canal.

The tracts of the Free Officers approved the Wafd's move. The guerrilla campaign gave free reign to the activist fever of Gamal and his companions. In an article in the review *Al-Tahrir,* published in 1955, Saroit Okasha has evoked this period: "We had become a beehive of activity: training commandos, aiding the partisans, issuing arms. . . ." In his house in Manshiet el-Bakri, Gamal Abdel Nasser, who had been promoted to lieutenant colonel in May 1951, installed a munitions cache and drew up maps with his companions. His representatives in the Canal Zone seem at that time to have been Kamal Rifaat and Lutfi el-Waked; they led commandos into combat. Yet interested as the Free Officers doubtless were in the struggle, they did not seem to take the part one might have expected of their type of organization, nor did they become involved on an order comparable to that of certain student groups or the Muslim Brethren.

Gamal wanted to conserve his forces; he was concerned above all to save his men for the overthrow of the government. Perhaps he judged the current phase too preparatory to engage in a battle costly in human lives, in painstakingly trained cadres. Two years later, when Abdellatif Boghdadi, president of the military tribunal which arraigned Fuad Serag Eddin, the minister of the interior in 1951 and the real chief of the Wafd, and charged him with having thrown the nation into the "battle of the canal" with insufficient preparation, the accused vainly replied that, after all, the army itself had hardly done its duty during the invasion. In fact neither the clandestine groups in the army nor the army's official forces, prudently maintained in reserve by the king, had shouldered their responsibilities, while the university volunteers and the *Ikhwan* (Muslim Brethren) were bravely paying with their lives.

Tension was rising. One year earlier, a scandal had burst upon the Alexandria cotton market. The cornering of a large part of the harvest had enabled a group of speculators— current gossip had it that one of them was the premier's wife, the vivacious "Zouzou"—to manipulate, lucratively, the market value of the national product. The king's court crawled with financial and sexual scandals; and Farouk was even hissed while leaving a cinema. Everywhere people wondered about the exploits of the political police, which, under the aegis of a miniature Fouché, Ibrahim Emam, abducted, tortured, and blackmailed its victims.

Wasn't the time ripe? The Free Officers had set themselves a period of five years to drive out the nation's masters. But the social upheaval had quickened to such a pace that it was necessary to review the schedule. After all, revolutions are not the Olympic Games.

As the hour of action approached, it was necessary for the conspiracy to find a symbolic figure. What kind of reception would the nation give a gang of young officers, even if they were its real liberators? Power had so long been gerontocratic in this land where patriotism was symbolized by Saad's white mustache and where no one even hinted that Mustafa Nahas was slipping gently into his dotage that the Free Officers could not dream of acting without the protection of a name and a face with popular appeal.

No one in political life was acceptable to them. The head of the Nationalist (Watani) party, Hafez Ramadan, was intransigent and incorruptible: but for the task at hand he was

really too old. In the Wafd there were quite a few respectable
leaders: for example in the left wing of the party, friends of
Ahmed Aboul Fath. But the best of them, Aziz Fahmi, had
just died in an accident which had aroused some suspicions
(the king was not fond of him), and the rest were as young
as Gamal and his people. There was no question of having
recourse to a leading Muslim Brother, nor to a communist
chief. Therefore, they had to look within the army.

Four names were brought up in the Officers' committee:
the old Marshal Aziz el-Masri and the generals Fuad Sadek,
Seif el-Din, and Mohammed Naguib. Ten years earlier the
marshal had been their mentor. But his natural eccentricity
had become exacerbated with time. He reminded one of
Bernard Shaw's *en culotte de peau*. Perfect for an after-dinner
party, but to rebuild the state? Seif el-Din was said to be too
tame; as for General Sadek, a fine officer of integrity, he had
just been named chief of the general staff by the king, who
had perhaps been warned that he was considering some sort
of coup. Promotion was an argument which General Sadek
would be unlikely to resist.

That left Mohammed Naguib. All the young officers admired his conduct in 1942 and his valiance in Palestine. Some
knew that he was the mysterious "unknown soldier" who had
denounced the regime's corruption in *Rose el-Youssef*. As a
member of Nasser's entourage, Abdel Hakim Amer congratu-
lated himself on the sympathy which Naguib now expressed
for the movement (at least as far as Naguib's scanty knowledge went). Although the general public hardly knew him,
he was the best possible candidate. When the time was ripe,
they would let him know he was their leader.

In the meantime, the committee of Free Officers needed a
test, if not of strength, at least of influence, against the crown.
An election was to take place in January 1952: that of the
president of the Officers' Club. It was a minor event, of

course. But Gamal pressured Naguib to present himself at the head of a list in which figured several Free Officers: Zakaria Mohieddin and Hassan Ibrahim. The general's name was well enough known by the king to act on him like an emetic. Farouk let it be known that he would not accept this mischievous leader as president of the officer corps. Nonetheless, Naguib was elected by a crushing majority[2] after an unprecedented campaign: Nasser and his companions even had campaign leaflets distributed in the barracks and at the exits of the army cinemas.

Furious, the king decided to scotch the election and designated *ex cathedra* a president of his own choice, General Hussein Sirry Amer, a symbol of everything the young officers hated, besmirched as he was by every court scandal. This time, it was war—and all the more so since Gamal, with the help of Ahmed Aboul Fath, wrote an account of the affair in *Al-Misri* which was quite humiliating for Farouk.

The *bikbashi* (lieutenant colonel) Abdel Nasser was to wage this war against the king and his puppets with an energy bordering on fanaticism, and without any squeamishness over the means. In his *Philosophy of the Revolution* he recounts with impressive frankness the story of the assassination attempt against the same Hussein Sirry Amer four months later, an attempt in which he himself took part despite the principled hostility toward terrorism which he had often opposed to the projects of Anwar el-Sadat and Salah Salem:

The detonation of our arms, immediately followed by the heart-rending cries of a woman and the sound of a frightened child, haunted me all the way to my bed and kept me awake all night. Remorse gripped my heart. . . . I stam-

[2] Nasser's two henchmen on the list, Zakaria Mohieddin and Hassan Ibrahim, were also elected, as well as one sympathizer, Colonel Mehanna, who was chosen as regent after the *coup d'état* and then brutally purged in 1953 for his overambitiousness.

mered, "If only he does not die." By dawn I had arrived at the point where I prayed for the life of the man I had tried to kill—how great was my joy when, feverishly searching the morning newspaper, I discovered that the man had not succumbed.[3]

But it was yet another event, not directly related to conspiracy, which was to determine its rhythm and its outcome.

9

The Bonfire Conspiracy

In the month of January 1952, Egypt was a triptych of suffering, anger, and humiliation. In the villages, the peasantry was being exploited unbearably (especially since the market price of cotton had fallen after a brief boom sparked by the Korean war). In the Canal Zone the guerrilla war against the British had assumed a ferocity very costly in human lives. (These were the days when a French daily published a news story from the Suez area under the headline, "Two English wounded," and with subhead, "Eighteen Egyptians killed.") In Cairo, the royal court pursued its depravity and intrigues to the point of nausea, and Egypt was about to vomit.

[3] A joy which must have been, or certainly should have been, mitigated. For this lamentable assault did leave a victim: the general's chauffeur, a fellow named Ahmed Moussa, wounded by a bullet shot from the sentimental terrorist (cf. Eliezer Beeri, *Army Officers in Arab Politics and Society*, New York, 1970, p. 90).

Between Port-Said and Suez, the incidents raged on, though they did not exactly constitute the "Egyptian Stalingrad" of which the Cairo papers spoke. But as of January 15, the guerrilla struggle expanded into a veritable battle. On that day a commando managed to infiltrate the large base of Tell el-Kebir, the principal arms depot of the British command, and blow up a magazine, leaving ten dead on the field. Four days later the guerrillas repeated the attack. General Erskine, the commander-in-chief of the zone, decided to stage reprisals: he encircled the Ismailia barracks of the *Buluk Nizam*—the Egyptian auxiliary police—in which was quartered a contingent whose complicity with the guerrillas was obvious. At 7:00 A.M., January 25, he let it be known that if this unit of three hundred fifty men did not surrender its arms within two hours, he would level their barracks with artillery fire.

Should they resist? The commander of the *Buluk* telephoned Cairo where the all-powerful minister of the interior, Fuad Serag Eddin, ordered them to hang on, no matter what the cost. Was this a reflex of natural dignity? Or perhaps a calculation aimed at putting the British in a morally indefensible position before the reopening of negotiations? Fuad Pasha certainly craved an incident, but General Erskine offered him a massacre: when the British tanks stopped firing, about noon that Friday, January 25, the *Buluk* had lost fifty dead and a hundred wounded.

In Cairo, where the news became known toward the end of the afternoon, the reaction was violent. The Wafdist Youth demanded a massive counterattack. A specially convened cabinet meeting adopted grave measures that evening: the severance of diplomatic relations with London, an appeal to the UN Security Council, and the arrest of eighty British "hostages." Cairo went to bed in anguish that night.

In the early morning a strange procession formed in the courtyard of the university: beside the students a column of

the Cairo *Buluk Nizam,* who had come to declare themselves
on a solidarity strike with their comrades of Ismailia, marched
on the center of the capital, demanding arms to fight on the
canal. They arrived before the chamber of the Council of
Ministers, where Abdel Fattah Hassan, the labor minister, was
haranguing the mob: "Today is your day! You will be
avenged!" Traditional eloquence—predictable audience response. Yet when the clever tribune cried out haphazardly,
mostly for effect, "And why not ask the Russians for arms?"
he was surprised to notice that he had aroused considerable
enthusiasm. He soon noticed that "his public" seemed oddly
changed that day, that it was studded with soldiers in un-
buttoned jackets with their forage-caps and helmets thrown
back, and an air of defiance in their looks. Shades of the
October Revolution.

A column of still bolder demonstrators marched toward the
royal palace of Abdim. The column was channeled toward
the Opera Square. Outside the Badia cabaret, the holy place
of belly dancing, a police officer was drinking in company
with a resident of the establishment. "Are you not ashamed,
constable," they asked, "to drink while your brothers are being
massacred on the canal?" He sneered. The crowd became enraged and invaded the establishment, setting fire to it. The
flames of the Badia were to spread far and wide.

A half-hour later the Rivoli cinema went up in flames in its
turn, and then the Metro. Toward noon it was the turn of the
Turf Club, where some influential members of the British
colony and the Canadian chargé d'affaires had gathered. They
tried to escape, but eight of them were pushed back into the
flames by a populace drunk with fury. By all accounts the
incendiaries were led by several ringleaders whom one could
see here and there, maps in hand.

At lunchtime it was the turn of the Groppi, a tea room on
Soliman Pasha Square where much of officialdom and the

haute bourgeoisie gathered every afternoon. At teatime Shepheards Hotel, the symbol of the British presence, went up in flames. One of the chiefs of the political police was looking idly on. When a journalist expressed his astonishment at the chief's phlegmatic behavior, the latter replied with a smile: "Let them play awhile." Soon it was the turn of Barclay's Bank, then the Curiel and Ade's department stores. And soon the looting began.

The city—the downtown district of the well-to-do, the Europeans, the businessmen—had been gripped by an incendiary plot, with all its attendant madness and terror. From noon on the police budged only once, around three o'clock, to block the way of a column of rioters marching toward the British Embassy. The idleness of the police: was it a result of incompetence? sabotage? directives from above? As for the army, it was not until after five o'clock that a few detachments appeared, although a single squadron of light armored cars positioned on the Opera, Ismailia, and Soliman Pasha squares in the late morning would have cut the catastrophe short. What can explain this ineptitude, which, objectively speaking, amounted to actual complicity?

A political answer was supplied by the minister of the interior, Fuad Serag Eddin—himself responsible for both the drama at Ismailia and the disorders in the capital. According to the Wafd boss, whose explanation was published February 10 in *Al-Misri* (which was forthwith suppressed), there were two opposed to the intervention of the forces of public order, especially the army: the king himself, and the king's war minister, General Haydar Pasha, the ex-director of prisons. When Serag Eddin entreated the latter to call the army, the general allegedly replied: "It would be impolitic to have the army march against the people, who might easily become hostile to it. And there is too great a risk that the army might join the demonstrators!"

Another interesting fact: while the minister of the interior
was pleading for the intervention of the army, Farouk was
giving a feast for six hundred officers in honor of the birth of
a crown prince. After all, his great-grandfather Mohammed
Ali had consolidated his power by defenestrating the Mamlukes from the summit of his citadel in Cairo at the close of a
banquet. Farouk's banquet hardly consolidated his power: but
he did succeed that evening in ridding himself of the Wafdist
premier, by forcing him into a position in which he was
obliged to resign. It was a paltry victory, however, and it did
not put a stop to the search for the guilty party.

We shall not linger here over history's verdict. Who burned
Cairo? The king? The English? The Muslim Brethren? The
socialists of Ahmed Hussein? We have tried elsewhere to reopen this dossier.[1] What concerns us here is the role played
by the Free Officers—especially the tight-lipped discretion
which they always showed on the subject of the terrible day
of January 26. Yet in vain have we ransacked the sources:
we have found practically no trace, that day, of any of these
men, nonetheless so militant during that period. Two of them,
of rather modest rank, and of little note in succeeding years,
Captain Abdel Hadi Negm Eddin and Lieutenant Baghat
Rifaat, were spotted at the front of the procession which was
headed that morning from the university to the cabinet
chamber.

But it is enlightening to examine the legal actions taken
by the July regime. Attentive as it was to denouncing the
faults of its predecessors, it refrained from investigating the
legal proceedings following the most horrible crime of the

[1] Jean and Simonne Lacouture, *L'Egypte en mouvement,* Paris, 1956–1962,
pp. 107–15.

previous epoch. The new regime released, after an almost mock tribunal, the man whom all the rumors indicated as being largely responsible for that nefarious day: Ahmed Hussein. Neither the trial of Fuad Serag Eddin nor those of the Muslim Brethren dwelled lengthily on the affair of January 26. Perhaps Gamal Abdel Nasser was indeed protecting certain members of his organization.

More than any other day (including July 23, 1952), it was the day of January 26, 1952, which felled the old regime. This day marked the beginning of the second Egyptian revolution. Far exceeding the sorry schemes of the petty Machiavellians of the royal palace and the foreign embassies, the tragic ruins which smoked that evening encompassed not only the *beaux quartiers* of Cairo: they were also the ruins of an epoch, a system, a regime, a society, a relation between a people and its rulers. They were the perverted fruit of a long revolutionary tension, which was to yield still more fruit in the future.

Whatever their behavior on that day, Gamal and his people saw it as a portent of coming revolution. But did they see its immediate implications? Several years later their spokesman Mohammed Hassanein Heykal gave a historic interpretation of that day which we must quote here.

It is possible that certain individuals, intentionally, and out of pure ill-will, put the capital to the torch. But this is a minor issue. In fact, after the first spark, the masses themselves rushed in to express their being, by feeding the conflagration, by looting and pillaging. The burning of Cairo was not, though it may seem so today, a simple criminal episode, but an explosion by those who had nothing against those who monopolized the very right to live. From that point on it is hardly astounding if the anger of the masses turned against the cinemas, the grand hotels, and the ele-

gant department stores—all places from which the masses
wanted to protest their exclusion.[2]

This "dignifying" interpretation, so to speak, of the sinister
day of January 26 is also the thesis of the most revolutionary
current of the Egyptian left. From their point of view, the
authors of *La Lutte des classes en Egypte de 1945 à 1968*
have written: "The main feeling behind the demonstration
was justified because it welled up out of an authentic need of
the disinherited masses . . . it is inevitable that the excesses
would multiply, and that the hatred would at times take on a
xenophobic or anti-Semitic form. . . ."[3]

The same authors demonstrate, without apology, another
revelation of "Black Saturday": not only the terrible frustration of the people but also the bankruptcy of the cadres of
the growing revolution. Where, they ask, were the Communists? This absence Gamal Abdel Nasser had also noticed. And
if Heykal, his closest confidant, who reflected, according to all
the evidence, Nasser's own observations, gave in 1961 such
a "political," if not sociological, analysis of the day of January 26, 1952, it is because the explosion must have been
studied from this angle by the Free Officers. Leaving indignation and fear to others, the Officers confined themselves to
evaluating the ill-directed energy of the masses, guiding it
and putting it to their own uses. The revolutionary parties
and organizations, the usual interpreters and tribunes of popular fury, seemed stupefied, somehow unable to capitalize on
this anger as a weapon of either confrontation or negotiation.

In brief—however "natural" (Heykal) or "justified" in its
origin (Mahmud Hussein)—the fury of January 26 did un-

[2] Mohammed Hassanein Heykal, *Azmat al-Muthaqqafin*, Cairo, 1961
(quoted by Anwar Abdel Malek, *La Pensée politique arabe contemporaine*,
Paris, 1970).

[3] Mahmud Hussein, Paris, 1969, 1971, p. 87.

doubtedly open a new phase of the prerevolutionary process. A gulf suddenly opened before all the revolutionaries and power-seekers, from the Free Officers to the Muslim Brethren, from the radical elements of the Wafd to the Communists. The British, in conjunction with the Americans, were to waste still another six months trying to remodel the king's image. They changed nothing. Egypt was for the taking—by the boldest, by the readiest, and by those disposed of the best on-the-spot intelligence and the best leverage abroad.

But let us return to Gamal and the Free Officers. Starting with a core of fifteen men whom we have briefly described, the committee now could count two or three hundred members. They were compartmentalized into highly discrete cells by the organization's ingenious creator, Nasser himself, and his two able staff officers, Abdel Hakim Amer and Zakaria Mohieddin. With the exception of the stewards of each cell the officers never knew more than four or five of their comrades in the entire network. Anyone with some experience of Egypt must admit that the preservation of such secrets for more than a year must have taxed to the utmost the talents of the *bikbashi* Abdel Nasser.

The revolutionary cadres existed. The opportunities were multiplying daily. The socio-political climate could not have been more propitious. But what about the plans of this well-articulated mechanism? In their devotion to organizational tasks, had the Free Officers spared the trouble to establish a plan of action? Yes. As vague as possible, it did however exist. It was presented in the "Six Principles" to which the victorious officers would often later refer. They were as follows:

1) In view of the British armies stationed in the Suez Canal Zone, the first principle was the liquidation of colonialism and the Egyptian traitors who supported it.

2) In view of the feudal despotism which reigned arbitrarily over vast territories, the second principle was the liquidation of feudalism.

3) In view of the attempt to exploit the revolution's resources of energy in the interests of a group of capitalists, the third principle consisted in putting an end to the domination of power by capital.

4) In view of this economic exploitation and despotism—the inevitable consequence of the above—the fourth principle was to establish social equality.

5) In view of the plots aimed at weakening the army and using its scant remaining power to threaten popular forces on the verge of uprising, the fifth principle consisted in forming a powerful popular army.

6) In view of the rigged electoral politics which falsified the facts of national life, the sixth principle was to establish a healthy democratic life.

Such was the political platform which Gamal Abdel Nasser and his companions advocated on the threshold of their great enterprise. It might not seem like much. But besides the Communists of the MDLN, and the two or three groups (*Dalshin,* PCE) made up of more frankly intellectual cadres, there was nobody who offered anything more precise to the Egyptians in this hour of explosive change. True, "the liquidation of feudalism," "the installation of social equality," "the establishment of a healthy democratic life," seem pretty vapid and could have been borrowed from the Wafd program, if not that of the Constitutional Liberals.

One can however detect certain interesting notions, which do reveal some political and critical direction in the authors of this document, Nasser and Khaled Mohieddin. These are the two sentences which treat the exploitation of "the revolution's resources of energy in the interests of a group of capitalists," and of "using the army's scant remaining power to threaten popular forces on the verge of uprising." Here we reach the heart of the debate which dominated the year 1952 and which we shall now try to summarize.

First, a short review. We have briefly evoked the conflicts of the "superstructure": the unconvincing battle against the English, waged by the establishment to drain off popular ardor, the occasionally criminal ruses of the palace in its bid for survival, the schemes of the Wafdist old guard leaders, and the blind pressure of agitational forces, such as the "Muslim Brethren" or Ahmed Hussein's commandos. But what counts much more were the deeper shifts within the society's infrastructure, essentially that is, the peasantry.

1951 was not only the year of the "battle of the canal" which captured the public eye, but also of something much more important: the beginning of a *jacquerie.* The patient Egyptian peasantry had moved almost by gusts of violence, onto the very lands which seemed the best controlled by the open alliance of local feudal lords, police chiefs, and *omdehs,* or village headmen. The movements were so violent that they provoked bloody repressions—as on the domain of Badrawi Ashur, Serag Eddin's brother-in-law. Similar repressions occurred on the estate of Prince Mohammed Ali, nominal heir to the throne, on that of Prince Yussef Kamel, with his 16,000 feddans the greatest of the latifundiaries besides Farouk and keeper of a pack of hounds of legendary ferocity, and even at Inshas, the loveliest domain of the king. It was rumored that one of these repressions, at Bahut, had left fourteen dead.

Let us again quote Mohammed Hassanein Heykal, the mirror of Nasser's mind. In the essay cited above, written in 1961, he writes: "What we have called the 'Bahut incident,' where the fellahs rose up against the landed proprietors of the village and burned the *daira* of the feudal lord, was not an ordinary village incident, but the spark of a revolt against the monopolization of the land. If the revolution had been slower in coming, one would have seen more Bahuts in every village where feudal lords controlled the land."[4]

It is only one more short step to interpret Heykal as saying that the movement of 1952 was launched to cut short these really deep and authentic revolutionary developments. But let us take care not to oversimplify, not to view the Gamal Abdel Nasser of early 1952 as a nationalist craving social order rather than social emancipation. He was more than a military man shocked by the double revolutionary uprising in the countryside (*jacqueries*) and in the cities (the burning of Cairo) and throwing his organization and the army before the bonfire, like a curtain between the clashing classes, to cut short the radical subversion.

This sounds like hero worship in reverse, but it is no less true than the popular image of the men of July 1952 as the revolutionary heroes of an Egyptian "Long March." Let us reiterate—without necessarily agreeing with—the description of Egypt in 1952 proposed by the authors of *La Lutte des classes en Egypte*. It is suggestive.

To understand the contradictions of this period and the historical significance of Nasserism, write the authors, one must not think of it as a strict contest between feudalism and capitalism, such as emerges from most Marxist analyses. One must bear in mind the concept of *transition*, allowing that "the structure of Egyptian society was entirely determined by the situation of a *blocked transition*." Because the relationship between producers and the means of production had not yet

[4] *Azmat al-Mutthaqqafin* (quoted by Abdel Malek, *La Pensée politique arabe contemporaine,* p. 188).

really been transformed, they continue, "a nexus between the owners of capital and the sellers of labor had not yet crystallized. There were only great landowners in the midst of a capitalist transformation, and disinherited masses in the midst of proletarization. . . ." Thus a "degraded feudalism" had managed only to half-ripen into a sort of "paralyzed capitalism."

Of all the strata of Egyptian society, it was the petty bourgeoisie which suffered the most from this retardation. Frustration ran especially high among the most modernized element of this class, the intellectuals and the small entrepreneurs, who feverishly awaited a major transformation "on the condition that the bulk of the changes would be introduced from above, and not initiated by the disinherited masses themselves."

Now as it happened Gamal Abdel Nasser and his companions belonged to this class, the petty bourgeoisie headed toward technology, economic development, and productivity. They were avid for economic as well as political independence; they also realized that the latter could not come without the former, and that no national emancipation would be possible without Egypt's withdrawal from a production and trade system controlled by the powers which dominated the world market.

The attempt to break through, to achieve a transition to capitalism by resorting to the use of state power against feudal power (or the power of "paralyzed" landed capitalism), while controlling the drive of the masses—could this be a plausible definition of the early, embryonic Nasserism? We shall see if it works.

But let us point out that the supporters of the most cynical thesis, that which depicts a Gamal Abdel Nasser consciously running interference for anti-Communist forces, contre-feu, find their best arguments in a remarkable book whose author was involved in the Cairo activities of the CIA in the years 1950–5, Miles Copeland.[5] According to this book a team of American agents sent into Egypt in early 1952 under the direction of Kermit Roosevelt, a CIA boss, rapidly made contact with the Free Officers, in whom Washington saw a growing force with which to oppose the revolution. In search of a "Muslim Billy Graham" (*sic*) likely to install a "good" regime of law and order, based on nationalism and Islam, the agents apparently believed they had found their man in Gamal—and his cadre.

It does not seem, according to Copeland, that the CIA made direct contact with Gamal Abdel Nasser himself before the takeover, but only with certain of his companions. It also seems that the CIA agents were not rebuked by the committee, which, once it was comfortably installed in power, formed especially cordial ties with a certain Major Steve Meade, as well as Miles Copeland's other collaborators.

If we are to believe Mr. Copeland, Nasser, in the course of their conversations, was at pains to discourage his interlocutors from exporting to Egypt an American-style "democratic" system. "To give liberty to this people," the *bikbashi,* or one of his spokesmen, is supposed to have told Steve Meade, and later Ambassador Jefferson Caffrey, "would be like leaving little children in the street." Mr. Copeland's account often has the ring of truth.

Revolutionary, counterrevolutionary, trailblazer of justice, or defender of law and order? Did he know himself? Whatever the answer, Nasser and the committee of Officers had yet to seize the state apparatus. In the meantime Farouk had appealed, in the deliquescence of the old regime, to three

[5] *The Game of Nations,* New York, 1969.

shrewd men who might indeed have procured for the crown a reprieve in an earlier day: Aly Maher, the Monsieur Thiers of modern Egypt, an astute nationalist, ferret-faced conservative and fertile inventor of political gadgets; next, Hussein Sirry, a gentle manipulator of intrigues and circumstances, much cleverer at this than he seemed; and finally, Naguib el-Hilali, the ex-Wafdist leader, whose behavior was subject to criticism, but whose integrity, talent, and energy were impeccable.

This adult merry-go-round enacted against a background of intrigues and debaucheries did not succeed in pacifying Egypt. An issue of *Rose el-Youssef* appeared, bearing on the cover a cartoon of the ex-minister Mustafa Nahas, leader of the Wafd, lowering a flag before a locomotive with the inscription *thawra* (revolution).

In the palace, a pitiful camarilla of Levantine procurers and Nubian valets arranged for the king's nocturnal entertainment, undid governments, and controlled nominations in the army. It was notorious that cabinet portfolios and the titles of bey or pasha were bought with gold, and not one important business matter transpired without Farouk playing some role in it. There was no longer a man in Cairo graced with a pretty wife who did not fear to escort her to a public place where the king might appear: for it was dangerous to resist his caprices. Farouk seemed to be suicidally drowning in excess, all his illusions contravened. One day in July he addressed to a singer girl friend a *billet-doux* signed: "F.F.: *foutes* Farouk." Poor washed-up Farouk.

At the end of June, the court took up its summer residence in Alexandria. From now on the political life of Egypt seemed reduced to a pathetic merry-go-round on the Corniche, from the San Stephano Casino to the Hotel Cecil. First came the Cadillac of Hafez Afifi Pasha, director of the royal cabinet: he was in quest of a champion, a man who would save the throne. Then came the cabinet attachés, followed by a few MPs in search of portfolios, and the journalists—not counting the numerous ladies of easy virtue. Pashas, procurers, politicians, informers—all wandered about directionless; a lavish death throe on the beach.

On July 21, Farouk witnessed Hussein Sirry try to call in General Naguib for the war portfolio—for Sirry had heard that Naguib alone could appease the mounting anger in the barracks and officer circles. Furious, the king dismissed him, snarling, "You bunch of pimps!" Next he called in Naguib el-Hilali. Now Farouk knew that this gentleman would refuse to keep Karim Tabet, a despised Levantine, in the government, and would bar the entrance of the eternal General Sirry Amer (who had recently escaped, as we have seen, the bullets of the Free Officers). But Farouk had no choice. So, obliged to abandon his two favorites and the scandals which their participation in the government would have entailed, he contemplated another coup of a special sort.

On July 22, toward five o'clock, fifteen gentlemen in gray smoking jackets, the members of Hilali's cabinet, entered the drawing room of the Ras el-Tin Palace to be sworn in before the king. A seventeenth personage soon appeared beside them —a certain Colonel Sherin, a brother-in-law of Farouk. "Sire," asked the head of the government, "what is the colonel doing among us?" "He'll be your minister of war!" replied Farouk with a guffaw. So reigned Farouk. Yet he had very little time left to indulge in this sort of whim. When the ministers left the palace twenty minutes later, with preoccupied looks on their faces, speaking of "grave moments" and "critical situations," they still believed that they governed Egypt. Only the following morning did they learn that political power had changed hands, and not only power, but the very source of power.

At six o'clock the chief of state was still convening with

his ministers in his villa, with its charming view of the sea; two hundred miles away, in the blistering Cairene suburb of Manshiet el-Bakri, eight young men in shirtsleeves were listening to a comrade read a detailed plan: that of the seizure of army general headquarters and the radio station. They were in the house of Khaled Mohieddin. The reader was Abdel Hakim Amer. The hour for action had come.

10

A Putsch *in Shirtsleeves*

The final phase of the takeover plan began in the early days of July. Various dates had been proposed and debated. Khaled Mohieddin suggested that they await the general elections—which the king could hardly defer much longer—in order to fit the operation into a climate of popular agitation and democratic choice. This was rejected as unwise—the clues obtained by the political police and General Haydar, for whom Salah Salem worked, were multiplying daily. Mortada Maraghi, the extremely thorough minister of the interior, might strike at any moment.

The court had just left for Alexandria—that would facilitate things. Also the two army units whose commanders sympathized with the views of the movement, the Thirteenth Infantry under Colonel Ahmed Shawki, a friend of Naguib's, and the First Motorized Battalion under Yussef Saddiq, a Free Officer himself, were scheduled to move toward Cairo on the evening of July 19. Now this was an eminently favorable circumstance. For what the conspirators, almost all of them general staff officers, needed the most was a massive deployment of troops—and here it was. Another prestigious army commander, however, the artillery colonel Rashad Mehanna, whose influence and whose batteries might have proved very useful, absolutely refused to march. They decided to forgo his help. "On July 10," recounts Saroit Okasha in an article published by *Al Tahrir* in 1955, "Gamal and Khaled Mohieddin dropped by and asked me, as they often did, to put on a recording of *Scheherazade* by Rimsky-Korsakov. Soon they were entranced by the charms of the music. Gamal listened, absorbed but dreamy-eyed. As soon as the last note had sounded, he rose, replaced the arm of the phonograph and declared abruptly: " 'We shall move at the beginning of next month.' " Why then? Quite simply because Gamal knew that the officers would prefer to pocket their pay before rushing into an adventure. Thus the peasant spirit revenged itself on the music-lover whom Slavic melodies had spurred into action.

As it turned out, the officers' pay was going to be a bit difficult to collect. For on July 20 Ahmed Aboul Fath telephoned his brother-in-law Okasha from Alexandria that the king was preparing to take on General Sirry Amer as war minister in a new government, and that the arrest of several Free Officers would promptly follow. Okasha dashed headlong to Gamal's house: luckily Gamal was surrounded by friends, and they decided at once to take action within forty-eight hours.

Several eyewitnesses have described Gamal Abdel Nasser correcting his students' papers in his office in the general staff college on July 21, while in a nearby house Abdel Hakim Amer and Khaled Mohieddin were putting the finishing touches on the plan for the coup. On the twenty-second, the day set for the operation, the last of those innumerable war councils which had brought the khaki-clad companions together for the last three years took place. It was held at Khaled's house, and was made up of Gamal Abdel Nasser, the two Mohieddins, Abdellatif Boghdadi, Hassan Ibrahim, Kamaleddin Hussein, Abdel Moneim Amin and Abdel Hakim Amer, who read the plan he had drawn up with Zakaria according to Gamal's directives. Anwar el-Sadat, as he himself has since recounted, was at the movies. As for the Salem brothers, they were in the El-Arish garrison, charged with carrying out the coup in the Egyptian army's most important outpost on the Israeli border.

The operation was set for midnight. As we have seen, its principal executors would be the two army officers Ahmed Shawki and Yussef Saddiq, plus Hussein el-Shafei, the tank commander of the Cairo fortifications. But about seven o'clock Captain Saad Tewfik informed Nasser that General Hussein Farid, whose arrest was one of the plan's first targets, had called an urgent general staff meeting for ten o'clock: by all accounts, he had got wind of the project. Friendly journalists soon notified Gamal that the ministry of the interior had been placed under a state of alert. Gamal decided to set the operation forward by one hour: then Hussein Farid's meeting would enable the Officers to net with one swoop the entire enemy clique. He tore off in his little Morris to warn his companions: luckily, he was able to pick up Anwar el-Sadat as he was coming out of the movies.

"Toward nine-thirty," Saroit Okasha recounts again, "I saw a tall young man in sports clothes pull up outside. It was Gamal. He was very calm. He told me that the time for the operation had been advanced, and added in English: " 'Saroit, don't let your feelings run away with you. And don't imagine that you're at the cinema. We have 99 chances out of 100 of succeeding.' "

Since then Gamal Abdel Nasser has told the story—with that bizarre humor which spurts up from time to time in his more confidential moments—of how he and Amer, embarking at last on their brilliant scheme, were leaving their office around eleven o'clock when suddenly they ran into a blacked-out column of armored cars heading toward general headquarters. All was lost! As they were about to open fire in wild desperation, a voice rang out: "Peace, brothers! I have already taken some prisoners!" It was Yussef Saddiq, a bit ahead of schedule!

The same officer, covered by Colonel Shawki's Thirteenth Infantry—the spearhead of the operation—burst, revolver in hand, into the office of Hussein Farid. Refusing to surrender, the general leaped behind a screen and fired three shots. But not one more . . .

Meanwhile the armored cars commanded by Khaled Mohieddin encircled the military zone of Abassieh-Koubbeh-Manshiet el-Bakri-Heliopolis, while the tanks of Hussein el-Shafei invested the city's strategic points, especially the radio station, to which Anwar el-Sadat, as a communications officer, was dispatched. Except for one exchange of gunfire at the entrance to the army general headquarters in which two sentries were killed—the sole victims of this practically model *Putsch*—the army and the city passed from Farouk's to Gamal's hands without a single blow.

Toward three in the morning, seven of the Free Officers met at the army general headquarters—now lit up as bright as day—to gather around Gamal Abdel Nasser for a toast. Twelve generals—one of whom was Aly Naguib, the brother of the future president—had been arrested and were being detained. One of them, however, had managed to escape, a conspicuous gap in the putschists' trophy collection: the inevitable Hussein Sirry Amer (who was to be apprehended the following day while trying to cross into Libya). Who then was missing? Only the "boss," the figurehead without whom the entire operation would seem a bit lightweight.

About three-thirty a jeep went off to pick up General Mohammed Naguib, whom the minister of the interior, Mortada Maraghi, had already awakened a half-hour earlier with a phone call from Alexandria. Maraghi belonged to a rich family which had helped the future general in his early youth. He still thought he had Naguib under his thumb, and addressed him rudely over the phone: "Well, now, general, why don't you calm your boys down!" "What boys?" "Don't play dumb. I'm passing the receiver to the head of state, Hilali Pasha." Hilali had been Naguib's professor of law at the Military Academy. Now he adopted a paternal tone. "Now, now, general, don't you see: this business can't lead anywhere." "I assure you, Professor (*ya Ustazi*), I don't know anything."

Mohammed Naguib did not have the time to fall back asleep before the victors' jeep arrived. "*Mabruk,* my boys," Naguib blurted out as he entered the general headquarters, "I congratulate you." And he entertained his young companions with his own tale of the night. At four o'clock, Ali Sabri, then one of Naguib's close collaborators who, as an information officer in the airborne troops, was in constant contact with foreign embassies, telephoned David Evans, the American naval attaché, and informed him of the operation. The Free Officers have taken control of the army, he said; General Naguib has been named commander-in-chief, and if the foreign powers refrain from intervening, order will be maintained and foreigners' lives will be safeguarded. Several minutes later, Abdel Moneim Amin transmitted the same message to the British chargé d'affaires, Mr. Hamilton.

On the first floor of the modest yellowish building in which the general headquarters was installed at that time, the sun rose in a burst of feverish joy. Two journalists were already there, two friends of the movement—Ahmed Aboul Fath and Ihsan Abdel Kouddous, who had made *Al-Misri* and *Rose el-Youssef* into real weapons for the conspiracy. The first photos were taken for the midday extra issues. In them you can see Naguib, a bit foppish in his elegant cap, with Gamal Abdel Nasser and Ahmed Shawki seated beside him, while opposite sit Zakaria Mohieddin, Abdellatif Boghdadi, and Yussef Saddiq; and all around these, standing, you can make out Abdel Hakim Amer, Kamaleddin Hussein, Gamal Hammad, Ali Sabri, Abdel Moneim Amin and Anwar el-Sadat.

Abdel Kouddous, a shrewd observer, remarked that all this had the feeling of a family reunion, and addressed the general—who had been his collaborator in *Rose el-Youssef*—in a familiar tone of voice:

"Well, Naguib bey, what are you planning to do?"

"Preserve the constitution and reform the army and the state."

"Will you effectively take power?"

"No, the constitution does not permit it."

"What will be your first measure?"

"I think we should recall the preceding parliament, our last link with the constitution."

"But whom are you considering as premier?"

"Aly Maher, perhaps. What do you think?"

"Bravo, he's the man for a crisis. And the king?"

"He'll have to be kicked out."

So went the first of innumerable press conferences granted by Naguib and the Free Officers, which are much more helpful than official texts in defining the confraternity, its style, and its aims. But if this press exposure openly revealed the fumblings of the victors and the relative timidity of their objectives, it is also true that Nasser's briefings of Naguib were as yet too infrequent for the general to claim really to represent the spirit and the aspirations of his young companions. But, as we shall see, he was not ill-informed, at least in the short run, for an eleventh-hour joiner.

While Naguib chatted, Abdel Hakim Amer, under Nasser's watchful eye, sat in a corner and scrawled out the text of the communiqué which would inform the Egyptian people of its altered public life. About six o'clock Anwar el-Sadat, the communications man, once again dashed off to the radio station to announce the event to the citizens of Egypt.

In Cairo, it was the "hour of the first Koran," Koranic verses always being read before the first news bulletin. The new summer day had already begun when, a bit before seven o'clock, an unknown voice—that of Anwar el-Sadat—suddenly appeared on the radio with some surprising information:

"To the Egyptian people: Egypt has just passed through the most somber period of its history, debased by corruption and disaffected by instability. These causes of dissolution infected the army itself, constituting one of the reasons for our defeat in Palestine. Commanded by ignoramuses, incompetents, and traitors, the army was no longer capable of defending Egypt. That is why we have purified ourselves: the army is now in the hands of a man in whose competence, integrity, and patriotism you may have perfect confidence. Egypt shall welcome our movement with satisfaction. The army shall be guarantor of the national interest. Those of its ex-leaders whom we have seen fit to arrest will be released as soon as circumstances permit.

"I take advantage of this opportunity to warn the Egyptian people against its enemies and to ask you not to tolerate any acts of violence or of destruction, for such acts will only hurt Egypt. They shall be considered as acts of treason and will be punished with the greatest severity. The army, in cooperation with the police, shall ensure respect for the law. Above all I take occasion to reassure our foreign friends in affirming to them that the army considers itself entirely responsible for the security of their persons, their property, and their interests. I entreat my fellow citizens not to listen to malevolent rumors, for calm reigns everywhere. May Almighty God aid us." It was signed: Mohammed Naguib, commander-in-chief of the army.

A highly significant text. When Nasser seized power he was a man of order, a strict officer, much less concerned to proclaim the progressive thesis which colored the tracts of 1951 than to prepare a flexible and peaceable takeover of the state by the army. If the first proclamation of July 23 does not allow us to retain any of the three hypothetical explanations of early Nasserism—a revolutionary operation imparting a rational structure to a powerful mass uprising, directed against both imperialism and feudalism; or an attempted rechanneling of the menacing revolution in the interests of a petty bourgeoisie in uniform; or, again, a preventive, counterrevolutionary operation incited by certain Egyptian nationalist currents supported by the United States, with the aim of preempting and imprisoning popular energy —in any case, this statement is an uncomfortable one for the thesis of a truly revolutionary movement. Nationalism, corporatism, discipline: we are closer to Pilsudski than to Lenin. But we are getting ahead of ourselves.

At the general headquarters of Koubbeh Bridge, however, the fever was rising. The problem which Abdel Kouddous had broached in his first interview with the new commander-in-chief would have to be solved: since, as Naguib had said, the army itself could not rule constitutionally, who should take charge of the government? Naguib returned to his first idea: "Ihsan, we would like to contact Aly Maher Pasha. We do not know where or how to find him. Would you take one of our officers to him?"

The journalist accepted at once. But with whom should he approach Maher? A moment ago he had noticed an officer with the olive complexion of the Saïd who from time to time drew Mohammed Naguib aside. He was, they said simply, the *bikbashi* Gamal Abdel Nasser. "I'd like him to accompany me." One of the officers interrupted: "No, not him. Leave him alone." The journalist, who was no fool, realized that this tall devil of a colonel, silent in the midst of the tumult, meditative in the midst of chaos, at once painstaking and phlegmatic, and so carefully protected by his comrades, was probably the operation's key man.

It was the indefatigable Anwar el-Sadat, back from the broadcasting center, who eventually accompanied Abdel Kouddous to Aly Maher. The interview was tense. Aly Maher wanted to leave the matter up to the king. The officers' representative launched into a violent philippic against Farouk (whom certain officers such as Gamal Salem already wanted to have shot). The journalist tried to calm him. "No," cried Sadat, "he must know that a revolution has taken place." The misunderstanding was to persist for a long time. In fact, was this really a "revolution," this movement which was now calling upon one of the palace's liege men to run the government?

Naguib's proclamation, and the appearance of some tanks in the streets of Cairo, were well received. Not as a revolution though, but as a sanitary operation, a scalpel removing a smelly wart. A sort of sigh of relief rather than any enthusiasm dominated public opinion. And indeed, what was to become of Farouk in all this? The proclamation did not even mention him.

In Alexandria, the king, hearing about the events on the radio, had immediately telephoned Haydar Pasha—the only person in the regime who had so far officially lost his job, of which Naguib had deprived him. "What's going on?" "Uh

. . . a tempest in a teacup." But Mortada Maraghi, the minister of the interior, hurried off to Cairo and soon verified that the officers had the situation well in hand. Moreover, a Naguib-Maher interview that afternoon gave an appearance of legality to the ouster.

Decidedly, more was at stake than *Putsch* of one section of the army against another. The newspapers, distributed around five o'clock, gave a reassuring picture of the events, as polished up by Nasser and Amer. And Naguib's face, splashed grandly across the front page (the others appeared as anonymous backers), was calculated to give a good impression.

In the embassies—except in the American, of course—chaos reigned. Why were these persons rushing about in midsummer, in Cairo, when it was so pleasant in Alexandria? The chargés d'affaires peevishly summoned their military attachés. The file clerks were hastily queried. "Mohammad Naguib, yes, we know the name. He was much discussed during the Officers' Club affair. They say that Hussein Sirry Pasha wanted to make him war minister. A good officer, popular in the army. He seems to have fought in Palestine. Of course he is less well known than his brother Ali, the commander of the Cairo garrison. Their mother was Sudanese. He's said to have connections with the Muslim Brethren. He has written two or three manuals of military tactics. He's known to be very anti-British. He speaks English, French, and Italian. That's all I have in my files." "And the others?" "Well . . . the name of Anwar el-Sadat has turned up—he's been mixed up in several terrorist incidents. His name has been mentioned in connection with the assassination of Amin Osman. Sadat is a fanatical Anglophobe. Colonel Shawki's in the group, too—Shawki Pasha's son, a relative of Aly Maher, and a real hothead. Also Ali Sabri, a cousin of Queen Farida, a good communications officer. All in all, not a very imposing bunch."

The English did not hide their irritation over having been caught napping. To think of the era of Russell Pasha! And that was not so long ago! The Americans, on the other hand, were euphoric. Ambassador Jefferson Caffrey, then finishing his brilliant career in Cairo, would be able to give free rein to his talents. On his way to the office he looked commiseratingly over his shoulder at the British Embassy. Hopeless— those poor English.

Even more unprepared was international opinion. The Communists thought they whiffed a distinctly American smell, and—with the curious exception of Radio Bucharest—the Eastern bloc soon began to speak of a fascist-type movement remote-controlled from Washington. The Western press trucked out the old phrases. The *Times* of July 24 assured its readers that "these events have nothing to do with the Anglo-Egyptian conflict" and were "of purely domestic origin." It predicted that "the coup's beneficiaries would be the progressive wing of the Wafd." As for *Le Monde* of the same day, it held that "if the authority of the king has been challenged, his personal position remains secure. The choice of Aly Maher, Farouk's personal friend, shows that the army has chosen merely to limit the consequences of Farouk's undisciplined behavior. The army remains monarchist." It went on to predict an upcoming free general election, with "the Wafd returning in triumph." (The journalist's greatest misery is to be quoted twenty years later.)

What about Farouk? At general headquarters in Cairo, during the night of the twenty-fourth or -fifth, the officers took stock for the first time—and with satisfaction—of the two first phases of the operation: the military takeover, and the choice of a head of government docile enough and prestigious enough to ensure a civilian cloak for the enterprise. But there was still article 3: to decide the fate of Farouk. It was here that, for the first time, the extraordinary tactical talent of Gamal Abdel Nasser revealed itself. Up to then he had directed an almost banal operation, a sort of padded pronunciamento, adroitly garnished with indispensable political reprieves. But "operation Farouk" was to be a real aerial stunt (reminiscent of that which de Gaulle staged on May 13, recalled to power by his own political victims).

First he had to convince his colleagues not to kill the fat king. Several among them—especially Gamal Salem and Anwar el-Sadat—favored exemplary justice: purification should begin at the highest levels. But Naguib, Gamal, and Khaled Mohieddin emphasized that the king had already committed political suicide, and that they should avoid martyring this dishonored figure, a deed which would only stain with blood a revolution which should imitate neither Cromwell nor Robespierre.

Here the choice of Aly Maher became plain. The *bikbashi* Abdel Nasser wished to avoid the vexations which the eviction of the king might bring on. He knew that the ex-premier, also the sovereign's cabinet chief, was perhaps the only man still to have kept a little pull with Farouk, the only man who might persuade that barbarian to swallow an accommodating abdication. The young colonel planned to use the old statesman as a form of lubrication.

On the afternoon of the twenty-fourth, Aly Pasha entered the king's chambers, cabinet list and program in hand. Back in Cairo at nine o'clock, he announced to Naguib that "His Majesty has deigned to accept the army's requests" (a new government, the nomination of Naguib to the head of the army in place of Haydar, and the dismissal of the royal entourage). A second proclamation posted on the streets of Cairo detailed the movement's program: "a purification within the framework of the constitution, and the restoration of individual liberties" accomplished "by a group of loyal and devoted men, whose experience and youth has prepared

them for such tasks." Soon Mohammad Naguib boarded a
plane for Alexandria. Here he received an overwhelming
welcome. It was at this moment that the new army movement received the baptism of the people. The "liberator and
savior of the homeland" was almost smothered to death by
an ocean of well-wishers. But he still had a grave mission to
fulfill.

A column of armored cars which had left Cairo the previous evening cornered the royal palace of Ras el-Tin. This
time it was no longer English tanks which menaced Farouk.
Terrified, the king appealed to the American ambassador
who, after a discussion with Aly Maher, assured Farouk that
he had obtained the guarantee of his life and those of his
close relatives and friends. On the twenty-sixth, at nine in
the morning, the commander-in-chief gave Maher an ultimatum addressed to the king:

"In consideration of your bad rule, your violations of the
Constitution, your contempt for the will of the people, to
the point where no citizen feels secure in his life, property,
and dignity . . . and of the scandalous fortunes which traitors and prevaricators have amassed under your protection
. . . the army, representing the will of the people, has given
me the order to require Your Majesty to abdicate in favor
of the crown prince, His Royal Highness Ahmed Fuad, this
same Saturday, the twenty-sixth of July, and to leave the
country this same day before six o'clock. In the event that
this ultimatum be rejected, you shall be held responsible for
the consequences. Signed: Mohammed Naguib."

The Nasserian style had picked up a certain vigor since
the tame proclamation of the twenty-third. A Jacobin echo.
Aly Maher was shocked: but it was too late to retreat. Besides, Farouk did not try to resist: he attempted to obtain
several considerations: the safekeeping of his property, the
departure at his side of several companions, the right to re-

turn to Egypt as an ordinary private gentleman. In vain. When it was pointed out to him that the act of abdication was drawn up in the form of a royal receipt, implying the expression of a sovereign will, he seemed relieved and readily signed.

A little before six o'clock, flanked by the American ambassador and followed by Queen Narriman, who carried in her arms the new six-month-old king, Farouk boarded his yacht, the *Mahroussa,* where he was shortly joined by Mohammed Naguib, himself accompanied by three officers representing the three armed forces: the foot-soldier Ahmed Shawki, the cavalryman Hussein el-Shafei, and the aviator Gamal Salem. The general reminded the dethroned sovereign in a respectful tone of voice that he himself had offered his resignation, in February 1942, to protest against the English *coup de force.* Farouk replied: "Take care of the army." "She is in good hands now, Sire." Then, trying to slip in the last word, Farouk said: "What you have done to me I was preparing to do to you."

When Naguib reached the pier he was enveloped by the joyous crowd. In Cairo, in the office which he had just had installed next to that of the commander-in-chief, the *bikbashi* Gamal Abdel Nasser took stock in silence. Here was the power, right in his own hands, barely camouflaged by the name of Aly Maher and the nice smile of Mohammed Naguib. The power. But the power *to do what?*

PART THREE

---◆◆◆∞◆◆◆---

A Patriot Without a People

11

The Power to Do What?

A man and a nation were face to face. But here were no egalitarian conjugal responsibilities such as de Gaulle accepted, or thought he accepted. Nor was this the "ein Volk, ein Führer" type of relationship which, despite the obvious differences, was to assert itself in 1956. There was nothing of that powerful and total seizure of the state and people which Mustafa Kemal Ataturk had effected thirty years earlier.

When the *bikbashi* Gamal Abdel Nasser moved into general headquarters in late July 1952, he was not only the heart and brain of the *Maglis el Thawra* (Council of the Revolution),[1] but also the hesitant delegate of forces which he did not thoroughly understand and which were still unaware of him. Of course he overflowed with ambition. But ambition to be what, to do what? While waiting to find out, he immersed himself in daily tasks. And the people heard that at last the new leadership was getting something done.

We have spoken of the mounting wrath of the people, fanned into incandescence six months earlier and since then

[1] The following then sat on the Council of the Twelve: Mohammed Naguib, president; Gamal Abdel Nasser, Zakaria Mohieddin, Khaled Mohieddin, Abdellatif Boghdadi, Gamal Salem, Salah Salem, Hussein el-Shafei, Anwar el-Sadat, Kamaleddin Hussein, Hassan Ibrahim, and Abdel Hakim Amer.

cooled down to anxious expectancy. Exploited in its peasant depths, repressed in its elites, and still occupied by foreigners, it had experienced four upsurges in ten years: the rather limited, nationalist one of February 1942, which quickly collapsed; the popular, political one of February 1946, which advanced the cause of the progressive Left; the peasant uprising of 1951, which left only corpses behind; and that of January 26, 1952, the savage outcry of misery scorned by insolent luxury. Was not the movement of July 23 another one of these upswings, newly modernized and retailored by technique and discipline?

Ten years later, in his presentation speech for the 1962 Charter, Gamal Abdel Nasser set forth a heavily populist interpretation of the events of July 23: "The armed forces which undertook the revolution were not its real maker but merely the people's tool. In that memorable night, the revolution succeeded because of the presence of the army in its natural place, under the aegis of the people and its aspirations." And it is true that during the summer of 1962 the Egyptian people did come to feel represented and revivified by this cohort of young men in khaki cotton, who ate the same favas and the same farmer's cheese, and drank the same black tea and laughed at the same *nokat* (jokes).

For the first time in centuries, perhaps twenty centuries, Egypt was ruled by the Egyptians: Hellenistic sovereigns and Yemeni conquerors, Circassian Mamlukes and Turkish colonizers, French invaders, Albanian pashas, cosmopolite dynasts, English occupiers—the alienators were at last replaced by these suntanned lads who, though no more Egyptian than Zaghloul, Nahas, or Mohammed Mahmud, had at last actually kicked out the alien Crown, acquired in an alien land and serving an alien people.

The Egyptian people knew this in its bones, and were affectionately grateful to their new bosses as long as they continued to rule lighthandedly, as long as the international, multiple, and complex values of this numerous people were not, under the pretext of Egyptianism, and later Arabism, subject to elimination. But the image of Gamal Abdel Nasser presented its own very real problems.

In July 1952, the *bikbashi* Abdel Nasser was thirty-four years and several months old. He was a good staff officer whose course at the Abassieh Academy had impressed most of its auditors. He liked his work, and had a good pedagogical sense as well as a sense of authority. But he was still shy, at least with strangers; that is, with people outside his class and milieu.

He had no vices—not even the passion for hashish rather widespread among the officers (including two or three of his colleagues). The package of Craven A which he consumed every day could hardly be termed an excessively bad habit. He did not absolutely eschew whiskey, but he was a good Muslim who said his prayers and eventually made, eighteen months later, the pilgrimage to Mecca for reasons not purely political. His habits? Chess, to which he devoted long hours with Abdel Hakim Amer. He played ping-pong, and went swimming at Marsa-Matruh. He was athletic too, and prey to flabbiness if he neglected to exercise.

Undoubtedly he was a fine husband. If, in a political context, he did not fail to notice love affairs, they were, and would remain, the love affairs of others. He observed them but he kept out of them, and not only because a Caesar should, by his wife, be above suspicion. He was genuinely virtuous. Tahia, his wife, was not pretty. Tall, strong, and dark, she occasionally appeared (beginning in 1955) at his

side. In any case her discretion was exemplary, which is by
no means commonplace in Egypt: who can measure the dam-
age Mustafa Nahas' wife caused him?

In 1952, Gamal and Tahia already had four children (a
fifth, to whom he gave the name of his best friend, Abdel
Hakim, was born in 1955). The older two were girls, Hoda
and Mona. The next two were boys, Khaled and Abdel Hamid.
This good husband was also a good father. He spent as much
time as possible with his family, who continued to live, right
up to the end, in the professional villa in Manshiet el-Bakri,
near general headquarters, which he had acquired as a young
lieutenant colonel. When he became the *Raïs* he simply
added on, from one year to next, new rooms and annexes.
The house never lost the respectable banality of a high official's dwelling in a country where the underdevelopment of
the masses no longer caused their leaders enough anxiety to
hastily bother to provision themselves against the eventual
return of ill-luck. If this Muslim had gone to confession, as
our European monarchs once did, his confessor would have
known that he sinned only in his almost naïve taste for deviousness and in a harshness of spirit which could throw him
into uncontrollable rages. His deviousness was a vice which
must have served him well up to 1952 in dealing with political police inspectors and the upper echelons of the army.
There is something troubling about the more than three
years during which this conspirator melted into Egyptian
daily life without even being detected by the press's most
omniscient observers, such as Ihsan Abdel Kouddous. It was
an admirable gift, but one which Nasser distorted, once in
power, into a disproportionate taste for intrigue and dissimulation.

We have seen that his violence could be very impolitic:
the reprieve of Farouk did not come naturally to him. But
time only exacerbated his tendency to vindictiveness. His fa-

ther and his brother el-Leehy were to suffer from his rancor, not to mention the political leaders of the old regime, not all unworthy of their tasks, as well as the Muslim Brethren and the Communists. His might was by no means benevolent—we shall return to this. For the moment this tall young man intimidated others as much as they did him. He was not taken for what he was—the real boss—until about three months after the coup, when *Rose el-Youssef* revealed his true position to its readers in three or four pointed anecdotes. Onlookers would sometimes spot him walking behind Mohammed Naguib, who would receive the applause or the complaints. Perhaps he was considered the *éminence grise.* A Sadat or a Salah Salem had more volume, and spoke a great deal more.

He would walk along, his somber eyes with their green highlights sheltered under his eyelids, his shoulders almost vaulted, his long, feral gait a bit heavy. Under his brown helmet his long nose looked rather like a scimitar. And his formidable jaw led one to think he might have a literal appetite for authority. He had in him nothing of the populist leader, not to speak of the revolutionary apprentice. He was a grave staff officer whose plans were darkly ripening, and whose odd charm, though it struck his visitors and fascinated his companions, did not project out to the masses.

The crowds saw only a heavy-set, gray-templed fellow, a pipe in his mouth, his shirt half-opened on his hairy chest, his wide, weathered face cleft by a broad smile, his eyes laughing under their heavy black lashes. In early September, 1952, *Time,* claiming to reveal the cards in the regime's hand, wrote that the real strongmen were Anwar el-Sadat and Rashed Mehanna (one of the three "regents," along with Prince Abdel Moneim and Bahieddin Barakat—Mehanna was soon eliminated).

Yaish Mohammed Naguib! The man in khaki would wave his helmet, kiss a newborn baby thrust in his direction by a pair of outstretched arms, slip his swagger stick under his elbow and, escorted by two or three taciturn captains, disappear into the depths of his limousine.

We shall see that it is possible to define the early regime only by its deeds, in a "blow by blow" fashion. In the meantime two events disclosed Gamal Abdel Nasser's current orientation. On July 26, while five members of the junta were in Alexandria sealing the fate of Farouk, a lively debate arose in Cairo among their seven comrades on the theme of an eventual return to a classic form of democracy, a cause championed by Gamal. The majority, however, declared for an authoritarian regime. The *bikbashi* hastily dispatched a note to his friend Khaled: "Return at once. We must block the way to dictatorship." (In 1952!)

Two weeks later, on August 12, a fever raged at Kafr el-Dawar, one of the great weaving factories in the Alexandria region. It is dangerous to talk revolution to the alienated masses: instigated by a militant revolutionary, Mustafa Khamis, the workers formulated a series of revindications "in the name of Mohammed Naguib." Sharp tension reigned, and the buildings were occupied. The following day the army appeared. The workers refused to answer to summonses, the troops fired: eight dead. After a summary trial, Khamis and Ahmed el-Bakri, a randomly selected comrade, were condemned to death. Should they be spared?

The Twelve confronted each other all night, with Nasser and Amer pleading for clemency.[2] At dawn, the two workers were hung in the Alexandria prison courtyard. One of the Egyptian Marxist organizations (the MDLN) vainly denounced "the military dictatorship which, having spared Farouk, the feudal lords, the traitors and the profiteers, now stains its hands with the blood of the workers." Gamal, in

---

[2] These data, like the above, were furnished by Saroit Okasha, the *Raïs's* faithful friend. There is no reason to doubt them.

the minority opposition but still linked to the deed, had entered a path which would lead him far.

How can one define this collective rule, which seized power stammering? Perhaps the severe judgments of Westerners originated in their difficulty in pigeonholing, cataloguing, and explaining the phenomenon. How comfortable it would be, a few years later, to define analogous movements as "Nasserist." In fact there is no way to evaluate the July regime except by its acts, themselves so very ambiguous. But, for now, let us consider the system of national and international power in which the regime fitted, as well as its manpower and political advantages.

In Egypt itself, it is easy to see who lost the game against this bayonet-brandishing third estate: the king, the king's men, the upper echelons of the army, the big feudal lords—and, so it seemed, the English. But it is not so easy to tell what political tide was carrying them. We have quoted some reliable foreign observers who believed the Wafd to be the beneficiary of the adventure. But little time elapsed before the mutually allergic reaction of the colonels and the leaders of the old party—even the more or less left-leaning ones—became apparent.

Hurriedly returning from medical treatment in Europe to hail the officers' victory, which they assumed would shortly be their own (only two forces existed in Egypt of course, so whatever thwarted the king necessarily boosted the Wafd), Nahas and Serag Eddin quickly lost their illusions. Not only had the real power passed into the officers' hands, but the very image of the pipe-smoking general was rapidly dispelling the fading rays of the old leaders. Three months later the Wafd was dissolved, broken, its cadres outwitted and jailed. One year later it was no more than a state of mind (although in an interview which he granted us in late 1953, Gamal Abdel Nasser admitted that if elections were to be held in the near future the Wafd would still stand to win).

As for the Muslim Brethren, several of the Free Officers had belonged to the confraternity and remained attached to it. From July 23 on, the leadership of the *Ikhwan al-Muslimin* gave the junta its stamp of approval. But three weeks had not gone by before they too began to change their tune: the junta was resisting their attempt to place Koranic precepts at the foundation of the new regime. Their attempted trusteeship having failed, the confraternity forbade its members to enter the new government then being formed: Sheikh el-Bakury, the youthful Nasser's old comrade, was obliged to resign from the society to be able to enter the new regime's ministry of *Waqfs* (religious foundations). Here too, early misunderstandings were to lead to a much worse end.

The Egyptian Communists did not react in unison. As often happens, the two principal currents splintered. The MDLN, or "Hadetu," more labor-oriented and more populist, willingly supported Farouk's vanquishers, especially since several of them were considered militants or fellow-travelers of the organization: Yussef Saddiq, Khaled Mohieddin, Ahmed Hamrush, and others. The other current, composed essentially of intellectuals—some of them very brilliant—saw the military victors as a group of petty-bourgeois in the service, whether consciously or not, of American interests.[3] Perhaps the extremely negative reaction of the U.S.S.R. should be attributed to the influence of these groups (*Dalshin,* PCE). Soviet leaders often prefer to consult their own direct sources.

---

[3] Maxime Rodinson has told the story of how he was delegated to Cairo as the observer of the CPF and returned with an evaluation which seemed a bit too intricate: "Do you know of a single *coup d'état* in the Middle East that was not engineered by the Anglo-Saxons?"

Besides, the Communist element which was sympathetic to the officers never amounted to much more than an ephemeral traveling companion. It was later, in 1955, and again in 1964, that the grand alliances between Nasserism and Egyptian Marxism were formed. In 1952 the cold war implacably separated all social forces into two groups, separated by an omnipresent iron curtain. In the movement itself, certain leftists were soon eliminated: Yussef Saddiq, the major executor of the July 23 operation, was dropped in the first few weeks for "leftism"—as was Abdel Moneim Amer, for the opposite reason. (A consequence of the mechanical schema of the "third camp.") Khaled Mohieddin stayed at Nasser's side—but only until 1954. As for the MDLN, it veered away in January 1953, and then broke completely with the officers in March 1953, after the first raid on leftist cadres.

That left the fragments of various parties, leagues, organizations, sociological and economic study-circles. Residues of the "Green Shirts" were picked up. Fathi Radwan, released by Nasser from the prison in which he had been thrown after the arson of January 26, was promoted to the ministry of National Orientation, thus clearing the way for several militants of the old national party al-Hish al-Watani of Hafez Ramadan, one of the most eloquent adversaries of the 1936 treaty. Several technocrats of the "Pioneer" group, Sayed Marei, Abbas Ammar, Fuad Galal, the authors of a reform plan for Egypt, also made their way into the government. Beside them were some highly valuable top civil servants, such as the economist Ali el-Greitly and the jurist Bahgat Badawi. One is reminded a bit of the Gaullist government of 1958, with its mixture of ultras and brain-trusters.

It was difficult at this time to make out the forces which supported the July regime. The army, its foundation and skeleton, rapidly slipped into the state apparatus, sinking into

its structures like concrete, hardening them and making itself
the absolute arm of all action. What about the working class
(about ten per cent of the salaried labor force) and the peasantry (about seventy-five per cent of the social body)? It
would be premature to claim to unravel these strands which
were still mere potentialities. True, since the beginning of
September, Mohammed Naguib's tours in the delta, in the
heart of the zone which the Wafd had held as a bastion of its
power, brought off a lively success. But what do crowds
mean?

Moreover, a number of the general's "triumphs" were organized by the Muslim Brethren, who, however deceived they
may have been by the coolness of the regime toward them,
had not despaired of colonizing it. But it was only after the
first stages of the agrarian reform and the building of the
labor unions that one could speak of the actual support of
certain sectors of the population, or at least of rural petty
bourgeoisie and the salaried labor of big business whose employment was to be stabilized.

In the weeks and even the months following the *coup
d'état,* it was impossible to get a global view of the tendencies of the system or of the socio-professional forces upon
which it rested. One could only evaluate it in terms of each
one of the gestures which it accomplished. Within a framework which might be summarily defined by two formulas,
national populism and authoritarian reformism, it was, within
two years, to achieve most of the tasks which it had assigned
itself in the six-point program of 1951.

Let us briefly review these six principles, which seem then
to have been Gamal's and his colleagues' only clear ideological and conceptual baggage: 1. to liquidate the British occupation; 2. to eliminate feudalism; 3. to put an end to the
domination of political power by capital; 4. to install social

equity; 5. to build a powerful army; 6. to establish a healthy democratic life.

The first principle obliged the Free Officers to negotiate with the English, which led, after the settling of the Sudanese question, to the evacuation treaty of October 1954. The second, third, and fourth obliged them to realize an agrarian reform; the sixth, to destroy the old political parties. It might seem a little odd, at least to anyone who did not follow the evolution of early Nasserism, that the fifth principle, urging the creation of a strong army, was neglected the longest.

The reasons for which the *bikbashi* Abdel Nasser, an excellent staff officer, left the armed forces in the state in which they remained up to the Gaza surprise attack (February 1955), then the Suez campaign, and finally the Six-Day War, we shall see as we go along. Let us say for now that two principal motives explain this: the need to have recourse to the army cadres for the reconstitution of the state apparatus and the creation of the structures of the nationalized economy; and the mistrust of the man of the July *Putsch* for anything which might make the army an alternative power, a state within the state. To place officers in government positions, yes; to build an army strong enough to be autonomous, no.

12

The River and the Canal

"First, we must resolve our litigation with England. . . ." So said one of Nasser's companions during our first interview. In early August 1952, London offered the Free Officers—who, all in all, did not look like such a bad lot—to resume negotiations on the future of the canal. Naguib answered that he preferred to dissociate the two problems, that of the occupation of the Suez Canal Zone and that of the Anglo-Egyptian cohabitation in the Sudan.

If the men of July wished to reinitiate a dialogue on the second matter, a result of their strong attachment for Khartoum (Naguib's mother was born there, the Salem brothers came from Port-Sudan, Nasser and Amer had served in that land), it was because they thought they had the key to it. To dislodge the British from the canal was, they thought, another matter entirely. They would have to consolidate their power before waging this decisive battle.

Actually the Sudanese question was the decisive one. By involving themselves in it without sufficient preparation, Nasser and his men forfeited that grand policy of contractual unification of the two lands of the Nile which had been the major historical objective of every Egyptian patriot, and which, from the geopolitical and economic standpoint, was at the base of any modern development. Not that the Sudan policy of the officers was clumsy or aggressive. It revealed, on the contrary, their intelligence and tactical good sense. It was to bring them a degree of success—the detachment of the Sudan from English influence by a substantially democratic process. It even laid the cornerstone for the system of proto-federal alliance established in 1969 and consolidated in 1970.

In trying to impose their own views on others too rapidly, in playing exclusively on only one of the two great confraternities which dominated Sudanese Islam, the *Khatmia,* against the *Ansar* of the Mahdi (the posthumous son of the famed warrior of the end of the last century), the Egyptian officers caused the Sudanese to rear up against their enterprising friendship. A smiling Mohammed Naguib, arriving in Khartoum one fine day in 1954 to pick the fruits of his personal popularity, provoked a sort of feudal riot: the *Ansar,* weapons in hand, rushed into the airport where his plane was landing and massacred everyone within reach of their spears. Thirty dead were counted. The break was complete. The Sudan was lost, at least temporarily.

But despite the deafening chants for the Egyptian-Sudanese marriage during cinema intermissions, the Egyptians were still primarily obsessed with the Canal Zone—that Alsace-Lorraine, that excuse for the worst governments and stumbling block for the best. Gamal Abdel Nasser and his companions— Amer, Boghdadi, Gamal Salem—attacked the question with a professional realism which led their principal interlocutor, the British ambassador Sir Ralph Stevenson, to declare when he received us in March 1953: "These boys are the first serious interlocutors we've ever had to face."

February 10, 1953, the military junta published a "strategic note" which summarized the thinking of Gamal and his men. To sum up its contents: Egypt is perfectly capable of defending the canal; it is out of the question for her to pay for the evacuation of the zone by form of any adherence whatsoever

to a pro-Western military part. Since Cairo is only claiming
a debt, the talks can cover only two points: the procedure for
(1) the evacuation, and (2) the eventual maintenance, of
the British base, a triangular zone situated between Suez, Port-
Said, and Tell el-Kebir where over 80,000 soldiers had been
billeted since the war. (According to the terms of the 1936
treaty, the contingent was not to exceed 10,000.) The first
phase of the discussions lasted ten days (April–May 1953).
When they were broken off, Winston Churchill berated
Naguib with a telling aphorism: "The trouble with dictators
is that they can never really dictate anything." To which the
"dictator" replied in the traditional style of his own part of
the world: "Independence is not won with a piece of paper,
but with the shedding of hot blood!"

Six months later the negotiations, this time prudently
labeled "informal talks," were resumed. On the way out of
one of these discussions, which were held in a pavilion near
the Pyramids, a fiery-eyed Gamal blurted out to me: "Impossible!" Several months later the *bikbashi's* tone had changed:
"The last obstacle," he confided to us in January 1954, "is
that the English now claim the right to keep uniformed technicians on the base, which would symbolize, in the people's
eyes, the perpetuation of the hated occupation." It was not
until the following July 27, on the occasion of the anniversary
celebration of Farouk's exile, that the protocol of the agreement was initialed.

As always the principle of mutual concessions had prevailed: if London would agree to withdraw its troops and
"military experts" within twenty months, Gamal Abdel Nasser would submit to the "Turkish clause," that is, he would
allow the "reactivation of the base" in the eventuality of an
attack by a power "foreign to the Middle East" (Israel was
thus placed between parentheses) against an Arab state (the
Egyptian thesis) or against Turkey (the Anglo-American

thesis). By capitulating on this point, Gamal agreed to link himself to the Western camp, for the defense of Turkey could not be camouflaged with any pretended solidarity other than a "common defense" against the U.S.S.R.

When the treaty was signed on October 24, 1954, the most morose face was not that of the English diplomat who had just accepted the liquidation of three-quarters of a century of occupation and protection, whether *de jure* or *de facto,* but that of Gamal Abdel Nasser. "Now what?" we asked him. "Now? We must rebuild our country," he said in a defeated tone. In the press conference which followed, it was not he, but Abdel Hakim Amer who answered our question on the likelihood of an expansion of the army: "It is not tanks that we shall buy, but tractors: they are more useful."

And so the alumnus of the *En Nahda* school had himself signed a treaty similar to the 1936 treaty which he had so violently opposed. It was a bitter victory over himself. He apparently proposed to shift Egyptian energy from the military front to economic and social reform. A dangerous game— but consistent with his evolving power and his isolation from the people—to which we shall shortly return.

In the acceptance of the Anglo-Saxon artifice there was an element of ideological collusion, the will to block the path of a violent social revolution by supplanting it with an active technical reformism. In the mind of both parties (or, rather, of all three parties, since the American part in the debate was obvious) it was less important to block the intervention of Soviet armies than it was to smother any possible hatching of a Mao Tse-tung of the Nile Valley. But the thirty-six-year-old dictator also wished to take a technical shortcut in winning the economic means for a struggle against the misery of the masses.

The least one can say is that the masses themselves did not adhere to this political strategy. If Nahas had been able to find support for the 1936 treaty with a plebiscite which was vigorously opposed by only a few hundred extremists like Gamal Abdel Nasser, the leader of the July regime could, in 1954, only summon up what my Greek barber, an old Cairene, called "a two-piaster hurrah." Never was the *bik-bashi* so isolated, in the eyes of the Egyptian people, as the day when he presented his evacuation plan. He had pressed the button which he thought would lead to his being adopted by Washington. It is here that one can measure the depth of the gash left by the revolutionary days of February 1946. The wound seemed entirely closed—but for one thing: the intractible popular condemnation of any adherence to a pro-American military pact.

Egyptian public opinion, so delicate and demanding, was affronted. From university professors to porters, from students to Nubian doormen, from the terraces of the coffeehouses to the teeming sidewalks of the Sayeda Zeinab district, the impassioned commentaries, oaths, and jests threatened to undo the most delicate political manipulations. It was the same enormous complaint which had forced King Fuad to appeal to Zaghloul, which had obliged Farouk to recall the Wafd, and which had forbade Nahas from signing in 1951 a more "Western" treaty than the 1936 one. Public opinion had seemed becalmed, entranced, half-terrified and half-chloroformed. Yet here it was again, reborn, and more prodigious than ever. Rarely in the history of Egypt has the affronted cry from the street so strongly contravened the will of an isolated ruler.

However unpopular or misunderstood, Nasser's choice seemed definitive. A Turkish delegation was invited, indirect contact was made with the Israeli premier,[1] the policy of the french *président du Conseil,* Pierre Mendès-France, was

---

[1] See Part Six, "Confronting Israel."

pointedly eulogized, every move seemed to consolidate the new orientation. Gamal Abdel Nasser's closest collaborator, his cabinet chief Ali Sabri, said to us then: "Have we not turned to the West rather than to the East? It can't be helped if our relations with the U.S.S.R. deteriorate" (November 1954).

13

———···◁∞▷···———

For a Few More Feddans

Having fared forth on the road of collaboration with the West (of course 1953–4 was not 1970, and the balance of power in the eastern Mediterranean left little margin of action for a politico-military strategy armed with feeble means), Abdel Nasser and the Council of the Revolution conducted, however, a firmly reformist domestic policy, whose principal accomplishment was the law of "agrarian reform" of September 8, 1952.

Since the regime's second and third objectives after the eviction of the British consisted of ensuring "social equity" and the "destruction of feudalism," agrarian reform became inevitable. Whether the system of production practiced in the Nile Valley proceeded from classic feudalism, or whether it was closer to what Ibrahim Amer calls "agrarian capitalism" and Anwar Abdel Malek calls the rule of the "landed gentry," the fact is that its two chief characteristics were the radical alienation of the producer and the confusion of property and

power. "The English," Marshal Allenby said, "can evacuate
Egypt with complete peace of mind: they have created a class
of big landowners on which Great Britain can count to up-
hold her Egypt policy." Thus the destruction of the colonial
system also raised the issue of landed property.

Yet to hold that such a measure was "revolutionary" is
going too far. The Egypt of 1950 was teeming with projects
for agrarian reform. Some were advanced by liberal bourgeois
like Merrit Ghali; others came directly from American experts. Three very different men were responsible for the
document of September, 1952: Gamal Salem, the most technocratic of the Free Officers; Ahmed Fuad, Gamal's most
Marxist counselor; and Rashad Barawi, an economist with a
socialist background. The principal effect of the law which
they elaborated was the following: no one could possess more
than two hundred feddans (about two hundred acres), or
three hundred per family (the king had 55,000, Prince
Yussef Kamel, 16,000, Badrawi Ashur, 9,000). Now it is
important to realize that the better acreage of the delta, which
yielded two harvests a year, was worth as much as 10,000
francs per feddan. Was the law a genuinely revolutionary
measure?

In certain respects, yes. A young latifundiary, Adly Lam-
hur, refusing to submit to the redistribution project, set his
dogs on the government surveyors. He was apprehended and
sent up to Cairo in chains. The appearance of this chubby
aristocrat at the gate of the Cairo railway station was one of
the regime's finest celebrations, the sudden appearance of a
truly revolutionary spirit. But for every such plebeian upsurge,
how many calls to military discipline there were!

This agrarian reform soon proved itself one of the most
characteristic measures of the new regime. During the first
interview which he granted us, in the train which was taking
us all back to Cairo after a successful public appearance near

Tantak in June 1953, General Naguib told us: "In essence, the reform's basic objective is to force a transition from real estate to industry. Egyptians are land-crazy. This passion must be checked; their accumulated capital must be fed into the industrial sector." Whether this proposal emanated from the good general's brain or was passed on to him by Gamal Salem or Abdel Nasser, it was at the heart of Nasserian ideology and practice during the regime's first phase. Not industrialization for justice, but justice for industrialization. The ends were technical and production-oriented.

The third principle, or imperative aim, was the destruction of the political organizations and parties of the old regime. But to build a "healthy democracy"? Nobody would have disputed that the Wafd of 1952 was no haven for virtue, or that the Muslim Brethren did not haunt Egypt with factious atavism and factitious fanaticism, or that the Communists were trapped in their own dogmatism and burdened with internal rivalries. But to go on and claim to build a "healthy democracy" on the corpses of these organisms, on the incarceration of their chiefs and the transformation of the nation into one enormous barrack!

First, the liquidation of the Wafd: blackmail, confiscation, trials, a smothered press—nothing was missing but bloodshed. From the trial of Ibrahim Farag to that of Fuad Serag Eddin, we saw a parade of every Egyptian public figure in thirty years, with the exception of several people whom Gamal did not dare to touch: Mustafa Nahas, Hussein Heykal, Abderrahman Azzam. This was not Vichy, not the Riom trial.

The dismantling of the confraternity of the Muslim Brethren was more costly: it was a veritable fortress of zealots, and fire-eaters. Since the July *Putsch,* however, Gamal had been lying in wait for the Brethren to make a fatal mistake, for, although they had been his allies, they now clearly intended

to snatch away the power won by him and his men. Good
Muslim that he was, the *bikbashi* Abdel Nasser already
keenly mistrusted these muddled and atavistic enthusiasts. He
told us in December 1953: "I really don't know how one
could possibly govern according to the Koran."

This fatal mistake the Brethren committed exactly three
weeks later by fomenting a brutal disturbance in that explosive terrain, the university. Nasser parried by dissolving the
society, and Zakaria Mohieddin, the minister of the interior,
put into operation a machine of investigation and repression
which nobody had suspected was so powerful. As the arrests
and arms discoveries went on, Gamal Abdel Nasser declared
to us in late January: "The real crime of the Muslim Brethren is to have tried to infiltrate the police and the army in
order to seize power forcibly. What they tried to wage on us
was holy war."

Nine agitated months passed, during which Nasser broke
with Naguib, partly as a result of the confrontation between
Nasser and the Brethren. Nasser signed the treaty with London, against which the Muslim Brethren unleashed a campaign which was especially pernicious since it was directed by
clandestine cells and was based on widespread popular discontent. On October 26, in Alexandria, Gamal Abdel Nasser
was addressing the crowds on Mohammed Ali Square justify-
ing the signing of the treaty with the English. In the half-
light, eight shots rang out. A light bulb above the speaker
was shattered. A Sudanese minister, sitting nearby, was hit.
A short, frightened silence followed. Then Gamal's voice was
heard again, altered now, sharp and tense with anguish:
"They can kill Gamal. But ten, a hundred, a thousand Gamals
will rise up to liberate Egypt."[1]

The man who had fired the shots did not resist the police.

[1] By chance this episode was recorded: it was perhaps the only attempted
murder in history which was broadcast.

His name was Mahmud Abdellatif, and he was a highly placed henchman of the Muslim Brethren. He had been six rows down from the speaker's balcony, a mere twenty yards away. Was it a plot? The act of an isolated fanatic? A police fabrication to restore Gamal's popularity and provide a pretext for repression? The latter theory has been advanced by Ahmed Aboul Fath. But the demeanor of Nasser, who, brave as he was, controlled himself with difficulty, as well as the statements of the accused, testify to the opposite. The Brethren suggested nothing of the sort before the judges, Gamal Salem and Anwar el-Sadat (their ex-colleague). Six of them were condemned to death, among them one of the most important and perhaps respectable members of the organization, Abdelkader Auda. Before the gallows, where, for my sins, I saw them conducted, they behaved with exemplary firmness of spirit. "O Gamal, may our blood be upon your heads," Abdelkader Auda cried out, before being gagged with the black hood.

From then on it was mostly in the regime's prisons—where several thousands of them were thrown, and often tortured—that the Muslim Brethren survived. A new wave of repression, in 1965, was to send to his death their best theoretician, Sayed Kotb. Perhaps the long cohabitation with the Communists in the world of Nasser's concentration camps brought them that ferment of intellectual curiosity which they had sadly lacked. Perhaps their clandestine cells survived the repression, albeit in rags and tatters. For Gamal Abdel Nasser, in any case, the problem was virtually solved by the end of 1954.

14

The General and His "Children"

The fall of the Brethren prepared the collapse of one of the regime's important buttresses: the figure of Mohammed Naguib. Even today it is quite hard to evaluate the role which the general-president played in founding and defining the military regime of 1952. We have seen that he was entirely an eleventh-hour—possibly even a thirteenth-hour—joiner. But neither Nasser nor any of the Twelve could forget that the prestigious general, approached by Saroit Okasha one month before the coup, had answered simply: "Use me for any job at any level. I want to help you." (A Frenchman is reminded of Catroux placing himself at the disposition of de Gaulle, his junior, although Catroux was not of the highest rank.)

Mohammed Naguib soon showed that he deserved the nomination of Nasser's scouts. His down-to-earth charm, his craftiness, his peasant practicality, and his unimpeachable Egyptianness gave the July regime a seductive front. Without him, the austerity and the harsh single-mindedness of the *bikbashi* might have undone the regime, which had no popular underpinning.

From the summer of 1953 on, however, relations between the general and his twelve junior officers became strained. His unique appeal to popular affection encouraged Naguib to feel that the regime was embodied in him, and in him alone.

But the cracks which began to appear between the president and the colonels were more than mere personal differences. Indeed, what separated Naguib from Nasser and his companions was more than an age difference and almost a class difference.

Not that Naguib was from a different background: he had been a poor child, a half-Sudanese with no social advantages helped out by the rich Maraghi family (one of whose members, Mortada, minister of the interior on that morning of July 23, tried to exploit this advantage to nip the movement in the bud). But Mohammed Naguib was already a general during the old regime; he had the title of bey; when Gamal's father was earning six pounds his soldier's pay was seventy-five; he had already hoisted himself out of the military quasi-proletariat to which the authors of the coup remained loyal. He was, despite his independence and loyalty, a vestige. Hence his repugnance for the methods adopted by Gamal and his henchmen against people who had been his friends. He loathed the ferocious manhunt against a political class to which he felt himself bound and the Muslim Brethren who had fought so well in Palestine and on the canal.

There was another, still deeper cause of dissension. As a tradition-minded career officer, Naguib looked on with irritation and anxiety when the new regime recruited its cadres from the backbone of the army. What was to remain of this already mediocre body if they gleaned it of its few talents? "That's enough! Back to the barracks, or the army is through!" This he often cried in alarm throughout 1953. "These children are imprudent," Naguib chided the new policy-makers. "They're rushing into impossible adventures. They're leading us toward disaster."

On February 24, 1954, at about midnight, a sour-faced Naguib stormed out of a session of the Council of the Revolution. He had just tossed his resignation in Gamal's face, after having been refused the veto power which he had demanded for himself alone. Salah Salem told us the day after: "Naguib demanded a dictatorship. We blocked him." Dictatorship or no, public opinion reacted badly: the streets of Cairo were draped in mourning. But more serious for Nasser was the powerful wave of feeling which the leadership crisis provoked in the army. The "return to the barracks" thesis which Naguib championed was finding more and more converts among the soldiers; among them was the same Colonel Shawki who had played such an important role on the evening of the *coup d'état*. Named to the key post of commandant of the Cairo garrison, he had recently been ousted, causing murmurs among the officers. Still more important from Nasser's point of view was that his faithful friend Khaled Mohieddin, who as a leftist was anxious for a return to more normal forms of democracy, had also rallied to the "return to the barracks" idea.

Khaled was an officer of the motorized cavalry: it was from the tank park—the traditional source of modern *coups d'état* —that a disquieting tumult arose on the following evening. Raw discontent had surfaced. "Where are they leading us? Naguib's resignation is a grave warning. Let's take things in hand." The voices rose; rash projects were suggested: Hussein el-Shafei, a Nasserist cavalryman, telephoned Gamal: "Come quickly or all is lost." The *bikbashi* faced an angry tribunal: "You prefer the government to the army. You're replacing Farouk's autocracy with your own. Only Naguib could reassure the people. Recall him or quit!"

Informed that tanks had surrounded the Cairo garrison, that he was trapped by his friend Khaled, Gamal saw that he was out of his depth. It was only with the greatest difficulty that he passed through Khaled's barricades: he did not even know the password. Meanwhile a loyal band had staged a counter-operation, and seized Naguib and Khaled Mohieddin, who was conducted under heavy escort to the Council of the Revolution. Mohieddin gave himself up for lost. But all he found was a disabled, resigned Gamal, despairing over the army's cravenness. The game was up. "Khaled can get Naguib and liquidate the 'revolution.' The spirit of July is finished."

The news swept the city: "Naguib is coming back, Naguib is here, *yaïsh Mohammed Naguib!*" It was a wave of enthusiasm such as even Farouk's departure had not aroused, and which older Cairenes compared to the joy which had greeted Zaghloul's return from exile. In Cairo, on the evening of Saturday, March 24, there was a sort of popular wedding between a man and a people: there was singing, sword-dancing, whole crowds fervidly embraced! But it was not as spontaneous at it at first appeared to our naïve eyes. Behind this onrush of popular tenderness there was at least one hidden manipulator. The fog rose the following day, a day which one of our friends, a sharp observer of his homeland, called "the Sunday of the Coran," though everybody else called it "the people's Sunday."

From the immense crush which had gathered since daybreak under the balcony of the Abdin palace, where Naguib had promised to make an appearance, a cry rose which counterpointed more and more frequently the *Yaïsh Naguib:* it was the *Allahu Akbar!* (God is the greatest) of the Muslim Brethren. We were surrounded by beards, rosaries, gray kaftans, turbans. When Naguib appeared, the clamor was deafening. But it crescendoed when a robust, bearded gentleman suddenly arose beside him waving a red-stained handkerchief. It was Mohammed Auda, shouting: "It is red with the blood of our brothers, shot down by the police!" Would Naguib's triumph enable the *Ikhwan el-Muslimin* to revenge themselves upon Nasser?

But things took a different turn. The confraternity had indeed whipped up the mob. But the masses had their own

life, their own aspirations. (Unless the Communists were
one day to succeed . . .) In short, the celebration had reached
a paroxysm when Naguib, towering above the tumult, called
out to the crowd: ". . . and we shall invite the people to elect
a parliament." This tactless remark was to be ruinous for the
good general. His re-advent had been the fruit of a tense
negotiation, which had taken up the entire night, but the
Twelve had never authorized him to make such a promise.
Pageants of reconciliation took place all day long between the
pipe-smoking general and a Nasser borne aloft for the first
time by the popular tide. But Gamal, sanguine once again,
now knew that he had to deal with a man who was more
than the junta's jolly figurehead, a popular leader in his own
right, imposed and supported by the masses.

But the game had hardly begun. Its preliminaries were to
last a whole month; yet soon the astounding tactical brilliance
of the *bikbashi* Abdel Nasser, which we have already seen in
the settlement of the Farouk affair, was once again to seize
center stage. Having recovered from his loss of nerve of
February 26, he now began to prove just how much he really
outclassed his rivals. In the beginning he had almost everything against him: the people, who were in love with Naguib;
the majority of the army, which had rallied behind the general; the foreign embassies, who were banking on the smiling
general—except the Americans, who were concerned about a
possible upsurge of the left in Naguib's wake; all the political
parties, from the Wafd to the Brethren and the Communists;
and finally the propertied class, which found the easygoing
pipe-smoker reassuring.

Nasser had only two or three assets: the vast majority of
the Free Officers, who already manned many of the levers of
the state apparatus; the police and its various ramifications;
and the labor unions rearranged and manipulated by a few
roughnecks like Abdallah Toema, a clever instigator of riots.

Gamal Abdel Nasser won out by breaking down his game
into smaller gambits. First he went about appeasing the
masses, then he reconquered the army, and finally he lured
his adversaries into making the sort of mistakes which lead to
internal division. He conducted this strategy with all the craft
and prudence which he needed to compensate for his handicap
at the outset.

The crowd he appeased twice, with stunning boldness. The
first time, March 5, he officially acceded to Naguib's demands to have parliamentary elections, to eliminate censorship, and to liberate a large number of political prisoners;
the second time, on March 25, he publicly announced "the
end of the revolutionary period" and the dissolution of the
Council of the Twelve. The first act was half-sincere, aimed
at avoiding a fiasco—a strategic retreat. But the second was
pure play-acting, to draw his adversary out into the open and
compromise him. It was the beginning of the counterattack.
(Reading today through the pages of this dossier, one thinks
often of Charles de Gaulle in Algiers, flouting General
Girand, who had every advantage, or withdrawing, for a
calculated moment, before the May revolution.)

The evening of March 5, after the announcement of the
approaching return to electoral procedures, we met him on the
front steps of his house in Manshiet el-Bakri, the first time we
had seen him in civilian dress. A constrained smile barely
concealed his anxiety.

"Do you consider that the army has achieved its purpose?"

"Yes, when they have put some finishing touches on the
work already accomplished."

"Do you really think this decision is wise?"

"Yes."

"You don't find it precipitous?"

"We have been working for the past forty-five days to find
a good formula for popular decision-making."

"But you hadn't foreseen such a rapid achievement."

"That is true."

"Do you believe that the re-establishment of the parliament will facilitate the solution of the Anglo-Egyptian problem?"

"I know that in any case Mr. Churchill would not be able to treat us as Nazis and fascists. Any stabilizing element serves the Egyptian cause."

"Do you propose—you and your comrades—to try and pursue a political career with the electorate?"

He laughed: "Some of us will return to our barracks. Others will enter the political arena."

The whole story of that month can be summarized as follows: Naguib, caught up in his idea of restoring the old democratic freedoms and sending the army back to its real task, gradually became so reconciled with the old regime politicos that they compromised and ensnared him. Nasser sought only to gather the army around him by playing on a sort of class consciousness and flattering the officers' corporatist spirit. What were you before? Nothing. What have you become, what could you become again? Everything. Do you wish to fall back into the shame of the past, ill-commanded, ill-paid, forgotten, despised? Do you long for the days of Haydar Pasha?

Then Nasser alerted the labor unions: the choice was between the continuation of the military revolution, he said, or the return of the pashas. Did we throw out Farouk to pave the way for the rotten old politicians and the decadent old leaders? It was like Mark Antony before the plebeians, defending the cause of the dictatorship over Caesar's dead body. If he had forgotten the lines which they had recited at the *En Nahda* school, Gamal might recently have refreshed his memory: a Cairo cinema was showing Mankiewicz's *Julius Caesar* that week, and it was whispered that all the leaders of the regime had discreetly gone to see it.

Finally, on March 25, all was ready for the last act. Nasser had announced the "end of the revolution." But the crowd—this time, *his* crowd, well prepared by his agents—would have none of it. Instigated from above, a general strike was declared. The entire city, consumed with passion and infiltrated with paid provocateurs, whirled about in near-madness. Columns of demonstrators waved Nasserist banners eulogizing the Council of the Revolution, while other pro-testers shouted, "Down with the basic freedoms!" A band of hooligans—were they really spontaneous?—went off to at-tack the president of the council of state, Abderrazak el-Sanhuri, Egypt's greatest jurist, and one of Naguib's closest counselors during the crisis. A day of madness.

An official communiqué, prepared by the finally vanquished Naguib, put an end that very evening to the *"ideas* of March." The general remained titular president of the republic, but the executive was divided, with Nasser as president of the council. As for the legislative branch, the elections were postponed: a vague "council of national deliberation" was to be established. Censorship was reinstituted. The *bikbashi* had won. Authori-tarian "revolution," *nabut* (blackjack) reformism, and virtue in uniform had successfully stemmed the rising tide of civil liberty.

This left-leaning militarism, based on both the political police and the half-colonized labor unions, this petulant popu-lism, evoked dismal memories at the time. Did they mask some sort of fascism, were they destined to be subsidized by the Americans, or infiltrated by the AFL-CIO or the CIA? That was our prognostication at the time. It was too simple. It invested too much significance in only one of the regime's faces, the one Miles Copeland describes with all the heat of an expert caught up in his field in *The Game of Nations.* We too were obsessed by the intimate contacts between the Free Officers and the Lakelands and Eichelbergers, dispatched to Cairo by Kermit Roosevelt and the virtuosos of the CIA, not to mention German—and possibly Nazi—agents like Otto Skorzeny.

Was this the regime's real face? Was this the real early Nasserism, a simple German-American operation to transfer Egypt from the British Empire, which was powerless to control the revolutionary onslaught, into the sphere of influence of the United States, the purveyors of dollars, "wise" reforms, and modern arms shipments?

Nasser and Nasserism remained—right to the end—too mobile to lend themselves to such a definition. But at each decisive turn it was possible at least to try and sketch the outlines of the man and the social groups which he played upon. Let us now try to take a snapshot of these days of April 1954, at the very moment when the *bikbashi* had, by triumphing over Naguib, just eliminated the only figure who could have threatened him, and controlled at last the entirety of the state machinery.

15

Early Nasserism: A Snapshot

The army was the beginning, if not the end, of everything. Gamal had just won it over to his side by shrewdly limiting his contest with Naguib to the struggle for the control—and, in the long shot, for the actual use—of the armed forces.

The regime was pyramidal. At the summit was the *bik-bashi*-premier who (after the definitive elimination of Naguib in late 1954) dominated and reigned over the two decision-making bodies, the Council of the Revolution and the ministerial cabinet—the former, of course, being rather more important. Some of Nasser's companions of proven ability belonged to both bodies: Zakaria Mohieddin, minister of the interior and chief of the army's special services; Abdellatif Boghdadi, who played Baron Haussman in marking out wide new avenues in Cairo; Gamal Salem, a sarcastic maker of plans; and Abdel Hakim Amer, whose stunning promotion to head of the army was due in part to his own real talent. With the technical assistance of several civilians, a Kayssouni for finance, a Sayed Marei for agriculture, and a Mahmud Fawzi for foreign affairs, they guaranteed the relatively smooth functioning of the higher machinery of state.

The upper story of the pyramid rested upon a fairly coherent collective base, made up of three organisms: the *Dhobat el-Ahrar*, or Society of Free Officers, which comprised about two hundred fifty members of very uneven value, but who, once Gamal had farmed them out into various key positions, constituted a semiclandestine ring which increased his control and his direct command; the *Haïat el-Tahrir,* or Assembly of the Liberation, a kind of rough sketch of a simple party bureaucracy which, though it had no real power, served as a communications network for the Council of the Revolution and the Free Officers; finally, the *mukhabarat,* the collection of special services which penetrated the two preceding organisms and regulated the purely repressive power of the minister of the interior.

To these three instruments of power should be added, first, the labor unions, whose Francoist-type framework we have already described, which were under the thumbs of two strongmen, the commandants Tahawi and Toema, and, second, the special network which Gamal created for his own purposes (not that he suspected Zakaria, but ten precautions are better than one).

Last but not least was the propaganda machine under the authority of Major Salah Salem, the regime's "roarer," who was to be eliminated in 1956 after a rambunctious career embellished with nude dancing in the Sudan (to inveigle some animistic tribes), several monumental lies, and untiring attempts to be taken as a holy terror by foreign correspondents—although he was closer to a Marseilles *député* than to Dr. Goebbels.

In March 1956, a few weeks after being dismissed from his command by Hussein of Jordan (under pressure from Cairo), Glubb Pasha insisted in utter seriousness: "Great Britain is being chased out of the Orient by words." Perhaps this remark reflected the "dancing major's" posturing, perhaps the contribution of his successor, Fathi Radwan. In any case, each one of those words was dearly paid for by the peasant of the Nile Valley, not in devalued piasters, but in balls of cotton.

But the bottom level of the pyramid, the foundation of the regime, was the army as a whole. It was everywhere, whether in or out of uniform, in the banks, in the committees for social reform and the encouragement of the arts, in the nurseries and the prisons, in the trade unions and in the casinos, and even at the Israel border. It owed its all to the regime, as Gamal had reminded certain of its officers on February 26, 1954. Before July 23, 1952, it had been, as in the time of the Middle Kingdom, a lower order, well below the priests and merchants, perhaps a bit above the road-makers and the water-carriers. In those days no solid citizen cared to see his daughter marry an officer. The pay was meager, as was the prestige (the Palestine war had hardly altered that), and, in a milieu where everything English was hateful, nothing in Egypt seemed more English than the army.

Then came July 23. The helots became conquerors, or, as the ancient Thebans said, "scribes and lords of the secrets." From now on, under the aegis of the *bikbashi* Gamal Abdel Nasser, they began to assume the habits of a ruling class, a corps of vehement major-domos. At first an isolated class, then after 1936 linked by social origin and living habits to the daily life of the common people—the middle or petty bourgeoisie—it now began to become particularized, and, perhaps, isolated once more. To the degree to which it imposed itself—or rather was imposed—as a dominant social order, it also began to take flight from the human terrain which had nourished it.

We should point out that these officers were less incompetent than rumors and *nokat* (popular jokes) had it. They were annoying but they worked hard. They were pretentious and clumsy, but they applied themselves, and improved. Half of their efforts were struggle against sabotage (real or imagined) from the older, now declassed, civil servants, but the other half escaped from the persistant nonchalance of their predecessors. Thus five hundred officers, working ten hours per day, often feasting on one mere sandwich of *ful* (fava) tucked away in a drawer of their Empire desks, administered, heavily but not unsuccessfully, an Egypt now forgetful of the old vices, and hungry for change.

Their hard work was well paid. Advancement, pay hikes, job annuities, clubs, social services, entry to the councils of administration—it was good, in Nasserite Egypt, to be an army officer. Now fathers wanted them for their sons-in-law. Even the lowliest privates, the fellahin barely out of the villages, felt the rays of the military order shine upon them. General Abdel Hakim Amer was a true benefactor; new uniforms, lots of food, clean barracks, playing fields, movie shows, and, even in the unhappiest regions, the admiration of tots and governesses—what a royal temptation for the peasants' sons of Beni-Morr!

But this order cannot be labeled militarism, which makes the military caste the arbiter of national life. It was said of Frederick's Prussia that it was not a state with an army but an army with a state. That formula does not apply here. Nasser did not militarize Egypt, he merely used the army to build a modern state, or what he thought was a modern state. The army did not overshadow public life, did not manipulate the machinery of the state: it was raw material for the state, and, indeed, it was the state's ingestion of the army which had so alarmed Naguib.

Which devoured the other, the cobra-state or the boa-army? The first, unquestionably. It was no mere accident, nor a simple dissimulation, that military uniforms disappeared after 1955, that Gamal and almost all his companions resigned from the army, that the *bikbashi* became the *Raïs*—a head of state who would never again be seen in military garb—and that he dressed in a jacket which looked commonplace beside the uniforms of Tito, Hussein, and Hassan II, or the battle dress of Castro or Ben Bella.

Was the new order a form of reformist populism? The definition is over-precise. A few weeks before his ouster, on January 23, 1954, Mohammed Naguib delivered a grand speech in which he declared, in utter seriousness, that the Egyptian government was "neither fascist, nor Communist, nor Nazi, nor socialist, nor capitalist." What were the interpreters of this speech to say when they had to confront the real dilemmas of power without the charms of oratory?

Was it a merely opportunistic regime? Yes and no. Yes, for up to 1955, Nasser and Nasserism could be defined only by their deeds. No, for these deeds were achieved in the context of circumstances beyond the control of Egypt's masters. (It was at this time that John Campbell, in the *Observer,* described the *bikbashi* as "a man of reaction rather than a man of action.") This game of ripostes and counterattacks took place within a system of countervailing power.

The *bikbashi* was hemmed in by London's pressure and Washington's maneuvers, by requirements for subsistence, by infatuation with his international leverage, by the constraints of demographic pressure and the ambition to industrialize. He navigated cautiously, himself the uncertain delegate of an uncertain class of small landowners swelled by his own agrarian reform. A patriot without a people, a populist with a clientele rather than mass support, an upholder of the rule of law who himself ruled by the rod, a militant enthralled with national independence yet dependent upon the good offices of the greatest foreign power of the era, Gamal Abdel Nasser was, at the end of 1954, a "pragmatic autocrat,"[1] powerful but solitary.

But we should avoid picturing him as mired in total op-

[1] Anwar Abdel Malek, *La Pensée politique arabe contemporaine,* Paris, 1970, p. 111.

portunism, a cynical practitioner resigned to "pure politics," to naked manipulation, a son of Mustafa Kamel transformed into an Ismail Sedky. Inside the Gamal of 1954—the virtuoso maneuverer of the spring, the realistic negotiator of the autumn, the implacable vanquisher of the Muslim Brethren —the nationalistic cadet hungry for freedom, justice, and grandiose dreams continued to persist.

Let us not forget that the publication of that astounding document the *Philosophy of the Revolution* was in the early summer of 1954. The fact that it had been drawn up a few months previously, with the help of Mohammed Hassanein Heykal, does not detract from its contemporaneity with the period in which Nasser chose to impose himself as absolute boss. The moment at which he chose to publish this manifesto counts above all. The seeker of notoriety redefines himself as soon as he projects his new image, even if it is only to retouch an earlier image which his behavior may have created.

European readers (and a good number of Gamal Abdel Nasser's compatriots) were struck by the naïveté and grandiloquence of these ninety-odd pages. The language was surprisingly gauche for a man who had just evinced his political virtuosity in his elimination of Naguib and his clique. Could it have been the same man who, so terribly adult in politics, had just published this adolescent document? Was this the self-contained negotiator of the treaty with London who now was unveiling such a spontaneous and unreservedly displayed will to power under the alternating banners of pan-Arabism and pan-Islamism?—the whole business packaged in a hero worship all the more worrisome since the hero in question had his finger on both a pen and a trigger.

Of course the author hastily explains in an introductory page that the word "philosophy" (*falsafa*) was misleading. Everything about the book suggested that it was hastily assembled, at a moment when Gamal felt that he would have to come out into the open, out of the comfortable shadow which Naguib had cast across his various doings. The pamphlet was probably thrown together from speeches, rough drafts of articles, and diary leaves, allowing this pragmatist, who had moved for fifteen years among national-fascists, Communists, Muslim Brethren, and democratic Wafdists, without bearing the stamp of any one of them, to adopt for both domestic and international public opinion "a style," a coherent account of history, and a rudimentary doctrine, or vague system of reference.

In this "philosophy"—in which one can still hear the echo of the frustrated young cadet—there are two very distinct sections. First, the confidences of a young nationalist revolting against corrupt power and foreign occupation, hesitantly preparing the tools and methods of liberation. There is a sort of typically Egyptian and rather noble romanticism here. This patriot, ashamed of earlier acts of terrorism, is worthy of respect.

The second part is mostly made up of curious and informative reflections on the attitude of the Egyptian people toward the July "revolution." Here Nasser's boyish élan softens into lucid melancholia. One is tempted to call this second part an "elegy for a revolution." In these broken illusions one can perhaps find the key to a stunning development: the young *bikbashi* of the period right after July 23, who dreamed of recalling parliament and voted clemency for Khamis, the workers' ringleader, had, six months later, become the cold-blooded wielder of undivided authority.

"We had breached the wall and nobody followed us. . . . I thought that after a few hours great crowds would join us in the sacred march forward. Farther still, my fertile imagination overheated to the point where I thought I heard the deep and distant sound of the masses advancing in solid ranks. . . . But the events following July 23 were disappointing. My heart was torn by suffering and bitterness. The spark had been kindled, the front lines had stormed the fortress of tyranny and dethroned Farouk. We needed unity, and discord was at our heels. We needed zeal and ardor, but we found only laziness and inertia in the masses."

The first section is in a sense the leader's childhood. The second, the realistic, adult discovery of the ingratitude and passivity of the crowd. In the third section, the leader dreams. But would he not have fared better wide awake? Here we read of crowds assembled for the holy pilgrimage and the holy vow—the entire Islamic *umma,* the entire Arab world —although Nasser himself had just confessed the utter apathy of the Egyptians. Mathematical operations followed, trying to show that Arab soil harbored the great part of the world's oil, and that the masters of this treasure could draw from it vast political and strategic consequences. Then he wrote: "This circle is awaiting its hero. We have answered its call," and added that "the Arab world is united, from the Persian Gulf to the Atlantic."

Soon after our first reading of these pages, in October 1954, we interviewed one of Gamal Abdel Nasser's closest collaborators, without trying to conceal our surprise at this exalted document.

He answered that a leader confronted with the backwardness and the deficiencies of Egypt in 1954 could not afford to overlook anything, including eloquence, lyricism, even daydreams, to raise up and lead forward the enervated masses.

Perhaps. But this *Philosophy of the Revolution* not only shows how much the new premier was still groping about for an idea, a doctrine, a general strategy; it also shows how badly he understood the relationship between a leader and the masses. For example, he did not grasp the fact that the masses could not follow, share, or back a movement which provided no explanation or blueprint; that a crowd which one merely

manipulates can be lost as quickly as it is won over; that the
so-called "ingratitude" and "passivity" of public opinion is
the normal attitude of a collectivity faced with a conspiracy's
fait accompli, a secret society which, even installed in power,
remained shrouded in mystery.

The *bikbashi* Abdel Nasser had not yet discovered in 1954
the virtues of self-criticism, nor those of mass communication.
Merely solitary, he saw himself as positively isolated. His
virtuousness, of which he was fully aware, was piqued by his
being unloved. As misunderstood as he was nonunderstand-
ing, this harsh surgeon was trying to heal the Egyptian people
without even telling them about it, and on the condition that
his patient stop breathing, and docilely put itself in his hands.
He wanted the initiative to come only from above, and contained or repressed it when it tried to gush out of the masses,
to spurt spontaneously from its deepest strata. He was still a
sort of auto-colonialist who filled the prisons as fast as he
filled the schools, and who preferred to lean on a probably
faithful repressive apparatus rather than a possibly unfaithful
public opinion.

This virtuous dictator, struggling to create for his country
a "third way" between colonialistic capitalism and a still much
despised communism, this man of productivistic social justice,
working in stages toward independence and development, was
still situated, no matter how you look at it, in the Western
camp. It was Nasser himself, not only his friends, advisers,
and American contacts, who was responsible for the virulent
anticommunism of the preface to a pamphlet called *Communism as It Really Is,* drawn up in late 1954:

"The Communists," he wrote, "have become machines
within the factory of collective production, even though they
were once human beings with free will. How far the truth is
from the picture given by their propagandists. What separates
us from communism, in the theory of government as in the

way of life, is that communism is a religion and we have our own religion. We will not abandon our own religion for that of communism."

And yet, less than a year later, Gamal Abdel Nasser would be engaged in a profound strategic shift, both political and diplomatic. The solitary reformer loyal to the West will have become a protorevolutionary leader, an adulated partner in the socialist camp.

1955—the turning point.

PART FOUR

The Raïs

That June day of 1956 the ex-postman Abdel Nasser Hussein stood, ballot in hand like everybody else, outside the Abassieh poll. With his bright new fez and his elegant black suit, he was one of seven million Egyptians ready to elect a president —rather, to elect the *president, for there was but one candidate, Nasser Hussein's eldest son Gamal. By that evening only two thousand Egyptian citizens had chosen to deposit the sinister-looking black ballot which signified a negative vote. Of all the voters 99.8% had, for various reasons, preferred the pretty paper with the red markings: "yes" to Gamal.*

At the same time that he was elected president, a constitution went into effect. Was it the charter of a fascist regime? "Fascism, no," said one of the finest French specialists in public law, Georges Burdeau, then a professor in Cairo; "it's more like technical Caesarism." It was to be a model for the constitutions granted by the majority of the new African states in the coming years. The text, already published in January 1956, aimed primarily at uniting in a single leader the offices of chief of state and head of the government, and to convert any organism which might eventually serve as a check or balance into a harmless phantom.

But it was neither this text nor the election which had made Gamal Abdel Nasser the absolute master of Egypt and the pretender, so to speak, to the Arab crown. It was rather the sixteen months of history, from February 1955 to June 1956, which had changed the bikbashi *into the* Raïs, *had changed the acerb pro-Western reformer into the leader of the most cyclonic revolutionary force in the Mideast.*

16

The Surprises of Bandung

On February 24, 1955, an incident occurred which, in comparison to other great moments in the story of Gamal Abdel Nasser, is all but forgotten. Yet it was among those which determined three of the most important choices in his career: his first rebuff to the West, his first rapprochement since August 1952 with the forces of the Left, and the discovery of his Arab destiny.

This event was the signing of the Baghdad Pact between Iraq and Turkey. We have already mentioned, in connection with the agreement of the previous year between Nasser and the British, how Egyptian progressives had depicted membership of an Arab regime in any pact with the West as an act of treason. This doctrine had been carried to a point where the single "Turkish clause" of the Anglo-Egyptian treaty weighted on the *bikbashi* like a sin. Gamal defied the anathema; but he could not tolerate another Arab leader's doing what he himself had done.

If Nasser had accepted to go along with London, it was with the intention of limiting London's power. But the premier of Iraq, Nuri Saïd, adhered to the pact with the declared purpose of making his alliance with Turkey the center of a Middle Eastern coalition against the U.S.S.R. During the following year, in fact, the Iraqi-Turkish axis was transformed into a Holy Alliance, into which entered its British, if not its

American, godfathers, and finally Karachi and Teheran. It was thus that CENTO was born, the central link in the chain which connected NATO in the West to SEATO in the Far East.

Although he could not pretend great surprise, since the announcement of the imminent signing of the pact dated from the preceding January 18, Abdel Nasser's reaction was violent. Rarely was there a more lively press and radio campaign than that which he unleashed against the Baghdadi "lackeys of imperialism." To the ambassador of a Western power completely uninvolved in the Baghdad operation, he declared on February 25: "Until then, as you well know, I was your friend. You may no longer count on me." We must seek to understand the reasons for this anger, which caused the United States ambassador to Cairo, Henry Byroade, to say upon receiving us several days later: "The pact is not a defeat for Egypt. It is Nasser's reaction that makes it a public failure for *him. . . .*"

Both the *bikbashi* and the ambassador were right. Henry Byroade's statement was valid because Baghdad's adherence *was* a partial victory for Nasser, who had succeeded during the preceding two months in preventing three other Arab countries, Jordan, Lebanon, and Saudi Arabia, from joining the coalition established by Dulles. But Abdel Nasser, having prevented the whole Arab group from passing under American control, had not been able to prevent the Baghdad operation itself, which threatened an extensive revision of the balance of Near Eastern forces, to the detriment of Cairo.

As he signed the agreement with London several months earlier, Nasser had silenced his own repulsion. He thought that the withdrawal of the British, the arms they were leaving him, and the collusion thus established with Washington made Egypt the fulcrum of the Middle Eastern strategic group, a position on which he could play as he wished.

American emissaries had not concealed from him that by initialing the treaties conceived by John Foster Dulles, he became the pivotal man in the region.[1]

The Baghdad Pact cruelly transferred the axis of Near Eastern strategy onto the Euphrates. Washington had preferred to invest in her declared friends, rather than evasive partners such as Nasser. Moreover, the new weight acquired by Iraq threatened to draw into the orbit of Baghdad, and of the Hashemite monarchy then in power, fragile Syria and especially Jordan, which Nasser had with great difficulty restrained from signing the pact in January. The Fertile Crescent was to be pushed by these Mesopotamians into a policy of allegiance to the West.

In this emergency because the Arabs of the northern tier were being wrested from him in the name of the West and of anticommunism, Gamal Abdel Nasser (that "man of reaction rather than action") rediscovered his passion for Arabism, his revolt against the West, and began to consider Marxism and its diverse representations in a new light.

At the same time, this deeply troubled man, who was beginning to re-examine all his values, and whose relative isolation made him all the more impressionable for outside opinions, received two visits in February—from Marshal Tito and from Prime Minister Nehru—which were to influence the course of his thought. The former head of the Croatian partisans was to affect greatly the career of Gamal Abdel Nasser. Nehru's influence was less keen, but the five hours the two men spent on the Nile on February 13, 1955, were to plant in Nasser a spirit which would inspire him in the course of the following years—the spirit of Bandung. The brilliant Indian statesman left him with a still more hostile

---

[1] Solicitations were then formulated by the Turks, armed with the clause relative to them in the treaty of 1954. An invitation to Ankara was addressed to Nasser, who curtly refused.

attitude toward all pacts, and especially to that of Baghdad.

Nasser was utterly inflamed—one could almost say bleeding—from the Baghdad operation, and gripped by an obsession with Western plots, when he learned that an Israeli
commando raid, penetrating at dawn into the Gaza zone controlled by Cairo, had left thirty-five Egyptians dead. The episode left Nasser in deep distress. He was unable to respond
to such a challenge because of the disrepair and unreadiness
of the Egyptian army thirty months after his accession to
power.

But the *bikbashi*-president did not see only the military and
technical side of the matter. He considered above all the
political-diplomatic aspects. There was no doubt in his mind
that the Israelis had struck in the capacity of a Western
militia, ordered by the Americans to remind him that without
arms he had little weight, that he needed the support of the
United States, that he needed to commit himself to the coalition just formed in Baghdad.

It was perhaps an absurd hypothesis, but like the majority
of his compatriots, Gamal Abdel Nasser always underestimated the specific character of Israeli politics and the original-
ity of the initiatives taken by Tel Aviv. But in any case his
version of the event was to orient his conduct profoundly in
the months to come. He considered that a trap had been laid
for him in Baghdad, and that the Gaza affair was but another
phase of the operation, a second trap.

He did not react by immediately running to Moscow to
demand revenge, as those who have followed his career and
its vicissitudes since that time might believe. The degree of
involvement which he still felt vis-à-vis the West is best
illustrated by the fact that following both these ordeals, he
dispatched his closest collaborator—then director of the presidential cabinet—Ali Sabri, to the West, to request a purchase
of arms. His envoy was rebuffed in Paris, where it was empha-

sized that the situation in Algeria did not predispose France to become the purveyor of arms to Egypt, and also in Washington, where he was reminded of the necessity for preliminary membership in a pact. Only after these refusals did the leader of the Egyptian government consider addressing himself to other suppliers. And even then it was Daniel Solod, the Soviet Ambassador to Cairo, who first openly broached the question during one of the many interviews he held with Nasser starting in February 1955. But we are getting ahead of ourselves.

For Gamal Abdel Nasser the spring of 1955 was not only a season of arms-seeking and of profound reflection upon Egypt's role in the world and his own diplomatic and strategic ideas; it was also the time of his first venture outside the Arab world, if not Egypt (he had fought in Palestine and visited Mecca): the journey to Bandung.

It is an understatement to speak of a journey. It was more accurately a flight, a transference, mutation, for these few days were to mark the *bikbashi* even more profoundly than the Baghdad pact, the Gaza operation, or the arms affair. They were to open new perspectives to him in the matter of the world situation of his country, the international relationship of forces, his own prestige abroad, and his stance vis-à-vis the progressive or revolutionary forces in Egypt.

For Nasser, the Bandung drama was played out on two fronts, domestic and foreign. Despite what has been thought, the most important incidents did not occur abroad. True, the timid *bikbashi* learned excellent lessons at Bandung from statesmen such as Nehru, whom he knew, as well as from others, whom he did not know, such as Chou En-lai. Nasser, a fervent anti-Communist, who had just written the vitriolic preface to *Communism as It Really Is,* from which we have quoted, found himself in immediate agreement with the Chinese premier. He witnessed the representatives of the two greatest powers in Asia and the most populated nations of the world in open dispute for his favors.

Chou offered to buy Egyptian cotton, in exchange for which, he said, the *bikbashi* might be inspired to recognize the Peking regime. But Nasser had already learned some tricks: he very politely let it be understood that this was a very high price for a few tons of cotton, since the Egyptian fellahin would hardly appreciate the Chinese tea offered as payment. Chou easily grasped his intents, and they separated the best of friends.

During the entire conference, Gamal Abdel Nasser received an enthusiastic welcome—such as neither Cairo nor Alexandria had ever given him—from the Javanese crowd, whose amplitude and propinquity Sukarno, as a true leader of the people, had encouraged. Nasser's brief appearances on the podium, in the hallways or in the streets, were the occasion of hearty demonstrations. Along with Chou En-lai, he was the man of the day. He who had arrived anxious, obsessed that he might appear inferior to the Iraqis or the Turks, left as the hero of what was barely beginning to be called the Third World. He had succeeded in putting to a vote an anti-Israeli (though nonaggressive) resolution, without piquing the Burmese, then fervent Israelophiles, as well as a motion hostile to "Communist colonialism," without breaking with Chou En-lai, who saw it as an attack directed against the U.S.S.R. His seven-point program, of admirable insignificance, was approved by referendum. But, much more important, Bandung had been for him, more than for anyone, what Léopold Senghor called "the end of an inferiority complex."

But the Bandung episode assumed its deepest significance for him when he returned to Cairo. We had often been witness to encounters between the *bikbashi* Abdel Nasser and the Egyptian masses. Until this time, these confrontations had never lost the stiffness imparted by Gamal's behavior. Yet on

April 27, 1955, a warm breeze seemed to pass between the man and the crowd. On the *Midan Tahrir,* where triumphal arches bearing the names of Nasser, Nehru, and Chou En-lai had been erected, a jeep emerged bearing an erect Nasser, his bronze face relaxed into a broad laugh, carrying after him the unrestrained crowd which had so often trailed after Nahas and Naguib.

This surprising modulation of the regime followed upon an even more surprising initiative taken by its adversaries. One week before the *bikbashi*'s trip to Asia, before he was certain himself that he would go, a new raid had sent several scores of Communists to prison. On the day when Nasser finally made his decision and was leaving for Indonesia, a telegram signed by the majority of these prisoners arrived on his desk: "Long live our militant in the anti-imperialist struggle! We salute you."

This rallying of the incarcerated Left coincided with his rapprochement with Peking, the advances then being made to him by Soviet diplomacy, and the friendship which he had just formed with Tito. These were factors well designed to orient Gamal Abdel Nasser toward a profound and all-inclusive re-examination of his political strategy, foreign and later domestic. One cannot overestimate the influence of his two experiences with the masses, first in Bandung, as a symbol of the anger of Arabism against the West, and then in Cairo, as an embodiment of the rejection of "imperialist pacts."

Even at the moment when Nasser renounced forever his rank, pay, and uniform, he remained steeped for some time in the ideas and preoccupations of a general staff officer; he did not forget that the survival of his regime still depended on the loyalty of the army, which in turn depended in part on arms and equipment still being awaited. Hence for Nasser the next episode would be still more decisive: the sale of arms to Egypt by the socialist camp.

.   .   .

Even before the Israeli operation in Gaza, Nasser and Amer
had attempted to buy arms from the Western powers. Washington and London had demanded that in return he adhere
to a common defense agreement. Paris had insisted that he
cease his aid for the North African nationalist movements.
These conditions had discouraged Nasser and Amer. Then
occurred, on February 28, the brutal demonstration of Egyptian military weakness. Negotiations with the U.S.S.R. opened
in May 1955. In the journal *Akher Sa'a,* Gamal Abdel Nasser
described the early stages:

"On the occasion of a diplomatic reception in May, I was
approached by the ambassador from the U.S.S.R., Daniel
Solod, who, taking me into a corner, very frankly asked me
whether my government was disposed toward buying arms
from the Soviet Union. . . . I answered in the same tone, since
this suggestion seemed to me extremely interesting, that I
was ready to enter into negotiations on this question."

Two months later, on the occasion of the anniversary
celebration of the *coup d'état* of July 1952, *Pravda* dispatched
a special envoy to Cairo. This was Editor-in-Chief Dimitri
Shepilov who, before becoming a rather ephemeral foreign
minister, was one of the "brains" of the post-Stalinist ruling
group. Shepilov patiently played his role as journalist and
regularly attended meetings, speeches, and military parades.
Then, on his last day, he requested an audience with the
premier and discreetly informed him of the Soviet acceptance
of the principle of an arms deal.

Yet Nasser still hesitated. He dispatched one of his last
buying missions to France, who had just proclaimed her hostility toward the Baghdad Pact. But excessive preaching about
the Maghreb caused the visitors to break off an arms contract which had already been signed. Then, receiving us dur-

ing the last days of August, the director of Nasser's cabinet, Ali Sabri declared: "If during the coming week the Americans do not make the gesture which we have requested for the last time, we shall have to buy our armaments from the Communist countries."

As night fell over the stifling city on September 26, Gamal Abdel Nasser inaugurated the "Army Fair" in Cairo. Five months earlier, his return from Bandung had made the crowd tremble with emotion. This time, his words sent it into a turmoil. We were listening to his speech on the radio. The bursts of applause sounded like static on a stormy night: "The West refuses us the means to defend our existence: we have just signed an arms contract with Czechoslovakia!" Coordinating their efforts for the first time, the propaganda services and the movements of the Left had prepared the audience and helped to stage its spirited reactions. But Gamal would have been able to do without hired applause that evening. He aroused something of which the Egyptian people had long been deprived: the hope of recourse, the conviction that there existed an alternative, a freedom, outside a colonial or semicolonial setting.[2]

This was the first time that a gesture had been made which upset, not alliances, but markets, the most important being the arms market. This act sealed an alliance between Gamal and the people which was to become a marriage, a fusion, an incarnation and possession. But it also upset the status quo in what was then called the "Middle Eastern equilibrium," that is, Anglo-Saxon domination with the intermittent complicity of Paris.

The West reacted lamentably to this terrible defiance, though it was even more serious and decisive than that which would later follow the Suez crisis. Washington sent one of

[2] We have already noted the favorable reactions of the crowd when a Wafdist minister spoke on January 26, 1952, of buying arms from Moscow.

its most notorious diplomats, George Allen, to Cairo with a threatening note. Gamal responded to this by making the messenger wait, then intimated harshly that he would only be received if he kept his message to himself. The *bikbashi* had not only taken the measure of his freedom to maneuver and the breadth of action made available to him by the East. He had also assessed the mediocrity of the retaliatory measures at the disposal of the West, even though this led him to draw certain exaggerated conclusions which would later cost him dearly.

17

The Challenge from Alexandria

Neither Washington nor even London had given up the possibility of eventually winning back the Egyptian leader. Henry Byroade, the amiable American ambassador, continued to maintain friendly relations with him, and the very intelligent representative of the Queen, Sir Humphrey Trevelyan, repeated on every occasion that one leans only upon that which resists. Gamal himself had chosen neutrality rather than alliance with the East. His first opportunity to demonstrate this was the construction of the High Dam at Aswan.

  The first plans for this project came from a picturesque engineer of Greek origin, Adrian Daninos, who had been snubbed for many long years by the governments of the old regime. The decision to construct the dam had been one of the first taken by the Free Officers, whose youth and patriotism were aroused by the fabulous prospect of a modern popular pyramid. The problem was the cost of the enterprise, first estimated at $500 million. Negotiations were opened with a Franco-Anglo-German consortium. French bankers came to Cairo; then the Americans entered the scene. Since they were eager to win back the *bikbashi*-president, the moment for dollars without arms had arrived.

In November 1955, two months after the announcement of the arms purchase in Prague, Mr. Kayssouni, the Egyptian Minister of Finance and a man favored in the West, was cordially welcomed in Washington. This welcome portended perhaps a loan for the dam, perhaps even a gift. A month later, on December 19, benevolent Uncle Sam announced that he was making $54 million available unconditionally to the Cairo government for the construction of the Aswan "pyramid." He had also persuaded London to offer $16 million as her share, a sum intended to pay for a part of the first phase of the construction. The offer was intended to make the Egyptian state a solvent borrower vis-à-vis the large international credit organizations.[1]

In January 1956, Gamal Abdel Nasser presented to the Egyptian people "his" constitution, which was to make him legally the *Raïs,* or "boss," without the counterweight of the nation and the state. At the same time Eugene Black, President of the International Bank for Reconstruction and Development, landed in Cairo. Black was a useful contact, for a month later, on February 11, the visitor signed a general agreement in which the International Bank loaned Egypt $200 million at 3½ per cent interest, payable in twenty

[1] In his *Egypt* (London, 1958), the astute Middle East expert Tom Little maintains that neither Washington nor London ever believed in the possibility of constructing the dam, and were simply giving Nasser a "political tip."

years. Curiously, this text, like the evacuation treaty of 1954, was satisfactory only to the giver and not to the beneficiary, though the Arab version of the text specifically stated that Egypt would have recourse to the loan only when she wished.

In order to understand Egyptian reservations, one must think less of the "treaty with imperialism" aspect of this agreement than of the history of Egypt in the nineteenth century. The statutes of the International Bank provide (articles thirteen and fourteen) that the borrower must allow his budget to be supervised by the lending organization. Yet Gamal and his friends had grown up haunted by the foreign debt accumulated by the Khedive Ismail. Ismail's reckless borrowing had been the pretext for the British (originally Franco-British) seizure of Egyptian sovereignty.

Surely better conditions could be expected from the Eastern countries, who also had more than arms to supply. Shepilov had promised to return in June. Meanwhile, Daniel Solod was consulted; he seemed less eager to discuss money than cannons. In Washington, however, Egypt's adversaries, notably the Israelis, besieged the Senate and the State Department, demanding to know whether this "red pharaoh," this friend of Tito and Chou En-lai, was to be financed with liberty dollars. London and Paris, exasperated by the Arab politics of the *Raïs* from Casablanca to the Persian Gulf, joined in the refrain. The leaders of both the French and British diplomacies had just undergone bitter experiences in Cairo.

Returning from an official visit to India on March 11, French Foreign Minister Christian Pineau was received by the *Raïs,* to whom he suggested that he moderate his intervention in Algeria. Charmed by his host, and having received a promise that Cairo would grant no strictly military aid to the Front de Libération Nationale, Pineau returned quite satisfied to Paris. There he commended Gamal's "word as a soldier," and advocated a rapprochement with Egypt. Several days later, the French special services published information that Algerian commandos were being trained in Egypt. The foreign minister's humiliation was to color his later reactions.

A month later, Pineau's British colleague Selwyn Lloyd was received before Nasser's desk. The British minister pointedly denounced Egyptian intrusions into the Persian Gulf. Then he said in a solemn tone:

"Do not forget, Mr. President, that we still have several trump cards in the area. At Amman, for example, we have Glubb Pasha . . ."

"No, Mr. Lloyd, you do not have him: you *had* him."

And Nasser smilingly held out to his interlocutor a telegram which the butler had received as they were being seated, announcing that King Hussein had sacked the British general. On this day, as on March 11, Gamal Abdel Nasser did not make a new friend.

The Egyptian ambassador to Washington, Ahmed Hussein,[2] counseled Nasser in June that he should abandon his reserve and accept the offers of the West: if the loan was not approved by Congress before July 1, it never would be. The Egyptian head of state instructed his ambassador to attempt to lighten the Anglo-Saxon conditions without breaking off the negotiations, adding: "There is not one chance in a hundred that they will finance us. . . ." In fact, on July 10 Dulles intimated that the credits which had been offered might now be withdrawn. On the seventeenth, Nasser, then visiting Marshal Tito in Brioni, cabled Ahmed Hussein to accept any conditions set by the West.

On the following day he received the harshest insult ever inflicted upon him, worse than the Baghdad Pact, worse than the Gaza incident, worse than the refusal of the West to sell

---

[2] Not the fascist leader of the same name.

him arms. The U.S. State Department released a communication directly to the press, without any preliminary notification of Cairo, which announced with unparalleled cruelty that because of the "weakness of the Egyptian economy" and the "instability of the regime," Washington had decided not to help finance the High Dam. Gamal's reaction could not have been angrier. He heard the news while disembarking from the plane from Brioni, and forthwith locked himself in his office with three or four advisers.

On July 22, he sat down at his desk and began to draft the first formulation of the decision he had just taken: the nationalization of the largest enterprise in Egypt, the Suez Canal Company, which represented holdings of several hundred million dollars in Egypt as well as in France and Great Britain. This act would procure for him both the revenge for his wounded prestige, which meant so much to him, and the financial assets needed for the great Aswan project. As for the possible risks of the operation, Nasser explained thus the terms of his note of July 22 in an interview eight years later with our colleague Kennett Love:[3]

"I imagined myself in the place of the British should they have recourse to force to recapture the canal after its nationalization. I concluded that such a recourse was impossible. By allying themselves with the Israelis in such an undertaking, the British would compromise all their positions and all their interests in the Middle East, which were considerable. . . . In any case, I arrived at the conclusion that it would take the British forces two months to mount an expedition against us. I thought that these two months would suffice for us to come to an agreement by diplomatic means."

As for the French: "France was hostile to the Baghdad Pact. . . . We had not yet understood to what extent the

[3] Interview published by *Le Nouvel Observateur,* July 20, 1966.

French were embittered by the Algerian affair. . . . At the same time, I thought that they were too busy in Algeria to be able to participate in an expedition against us."

And the Americans: "We had the impression that they would reject any use of force." The *Raïs* summed up his re-assessment of July 22, 1956: "Israel would do nothing, France would do nothing, the United States would do noth-ing. As for the possibility of a British intervention, we still have two months ahead of us."

Still, according to Nasser's account to Kennett Love, on the following day Nasser assembled his closest friends in the Council of the Revolution and informed them of his plan. "There are three solutions," he told them: "to nationalize the canal, to nationalize fifty per cent of it, or to announce that it will be nationalized if we do not obtain the loan for the Aswan Dam." Fearful of being trapped in an escalation of ultimatums and counterultimatums, Nasser convinced his lieutenants to opt for total and immediate nationalization.

The next day, July 24, the *Raïs* summoned Colonel Mah-mud Yunis, one of the military "managers" in whom he had the greatest confidence and whom he had made the director of oil development. He announced: "Mahmud, I am going to nationalize the Suez Company!"

"I remained rooted to the spot," the engineer recounted;[4] "then I kissed him on both cheeks. . . . He said to me: 'You are the one who will lead the operation. Prepare a plan of action and come show it to me tomorrow morning at nine. . . .' "

That evening, in a village near Cairo where he was inau-gurating a new oil refinery, Gamal Abdel Nasser impro-vised a philippic which caused foreign observers to sit up and take note: "The American broadcast lies about the sup-posed fragility of the Egyptian economy, thereby trampling

[4] Kennett Love interview, July 20, 1966.

over all the principles of decency. I shout in their faces: You may choke on your fury, but you shall not dictate the future of Egypt!"

It was unclear whether he was preparing an alliance with the U.S.S.R. or a rupture with the United States and all organizations tied to it. It was whispered that the canal was threatened, but the two journalists[5] who noted this were soundly reprimanded by Suez Company spokesmen. On July 23, an informant from the French Embassy who claimed to have inside dope was heard with courteous irony. In any case, everyone knew by this time that the *Raïs*'s forthcoming July 26 speech in Alexandria, on the occasion of the fourth anniversary of Farouk's exile, would be "sensational." This was the word used by a member of Nasser's cabinet whom we interviewed. He added: "It will be the most important speech since the beginning of the regime. . . ."

The plan submitted to the *Raïs* by Mahmud Yunis was marked by the somewhat romantic quality that is one of the charms of the Egyptians, and by a taste for spy novels hitherto unsuspected in this excellent technician. He had prepared five assault troops of five members each, to whom envelopes were distributed to be opened successively (1) upon Nasser's arrival in Alexandria, planned for 4:00 P.M., (2) at the beginning of his radio speech, and, finally (3) when he pronounced the words "Ferdinand de Lesseps." At that very instant, the last group would enter the premises of the director of the Canal Company and seize them, affixing seals on all available property and papers. The plan truly was really too magnificent to be executed.

That evening at about seven night slowly began to fall on the immense Mohammed Ali Square as the crowd gathered in the places marked off by heavy police cordons. It was the

[5] Simonne Lacouture, in a note in *Echos,* and François Courtal, in *L'Orient* of Beirut.

same spot where Mahmud Abdellatif had fired eight shots
at Abdel Nasser just twenty months before. A gentle breeze
revived those, like us, who had just undergone one of the
most stifling and nerve-wracking weeks Cairo had ever seen.
On the terrace where we were standing—next to members
of the government and the Council of the Revolution—Gamal
Abdel Nasser slowly climbed the three steps to the platform
and grasped the microphone in his right hand. At about
7:40, he began his speech.

He spoke in a familiar tone, what Egyptians call *baladi,*
the popular language, this time, not straining for a noble
style as he had done before. We had come to hear a tragic
monologue; he was offering us an anecdotal tale. "And now
I shall tell you about my unpleasant dealings with the American diplomats. . . ." Here Gamal the austere disciplinarian
was transformed into a popular singer. "Poor Mr. Allen! He
comes into my office with the note—I drive him out; he returns without having delivered the note—Mr. Dulles drives
him out. What can be done for poor Mr. Allen?"

The crowd roared with laughter. All around us, Egyptian
journalists steeped in the severe style of the *Raïs* shook their
heads in astonishment: "*Kuwayyis awi!*" (very good). Gamal
went on, mimicking diplomats and caricaturing their statements. This timid man had just discovered, in the depths of
his anger, how to talk to the people. Below us, in the dark-
ening basin of Mohammed Ali Square, there grew, not the
seething fury which we had foreseen, but a hearty laughter
that mounted every minute.

Suddenly the tone changed. An ironic description of his
last meeting with Mr. Black brought the *Raïs* to the sentence awaited by the teams lying in wait along the canal,
transistor in hand, at Port Said, Ismailia, and Suez: "This
gentleman reminded me of Ferdinand de Lesseps" (pronounced "Lissips," with a hiss). The speaker had passed

from a jest to an indictment; now he was harshly denouncing "mortgage colonialism." And then the crescendo: "We are going to take back the profits which this imperialist company, this state within the state, deprived us of while we were dying of hunger. . . ."

So that was it! "I announce to you that at this very moment our official newspaper is publishing the law nationalizing the company, and, as I speak to you, government agents are taking possession of the company. . . ." Everything exploded around and below us in the darkness. Newspapermen known for their skepticism toward the regime climbed onto their chairs to roar their enthusiasm.

Gamal was suddenly shaken by an irrepressible laugh: the thrill was enormous, the move surprising even to him. He shouted his defiance: "The canal will pay for the dam! Four years ago, in this very place, Farouk fled Egypt. Today I seize the canal, in the name of the people. . . . This night our canal shall be Egyptian, controlled by Egyptians!"

One could no longer hear his words nor his laugh. In a tornado of accolades and embraces he tore himself away from the rostrum, where nearby, we overheard a French MP murmuring repeatedly, as if to exorcise a demon: "He has no right, he has no right . . ."

For over an hour Mahmud Yunis's commandos had been in operation, from Port Said to Suez. At Ismailia, Nasser's right-hand man had taken possession of the directorial offices where the administrative director, M. Menessier, was somewhat surprised to see him enter. Yet the British cruiser *Jamaica* was anchored by chance at the wharves. And toward midnight on the terrace of the Hotel Cecil, an Alexandrian friend who had seen many other warships muttered: "This is a courageous act. But may God help us. . . ."

All Alexandria jumped for joy around us. Nasser's burst of laughter passed on to hundreds of thousands of hungry mouths and bellies. The grandson of the fellah of Beni-Morr, the son of the postal employee of Bacos, had just shouted his defiance at the high and mighty and rich. He had dared; he had broken into the coffer. By ruse and by force he had taken the master's place. In his own surprised laughter he had just recovered his totally Egyptian personality, his true citizenship in the country where one laughs at one's poverty even while planting one's beans. He was Goha the clever and Sinbad the prodigious. The little people clapped their hands in rhythm, prolonging into the night the grand insolent laugh of President Nasser, now become Gamal.

But well calculated were the risks taken on July 22. At the rostrum in the Palais-Bourbon, at the desk in the House of Commons, Mollet and Eden vituperated against "the new Hitler," the "insolent plunderer," the "barking dictator" who would soon be obliged to "disgorge" what he had swallowed. Jurists convened to decide whether he had total, partial, or no right to do what he had done.

We shall not go into this question here. It is enough to recall that Cairo was bound by two sorts of texts and obligations. On the one hand there were the *firmans,* or Ottoman decrees, of 1854 and 1856 which conceded to the Universal Suez Canal Company the development and revenues of the as yet unexcavated canal for ninety-nine years after the opening of the waterway, that is, until 1968. On the other hand, there was the International Convention of Constantinople of 1888, which placed Cairo under the obligation to assure free passage to all ships, without discrimination, even in time of war.[6] England had herself violated this obligation when she

---

[6] This convention, signed by Great Britain, Germany, Austria, Spain, France, Italy, the Netherlands, Russia, and Turkey (then representing Egypt), internationalized the application of the 1854 *firman* of concession: "The Canal and its dependent ports shall always be open as neutral passageways to all ships, and shall be open to all vessels of commerce without distinction."

controlled the canal during the two world wars, and since 1948 she had allowed Egypt to violate it vis-à-vis Israel at a time when she was still protecting it.

Concerning the "ownership" and the "nationality" of the Company, the dossier was complex to say the least. Witness the astonishing formula used in 1940 in *Suez, Panama and the World Maritime Routes* by Andre Siegfried, a circumspect writer who was far from hostile to the rights of property: "An Egyptian company, in point of fact French. . . ." Was Nasser seeking the revenge of "right" against "fact"? Perhaps he was simply taking from the rich and giving to the poor. This "revolutionary morality" has a certain generosity and appeal. But we must remember that Gamal was acting at a time when such a moral code belonged only to a small minority, and by scoffing at the conventional code, if indeed he did scoff at it, he placed himself and especially Egypt in a perilous situation.

We have seen that he took calculated risks, and that he also conducted his operation very well from a technical point of view. But at the time of the lengthy interview with Kennett Love cited above, Gamal Abdel Nasser laughingly admitted that he had committed many errors during his long meditation of July 19–26. In fact, certain unexpected developments were to occur. Gamal was better equipped to predict the reactions of the partners whom he knew well, the British and the Americans, than of those whom he knew only slightly, the French and Israelis. He barely escaped learning at his own expense the cost of poor intelligence in an overly bold analysis.

The following day witnessed a genuinely popular rite, the triumph accorded by the people of Cairo to its defiant leader. Nasser was to know many more triumphs. But never, until June 1967, or perhaps October 1, 1970, would his name be acclaimed more fervently than on that day, as he and his companions, perched on a jeep, inched their way through the crowd, jostled by fond embraces. They had just crossed the delta by train; at every station, sometimes even in the middle of the countryside, they had had to halt the convoy. Gamal, sometimes mounted on the locomotive, would once again resume the much-told tale, flouting foreign governments and bankers. Now and then he would add an especially harsh word for France: "As for her, the Algerians will take care of her!"

To understand the style of the operation, the popular adherence it found, and Nasser's strident triumph, one must imagine what the canal meant to Gamal Abdel Nasser and his compatriots. The canal—which our history books present to us as a considerable asset made available to Egypt by the European enterprising spirit and technical genius—was seen by almost all Egyptians as a mortgage on their independence. It was by using the canal in 1882 that General Wolseley had outflanked Arabi Pasha to crush the leader of the Egyptian independence movement. The occupation began *by* the canal and was to continue *for* the canal. The very word seemed synonymous until 1919 with debts and foreign control, and until 1954 with occupation and intervention.

One of the most distinguished Egyptians to have adopted Western culture, Hussein Fawzi, author of *Sinbad the Egyptian,* told us: "The canal has never ceased to cause suffering to the people who dug it." And despite the admirable labor accomplished by technicians, administrators, and even the town planners of Ismailia, it was not entirely by chance that the most xenophobic movement in modern Egypt, the Muslim Brethren, was born in the Canal Zone. Foreign profits, wealth, and paternalism were highly conspicuous there. From Mahmud Yunis's calm kisses on the twenty-fourth to the cheers of the Cairo masses on the twenty-seventh, an immense grievance, metamorphosed into an effulgent gaiety, at last found expression.

When the first fever had subsided, Egyptian officials quickly recovered their sanguinity. Less than a week after the noisy evening of July 26, one of the lieutenants closest to the *Raïs* declared while taking his breakfast in a Cairo café:

"Come now, why all this fuss? The Canal Company was Egyptian, and we have nationalized it. As for your shareholders, they shall be compensated at an excellent rate.[7] And as for the freedom of the canal, consider that we formerly had no direct interest in protecting the shipping that brought us hardly anything. Whereas now . . . all the sanctions you could prepare against us, such as boycotting the canal, or restraint of goods, would cost you more than it would us. . . ."

In any case, in Paris as in London a strong movement of public opinion was urging the governments to take up the challenge of Alexandria. The insolence of the weak, or those whom we suppose to be so, is so much more unbearable than the arrogance of the powerful. Yet for the French government, the problem was different. "Alexandria? The Company? They played no role!" Guy Mollet declared to us recently:[8]

"When we decided to act, it was for three reasons: Algeria, Spain, Munich. . . .

"Algeria? There is no need to emphasize this. We did not take Nasser to be the sole driving force behind the Algerian uprising, but we knew the full scope of the role he played as supplier and ally of the FLN. Besides, how could we have

[7] That of the French Bourse on the evening of July 26, 1956.
[8] October 27, 1970, in Paris.

carried French opinion in the projected operation had it not been for the cause of Algeria? Algeria alone was capable of mobilizing the French. Poor Mr. Eden understood this well, he who had no similar objective and was deserted by his people. . . .

"Spain? It was to the Spanish republic, threatened and then betrayed, that we compared Israel. We socialists had suffered too much in 1936 for nonintervention. We would not but choose to prevent a tiny imperiled democracy from being crushed, this Israel whose annihilation by Nasser the experts had convinced us was certain, and even at a precise date.[9]

"Munich? It was reading the *Philosophy of Revolution* by Nasser, a sort of *Mein Kampf,* much more than the coup of Alexandria, that persuaded us to act. It was too risky to allow this adventurer, this miniature Hitler, to develop. It would have meant shirking our responsibilities. . . .

"And make no mistake: this is the key to Eden's attitude, so inexplicable to many. Without this key, it is impossible to understand my colleague's decision. He had been courageously anti-Munich and wished to remain loyal to his past."

Munich or no, a campaign against the intervention was launched in London on August 5 by the Labourites who had again become socialists now that they were no longer in power. Too, American diplomacy, and that of certain members of the Commonwealth such as India and Canada, was working for appeasement. Moreover, the general staffs, especially in London, were asking for at least six weeks to set up an intervention force. Nasser's calculation on this point had been correct, but it remained to be seen whether he

[9] In fact, Israel was not very much interested in the crisis. Harassment by *fedayin* had taken place shortly before, but less frequently than at the beginning of the year. And a broadcast in Hebrew from Radio Cairo the day after the nationalization suggested a "settlement of the problems between the states in the area."

would gain the full two months on which he was counting in order to carry off a diplomatic solution. In conferences in London and in parleys in Washington and Cairo, a "users' association" was organized. One of its delegates, Australian Prime Minister Robert Menzies, was snubbed by Nasser as if he had been an Iraqi diplomat, despite his white hair, his respectability, his dollars, and his pugnacious humor. During these weeks, the *Raïs* appeared at times to be taxing his ingenuity to its utmost in an attempt to resemble his caricature in the *Daily Mail* and the *Populaire*.

With the aid of Washington, an agreement was finally signed on October 12, which included "six principles" involving the renunciation by the French and British of their demand for "international control," and hence the recognition of the nationalization. The plan required, from Nasser's side, the acceptance of the following essential principle: "The functioning of the canal must not be subject to the politics of a single power." But in their haste to win over the *Raïs* once more, the Americans, who had themselves triggered the crisis on July 18, exasperated the French and British negotiators by requiring them to accept, as a preliminary to any negotiation, that the "users' association" return ninety per cent of all tolls to Egypt. Thus they were suggesting to London and Paris a capitulation which might have seemed reasonable in July, but which seemed humiliating in October, after so many rounds and debates, so many bugle calls and military marches.

These sounds were in fact beginning to materialize, as the general staffs finally put their brains and bureaus to work. Four Franco-British divisions referred to as the "means" had been collectively mobilized in Cyprus. At this moment the seizure of the *Athos II,* a cargo vessel from Cairo carrying arms intended for the Algerian insurrectionists, revived anti-Egyptian feeling in France. The capture on October 22 of a plane carrying Ben Bella and several leaders of the FLN raised the war fever to the highest pitch. Though the *fellaghas* could trounce French troops in Algeria, France had discovered a fine target in the sneering dictator in Cairo. The hour had come.

Great Britain, excepting perhaps Eden himself, was not the victim of such demons. But a rearrangement in the Near East did not displease the Foreign Office, which believed it might have found the opportunity to realize its old plan for an Iraqi-Jordanian *Anschluss* (and now with the consent of the French, who were involved in the common operation). Thus the British would receive compensation for their Suez losses as well as carry out a reprisal against Nasser. The operation made sense.

Yet the interventionists, French and British, might nevertheless have heeded the age-old whisper of caution if another power had not intervened: Israel. David Ben-Gurion had two urgent reasons for acting. He wished to forestall any British operation which would tend to group a large Hashemite Kingdom, much too powerful a neighbor for Tel Aviv, around Baghdad. He also envisioned, through a combined operation with London and Paris, crushing, if not Nasser's regime, at least his ambitions in the broader Arab tier. Nasser might install himself on the banks of the Nile if he wished, but only on condition that he remain confined within his valley, like Nuri Saïd in Mesopotamia.

By dragging London as well as Paris into the daring strategic enterprise, the Israeli leaders hoped to strike a double blow. London would thus be diverted from her Hashemite scheme toward another target, and Paris would be given the illusion of settling with Cairo the account accumulated in Algeria. Hence Tel Aviv would loosen the double hold of dynastic Arabism in the north and revolutionary Arabism in the south.

Gamal Abdel Nasser seems not to have very clearly dis-
cerned the rise of these perils. On October 16, Mollet and
Pineau received Eden and Lloyd in Paris, and soon arrived
at an agreement on the principle of a military intervention,
projected for the last week in November. On that very day,
the *Raïs* announced to his entourage that the danger was
over, and that henceforth it was Jordan who was threatened.
On the following day, receiving the military reporter for *The
New York Times,* Hanson Baldwin, he jeered at Ben-Gurion
for calling him a "fascist dictator."

On October 21, the Jordanian electorate returned a pro-
Egyptian majority to the Parliament in Amman. The Palestinian population was already making itself heard. Gamal
rejoiced, thinking that now neither Nuri Saïd nor Ben-Gurion
would dare to attack Jordan. Was he aware that it was he
who had again become the principal target? In any case, a
week later his confidence declined as the Israeli government
decreed a mobilization for an uncertain purpose. The next
day, the *Raïs* went to relax with his wife and children at official property at Barrages, near Cairo; a telegram was delivered toward noon. Upon reading the first words he was
thunderstruck: the plane carrying Abdel Hakim Amer, whom
he had sent on a mission to Amman to assure the new Jordanian cabinet of Egyptian solidarity, had been shot down by
an Israeli fighter near Tel Aviv: there had been no survivors.
But as he reached the end of the telegram, he learned that
Abdel Hakim had delayed his departure and had not been
aboard.[10]

In the evening, the family celebrated the birthday of one
of the boys, Abdel Hamid. A little after 9:00, the telephone
rang. Abdel Hakim Amer, having returned less than two

---

[10] Robert St. John, *The Boss,* New York, 1960, p. 257.

hours earlier from Jordan, was calling from his office: "The Israelis are attacking."[11]

Since 8:30 P.M., in fact, two Israeli brigades had been racing across the Sinai Peninsula, from the small post of Kuntilla near Akaba, toward Nakhl and the canal. The sector of the northeastern front was weakly defended by Egyptian forces. In less than twenty-four hours Moshe Dayan's tanks would be on the canal. At the very least, one could say that neither Paris nor London was taken by surprise, although the Israelis had acted several days in advance of the established plan in order to take advantage of the shock produced throughout the West by the Soviet intervention in Hungary. The aggression in Budapest would make their own offensive appear relatively blameless.

Though somewhat shaken by this Israeli dynamism, the French and British did not have to improvise their reactions. They had only to enter the next phase of the operation, which had been prepared long before. An ultimatum was addressed to both parties on the twenty-ninth, enjoining them to withdraw to a point ten miles on either side of the Suez Canal.

Nasser was outraged by this "equal treatment" of attacker and attacked. It was understandable that Eden and Mollet would support their friends under the circumstances: Cairo had given them reasons to seek revenge. But to pronounce this judgment of Solomon in a neutral guise, nobly deciding between the accomplice and the target, was carrying hypocrisy too far.

Gamal Abdel Nasser could not have acted otherwise. He immediately summoned the British ambassador, Sir Humphrey Trevelyan, and the French chargé d'affaires, Guy Dor-

[11] See Part Six, "Confronting Israel."

get, to inform them that their governments' ultimatum was rejected, and that Egypt "would defend her dignity." Twenty hours later, British and French planes began to strafe Almaza airport, and the Cairo radio installations (which they so much despised), without entirely overlooking the suburb of Heliopolis either. This same Cairo radio announced that the Israelis had been repelled in the Sinai Peninsula, and that the air force of the Jewish state had been destroyed, but five million Cairenes saw the enemy planes whirling overhead.

Gamal Abdel Nasser faced the fact of a complete military disaster. On the diplomatic front, however, definite progress was being made. In the House of Commons, Anthony Eden came up against sustained opposition from within his own party. Alerted by a discreet but moving appeal made by Nasser to Eisenhower, Washington was redoubling her warnings and admonitions to the two allied capitals. No one was more indignant than Dulles, the inventor of the entire disaster, who until October 29 had done nothing to divert the French and British from their undertaking. Only Dwight D. Eisenhower, frightened puritan, offended gentleman, and supercilious military man, was perhaps equally outraged. On Friday, October 31, the *Raïs* addressed the masses from the mosque of Al Azhar. He spoke of his confidence in the invincibility of Egypt: the crowd celebrated, saluted, and acclaimed him, bearing him aloft as it had done after the speech in Alexandria, and as it was to do after the Six-Day War.

On November 4, Franco-British airborne troops attacked Port Said, supported by a naval bombardment. Several hours later, Moscow delivered an ultimatum threatening London and Paris with atomic retaliation if the operation continued. Anthony Eden's conservative majority broke down, undermined by hostile public opinion. Finally the American government, having again been alerted by Nasser on November

4, began to bring all its weight to bear for appeasement. Under its auspices, a United Nations peace-keeping force was formed to end the operation in Port Said, where the common people had spontaneously risen and were bravely fighting against the invasion. As for the Israelis, having achieved the conquest of Sinai, they judged that the affair had lasted long enough.

Pressured by London, Paris accepted the cease-fire at midnight of November 6, thus breaking the *élan* of Massu's parachutists (who were soon to find other targets, beginning with the Algerian casbah). Nasser was saved. Speaking again at Al Azhar on the following Friday, he no longer hurled forth a cry of unshakable confidence, but struck up a song of triumph: Egypt had vanquished her enemies.

When Kennett Love asked him eight years later what force, what event had saved him in early November 1956—the Russian ultimatum, British opposition, the United Nations, India, the Arabs—he coolly answered: "Eisenhower."

Speaking to a Soviet, he might perhaps have given a different answer. For the intervention of Moscow on Nasser's behalf in November 1956 was far from negligible. The Soviet consul in Port Said himself distributed arms to the population. And, if one believes Khaled Mohieddin on this point, while several of his friends were counseling Gamal to take a plane for Yugoslavia and let them deal with the assailants, the Soviet ambassador begged him to "hold on" for forty-eight hours more to permit the Soviet UN delegate to deliver the comminatory note of November 4.

18

The Uses and Abuses of Arabism

A long debate has centered around whether Egypt is an Arab nation. The commander-in-chief of the Egyptian army in 1840, Ibrahim Pasha (the son of Mohammed Ali and hence of Albanian origin), while marching across the Orient toward Turkey reassured his anxious father that he would limit himself to "Arab" countries. And when the Cairo envoy asked him, "What do you mean by 'Arab'?" he replied with a definition which still echoes across the East: "I shall lead my troops forward into any land where Arabic is spoken."

The idea of an Arabism founded on language has been contested by several Egyptian nationalist leaders, among them Mustafa Kamel and Saad Zaghloul, both of whom denied that Egypt was Arab. "The Egyptians," wrote the Syrian theoretician Sati el-Husri, "have no right to turn their backs on Arabism by asserting their link with Pharaonic civilization. Arabism is not part of a mummified past. . . ."

This thesis was to win the approval of, among many others, Makram Ebeid, a Wafdist leader and direct heir of Saad Zaghloul, whose Coptic origins may have provided him with a thoroughly Egyptian sense of identity. Yet this secretary-general of the Wafd wrote: "We are Arabs, united by sufferings and hopes, welded together by catastrophe and sorrow, forged in the same crucible by injustice. . . ."[1] Thus an

[1] Cited by Anwar Abdel Malek, *La Pensée politique arabe contemporaine,* Paris, 1970, p. 205.

Arabism of sympathy corresponds to a linguistic Arabism.

Yet neither one could capture two of the best minds in contemporary Egypt, Taha Hussein and Hussein Fawzi. For the former, Egypt is above all Mediterranean, "community of religion or language being unable to constitute political unity."[2] As for the latter, his Sinbad is the eternal symbol of a strictly Egyptian continuity.

The debate between what one might call Arabist extroversion and Nilotic introversion was wide open when Gamal Abdel Nasser emerged into public life. Apparently as a young man he participated in demonstrations against the Balfour Declaration in the name of solidarity with the Palestinians. Hence he must have considered the latter to be Arabs.

But one notes that in his memoirs of the Palestine war cited above he was astonished to see the High Command send Egyptian units to the rescue of Jordanian forces in distress: hardly an Arab reflex, particularly since the text was published in 1954.

One wonders when Gamal Abdel Nasser discovered Arabism, driven by what force, and with what aim in mind. Of course, those who support the thesis of Sati el-Husri or that of Makram Ebeid would observe that the question is an idle one, that Arabism occurs naturally, that it is simply, on the regional level, the collective consciousness of an historical grievance, of an identity to be recaptured.

But it seems that Gamal Abdel Nasser did not always think so. At the end of 1953, he confided to his friend of that time, Ahmed Aboul Fath: "Formerly I believed neither in the Arabs nor in Arabism. Each time that you or someone else spoke to me of the Arabs, I laughed at what you said. I could not believe the Arab peoples capable of anything. The Palestine war strengthened even more my conviction

[2] An opinion which he was to modify in 1954 by rallying to an Arabism which was at least tactical.

concerning the powerlessness of the Arabs. But when I realized all the potential possessed by the Arab States! That is what made me change my mind. . . ."[3]

It was during this same period that he wrote *The Philosophy of the Revolution,* with its central theme of the "three circles"—Arab, African, and Muslim—within which Egyptian power was to unfold. He stated with great candor that he decided to center his argument on the oil question after reading the thesis of a professor from Chicago. The following quotations, typical of the *Philosophy,* remind one of a board-of-directors' report: "The extraction of a barrel of petroleum costs the United States seventy-eight cents, South America forty-three, and the Arab countries ten . . . [that is why] the United States has secured a foothold in Arab regions which are endowed with inexhaustible oil fields and where the price of land and manpower are negligible. It has been established that half the world's oil reserve lies beneath the Arab zone. . . ." All these figures have been contested, but they emphasize Gamal's idea of the Arab potential and its profit-earning capacity. The thrust of "economism," however, was to last only a short while. The *bikbashi,* later the *Raïs,* was to base his Arab strategy on other foundations, though never forgetting the oil objective which always seemed to elude him.

One of his most significant texts on the subject dates from October 1952, at the very beginning of his climb towards the summit. This was a declaration made to an Indian journalist and republished seven years later when Egyptian Arabism was at its height, and when the United Arab Republic —not yet the *Raïs*'s first great failure—seemed on the contrary the symbol of his power:

[3] Ahmed Aboul Fath, *L'Affaire Nasser,* Paris, 1962, p. 239.

The Arab world is a crossroads, a world military route. . . .
Long ago, we directed our steps from the heart of the
Arab Peninsula toward Palestine, Egypt, Cyrenaica, Kai-
rouan, and Fez, then to the north, Cordoba, Seville, Lisbon,
and Lyon in France. . . . None of those who left returned
to Arabia, because they never felt like foreigners in these
countries. . . .

Later on, a caravan of builders composed of contingents
from the tribes of Beni Hilal, Beni Soulayn, and Beni-
Morr[4] spread out over the territory of the Arab homeland.
In each family, they left a paternal or maternal uncle.
. . . All these émigrés were "Arabs" in the judgment of
historians and politicians. When crusading Europe marched
on Granada and Jerusalem, on Antioch, Damietta and
Carthage, it was because all these countries, in the eyes of
the Crusaders, were Arab. They were right: these countries
are ours. The leaders and great men of Europe grow angry
today when we say so: yet they said it before us. . . .[5]

Between the period when these statements were originally
made by the modest young *bikbashi* and their eventual re-
publication in a work of the triumphal period, the daydream
had thrust itself into the political domain. To clarify this
development, we shall cite two more declarations by the
Egyptian leader. The first dates from the period of hesitation
between the policy of an Egyptian Egypt and that of thoroughgoing Arabism; the second from the phase of unification.

The first statement was made at our first interview with

[4] This is a remarkable reference to the modest ethnic branch which left its
name to the village from which Gamal's family originates. It is not by chance
that the *bikbashi* mentions this tribe; as a Saïdi, he was seeking an Arab reference. This is an eloquent one, though perhaps not verifiable from an ethnic and
historic viewpoint.

[5] Extract from *Le Nationalisme arabe pratique et théorique,* a collaborative
work prefaced by this text of Nasser, Cairo, 1959.

Gamal Abdel Nasser in late 1953. We had asked him whether he believed any of the innumerable plans for Arab unification then current could actually be realized. "No," he said frankly, "if only because of the rivalry between the two great reigning families, the Saudis and the Hashemites. Also because several Arab countries are still totally or partially under foreign domination. But unification can begin, in a modest way, through economic and defense agreements like those which you have in Europe."

The second declaration was made a little more than four years later, in early 1958, to Jacques Benoist-Méchin, who published it in his *Printemps arabe.* Benoist-Méchin asked Nasser: "You are planning to create a Pan-Arab Empire are you not . . . a new form of imperialism?" The president of what was still the Republic of Egypt retorted: "Not at all, not at all; I do not want to forge an empire, I want to lead a nation to self-awareness. Moreover, I do not like the word 'Pan-Arab,' which was created by analogy with Pan-German-ism and Pan-Slavism. . . . I wish to conquer no foreign land in the name of the Arab nation. I want only to assemble the members of this nation, who, once gathered, will have no need for an additional living space. . . . I am not a con-queror."

During this conversation, the *Raïs* seemed suddenly to re-capture the tone and inspiration of his predecessor, Ibrahim Pasha, whom he never sufficiently honored, when he de-clared: "Listen to me: I have an exact knowledge of the frontiers of the Arab nation. I do not place it in the future for I think and I act as though it already existed. *These fron-tiers end where my propaganda no longer rouses an echo. Beyond this point, something else begins, a foreign world which does not concern me.*" It was a remarkable manifesto, and Gamal was to abide by it. Where Ibrahim had "led his troops forward," Gamal was to cast his words. One could not better define a strategy in which the procedure and the objectives, the substance and the form, were more completely interdetermined.

Gamal's Arabism was at once an end and a means; round as a globe, smooth as an egg, one neither entered nor left it. The idea and the fact were identical. But we ought not to see it as a mere intellectual construction. This Arabism was first of all the articulation of a collective grievance forged in the "crucible of common sorrows," of which Makram Ebeid had spoken. It comprised three givens: community of language, of history, and of oppression. It would be audacious to maintain that it was a class-consciousness; for where could one situate the feudal or proprietary classes? (Such an attempt was made by another Oriental, Sultan Galiev, a Tatar Marxist and a Muslim. Forty years earlier he had been liquidated by Josef Stalin for having written that an Afghan feudal lord was more proletarian than a British worker.) These debates were resumed during Nikita Khrushchev's trip to Egypt in the spring of 1964.

Nasser's Arabism was certainly a mass consciousness, for troubled and dangerous as it was, it had a truly popular dimension. Optimists saw in it a kind of syndicalism on a subcontinental scale, a great in-gathering of the economically and legally disinherited, a coalition of the weak to confront the strong. Pessimists saw in it only a sort of plebeian eagerness for revenge, a petulant chauvinism, a preparation for the massacre of Israel. But what survived all these judgments was the feeling of having a common adversary. Arabism was simply the form taken at a certain moment by resistance to the Baghdad Pact, to Dulles's maneuvers, to French gunboats and to Düsseldorf bankers, even to Russian neocolonialism, and above all to the alienation and underdevelopment of the Arab people.

By turns populist, emancipating, chauvinistic, and internationalistic, the Arabism of Gamal Abdel Nasser took a historical leap in May 1953, when Naguib inaugurated the "Voice of the Arabs" on Radio Cairo. This sudden Arab awareness on Gamal's part explains both his immediate support for Ben Bella and his men, and also his refusal, during negotiations with the British, to tie the defense of Turkey to that of the Arab states, however unfriendly some of the latter might be.

But Arabism became a real strategy for Gamal Abdel Nasser only when he perceived that his fate was linked, even in the minds of others, to that of the entire Arab world. His decisions were not based on the services which the Arabs rendered, or even could have rendered, in the most dramatic moments of the Suez crisis. Never, between appeals to Eisenhower or Khrushchev, did he solicit the slightest gesture from Damascus or Baghdad. His determination was confirmed rather by the risks taken by, and for, the Arabs. He broke off relations with Selwyn Lloyd over Jordan, and with Christian Pineau over Algeria. It was not he who took possession of Arabism, but Arabism which took possession of him. It was Arabism that invented him, and established him as its hero.

Perhaps he should have remained deaf to this appeal, refused the temptation and, like Ataturk, restricted his efforts and plans to the national sphere.

True, our distinction between Egyptianism and Arabism, which we believe we can suggest by examining two texts or by comparing two conversations, was sometimes quite artificial. In the case of the negotiations with London, Nasser's politics were so exclusively Egyptian as to concede the "Turkish clause," in order to realize an immediate national interest. Yet this was the act which launched Egypt into "Arab politics," by raising the curtain of British forces which until then had separated Egypt from Israel. Henceforth, Cairo would

agree to confront the Jewish state, and all the "Arabist" conflicts stemmed from this.

A second example was the nationalization of Suez, a
strictly Egyptian, eminently nationalistic act accomplished
with a view to purely Egyptian interests. But the statements
Nasser made that day in Alexandria suddenly linked him to
the Arab world, making him finally the tribune of its mute
masses, from Bassorah to Khartoum. Egypt occupies a place
such that any dynamism in her politics will cast a shadow
over Arabism, and will project all the Arab expectations upon
her.

A genius of caution would have been required to circum-
scribe the liberation of Egypt's frontiers, legal fictions rendered still more absurd by radio and television. All revolutions must ford the Rhine, however ill they may fare beyond.

It would be unfair to speak of this Nasserist "Arabism"
without noting that over the years it became more and more
clearly distinct from its Muslim origins. As much in the
above-quoted text of 1952 (republished in 1959) as in the
most celebrated pages of the *Philosophy of the Revolution,*
the *bikbashi* distinguished ill between Islam and *uruba*
(Arabness). Whether he referred to the twentieth-century
political uses of the pilgrimage to Mecca, he constantly confused culture and faith, language and devotion. In his mouth
the word *umma* (community) referred almost as often to the
Arab circle as to the Islamic brotherhood. Yet after 1960
he no longer yielded to these temptations.

We have described Gamal Abdel Nasser as a good Muslim. But a lengthy effort toward self-control, as well as bitter
experiences with the Muslim Brethren and icy relations with
certain major Islamic states, such as Pakistan and Iran, were
to lead him, if not to Kemalist secularism or even to Bougui-
bist semisecularism, to a very independent vision of political
problems within the Muslim city. From one month to the

next—one might say from failure to failure—his concept of Arabism was purified of its Islamic references and even its Islamic loyalties.

This concept ripened into what could be called a broad "sympathy," experienced through the Arabic language, a means of communication between men who participate in a common drama and undergo the same trials, like prisoners who communicate from cell to cell in a code known only to themselves. Abdel Nasser himself pronounced on this subject three years before his death. When Emmanuel d'Astier asked him whether he felt more Arab than Egyptian, he answered: "I am Egyptian. And I feel Arab because I am deeply affected by the fortunes and misfortunes of the Arabs, wherever they may occur."

19

Syria: The Split and the Failure

Nothing on the level of principle condemned this Arabism "by affection" armed with a "syndicalist" strategy. But it must be evaluated on a factual level, and the facts, from Gamal Abdel Nasser's point of view, and even more from Egypt's, are not very generous.

The year 1957 had seen an American counteroffensive follow the storms of Suez, which had devastated the French and British positions. A declaration, termed a "doctrine," was then

published, which looked rather like a notice from an insurance company to the victim of an accident: the president of
the United States, principal salvager of the *Raïs* during the
Suez Crisis, made it known that he intended to draw on the
dividends of this investment, and that he assumed the right
to fill the "void" caused by the double eviction of London
and Paris.

During the summer, Undersecretary of State Loy Henderson, on a Mideast tour, distributed arms and promises to all
of Washington's allies. This was the big offer: there was
still time for Nasserian Egypt to accept. But the time had
passed when a Western power could act in the Mideast without provoking a repercussion: for on April 17, 1955, the
U.S.S.R. had also published its intention to be present in the
area.

At this juncture, one country stepped forward to serve
Russia, if not as a military camp or satellite, at least as a
hospitable base of operations: Syria, where a highly influential Communist leader of twenty years' standing, Khaled Bagdash—equally trusted by Moscow and Damascus, whose representative he had been since 1954 (hence for a long time
the only Communist in the Arab world)—had concluded a
sort of alliance with the most prestigious representative of
the big bourgeoisie, Khaled el-Azem. To defend Syria against
Anglo-Iraqi designs on the Fertile Crescent, and to foil an
American intrusion, this aristocrat with golden hands had
chosen to dine with the devil. So the Soviet transplant grew,
multiplying in proportion to the American efforts to weed
it out.

Washington and the Syrian bourgeoisie were not alone in
judging that the counterpoison was beginning to color the
glasses noticeably. This was also the feeling of the leaders
of the party which eventually became the arbiter of the policy of Damascus, the *Baath* (Resurrection), which had tried

to synthesize Arabism and socialism even before Nasser. The *Baath* was or gladly called itself anti-American. It was above all anti-Soviet. Its major objective was the Arab regrouping. And as for the Fertile Crescent, the unification of Syria, of Iraq, of Jordan and of Lebanon (while awaiting Palestine), its front-rank man, Salah Bittar, then said, "Yes, on condition that the Hashemite crown of Baghdad does not make of it an instrument of Iraqi imperialism." And this was indeed the case at the end of 1957. The regent of Baghdad, Abdul Illah, was looking for a crown. Why not that of Damascus?

Thus Syria was held in a quadruple vise: between Israel, the Iraqi threats (supported by Baghdad's ally, Ankara, which would have gladly seized Syrian land for itself), American pressure, and Soviet penetration. This situation was what the spokesman of the *Baath*[1] came to drive home to Cairo during the Afro-Asiatic conference in December 1957. Gamal Abdel Nasser had just vividly demonstrated his interest in protecting Syrian independence by sending a military contingent to Latakia, the Syrian port in which two Soviet ships had docked. But his Syrian friends were no longer talking about a protective gesture, but about actual federation or even union.

At the beginning of 1958, Gamal Abdel Nasser was still hesitant at least over the date and the means to effect the project. Upon receiving Benoist-Méchin, who asked him whether he believed the fusion of Egypt and Syria "probable," he answered:

"No, not probable but certain."

"When?"

"Perhaps during the course of 1958, perhaps later. It is not up to me to decide."

[1] Al-Hizb al-Baath al-Arabi al-Ishtiraki.

"How is that, 'not up to you'?"

"It is not a question of annexation, but of union. The matter is still premature. . . . I shall wait until the Syrians express a desire for it. . . . I am not a conqueror . . . I am, how do you say it in French, a 'magnet.' . . ."

"*Un aimant?*"

"That's it!"[2]

Two weeks later, on January 27, General Afif Bizri, chief-of-staff of the Syrian Army, put the problem thus to the chief of state, Shukri Kuwatli: "Either we shall have union with Egypt, or civil war. . . ." The elderly president proposed that he leave immediately for Cairo. But the general imposed a more expeditious procedure: he summoned each minister to a cabinet meeting "tomorrow in Cairo." And thus the full Syrian cabinet landed the next day at Heliopolis, where the disconcerted *Raïs* welcomed it. Kuwatli spoke: The Syro-Egyptian union must be sealed at once in order to protect Damascus from "imperialist aggression."

Nasser was not convinced. The visitors insisted: Nuri el-Saïd was multiplying his contacts with London, Washington, and Ankara, and the Iraqi threat had become imminent. Considering Abdel Nasser's feeling about Nuri Pasha and the Iraqi regent, and the danger he saw in this seat of English neocolonialism, home of the abhorred Baghdad Pact, one might well suppose the argument was convincing. Not enough. The Syrians further pointed out to him that the influence of the U.S.S.R., perhaps tolerable in periods of crisis, was becoming perilous for Arab independence. This he also knew; and he would consider it.

Possibly the Syrian envoys went on to present a third argument: the union would offer Egypt, obsessed as it was by overpopulation, an opportunity at last to provide land for its

2 Jacques Benoist-Méchin, *Un Printemps arabe, Paris,* 1963, p. 82.

peasants for less than the cost of constructing the dam. It is doubtful that this argument much impressed the *Raïs*. He knew the Nile fellahin too well to imagine them joyfully taking to the land between the Tigris and the Euphrates. (It was much less to guarantee land to his peasants than to assure markets for his nascent industry that the *Raïs* took the risk of assuming responsibility for Syria.)

Gamal continued to raise objections and to make preconditions. Then he impressed upon his visitors that this "fusion" would be possible only if total, and with the proviso Syria deliver herself up to him like a corpse to an embalmer. This was precisely what the visitors wanted: to give themselves up, to be delivered of their own fate.

Now it was time to sign, and the *Raïs* Abdel Nasser placed his signature next to Shukri Kuwatli's. Then the elderly Syrian statesman took him by the arm and whispered to him:

"If you only knew, Excellency, of what a burden you have just freed me, the burden of five million Syrians, half of whom claim to be leaders by vocation, a quarter of whom believe themselves prophets, and ten per cent of whom take themselves for gods. You will be dealing with people who worship God, fire and the devil. . . ."

"And you waited until I affixed my signature to reveal all this to me!"[3]

When, two years later, a reporter from *Life* magazine asked Nasser's wife, Tahia, whether her husband had ever been afraid in the course of his career, she answered: "Yes, when he agreed to unite with Syria. . . ."

On the first of February, 1958, the *Raïs* appeared on the balcony of the presidential palace, flanked by Shukri Kuwatli who, to his own great relief, was now only the very honorable "first Arab citizen." And so the creation of the United

[3] Edouard Saab, *La Syrie ou la révolution dans la rancoeur,* Paris, 1968, p. 92.

Arab Republic was announced. On February 22, 99.9 per
cent of the Egyptians and Syrians ratified this decision. Thus,
hardly had an Egyptian taken charge of Egypt, after so many
centuries, than he hastened to obliterate its name.

A month later, Gamal Abdel Nasser made an impromptu
landing in Damascus. He wanted to play Harun al-Rashid, to
take the measure in person of the union's popularity. The
crowd's response was overwhelming. Even Alexandria, on
July 26, 1956, even Cairo on the following November 9,
had not welcomed him this way. For days on end he had to
answer, from the balcony of the Difaa palace, the joyful
roars of hundreds of thousands of "Arab citizens," who had
come from all parts of the Middle East for this great festival
of Arabism, this carnival of triumphal unity. Was this the
zenith of Gamal's star?

Never did an enterprise begun with such enthusiasm collapse so quickly in rancor, hatred, and derision. The history of
this strange three-year republic vindicated in every way Nasser's apprehensions. Did he know his own defects so well that
he could thus strangle them in advance, and yet so badly that
he could let them ruin an almost impossible undertaking? In
any case, in the early days of the *Anschluss,* Khaled Bagdash had fled Syria, unconfident of the fate which Gamal,
that excellent friend of the Soviets, would reserve for the
Communist leaders in a country entrusted to his police. He
was not mistaken. After the Communists, it was the *Baath*'s
turn to be persecuted. Syria was no "northern province" of
the UAR, it was a protectorate ruled by a police officer,
Colonel Abdel Hamid Serraj, head of special services now
promoted to chief of the executive branch, and controlled by
a proconsul, Marshal Amer, the *Raïs*'s double.

Toward the end of 1959, Sallah Bittar, one of the archi-
tects of the union, confided in a grieved tone to Simonne
Lacouture in Cairo: "We had no choice. It was not an option,

it was an imperative to strike a blow against imperialism. But it was a failure. . . . The people are not associated with the enterprise. Everything should have proceeded from the base upwards. Besides, in Egypt popular movements degenerate into opportunism. . . ."

In fact, the Egyptian leadership treated Syrian society, infinitely mobile, sensitive, and proud, as a conquered people. Purges in the army, the destruction of existing political structures, intellectual domestication—nothing could have resembled colonialism (minus the cultural shock) more than this bizarre fusion. But it was perhaps not the more militaristic aspects of this policy which angered the "protégé." It was the evolution of the "southern province" toward a degree of socialism which provoked indignation in the Syrian bourgeoisie, especially since the latter had not been responsible for the fusion.

The extension of agrarian reform into the "northern province" had at first provoked a movement of dissent. But in Syria the landowners had lost their pre-eminence in 1954. It was now the urban bourgeoisie which was in control, via the army and the *Baath.* And it was the bourgeoisie which became enraged first over the application in Syria of state controls enacted in Cairo, including the control of currency rates of exchange, and then the reversal of the process imagined by the Syrian draftsmen of the union, in whose eyes solid and brave Egypt was to have become a field for the expansion of the agile Syrian economy. But now, it was the shrewd Egyptian businessmen who were profiting from the situation, sheltered behind a veritable customs barrier against Damascus products. In July, those measures of socialist aspect stopped by Gamal Abdel Nasser were to push to the limit people who, having recruited Nasser as a militiaman against communism, now perceived that they had imported a sergeant of collectivism. Bagdash had been right: why had they not listened to him?

Nothing could render more exactly the tone of these disintegrated relations, of this long and painful misunderstanding, than an extraordinary document published May 20, 1963, by *Al Ahram,* the newspaper of the *Raïs*'s confidant, Mohammed Heykal. The problem then was to try, twenty months after the failure of the first union, to revive it—not only between the two countries, but with the participation of Iraq. Was it in order to denounce in advance the risks of this new attempt that Nasser had the minutes of these tripartite conversations published, dominated as they were by a cruel settling of accounts between Egyptians and Syrians? Let us quote *Al Ahram:*

Abdel Nasser: ". . . Now it is the turn of our Syrian brothers to speak. I beseech each man to speak in all frankness. This is of the greatest importance for me and for the experiment in progress. . . ." A long silence followed this exhortation. "Must I speak on behalf of the Syrians?" (Laughter).

Abdelkrim Zouhour (minister of the economy): "The bureaucracy in Egypt has profound roots. It is necessary to the foundation of a state, but dangerous for a revolutionary country. This bureaucracy exists neither in Syria nor in Iraq. But the Egyptian bureaucratic apparatus has been installed in Syria, without taking into consideration the circumstances peculiar to this country and its people. . . . Moreover, and this is an even more delicate problem, but I am coming to it, we have always had the impression in Syria that the Egyptian powers wished to deal by means of police agents rather than revolutionaries. I am not contesting the usefulness of having police agents, but . . ."

Abdel Nasser: "These are very relevant reflections, brother Zouhour. But no police agent played any role in the Syrian province. When you accuse us of acting by means of agents, that is, of being a police state, you share, perhaps unwittingly, in the opinion held by imperialism, Zionism and the reactionaries—and also, if you will excuse me, the *Baath*. . . . I wish you would point out a single one of our 'agents' in Syria. Give me a single name?"

Ali el-Saadi (Baathist leader): "Many things have to be concealed from your Excellency; you cannot keep your eye on everything. Anim Ezzedin, for example, said in Damascus: 'Every man has his price!' It is a fact that the situation of a certain Hekki Ismail Hekki has greatly improved since his expulsion from the *Baath*. . . ."

Abdel Nasser: "It's impossible that the money came from Egypt!"

Taleb Shalub (Syrian minister of foreign affairs): "It's the case though. Hekki received and distributed tracts printed in Egypt."

Abdel Nasser: "That was healthy self-criticism! As long as we are on this topic, let's get to the bottom of it. . . . On the subject of money, we gave over important sums of money to the *Baath*. We did not ask it to be our agent, but to serve the national interest. . . . In 1959, 30,000 dinars were given to Michel Aflak. . . . What did he do with that money?"

Zouhour: "Michel Aflak never received anything!"

Abdel Nasser: "Who did, then?"

Taleb Shalub: "Iraq!"

Abdel Nasser: "But it was Aflak who served as the intermediary!"

Zouhour: "I didn't know all that. I think it was a serious mistake. . . ."

Abdel Nasser: "It happens that the special services do make mistakes. But in Egypt, our services don't operate with the methods of a concierge. In Syria, have you disposed of Shishakli's *Deuxième Bureau*? No! Its activities

are simplistic and unscientific. In Egypt, our services func-
tion in a technical and scientific manner. . . ."

(Rereading this dumbfounding text today, and remembering
the "scientific" performances of the Egyptian services in 1967,
one feels one is dreaming. And yet, Gamal Abdel Nasser was a
very talented statesman.)

From the month of February 1961, Abdel Hakim Amer
had warned his friend and chief that the experiment was
working out badly. It was too late to give the strong blow
that would have reassured the Syrians. And when it was
necessary to impose upon them the directives of July, the
Raïs could no longer count on the support of the socialists and
Communists, who alone could have agitated with conviction
for their acceptance. Amer dismissed a few officers, but the
crisis was already everywhere.

One man symbolized the regime, Nasser having presented
him to the crowd as "his" man, with the words, "He is
pure!"—Colonel Serraj was the protagonist in a strange business. The Saudis had approached him two years earlier with
a plan to "eliminate" Nasser. He pretended to go along, received his check, then came to deliver the story (and the
check) to the *Raïs.* One can imagine the credit he had
acquired with Nasser.

In September 1961, Serraj, hated and harassed by criticism
and threats from his Syrian compatriots, resigned from his
post as head of the executive committee of the northern
province. This was the signal for the stampede. On September
28, Syria, through the voice of several officers, declared itself
again independent. This *Putsch,* staged at dawn, opened the
way for a new wave almost as strong as the one which had
borne a triumphant Nasser into Syria forty months earlier.

The first reflex of the *Raïs* was to use force: an order was
sent to the general staff of the First Army of the UAR,

stationed in Syria and half composed of soldiers from the "south," to confront the "separatist revolt."[4] But it was quickly withdrawn. Abdel Hakim Amer, besieged in his residence, contacted Gamal and Gamal explained to him the game was lost and that a blood bath would be perfectly useless.

The next day, September 29, 1961, a Nasser such as the darkest days of the Suez crisis had never seen him, appeared on television livid, his features drawn, to announce to his stupefied (but perhaps relieved) people that "Arabs could not fire on other Arabs," and that he was withdrawing his troops from Syria, thus acknowledging the failure of the policy of union. But not without defiantly maintaining the abbreviation "UAR."

Would this split cause the entire Nasserian edifice to crack open? Damascus, the site of his absolute triumph of March 1958, seemed to be the source of the countercurrent. But Nasser's prodigious political vitality, his strategic imagination, and the popular forces that continued to support him assured the survival of the *Raïs*. Yet he was cruelly locked in still another struggle which for two years had pitted him, no longer against reaction, feudalism, or imperialism, but against another Arab revolution—that of Iraq.

On July 14, 1958, less than six months after the United Arab Republic was proclaimed, a military *coup d'état* felled the Hashemite monarchy of Baghdad and Nuri Pasha Saïd, Abdel Nasser's worst enemies. The triumph of the *Raïs*—which was contained anyway—was of short duration. The year was not yet over when it became clear that the new Iraqi regime was not an extension of but rather an alternative to Nasserism. Much more clearly than the operation of July 1952 in Cairo, that of July 1958 in Baghdad immediately assumed the aspect of a revolutionary movement. It was,

---

[4] Nasser declared three years later that these troops had received the order not to make use of their arms in any case.

wrote Maxime Rodinson, "the first true revolution of the Arab world."[5] Taking into account the differences in situation, sociological climate, and national temperament, it was in Iraq rather than in Egypt that the masses were observed amplifying and extending the action triggered by the military. Abdul Kerim Kassem very quickly transformed himself into a popular *zaïm* rather than a victorious general; the Communist leaders were released from prison, and a very active revolutionary tribunal was instituted. The atmosphere of Carmangola hovered over all this, and the spontaneity of the people pushed the Baghdad revolutionary regime still further.

Nasser's reaction recalled that of Moscow to the revolutionary exaltation of Peking. Were these epigones going to give her lessons in revolution? And Nasser denounced, with a violence sometimes bordering on frenzy, these "traitors to the Arab cause" who claimed to be more Iraqi and revolutionary than Nasserist. The *Raïs,* who extended an offer to the new Baghdad regime to join the UAR, at that time still young and prestigious, would never forgive Kassem for rejecting him, and still less the Iraqi Communists who, agreeing with Khaled Bagdash, published on September 3, 1958, a communiqué stating that "adherence to the UAR would alarm the Iraqi people, who see it as an obstacle to its development." The position taken by the Syrian and Iraqi Communists, followed by the increasingly overt support given Kassem by Moscow—sometimes even to thwart Nasser— are probably at the origin of the most violent conflict that ever pitted Gamal Abdel Nasser against the Egyptian Marxists, and also of the first estrangement between the *Raïs* and the U.S.S.R. since the entente of 1955. The entire Iraqi affair had, moreover, the magical power of spellbinding the Egyptian leader: Nasser multiplied his errors of judgment. He

[5] *Israël et le refus arabe,* Paris, 1968.

supported the mediocre Abdessalem Aref, whom he took for the Nasser of Iraq, against the heady Kassem, whom he believed to be the Naguib of Baghdad; and he also witlessly defended the *Putsch* fomented in Mosul by Colonel Shawaf, misled by his own obsession with Iraqi oil which, now that the monarchy was undone, could only gush forth toward Egypt, the leader of the Arab nation. . . .

Would Gamal Abdel Nasser, out of hatred for Iraq's Kassem and spite for his Russian support, make the second radical about-face of his career and turn toward the West? At the end of 1958, American aid to Cairo had been resumed, and the dispute with London and Paris had almost been liquidated. Nasser was impressed by the return of de Gaulle, and awaited the accession of Kennedy to the White House. West Germany displayed her somewhat heavy charms. In Egypt herself, the commercial bourgeoisie, which had profited from the "colonization" of Syria, pressed for this reversal. Within the Arab world, Gamal even dared to approach the most conservative regimes, those of Saudi Arabia, Jordan, and Yemen. He did not even hesitate to defend Kuwait by armed force against the pretensions of Iraq, which had turned the Nasserist argument against the little principality: Arab oil should sustain the revolution, not the reaction.

Was this then the end of militant Nasserism? Having been promoted from reformist to protorevolutionary by the mere force of circumstances, would he now regress toward a pan-Arabist counterrevolution (in which he saw nonetheless a widening and deepening of his own)? It was Egypt, and it was the resolution of Egyptian problems, that was to lead him back to the socialist and neutralist path.

It was increasingly clear, in fact, that the economic development to which he began to devote himself could not be assumed by the bourgeoisie. Native capital was weak and timid. It was still overly controlled by "Egyptianized" ele-

ments, who cast longing glances toward Beirut and New
York. Recourse to socialist procedures was inevitable. This
was fully demonstrated by the Syrian catastrophe, for it was
the Damascene bourgeoisie who had ruined the undertaking.
It had simultaneously rejected the socialist measures of July
1961, and the union with Cairo. But Gamal was not satisfied
with discovering his enemies. He also discovered self-criticism,
in the celebrated speech of October 16, 1961:

"We have been the victims of our excessive self-confidence.
We always refused to deal with imperialism, but we committed the error of doing so with reaction. We believed the
reactionaries to be sons of our fatherland, sharing in our
destiny. . . . We were mistaken. We directed our blows against
pacts and bases, while the enemy was hiding all the while in
the palaces and safes of the millionaires. . . .

"We have committed another error, no less serious . . . it
consists of the insufficient organization of the people. This
organization was the National Union, which should have
served as a barrier against class struggle. But we made the
mistake of opening the National Union to the reactionaries. . . .

"Our third error was not having mustered enough effort to
awaken in the masses a consciousness of their rights. . . . This
is why, after lengthy reflection, I have once again chosen to
brandish the flag of the revolution which we began nine years
ago. . . ."

A congress of "popular forces" was soon to be summoned,
which was to force, if not the regime, at least its political and
social strategy, to become more democratic. Then Gamal
settled the shoot-out in the Arab world: he moved away from
Saudi Arabia, broke with Jordan, and ended the vague federal
union which still united him with feudal Yemen, the third
partner of the 1958 alignment. But it was precisely there that
a movement was to break out which would be the beginning

of his hardest trial and which, aggravating the wound opened in Syria, would in the end undermine the entirety of his enterprise.

When, in the autumn of 1962, an insurrection drove out the Imam of Sanaa and proclaimed the Republic of Yemen, the president of the UAR could not remain indifferent. Nor could he remain inactive when this new regime, asserting a "nationality"[6] revolution inspired by Nasser, saw a militant group of royalists rise against it, instigated by the royal heir, the Imam Badr, and openly supported by Ryad. Of course the new Yemeni regime, even before being recognized by the big powers, had in its favor the attributes of legality, and by intervening, Nasser was only rejecting the isolationism so often reproached in other republics unable to rescue their friends.

True enough; but the enterprise was costly, even ruinous, for an Egypt in quest of its daily sustenance and self-development. We have alluded to Spain, and to the duty of progressive regimes to form a coalition in the face of any Holy Alliance, in order to protect the victories of their revolutions.

Yet one is reminded rather of another Spanish war by the long and cruel expedition in Yemen, which immobilized a third of the Egyptian army for five years across the Red Sea, and gave rise to atrocities which, though inherent in all such expeditions, were particularly distressing to attribute to a state which had been the advocate of deprived peoples, and had so often given lessons in morality.

We shall not reopen the debate on the use of asphyxiating gases by Egyptian forces: the British press became increasingly eloquent on this issue as the Egyptian threatened the British positions in Aden and its periphery. It is sufficient to recall the fact, as an element in the historic "trial" of the *Raïs*. The

[6] To adopt the ingenious formula of Anwar Abdel Malek.

Egyptian expeditionary corps was still bogged down in the Yemenite jebels when the Six-Day War broke out. Nothing justifies the assertion that these forces, had they been present in the Sinai, would have changed the outcome of the battle. But the Egyptian populace was entitled to tell itself that its young men's place was native soil, rather than overseas.

It was not until the end of August 1967, on the eve of the conference of Khartoum, that the *Raïs* succeeded in reaching a compromise with the King of Arabia which permitted him to recover his troops. But it was too late—at least from the Egyptian point of view. From the Arab, especially the Yemeni standpoint, it was possible that the uneasy sacrifice of Egyptian soldiers who blocked the path of the irregulars of the emir Badr had indirectly cleared the way for the revolutionary forces which were to assert themselves in Southern Yemen.[7]

Syria, Iraq, Yemen—soon Palestine: can the Arab policy of Gamal Abdel Nasser be analyzed as a long chain of disappointments, disasters, and unbearable sacrifices? Yet how skillfully the *Raïs* manipulated Jordan and its king, playing in turn on threats and charm, on violence and goodwill, helping to turn the kingdom into the base it became in 1967 for the national Palestinian movement—and all the while maintaining that crown which was and remained for long the best shield of the exiled.

It should also be pointed out that he played his hand with relative skill in Lebanon, forcefully urging on his friends (or, to use a word that we have seen hardly pleased him, his "agents"), without ever actually inciting, even in 1958, the dismemberment of the little state whose utility, both financial

[7] The decisive aid from Egypt to the revolutionaries of Southern Yemen was recognized as such by the latter even if they regretted the intervention—and how heavy-handed and clumsy it was!—of the Egyptian special services in the Southern Yemenite liberation movements, and in particular the support granted by *Flosy* (moderate) against the National Front (radical).

and political, he had long recognized. And this is not to mention the role of refuge that Lebanon played in an area where the reversals of public fortune were too sudden and consequential not to require the existence of a land of asylum. Where would revolutionaries be without Geneva or Beirut?

But it was in another domain that Nasser's Arabism was displayed with success, paid for or not by political and material advantages. This was in Africa. It was from Khartoum to Casablanca that Gamal truly left his mark. Not to say, of course, that he was everywhere welcomed as a liberator. We have recounted his rebuffs in the Sudan in 1954–5. And one must remember his long and bitter struggle with Habib Bourguiba, marked in 1959 by a plot against the life of the Tunisian leader, probably unsuspected by the Egyptian, whose special services were "scientific" enough to tolerate occasional accidents and failures.

But "African Arabism" was all the same an opportunity for Nasser to associate himself with a victory which had cost him so dearly, in 1956, and in all his relations with France, for him to have to derive some glory from it: the Algerian revolution. Here, from the point of view of the Arab collectivity, that "crucible of common sorrows," Gamal Abdel Nasser amply assumed his responsibilities—though French nationalism would long hold it against him. Always at the side of the founders and inspirers of the FLN, he was truly the "big brother" of whom the Front leaflets spoke. Whether or not he brought Algerian commandos into his camps[8]—whether or not he financed the arms purchases of Ben Bella and Boudiaf, the fact is that for a long time he made Egypt an insurgents' "sanctuary" without which there could have been no durable uprising.

Here again he made many mistakes, especially when the

---

[8] One should read, on this subject, the defense which he presented in his interview to Benoist-Méchin in *Un Printemps arabe*.

phase of political exploitation had succeeded that of combat. He was wrong to confuse a movement with a man, entrusting only Ben Bella with the confidence of the leader of the Arabs. This, among other things, had the effect of giving the first Algerian head of state the abusive reputation of being Cairo's henchman, and then of making of his defeat in June 1965 a defeat for Nasserism.

Two years before, Algiers had nonetheless witnessed a strange holiday. After one hundred thirty years of colonization, seven years of war, hundreds of philippics, operations camouflaged at times in leopard attire, generations of mythomaniacal literary men, and oaths about the maintenance of an eternally French Algeria, we saw the unimaginable accomplished: Nasser in Algiers. The cycle was closed, the war was really over: "big brother" was there—the fabled character, the werewolf of the colonial press, the militant archangel of the jebel vigils. He had arrived.

From El-Biar to the Boulevard Larbi Ben M'Hidi, the city flowed down to the water. The immense crowd scanned the sea where the yacht which had belonged to Farouk surged slowly forth from the mist. In the bow, a tall, massive personage, poised like a sea goddess upon a trireme, Gamal glided slowly toward the people whom his words and his specter had so long exalted. He disembarked; Ben Bella and all the Algerian ministers kissed him on both cheeks. But what a strange impression: side by side, or rather face to face, these visitors from Cairo, the ranks of a "revolution" born of a *coup d'état* and already installed in its own home, the wealthy Nasserian general staff, robust and sure of itself, and the slender Algerian hosts, a bit shabby, a bit weary, still covered with the dust of battle, aspirants to revolution welcoming the big exporters of slogans and myths. This was the big discrepancy—much less perceptible to the two leaders than to the two groups. The Egyptians, so true, lively, generous, and spontaneous at home, had not yet learned to travel.

The disembarkation of May 1963, so charged with significance, was to remain an abortive celebration. In order for a triumph to be meaningful, the hero must be fully present. On Algerian soil, which surprised him with its impressive appearance, and in that city which frightened him with its greatness (he often believed the slogans on the radio), Gamal constantly felt himself to be the object rather than the subject of the drama. Intoxicated with joy, a former refugee and protégé now master in his own land, Ben Bella assumed the role of theatrical director. But one might doubt that Shakespeare would have liked to play the role of Fortinbras. Nasser in Algeria was no more than one flag waved by another.

He would also be seen at Casablanca, speaking on African unity; at Bizerte in quest of the same Bourguiba with whom he had previously quarreled so intensely that it seemed hysterical on both sides, and whom he was to receive cordially in his turn in 1966. And it was with Algiers—in spite of the presence in Cairo of an exceptional ambassador, Lakhdar Brahimi, who was perhaps his only foreign friend—that he was to maintain the coldest relations in his final years. But on the day of his funeral, Houari Boumedienne was there, overwhelmed with grief, bearing witness to that "community of tribulation" which fuses the Arab fraternity.

20

Positive Neutralism

It was an old dream. From war to war, the rulers of Cairo tried to realize it, taking as many liberties as they could with their European "protectors" or "allies." "These combats, these causes, are not ours," protested Masri Effendi, a little man with a potato-like nose whom Egyptian caricaturists used to depict the average citizen.

Of course, Saad Zaghloul, who refused to pose the problem of nationhood as long as England was in peril, and then Nahas, who agreed to enter the struggle at Churchill's side, transgressed against this unwritten law. But the latter especially had paid heavily for it. And very soon, by 1951, the Wafd in fact tried to initiate preliminary discussions with the other side having the aim of placing Egypt on the middle road, which India had already traced.

By the time Gamal Abdel Nasser and his men seized power, it was a familiar theme: all ties with the West were anathema. Nehru had shown how to say no to Western military encroachment, and Tito to Stalinist colonization. Yet during the first two years of the July regime, "neutralism" was hardly mentioned in Cairo. On several occasions Naguib, Salah Salem, and Nasser himself pointed out to us that if they wished to be "neutral," it was with respect to any occupation or neocolonial recovery, but that they did not intend to bind themselves with a diplomatic doctrine such as neutralism.

We have seen how far the 1954 treaty with London stretched the principles of neutralism.

1955 was indeed the turning point. From the Baghdad Pact to the Gaza coup, from Bandung to the arms race, the *bikbashi* witnessed the deterioration of his relations first with the West, then with the East. Then two personalities appeared who symbolized the new neutralism: Nehru and Tito. Whatever the importance of the man who helped save Gamal Abdel Nasser during the height of the Suez crisis by threatening Anthony Eden with a diplomatic break with the Commonwealth, the visit of Josip Broz Tito merits consideration here for several good reasons.

For one, this visit was from the outset a picturesque business which touched us rather closely. We shall recount the following anecdote quite simply, without drawing from it any lesson other than the importance which a fortuitous event and a humble guide may assume on an important mission.

It was February 4, 1955. Premier Abdel Nasser was about to leave a large hotel in Heliopolis where a rather stormy interview had just taken place with his Sudanese counterpart Ismail Azhari. In the lounge of the hotel, we approached him to ask for news of the negotiations. As his look made it clear that it was best not to insist on this point, another question occurred to us. Marshal Tito was passing through the Suez Canal at this very hour: did he, Abdel Nasser, envision meeting with this transient and fortuitous guest in Egypt?

Gamal looked at us, a bit taken aback. Certainly the idea had crossed his mind. Yet when put to the question, and being an Egyptian not without the charming hospitality of that people, he answered politely: "Why not? I would be happy to meet President Tito. . . ." (In English, the language he used struck a very conditional, very evasive note.) Then, smiling, he walked away.

Our colleagues approached.

"What did he say?"

"In response to my question, he said he would gladly meet Tito. . . ."

One of them, a correspondent for Reuters, took note of this. That evening, while dining with some Egyptian friends, we received a telephone call from the Yugoslav ambassador, Mr. Nikezic (five years later promoted to minister of foreign affairs), who already maintained cordial personal relations with Nasser.[1]

"What did the President say to you?" Apparently a Reuters news dispatch received on board the *Galeb*[2] had greatly interested the marshal. "Does President Nasser really want to see him?"

Now I had only to reconstruct our earlier exchange of remarks, which could hardly pass for either a proposed discussion or an invitation.

"Ah . . . good. I shall relay the information."

This information was apparently deemed sufficient cause for Josip Broz Tito and Gamal Abdel Nasser to spend several hours together the following day, between Ismailia and Port Said, hours which were later to be followed by many others.

During the next fifteen years, in fact, the two statesmen were to meet not less than twenty-two times, sometimes in dramatic circumstances—but each time, in any case, with the feeling of adding an element, a touch, to what was always an exemplary political friendship. Between the former head of the Croatian Communist partisans, an ex-commander of international brigades who had become the somewhat pontifical president of a Marxist state, and the young colonel-president, there were many points in common: their modest origins,

[1] The Yugoslav diplomatic mission in Cairo had been elevated to ambassadorial rank only five month earlier.

[2] The yacht of the Yugoslav chief of state.

their professional soldiery, their fervent nationalism, their sense of the people and of authority, their steadfast behavior, and their sociability camouflaged in the one by decorum, in the other by laconicism. But there were also many contrasts.

Gamal chose to play the young admirer—which, in fact, he was. With a talent for this role which had charmed a hundred interlocutors more than any brilliant display of knowledge or conversational bravura, he asked questions about guerrilla warfare, the resistance to Stalin, neutralism, self-rule, federalism. . . . Tito, in the good-natured and sedate tone he had chosen to adopt, played the uncle wearied by tribulation, the old man heavy with a hundred secrets, the old warrior back from the campaigns. And how sympathetic the young Nasser was to this talk—how well he listened.

Tito's first state visit to Egypt, from December 28, 1955, to January 6, 1956, was, for Gamal, the cause of a significant gesture. Since the visitor was accompanied by his wife, the beautiful and robust Jovanka, an ex-partisan leader, the head of the Egyptian government also wanted his own wife to appear officially. The occasion was a performance at the Cairo Opera. True, Tahia had not been cloistered up to now. The *bikbashi*'s friends knew her well, as did her neighbors, local tradesmen, and her husband's colleagues. She lived like a true daughter of the urban Egyptian petty bourgeoisie. But this sudden participation in public life was a real event: here one sees Gamal, the introvert, the old-fashioned husband, trying both to honor Tito and to appear "modern" in his guest's eyes.

It has not been possible to learn from either source whether the Yugoslav marshal had any part in Nasser's decision of July 22, 1956. When the *Raïs* decided to nationalize the Canal Company, he was just returning, so it was said, from a week's stay at Brioni—his first official visit to Yugoslavia,

where, on the eighteenth and nineteenth, Nehru had joined
the two chiefs of state. Apparently, Gamal strongly doubted
that he would receive the loan promised by Washington. He
had not foreseen the provocative terms of Mr. Dulles's refusal,
but he was already prepared to seek an alternative (and he
had probably even raised the possibility of nationalization
during his last audience, in early July, with his ambassador
to Washington).

Did he ask Tito's advice? Did he receive his opinion? The
Yugoslav chief of state was not a man of aggressive stubbornness, or of defiant recklessness. But if his visitor already
had a plan, well then. . . . In short, Josip Tito was linked, at
the very least by a whim of the calendar, and probably much
more directly, to the most significant political act of Gamal
Abdel Nasser's career.

It was once again at the side of the Yugoslav chief of state
that the *Raïs* was to accomplish another important step: his
first—and last—sortie into the West, in September 1960 for
the fifteenth session of the UN in New York. Four years after
Suez, the Egyptian leader was awaited as a sort of bogeyman
in that city so susceptible to Israeli arguments. On September
19 the assembly, which Nikita Khrushchev dominated despite
his small stature, felt as if it were again in Alexandria, in
July 1956: it was Fidel Castro who spoke.

But—two days later—who was the dignified dark gentleman, dressed in a sober, close-fitting suit, who rose to the
rostrum? He read his speech from pages on the lectern in the
most even and restrained voice. Was he, Nasser, that sneering
buccaneer, that sharp-fanged Barbary pirate? "One would
think it was the House of Lords," murmured my neighbor,
the correspondent for the *Observer*. And of what did he
speak? Of peace, of international arbitration, of mediation for
coexistence. Was a more decent performance, or one more in

harmony with the ideals of the UN, ever heard within that international assembly? When these Arabs began to talk seriously, Khrushchev could find no occasion to bang down his desk top, to jump out of his shoes, or even to make a wisecrack.

Three days later, Nasser and Tito met again in a five-nation conference with Nehru (India), Nkrumah (Ghana), and Sukarno (Indonesia). The conferees initiated an appeal for peace to the Big Two, and suggested, politely but firmly, that they all meet. So now the poorer states were organizing the schedule of the great powers.

Mohammed Hassanein Heykal called this policy "positive neutralism." At the outset, this meant no more than that Nasser, a good staff officer with some knowledge of ele-mentary physics, was applying the basic principle of the lever. Bearing down on one force in order to raise another, he might bring pressure to bear on Washington to spring the British lock, then on Moscow to remove American pressure, then on Pankow to make Bonn open its purse, then on Bonn to set Moscow thinking, then on Paris to make Tel Aviv submit, and so forth.

But the word "positive" was not there for nothing. This strategy aimed at being more than "not negative": it claimed to be life-sustaining. Over and over again Nasser persuaded himself that "positive neutralism" was the heart of political wisdom and diplomatic ingenuity. And how right he must have looked on the day when, in response to the first Anglo-Saxon offer to build the High Dam, Moscow proposed to construct an atomic energy plant on the Nile; or on the day when, to counter the signing of a financial agreement with Soviet Vice Minister Nikitin, London accepted the liquidation on the lowest possible terms of its disputed post-Suez claims; on the day when, to foil German offers, the U.S.S.R. agreed to finance the first part of the Aswan construction. And this is not to mention the incident of November 4, 1956, when, supporting Eisenhower's efforts, Bulganin and Khrushchev also decided to come to the rescue.

This planetary diplomacy carried Egypt well beyond her pre-1955 role. But it did not grant her the place she wished in the world which is hers first of all, the world delimited by the three famous "circles" described in the *Philosophy of the Revolution:* The Arab circle, the Islamic circle, and the African circle.

One might evaluate the steps taken by the *Raïs* within the Arab circle by distinguishing those belonging rather to the Islamic circle, either in reality or in his mind. In the properly African domain, the plan for a grand Nile policy has been mentioned, founded on the unity of the valley, through Egyptian-Sudanese fusion or an alliance.

For a long time Egyptian avidity caused these projects to fail. And the construction of the dam, leading to the flooding of a part of the Sudan, was an opportunity for Khartoum to make Cairo dance to its tune: discreet or cynical, this blackmail was profitable.

The Sudanese revolution of 1969—the most radical movement, along with that of Southern Yemen, that the Arab world had yet known—opened the door to true cooperation, and on the day of Nasser's funeral, the most acclaimed politician in Cairo was neither Arafat, nor Kosygin, nor Boumedienne, but General Nemeiri, the Sudanese leader. Through many vicissitudes, reversals, and resurgences, Nasser had in the end contributed to the unity of the Nile Valley.

But his other African undertakings fell short of the mark. The fact that he was, in 1960, one of the most vigorous supporters of the UN intervention in the Congo to quell the Katanga secession (his ambassador to Leopoldville, Mourad

Ghalel, was one of the key men of the operation) did not suffice to alleviate the mistrust that surrounded, and still surrounds, Cairo's initiatives in the African world. Was this the effect of old anti-Arab rancors dating from the time of the *rezzous?* Was Israel, whose position in black Africa is very strong, working to undermine Cairo? Was it a specifically Egyptian clumsiness or excess? The fact is that, although involved in various rebellions such as in the Tchad or in Cameroon, Northern Nigeria, Guinea, or Niger, Nasserian politics never really led very far in Africa, outside the Arab-speaking countries.

The real Nasserian "circle," beyond the Nile Valley itself, was the Arab circle. Although Nasser experienced many failures in this area, policy here reveals an inner logic, as much in the search for markets for Egyptian industry and in the pursuit of a theater for diplomatic activity. Let us not forget: his policy was above all neutralist. And he was above all an Arab neutralist.

But what of Egypt?

Having become the UAR, Egypt lived in the shadow of the man whom one of our neighbors, a radio broadcaster, presented in these terms during a meeting in 1960: "That heroic and revered face which the light of the projectors renders almost incandescent, quasi-prophetic above us . . ."

Invested with the *hukm*—charisma won by personal daring and, since Suez, confirmed by the masses—Gamal Abdel Nasser towered high above the Egyptian political landscape. By his personal influence, by his constitution, by popular ratification, by the repressive forces he had created, consolidated, and endowed with innumerable responsibilities, he became the *Raïs,* the "boss." We shall try later on to discern the limits and the faults of this absolute power, and the several restraints, which he himself solicited, placed upon it after the Congress of Popular Forces in 1962.

The death of the great viceroy had been followed by rivalry between the palace and the foreign protector. Then, after the eviction of Khedive Abbas Hilmi, the open conflict between the sovereign and the intelligentsia paved the way for pluralism and even a measure of decentralization. (Of course this pluralism remained purely political, and always within the limits of the "hydraulic system.") This ever-present dualism—between Arabi and the Khedive, between Mustafa Kamel and the palace, between the Wafd and the king—was abolished by Gamal the *Raïs*.

Since there can be no unchecked power which acts totally without folly, even this talented man, endowed as he was with a lofty sense of his mission and his responsibility, committed several extravaganzas. For example, he was responsible at the end of 1961 for the arrest, imprisonment, and absurd trial of five French diplomats along with several well-thought-of foreign and Egyptian intellectuals, accused of having plotted against the regime and of having tried to direct the *Raïs*'s assassination. Six months later, Gamal Abdel Nasser admitted before Edouard Sablier[3] that it seemed improbable that the French government had really wanted to do away with him. "And especially not de Gaulle, whose high moral worth is known to everyone. How could a practicing Christian have contemplated my assassination?"

The signing of the Evian agreements produced an easing of tension between Paris and Cairo. The innocence of the convicts suddenly became clear to the Egyptian authorities, who released them. But, in the climate of confusion which followed the rupture with Syria, a gang of henchmen once again appeared in the shadow of the *Raïs*—policemen, bureaucrats,

[3] *Candide,* May 31, 1962.

judges—to transform his irrepressible need for vendetta into official inquests and trials. The personality cult was echoed by an all-powerful police, a corps of arbitrary investigators and schemers, and a bench of conniving judges. Was this, then, Nasserian socialism? Had he borrowed only the defects of the "fatherland of the revolution"?

PART FIVE

A Peculiar Sort
of Socialist

21

In Quest of an Ideology

For the people, but not by the people: such might have been the motto of Nasserism in its various domestic accomplishments. Both plebeian patriot and authoritarian reformer, Gamal often reminded one of those Russian populists, the *nurodniki,* whose concern for the people was equaled only by the distrust it inspired in them.

This does not mean that Nasser remained cut off from the masses: from his return from Bandung to his funeral on the banks of the Nile, the leader was to be followed, surrounded, and celebrated by the people. But throughout his strategic vicissitudes and ideological retractions, the same preoccupation recurs constantly, ever more secret but always present: the initiative must never pass to the masses, nothing must involve them which does not come from the leader and his men. The revolution is in the hands of the leader as water is controlled by a hydraulic engineer.

That the young officer's undertaking conceived in 1945, fully formed by 1950, and perfected in early 1952 had as its essential objective to ensure reform in anticipation of the menacing revolution (the peasant revolt of Bahout, the Cairo fire) and that that objective was to be achieved through a uniformed petty bourgeoisie, impatient to modernize Egypt while wresting it from European influence, is a hypothesis which may be judged too "coherent" and restrictive, especially since this his-

torical adventure was marked by improvisation, by pragmatism
and eclecticism, almost by mental "nomadism." But this hypothesis may at least serve as a point of departure, on condition
that the young strategist be recognized above all as a nationalist ardent for the emancipation of a country immobilized by
foreign occupation and humiliated by Farouk's autocracy.

This project was very quickly to become enriched by the
addition of a third aspect. To the eviction of the foreign army
and the purification of public life was added the necessity of
rescuing the peasant masses from "feudalism." The Six Principles which served until 1952 as the ideological platform and
operational plan of the Free Officers wax eloquent on this
point. But for a long time these principles marked the outer
limit of the conspirators' imagination.

Questioned ten years later on his program at the moment
of his rise to power, Gamal Abdel Nasser answered:

> There were two tendencies among us. Some wanted to set
> up a list of our demands, a program of political action.
> The others, who felt as I did, judged that a clandestine
> movement such as ours should avoid setting up documents
> and writings which could fall into the hands of the police.
> . . . Moreover, our political ideas varied according to our
> social milieu, the families from which we came, and our
> temperaments. In wanting to define our program of action,
> we would have become divided. . . .[1]

It was a classic argument. Yet Gamal did not believe he
risked possibly splitting the movement by entrusting the
writing of tracts, the basic ideological equipment of the officers
before the takeover, to the Marxists of the group, notably to
Khaled Mohieddin. The few copies that can still be found are
surprising: they could then have come from the Mouvement

[1] Georges Vaucher, *Gamal Abdel Nasser et son équipe,* Paris, 1959, II, p. 9.

de la Paix or any other organization of "fellow travelers."
Sandwiched between two philippics against the leaders of Farouk's army one finds a denunciation of bacteriological warfare
in Korea, or imperialist moves in Europe.

The twenty-third of July 1952 arrived, followed almost immediately by the removal of the most leftist element of the
committee, Yussef Saddiq. The declarations of Naguib were
soothing: the regime has not been overthrown, the monarchy
continues, the armed forces remain outside the political situation, even if only to make simple "suggestions." Here and
there the word *thawra* (revolution) is indeed heard, if only
because the leading organ of the new authority was the *Maglis
al-Thawra* (Revolutionary Council). But official rhetoric preferred the word *islah,* reform. In January 1954, Fathi Radwan, the official thinker of the regime, declared that "it is not
yet time to define Egypt's politics." Early Nasserism was as
circumspect as it was ambiguous. Nonetheless, the elimination
of Aly Maher, the application of the agrarian reform, and the
quarrel with the older political class set in motion mechanisms
which were to lead to the progressive radicalization of the
system. This was above all because the vast majority of the
intellectual elite looked ignorant of Proust and Eliot, Sartre
and Lukacs; because the most militant Muslims, those of the
ikhwan, had declared war on the officers; and finally because
the Americans, the purveyors, if not of ideology at least of
recipes, really claimed to be receiving excessive political dividends. It would be necessary to obtain some heavier ideological baggage than the *Philosophy of the Revolution* which, in
1954, merely introduced a personality, denounced apathy, and
offered various objectives, among them a vague Arabism.

And what of socialism? The word *ishtirakiya* hardly appears
except in certain marginal publications of the regime (*Al-Tahrir,* for example, an organ founded by the military and in particular by Ahmed Hamrush, a declared Marxist who was

reproved by Okasha, a liberal commanding officer with Wafdist sympathies). As far as Gamal Abdel Nasser himself is
concerned, it seems that he never publicly used the word before a speech delivered at the military academy, in February
1955; yet here it was used in a rather negative tone, as if it
were a question of some inevitable recourse against the incompetence of "the business elite" to assume responsibilities for
Egyptian development. Socialism was nearly made into a
shameful punishment, a sanction against economic irresponsi-
bility.

But Tito had visited Egypt, and now the Bandung Conference was meeting. This was a decisive moment, less for the
contacts established with Chou En-lai than for the rallying of
the Egyptian Left to the "militant of the anti-imperialist battle." Nasser appreciated the enthusiasm of these elusive masses.
He discovered above all those intellectual milieux that had
previously been wanting; here were the disseminators of ideas,
projects, and propaganda themes. At this point began what
the Egyptian Left has called the "Bandung period."

During the three years that passed between the Indonesian
trip and the conflict with Iraq, curious relations were established between Abdel Nasser and the Marxists. In the spring
of 1953, several leaders of the PCE (then the most radical
branch, and the closest to the Soviet Union, of Egyptian Marxist organizations) had been tried before a military tribunal
presided over by Colonel Ahmed Shawki, a friend of Naguib,
who had hardly hidden his sympathy for the accused. But the
press had been forbidden to mention even the word "Communist"; at the very most it could speak of some strange social
malady afflicting these wicked Egyptians. Two years later, several comrades of these "antisocial" elements were summoned
to cooperate with the *bikbashi*-premier. And beginning with
their liberation, which followed the publication of the constitution in early 1956, other militant Communists took their

place in the president's brain trust or on the editorial boards of the most influential newspapers.

It is hard not to speak ironically of the singular role of the militants—both martyrs and *éminences grises,* now inquisitors, now excommunicated, now champions, now torture victims. With this group, with the visionaries and Machiavellians, the *Raïs* had found the foil he had long been seeking, for they were at once bearers of information and of criticism. Sometimes court advisers, sometimes expiatory victims, the members of the little Soviet which camped on the outskirts of Gamal Abdel Nasser's office were to help push the enterprise slowly along toward a kind of socialism—a very peculiar one, to tell the truth, and very artificial, depending as it did on the leader's arbitrary will. The situation was reminiscent of the head-scribes of the Pharaonic regimes, or of Mohammed Ali's *Rumi* experts: Armenians, Frenchmen, Greeks, all of whom the viceroy played upon like a virtuoso.

But these scribes were very conscious and very profoundly linked to the national collectivity: although they themselves were being used, they also gradually changed the course of things. The nationalization of the Canal Company was certainly achieved without them, or any consultation from within their ranks, except perhaps for Ahmed Fuad, already more of a bureaucrat than a militant Marxist. But the nationalization could not have borne fruit or accomplished any economic or governmental results without the active presence of the Communists. Without doubt, what occurred was the establishment of state military control of the economy rather than a transition to socialism. But that the public sector, suddenly enlarged, could organize itself, however poorly, and defend itself, however brutally, was above all due to the cadres of Marxists who were then in office.

Not the least remarkable person on the steering committee the "economic body" assigned to develop the resources created by the nationalization of Suez and the confiscation of British and French interests was Ismail Sabri Abdallah, accused by the police of being "Khaled," the writer of anti-governmental Communist tracts. This Marxist economist had been arrested at the time of Bandung, tried in June 1956, and acquitted, not before having shown his judges, before a full audience, the marks of torture suffered during the preliminary investigation. Ismail Sabri was to be for thirty months one of the economic heads of the regime before being imprisoned in December 1958, then summoned to direct the national publishing house and, finally, the institute of social planning.

Between 1952 and 1955, the quarrels between Gamal and the Communists proceeded like a national occurrence. The *bikbashi* then spoke mostly of reform, and needed the Americans. But after Bandung, the Czech armaments, and Suez, the crises between them were of an entirely different nature, the ruptures and tensions of companions. Nasser now saw in the Communists men whom he had welcomed into the bosom of the state after making them swear at the moment of their liberation from jail not to engage in further political activities, men who in time of disagreement might betray his trust. In short, he saw them as traitors, and a witch hunt ensued.

From 1956 to 1958, cooperation proceeded undisturbed. It was challenged again in the very year of the union with Syria and the Iraqi revolution, for reasons due in part to these two events. When Nasser resolved to absorb Syria, Khaled Bagdash and his Syrian Communist Party turned against him. The leader soon left Syria, first to install himself in Bakou, later in Prague. Thus Gamal saw this perilous union, which could only succeed with everyone's support, doomed from the outset by the opposition of the major personality in Middle Eastern communism. His bitterness over this had bad repercussions for Bagdash's Egyptian comrades.

On February 28, 1958, the latter had just effected the unification of the two Egyptian organizations which claimed to be orthodox Marxist. Now they could securely avail themselves of the title of "Egyptian Communist Party," especially since Moscow had ratified the operation. But this new front was not at all to the *Raïs*'s taste. He could accept diverse and divided Communist organizations. But if these people united to the point of constituting a force comparable to that which he directed...

On July 14, 1958, the Baghdad revolution, with its elementary and outspoken violence, made clear to everyone the oligarchic and authoritarian character of the Cairo regime. The decline in popularity of the *Raïs*'s trusted Aref, the refusal of Kassem to adhere to the UAR, the leftist sentiment exhibited by the popular tribunal in Baghdad, all irritated Nasser and incited him against this popular revolution which was in a sense the negation of his own. Since he could not act in Iraq except through the intervention of agitators who were foiled time and again, he chose to take his revenge in Cairo against any Communists who joined in the applause for the Baghdad "carnival" (for a division had once again occurred in the PCE over the issue of Iraq).

At first threats were used: Anwar el-Sadat, then secretary general of the National Union, the second avatar of the sole Nasserian party, summoned the leaders of that fraction of the PCE favorable to the Iraqi revolution, and to the Iraqi refusal to adhere to the UAR. They were "advised" to join his organization. He encountered a polite refusal. From then on, repression drew nearer. On December 20, Khaled Bagdash published in the Beirut newspaper *Al Akhbar* an indictment of the Nasserian "dictatorship." Three days later, at Port Said, the

Raïs countered this by denouncing all "dividers of the Arabs, imperialists, and opportunists."

On December 31, Eugene Black landed in Cairo, carrying new offers of a loan from the International Bank. The same evening, a hundred of the best militants of the PCE—all the more well known and observed as they collaborated for the most part with the regime—were apprehended and sent to various internment camps.

Several days earlier, the minister of the interior, Zakaria Mohieddin, received Simonne Lacouture of *France-Observateur* in his Louis XV salon, sparkling with false gold; holding out a plate of petits-fours, he declared with a suave smile: "In Syria, communism is a danger. In Egypt it is only a problem. Here, we know all the Communists. . . ."

This problem was faced by this astute man by means of infiltration and harassment. The shadowing of the *mukhabarat*[2] had become so ubiquitous that suspicion and doubt rendered the presence of policemen and informers virtually useless. We knew men who literally tracked themselves down. That one, who had just left prison to become head of a minister's cabinet, what pledge did he give? And that other, was he now back in the police? The dragnet was thrown not only over the Communists, but over all sorts of men of the Left: the latter were deemed more dangerous, since they were not card-carrying members. And all this occurred despite the presence in power, or on the fringes, of companions of Nasser firmly attached to socialism or even communism, such as Khaled Mohieddin, Kamal Rifaat, Ahmed Hamrush.

The infiltration and surveillance were followed, at the beginning of 1959, by brutal repression. From the prison of Abou Zaabal to that of Kharga, in the middle of the great

2 Military intelligence.

western desert, in horrifying conditions of internment, the intellectual ranks of the Egyptian Marxists were subjected to the most destructive and demeaning existence. In an article published by *Esprit* in April 1960, we evoked the fate of these militants by referring to this incident: "One of the men who was starved and beaten in a camp in Egypt told us that one day, a warden cried out to the prisoners as he doubled a punishment: 'this is to make you pay for the campaigns that your friends who "care about you" are waging abroad!' " And, our article continued: "Will these few lines be worth new sufferings for Ismail Sabri Abdallah, Lutfallah Soliman, Mahmud el-Alem, Shohdi Attia and Ibrahim Abdel Halim?"

It was several weeks later, on June 15, 1960, that Shohdi Attia el-Shafei, often considered the major theoretician of Egyptian Marxism, and a professor of English known outside Egypt for his studies of classical literature, was slaughtered by the cudgel blows of his jailers. Shohdi Attia was, however, one of the Egyptian Communist leaders most ardently in favor of an active cooperation with a regime irrevocably committed, whatever vicissitudes might occur, to an alliance with socialism and popular forces. Before his judges, his declaration had been the most fervent and dignified defense for the "Bandung period" of Nasserism.

The internment camps of Barrages or Maharic were veritable universities, the best intellectual circles of Egypt. Beaten and starved, subjected to tortures or vexations, the painter Inji Efflatun and the caricaturist Zohdi, the writers and journalists Ibrahim Amer and Abdel Azim Anis, the lawyers Yussef Hilmi and Ali Shalakani, and many others formed behind their bars a countersociety, ghetto-like but not desperate, to which the state would again appeal when in need. And the majority, despite everything, though without illusions, were to set forth again by the side of the *Raïs*.

22

An Objective Statism

At the height of the repression, which he protected by his authority (for what remained in Egypt for which he was not responsible?), Gamal Abdel Nasser stepped up the conversion of the social system to what would soon be called, in this climate of the Syrian *Anschluss,* "Arab socialism." But what marked this period, by contrast to the one which followed, was that the measures taken and often applied counted more than the words. Beyond the ideas, the propaganda, and the appeal to suggestibility and collective emotions, what might be called "the force of things" asserted itself. It was the latter which seemed to be leading, from early minor alterations to a later complete reorientation and from coercive measures to the beginning of real planning, toward the objective socialism which colored this period, despite the re-establishment of relations with London and the rapprochement with Washington during the Kennedy era.

In 1959 and 1960, two measures emphasized the new public pressure on private capital and the acceleration of the takeover of the economy by the state sector. In January 1959, a law was passed forbidding corporations to distribute dividends greater than ten per cent to shareholders, who, besides, were obliged to devote five per cent of their profits to the acquisition of Egyptian state securities. In February 1960, the National Bank of Egypt was nationalized (an operation which was not in the least tautological, despite the title of this highly cosmopolitan organization) as well as the Misr Bank, which had been for almost forty years the instrument for the development of the Egyptian bourgeoisie. (It should be noted besides that the founder of the latter establishment and of many others, Talaat Harb, was so popular with the military regime that his statue in one of the principal squares of the city has recently replaced that of Soliman Pasha.)

As Anwar Abdel Malek[1] writes on this subject, the real cause of this nationalization was political. As the official newspaper *Al Ahram* maintained: "The Misr Bank had attained, via its subsidiary companies, a stage of monopoly sufficiently advanced to permit it to impose its will on the ruling power. . . . If the Misr Bank had not until then behaved as a monopoly, this was only because of the personal ideas of its leaders and of the government authority. . . ." And to show that it was indeed the state's authority in question, and that henceforth this authority intended to speak out, Marshal Abdel Hakim Amer stepped into the office of president of the "Superior Council of Public Organizations" a doubly symbolic act since he was highest officer in the army and the closest friend of the *Raïs*.

One more paradox could hardly matter in the grand puzzle of Nasserism. But this one is striking: the seizure of the economy by the military, which forced industrial capital to undergo what agrarian reform had inflicted on the agrarian aristocracy in 1952, was accomplished after the Bandung period when the Marxists were no longer present in the government. Could it be that Nasser was not tempted to convert Egypt to a planned economy until the Communists had been sent to prison? We know that despite the regime's personal character, and the arbitrariness of many decisions, the president of the UAR was above all a pragmatist, who acted or reacted according to the

[1] *Egypt: Military Society,* New York, 1968, p. 137.

circumstances and his own obsessive concern for equilibrium and independence. It was precisely when he had succeeded in re-establishing useful ties with the West that it was important for him to seize control of production, or a whole business world might have eluded him with the return of the emissaries of the International Bank, the city, and the Franco-Italo-German consortium.

He wished to play upon the latter as he pleased, according to what he judged to be the interests of the UAR: he already felt the pressure of a "local business elite," which would henceforth be doubled in strength because the Cairo business community tended to follow that of Damascus, already lost perhaps, but unwilling to give up on all fronts. And the *Raïs* secured all possible guarantees that the return of dollars would not be a revenge for those who brought them.

On July 22, 1961, on the occasion of the ninth anniversary of the 1952 takeover, Gamal Abdel Nasser announced, or solemnly confirmed, a series of measures which introduced what was then called its "third revolution." Needless to say, he had to remain sanguine and refrain from speaking of a transition to socialism. But some seventeen laws and decrees enacted between June 5 and July 23, 1961, profoundly radicalized the regime, modifying the relationship of social forces, completing the destruction of the upper middle class, and offering more chances for promotion to the rural petty bourgeoisie than the 1952 document.

There is no doubt that, for the *Raïs* Gamal, Egypt (or rather the UAR) had that day made "democratic and cooperativist socialism" its own. The latter formula was obviously inspired by the Yugoslav friendship of the chief of state. Without ever having attempted to insinuate themselves into the workings of the Egyptian economy or army, the experts and representatives of Marshal Tito enjoyed great prestige. Moreover, each of Abdel Nasser's seven trips to Yugoslavia was the occasion for visits and observations which influenced his own experiences.

From now on, asserted the *Raïs* on July 23, 1961, "there will no longer be one class sucking the blood of the other," although "all owners are not exploiters"; the regime was not "against property"; it prohibited "all kinds of class vengeance"; and he summoned the people to build socialism on the basis of "national friendship." It seemed that the *Raïs* was inviting his listeners to a festival. But the festival was costly to some.

Let us again consider the principal texts of June–July 1961: some threat of the redistribution of the national revenue, others of the agrarian structure, and others of the state sector. Income tax was levied on the basis of annual income of more than 4,000 pounds (approximately 30,000 francs at present) and could rise to ninety per cent in the above 10,000-pound bracket. No salary was to exceed 5,000 pounds. The group composed of the workers and employers officially was to receive ownership of twenty-five per cent of the property of all companies. The work day was limited to seven hours, and it was decreed that all officials must declare the source of their revenue for the past ten years. Perhaps these measures constituted more an equilibration of existing social structures rather than a real revolution.

One might well wonder, but not as far as the second agrarian reform was concerned, which henceforth limited land property not to 200 but to 100 feddans (about 42 hectares, or 103.74 acres), and necessitated the transfer of property of more than 200,000 hectares (494,000 acres). Besides, the state, nationalizing in one stroke the banks, insurance, all transportation companies, and fifty heavy industrial companies, claimed sole rights over import commerce and, of even greater interest, the monopoly of cotton transactions. The entire trade network of this staple product, the foundation of the wealth of the Egyptian bourgeoisie, passed into the hands of the state, which would henceforth control fifty-one per cent of the shares and hence the decisive vote in all companies dealing in cotton.

Was this capitalism? Certainly, although the measures ensuring working class advancement and agrarian redistribution had given a populist color to its laws. In November, 1961, a new series of decrees was to follow, more leftist in flavor and apparently inspired by the spirit of "class struggle" mentioned but apparently rejected in the July speech. In the new November measures, and in their presentation by the *Raïs,* the echo of Suez could be heard, the vengeful tone of the humiliated, the old defiance toward the "millionaires." This was without doubt a case of demagoguery. But it was necessary at that time to eradicate the memory of the Syrian debacle, and to strike a lasting blow at that Damascene bourgeoisie which, not without outside complicity, had just inflicted its greatest defeat on the regime.

Was this the liquidation of merely the "exploitive" and cosmopolitan bourgeoisie, or simply of the whole bourgeoisie? Or even, on a long-term basis, of private property itself? Was the UAR claiming to be an African Yugoslavia, or was it satisfied to replace the old Egyptianized Egypt with a new Egyptian Egypt founded on the power of the middle classes, and represented by a bureaucracy both in and out of uniform? We must not believe that these problems of definition and of strategy left Nasser the opportunist indifferent.

In this period, during which he delivered many speeches, one could sense in one after another an appetite for concepts, a desire for a durable explanation, and a plan of action which were all quite new in this pragmatist.

Nothing was yet clear. On the day following the presentation of the laws of June 1961, the *Raïs*'s second, Ali Sabri, stated during a press conference: "Our objective is property development. The public sector is not, for us, a way to liquidate property, but rather a way to expand its base. . . ."

Two months later, the tone was set by Gamal Abdel Nasser's other intimate collaborator. In a series of articles entitled "Communism and Us," Mohammed Hussanein Heykal attempted to define "Arab socialism" as opposed to Marxism. While the latter imposed "the suppression by one single class of the other classes" the former proposed "a process of dissolution of class contradictions within the framework of a national union."

Whereas for communism "the individual is but an instrument of work," Arab socialism considered him "at once the product and the agent of history."

And to the "dogmatism" which he declared inherent in communism, Mr. Heykal opposed the vision of a new doctrine forged in Cairo, and "open to the entirety of world culture."

At the same time Mohammed Heykal launched a very curious debate among several of the country's most famous intellectuals. In several articles he had demanded "more freedom, still more freedom!" (But was he not among those who held the reins?) In June, in fact, the familiar spokesman of the *Raïs* had published a series of articles on "the crisis of the intellectuals" which was a kind of courteous summons issued for the best minds of Egypt, liberals as well as Marxists. From this series of exchanges, which brought a breath of fresh, if not hot, air to this society so frozen by personal power and the agents of the *mukhabarat,* we luckily can formulate certain definitions of the relations between Nasserism and the intellectuals.

The following incident is characteristic. Magdi Wahba, a highly intelligent academic, summarizes the situation of his peers:

> Non-participation in the army movement of 1952; a feeling of failure and withdrawal, that is, a return of the intelligentsia to its cultural barracks; the economic poverty

of the Egyptian intellectuals, which forces them to play the role of propagandists rather than critics; the imitation of foreign models, . . . the intellectual feels that Gamal Abdel Nasser is in essence right. But at the same time, he feels by his very nature the need to formulate a certain measure of criticism. This internal contradiction . . . tears him apart and makes him an unproductive being.[2]

Could so much frankness be tolerated? Colonel Salah el-Dessuki, who had one foot in the police machine and the other in a cultural committee, thought not: "The attitude of intellectuals has always conformed to the interests of the milieux and the classes to which they belong. The army revolution was itself a revolution of intellectuals. Those intellectuals who went along with their class, at the side of the revolution, are more numerous and more powerful than the ruined men who resisted them. . . ."[3]

But the debate could not be ended by a simple argument *ex autoritate.* Gamal Abdel Nasser was well aware of this, and himself later launched the critical exchanges and examinations prompted by the Syrian catastrophe as well as by the adoption by the ruling group of a socialistic economic framework. What was the real meaning of "Arab socialism" in the light of what had just happened with the *Baath* and the Syrian left-wing elite? "Democratic and cooperativist socialism," "National Union": what did these formulas mean, the day after the violent measures against the "millionaires" and the "exploiters," in the name of a still silent people?

It is in this perspective that the convocation of a "National Congress of Popular Forces" on May 21, 1962, must be situated. Nasserism was ten years old. After three years of pure opportunism and three great strategic shifts toward neutralism

[2] Abdel Malek, *Egypt: Military Society,* pp. 195–6.
[3] *Ibid.,* p. 196.

and state control in 1955, toward Marxism in 1959, and toward "democratic and cooperativist socialism" in 1961, it was finally trying to equip itself with an ideological apparatus. This common effort was conducted in the big amphitheater of the University of Cairo, inherited from King Farouk. (One might wonder how it was that this regime founded, according to Colonel Dessuki, by "intellectuals," had never provided the city's cultural life with a new assembly hall.) The *Raïs* proposed to the ten million members of the congress a "Charter for National Action," which his sycophants immediately dubbed "a new Koran."

The charter was composed of ten chapters. The last two are devoted to foreign affairs, and we shall not pause to examine them here. But the eight others form a mass of historical explanation and political planning of great interest. However skeptical one might be toward evaluations of the past or the future, one must admit that the *Raïs* of the Charter makes it easier to forget the *bikbashi* of the *Philosophy of the Revolution*.

First, a historical point: Gamal Abdel Nasser maintained in his 1954 pamphlet that the Egyptian people had refused to follow the army movement of 1952; then, in a speech in October 1954, he held that it had "shouldered it with enthusiasm." Here, still keeping a safe distance from the facts, he maintained, not without a certain nobility, that it was thanks to "this great people, this masterful people" that the overthrow of the monarchy did not occur merely as a banal palace revolution or as the inauguration of a fascist-type military dictatorship." But the inevitable Egyptian revolution had other trump cards at its disposal: the brother movements of other former colonies, and the presence of the socialist camp, that "growing material and moral power," which would allow them more easily to confront "the menace and the plots of imperialism."

Having arrived at this point in his reasoning—which seemed to be leading toward a socialist position—the *Raïs* formulated two fundamental antisocialist objections. On the one hand he firmly protested against the principle of class struggle: "The Egyptian people reject the dictatorship of one social class, whichever it might be, and esteem that a true democracy is only possible if class differences are suppressed." On the other hand, he insisted apropos the rights of individuals that "political democracy cannot be separated from social democracy" and that "all religions recognize the rights of individuals." This indicated clearly that Islam would remain an integral part of the doctrine under elaboration.

Having dealt this double blow to class struggle and to materialism, Gamal Abdel Nasser went on to pronounce the most essential sentence of his speech, the one which gave it a really international reverberation: "In Egypt, the putting into practice of the principles of scientific socialism is an ineluctable necessity." Was "scientific socialism" only a new tack in the long race of the *Raïs* toward an ideology which could rationalize his enterprise? Was it only a simple formula, a tactical salute to his Soviet friends, a homage to his Yugoslav ones, an ephemeral guerrilla coup from his old Marxist braintrusters?

Gamal Abdel Nasser did specify, however, exactly what was "scientific" about socialism according to the new charter: scientific socialism was first of all the domination of the private sector by the nationalized sector, the latter being placed "in the service of the people and controlled by it; next, it would be planning in every domain, a redistribution of wealth such that the working class would be the exclusive beneficiary; it would assure priority of heavy over light industry, and the elimination of inequalities between cities and rural areas; and finally it would entail the rapid development of cooperative movements and of trade unions which would be endowed with genuinely political responsibilities.

This was altogether a very ambitious and quite coherent program. But was it composed more of pious vows than of precise directives? This time, the *Raïs* seemed to know where he was going. And he recommended—that is, he declared— the creation of a new party, the "Arab Socialist Union," to succeed the "National Union" which had already without any great success taken the place of the phantom "Liberation Assembly" of the early years of the regime. A socialist-type program, with an organization created solely for the purpose of realizing it: was this the decisive commitment to the "Egyptian socialist way," certainly very "special" but no longer folklore?

The most radical Egyptian Marxists, whose ideas find expression in *La Lutte des classes en Egypte de 1945 à 1968,* refused to recognize any real socialism in this adroit pastiche. According to the authors it was rather "the Egyptian capitalist way" that was being outlined. After having "provided themselves with the economic tools of the state apparatus," Nasser and the forces of the dynamic bourgeoisie which he incarnated then proceeded to equip themselves, according to Mahmud Hussein (one of the authors of *La Lutte des classes en Egypte*), with "the ideological tools of socialism, after transforming it into a system of abstract formulas, devoid of any class content." Mahmud Hussein concludes: "This 'socialism' without class struggle, which identifies the growth of the state with the people's cause, is the ideological expression of the class vision of the bourgeoisie."

The debate instigated by the *Raïs* over this text, whose acclaim he engineered, reveals the hunger for ideology and political thought which had for years been gnawing away at the Egyptian intelligentsia, reduced as it was to providing perpetual applause. The religiously devout extreme Right and the

Marxist Left confronted one another, not without striking along the way at the suras of the new Nasserian "Koran." While the sheikh el-Ghazali grumbled about the vaguely secular aspect of the presidential program, his elderly socialist rival Khaled Mohammed Khaled was demanding the re-establishment of the parliamentary regime, and the syndicalist Anwar Salama criticized the paternalist aspects of a program which made hardly any appeal to working-class initiative. The *Raïs* defended himself step by step, and not without revealing some interesting ulterior motives. Thus, on the subject of paternalism, he retorted that the peasant and working classes suffered from inequalities that were not only economic but also psychological. Had not long centuries of oppression and alienation rendered the disinherited too weak to defend themselves? Must the state not substitute for them in defense of their rights? (This step is not very different from Lenin's idea of the revolutionary avant-garde.)

The debate closed without the adoption of a single modification of the charter: no one would say that the new Koran had been susceptible to change by a few irresponsible intellectuals. Still more serious, the organization of the Arab Socialist Union had not even been begun in a collective setting which might have permitted it a relatively democratic base.

Once again, it was at the top that this instrument of the Egyptian revolution was constructed. No one was more aware of this than the leader who, four months later, again addressed the citizens of the UAR, announcing the formation of a government with Ali Sabri as president—as the *Raïs* designated —and of a "presidential council" which would also diversify power and responsibility; Nasser added with a sort of lassitude: "It is not easy to organize socialism. . . ."

No doubt. But this time the Cairo leaders could refer to two earlier experiences, both failures. The "Liberation Assembly" (*Haiat al-Tahrir*) had been created in January 1953, under the personal aegis of Gamal Abdel Nasser, who very quickly became its secretary general. This was his first official post. The assembly immediately assumed enormous proportions—two million members. Supposedly this was the "government party"; therefore everyone registered in it, to make extra sure of being in good standing with the *omdeh* (village headman), the *maamur* (local police chief), the union leader, or the public works engineer.

In January 1956, the constitution presented by Abdel Nasser had expressly provided (Article 192) for the formation of a new political organization, this time not intended to play a one-party role but to be the crucible in which the new Egyptian society would take form. It was called the "National Union"—a significant formula which tended to preserve the fiction of social and political unanimity, although the great trials of 1953–4, the crushing of the Muslim Brethren, and the first anti-Communist repression revealed how fractured the Egyptian social body really was.

The constitutional text specified in addition that "the modes of formation of this union will be the subject of a decision by the president of the republic." Rarely had the omnipotence of the leader and his summit strategy been expressed with so much candor. On July 18, 1960, the *Raïs* appointed the 600 members of the National Assembly (400 for Egypt, 200 for Syria). The president was Anwar el-Sadat. There were certainly no surprises in store, especially since the two governors-general (Marshal Amer in the North, Kamaleddin Hussein, the most reactionary of all the Free Officers, in the south) were entrusted with disposing the organizations of the Union. There are few states in the world as centralized and concentrated as Egypt, except perhaps France. But no state in the world had ever had a body offering so little chance for decentralization, in the pressure game of hierarchies and competitive elites, than this one, which demonstrated Egyptian power about as much as the pyramid of Chefren encroaches on the pyramid of Cheops....

While on the subject of the pyramids, let us accompany Georges Vaucher, who in 1960 visited the secretary general of the governing committee of the National Union in his office at the foot of the Sphinx. His first discovery was that the representatives in the "party" were simply the *omdehs,* the eternal village chieftains. And, as often happens, even in socialist Egypt, they were also the richest men in their respective regions. And what were they doing with this bundle of authority and local power? They were buying fertilizers, seed, and insecticides for the commune. This is what every *omdeh* had done since Mohammed Ali. As for a young people's club, "It is useless," said the secretary, "we can very well do without it...."[4] At Kafr el-Nassar one could see that the revolution was hardly proceeding with haste.

On October 16, 1961, in his first act of self-criticism, the *Raïs* delivered the funeral oration of the National Union; it was riddled, he admitted, with "reactionary elements." The following November 5, he formally announced its dissolution. The second attempt at regrouping the Egyptian masses had been as abortive as the first. The work was returned to the shop.

The Arab Socialist Union emanated from the Charter of May 1962, a text which the leader once again bestowed upon the people, but which awakened a semipublic discussion and thus received some popular ratification. In his speech of the following September 24, the *Raïs* expressed his intention of

---

[4] Georges Vaucher, *Gamal Abdel Nasser et son équipe,* Paris, 1959, II, p. 343.

basing the new organization on the village, the factory, and the union trade. Nasser observed that massive and uncontrolled membership was the worst danger that could confront such an organization ("to say, as at the time of the early committees, that everyone belongs to them, comes down to saying that no one belongs to them"). Nasser now emphasized the necessity of selection, of a painstaking procedure to avoid past errors.

What had become of this theory three years later? Kamal Rifaat, the vice-premier and one of the most Marxist of Nasser's companions, declared to Claude Estier: "We put the cart before the horse. We have six million members. Now we must find 20,000 militant cadres. . . ."[5] This was indeed the problem. How could ranks be forged, if not in a shared and dangerous battle? Could these cleaners of revolutionary trenches form an advance guard worthy of the name? Once more the *Raïs* was to appeal to the Communists and the socialists. Although he contemplated entrusting the direction of a new educational institute to Khaled Mohieddin, he eventually placed another leftist, Ibrahim Saadeddin, at the head of the School of Socialist Personnel, created in Cairo in April 1965. Nasser himself had come a long way from the National Union and from Kamaleddin Hussein. But had anything really changed in the provinces and villages?

The *Raïs*'s doubts were so strong in 1964 that he envisioned resigning from his state functions in order to devote himself to the reorganization and animation of the party. Re-elected president in March 1965, Gamal Abdel Nasser renounced this option. But he was disturbed by similar preoccupations when, on May 16, 1965, he presented a kind of balance sheet to the members of the parliamentary group of the Arab Socialist Union. Let us listen to him—it is Nasser at his best who speaks to us.

5 Claude Estier, *L'Egypte en révolution,* Paris, 1965, p. 68.

After having denounced various errors more or less inherited from the old regime, he listed his criticisms: ". . . There
are people who work for 10 piasters[6] a day. They will be
there tomorrow, and the day after. . . . And I know there is
seasonal unemployment in the countryside. . . ." (Voices in
the room: "There is no unemployment, seasonal or otherwise.")
"The peasant and the agricultural worker work 180 days
per year: there is therefore seasonal unemployment. . . . Our
duty is to provide work for them. . . . But I judge that the
stage of revolutionary administrative measures is now past.
The moment has come to find support in the popular conscience and not in governmental intervention. . . ."

And the leader went on, with that mixture of candor and
ingenuous cynicism which was his alone: "Should we create an
opposition party in the heart of the National Assembly . . . ?
I am seeking a way of our working together as colleagues, I
do not want personal power. . . ."

To create an opposition? This was the question which Czar
Alexander I had asked in 1815. But a century and a half later,
the *Raïs* had not entirely come to the point of resuscitating it,
but only of confirming the existence of vigorous currents which
lent their flavor to Egyptian political society. Abdel Nasser
hardly went beyond opening the gates of the concentration
camps where the Communists were herded. This gesture, accomplished on the eve of Khrushchev's arrival in Aswan, did
not fail to have long-term repercussions. These Communists
were again—and this time until the end of Nasser's reign—
to take part in the debate, such an important part in fact that
they could well afford to bow their heads a little at the outset:
the majority of them in 1964 declared themselves for the dissolution of the Egyptian Communist Party and its integration
into the framework of the Arab Socialist Union.

[6] One franc "lourd."

In doing this, they had a good precedent: that of their Cuban comrades. Moreover, the *Raïs* was offering them an exceptional chance to widen their influence. At the very heart of the Arab Socialist Union he established a clandestine apparatus (his ever-present taste for conspiracy), and invited them, whose role had so long been clandestine, to enter it. Several occupied important positions in it, until the so-called "sincere" elections of 1969, which brought them fully to light.

Beginning with the measures of 1964, the cultural ascendancy exercised by the Egyptian Marxists, from columns in *Al Talia* to publishing houses, became obvious. This was a second "Bandung period," consolidated by the physical presence of the Soviets and the sheer volume of Russian investments in the Nile Valley. Well before 1967–70, the period of Soviet "protection," experts, and missiles, the Soviets had at their disposal in Egypt a network of influence reassuring to their friends. Before implanting themselves on the canal, they had found a home in the upper valley of the Nile, at Aswan.

23

The Journey to Aswan

In May 1964, we were among several thousand witnesses to a prodigious event: the bed of the Nile was to be shifted. To complete the final portion of these works, which aimed at channeling the river's course into "Lake Nasser," a diversion canal had been dug in a high granite wall. All that remained was to knock down a thin dike, so that the divine river would leap across its old bed. The pickaxes which the fellahin had wielded for five years in terracing the Nile broke through the last obstacle: the water surged forward.

On the bank, perched on the summit of a rostrum, there were two men: Nikita Khrushchev and Gamal Abdel Nasser. For both, this was a great victory. Nikita, under the panama hat of a Chekhov hero taking the Crimean sun, was bursting with satisfaction. "His" engineers had accomplished this prodigious feat, and the Soviet Union had gained a foothold in Africa through the genius of its technology. He had not come here simply as a symbol. He was the first wave of an army of engineers who were to tear Africa apart and tame its rivers for the greater glory of the Soviet Union.

Gamal, at the side of the little red-faced man, who had become winded and was wiping his brow, looked like the king of the castle receiving an ingenious merchant. He had finally arrived at the last stage in the construction of the dam, which he had a hundred times called the great pyramid of modern Egypt.

He found nothing humiliating in Khrushchev's appearance there. And it mattered little to him that the construction foremen of the work were mostly Soviet; for the *gallabieh*-clad workmen themselves, calling to each other as they threw into the Nile blocks of stone which would change the course of history, these men were truly Egyptians. They were still peasants, unskilled miserable laborers; but no one could change the Nile without being changed in the process.

Khrushchev had merely sent him his engineers and his rubles. He was grateful to this powerful little moujik who could so easily have been a fellah. But the people in the real process of change, like the Ukrainian peasants of half a century earlier, were the children of the river.

Of course, this was only one brief moment in the very

complex history of the relations between Gamal Abdel Nasser and the U.S.S.R. Several months earlier, the *Raïs* had been
made "a hero of the Soviet Union." But he had certainly
filed away somewhere the interesting article from the *Great
Soviet Encyclopedia* of 1952 worded thus:

". . . Exploiting this situation, the American and English
imperialists carried out a *coup d'état* at the end of January
1952, and put their favorites in power in Egypt. On the night
of July 23, 1952, a group of reactionary officers led by General Naguib and in close contact with the United States,
seized the power."[1]

Toward February 1955, soon after the signing of the
Baghdad Pact, closer ties between Abdel Nasser and Moscow
were formed (formal diplomatic relations between the two
capitals dated already from World War II). This was the
post-Stalinist era, the time when the Soviet leaders were opening a window on the world. Egypt, key to the eastern Mediterranean if not to the route to India, was also opening up,
delivered not from a tyrant but from a colonial power and
quite anxious not to exchange one for the other. The new
Soviet partner seemed strong and distant enough to be a
supporter rather than an exploiter. Then came the arms affair,
the Bulganin-Khrushchev ultimatum of November 4, 1956,
the highly important Nikitin-Fawzi commercial agreement of
1958, and finally the loan granted to Cairo in 1960 for the
construction of the High Dam.

From one vicissitude to another, the Soviets had taken care
not to involve the problems of their Egyptian Communist
friends in that of foreign relations.

In June 1956, the second Shepilov mission, a decisive
episode in which lasting links between the two states were
formed, coincided with one of the waves of repression ordered

[1] Quoted by Maxime Rodinson in *Israël et le refus arabe,* Paris, 1968.

by the *Raïs*. And the Nikitin-Fawzi agreement preceded by very little the cruelest period of anti-Communist repression at the end of December 1958.

In fact, from the end of January 1955 to September 28, 1970, only one crisis seriously troubled relations between the *Raïs* and Moscow: the Iraqi revolution. At the end of autumn, 1958, it seemed in fact that Kassem and his regime were offering the Arab masses a different path from the one beaten by Nasser. And, even more serious for the Egyptian leader, the Soviets were leaning toward Baghdad. This was certainly not because the Iraqi leaders were giving free rein to the masses—which would have distressed Moscow—but because they allowed the local Communist movement a freedom of movement of which their Cairo comrades could not dream.

Here Nasser made no attempt to rival Kassem. Instead, he was to intensify the repression for reasons at once passionate and quite rational: if Khrushchev, he judged, could publicly make known his encouraging attitude toward Baghdad,[2] it was because the U.S.S.R. had secured a sufficiently strong position in the Arab world to "choose its allies." Hence his anxiety concerning the intentions of the U.S.S.R., a feeling which was not to abate until two years later, when the *Raïs* chose the Soviet offer to finance the High Dam over a competing West German offer, thereby honoring the "disinterestedness" of the U.S.S.R.

The news in June 1961 of the death by torture of the Lebanese Communist leader Ferjallah Helou in a Damascus prison (the Syro-Egyptian union had not yet broken up) was not sufficient to tarnish a dialogue which had been so successfully resumed. Khrushchev's visit to the Nile thus had the quality of an apotheosis.

[2] Notably in a speech delivered in Moscow on May 7, 1959.

This apotheosis did not proceed, however, without several storms. It was quickly known in the circles of the two leaders that Nikita Khrushchev had very harshly criticized the "scientific socialism" of which Abdel Nasser seemed so proud.

"What is this Arabism? What is a politics founded on an ethnic, not to say racist, notion? For a socialist, there are not 'Arabs and others,' there is 'the working class and others.' You ought not to be the ally, the supporter, or the comrade of any Yemeni or Moroccan, but of the Yemeni proletariat, the Casablanca worker. . . ."

The storm of abuse was harsh. President Nasser's collaborators hardly echoed his response. All that appeared publicly was the discrepancy in their views concerning Israel, which the visitor refused "in principle" to condemn, remembering that there were revolutionary elements of a proletariat to be found there too, indeed closer to true revolution than King Idris or the Sheikh of Kuwait.

Three years later, on the eve of the Six-Day War (in April 1967), Leonid Brezhnev declared to some East Berlin interlocutors:

Nasser is a bit mad in matters of ideology. But he is a good man and has proven to us that we could count on him. . . . We have certainly had to grant him several sacrifices, such as the fact that he persecutes Egyptian Communists. . . . But when the Arab masses realize their real interests, we will no longer have need of any Nasser. . . .[3]

Did later events modify the viewpoint of the Secretary General of the Communist Party of the Soviet Union?

.   .   .

[3] Erwin Weit (interpreter for Walter Ulbricht), *Ostblock Intern,* Hamburg, 1970, p. 165.

This "socialist" chief of state broke the landed aristocracy, put the mercantile bourgeoisie on the defensive, created an unrivaled militarized public sector—although the private sector in 1964 controlled more than sixty per cent of the total national revenue—gave to the "landless" fifteen per cent of the arable rural domain, and assured undesirable advancement to the salaried workers of the industrial sector, to whom the way to ownership (or what Gaullism calls the way to "participation") was now open. But had he accomplished the two tasks which all consistent revolutionaries assign themselves: collective development and modification of social relationships? The period before the great crisis of 1967, which opened the phase of the "1200 days," must be considered separately since such profound modifications occurred in the relations between the leader and the masses and in the immediate objectives of the leadership. But, aside from this, one might say that the *Raïs* had really destroyed an ancient social system and built a new system of production.

Let us isolate three contributions of Nasserism to see what benefits a collectivity, in principal "socialist," might have derived from them: agrarian reform, the construction of the High Dam, and industrialization. Gamal Abdel Nasser marked each one of these accomplishments with his seal and presented it as a major means to change Egypt and the Egyptians.

What of agrarian reform? When he spoke to us of it at the end of 1953, and again in early 1956, the *bikbashi* Abdel Nasser presented it not so much as the regime's answer to social injustice and poverty and the peasants' hunger for land, but as a political operation, aimed at destroying feudalism and bringing about the transference of Egyptian capital from land to industry. This was a strategic attitude toward development rather than that of a Boy Scout in pursuit of promotion. And it is true that the objectives were reached in both areas.

"The agrarian reform of 1952," wrote Mahmud Hussein,

"is the only factor accelerating the capitalist transition which occurred in the course of the fifties."[4]

But the same authors maintain that neither the first agrarian law of 1952, nor even the second of 1961, truly modified class relations in the rural Egyptian world. From their point of view, the principal result of these measures was to swell the small ownership sector while diminishing that of the small tenants, and to substitute relationships of authority exercised by the representative of the state government for those previously exercised by the latifundiaries. This view is limited, but not without validity. Below we offer three sketches or accounts of the new life initiated in the countryside by the Nasserian reforms.

In June 1956, Simonne Lacouture visited the village of Ussim, not far from Cairo. She found a rich settlement, on fertile land; and the harvest that year had been excellent. She noticed a group of fellahin who, they said, worked for the *omdeh,* head of the village and representative of the government; she asked how much they earned. "Twelve piasters for the men, eight for the women, five for the children." (Between one franc and 50 centimes per day, or nearly fifty per cent below the legal rate.) At less than thirty kilometers from the capital, the representative of the government thus violated the elementary provisions of the agrarian reform!

Two years later, President Gamal declared: "We must not forget those who live in the country...." Forthwith the daily *Al-Goumhouriya* began a series of stories on rural life. Nefissa Harak visited the village of Mushtuhur in the Kalubieh. It was provided with one of the famous "group units" which the agrarian law had created. They surrounded the sanitary centers, the local agency of reform. The inhabitants gave the following testimony:

[4] Mahmud Hussein *et al., La Lutte des classes en Egypte de 1945 à 1968,* Paris, 1969, 1971, p. 221.

Mohammed Raha: "The unit? It's a colony exploited by its personnel. . . ."

Ehsan Abd al-Aziz: "Two of my three children are dead after having been treated there. I will never return. . . ."

Abdel Rahim Mahmud: "A group unit? I have never heard of it. . . ."

In 1963, Eric Rouleau, investigating for *Le Monde,* spoke with a fellah who revealed to him that the rent he was paying was twice the ceiling fixed by law. Why did he not complain? "Who would protect me against the owner, so powerful in the village and his possible accomplices? The *maamur* (police superintendent), the *omdeh* (mayor) and the *ghaffir* (rural policeman) would have at their disposal a thousand ways to make me pay for my rashness. . . ." Perhaps in order to restore some order to this mess, the national lands should quite simply have been nationalized, as Mohammed Ali had done at the beginning of the nineteenth century. To this question, asked by *Le Monde's* special envoy, Gamal Abdel Nasser answered:

"The fellah is too individualistic, too attached to his secular dream of acquiring a plot of land to agree to such a measure. . . . Besides, the traditional mistrust of the fellah with respect to his government is such that we ought to avoid giving him the impression that we are seeking to make of him a state functionary. . ."[5]

"What would therefore be the solution?"

"Industrialization."

This was, to be sure, the key idea of Nasser's reign, the great hope of the class of bourgeois entrepreneurs, of the Third Estate with or without uniform which had chosen statism because it seemed to be a shortcut toward modern development as much as for reasons of egalitarianism or social

[5] *Le Monde,* September 18, 1963.

justice. This was the motivation for the Five-Year Plan of 1960, whose objective was to "double the national revenue in ten years." In this figure could be found an echo of Egyptian romanticism, and of the kind of propaganda which ends by getting caught in its own trap.

In his speech of July 23, 1963, Abdel Nasser asserted that industrial investment had tripled since the beginning of the regime. Yet this claim was true only if limited to public investments. In one of the speeches of his presidential campaign, in March 1965, the *Raïs* maintained that "the work force was now composed fifty per cent by industrial workers." As a statement concerning only the heads of families this was almost true. In the same speech, Nasser emphasized the building of heavy industry, which was to be at the origin of what he called the "great thrust." This is the *industrie industrialisante* theme which is found in most people's democracies and in Algiers.

"In 1970," added the *Raïs*, "we will have heavy industries; we will manufacture our own machines, and no longer have to pay for them abroad, we will have accepted the challenge of economic independence: already the iron industry and automobile manufacturing are pointing the way...." This was merely vain propaganda. With and without him, we have visited several times the metallurgical complex at Helwan, at the gates of Cairo, which the spokesmen of the regime call simply "iron and steel."

The Helwan factory was built to develop Egypt's richest resource (before the petroleum discoveries of 1966), the iron ore on the banks of the Red Sea, which was evaluated at 130 million tons with a grade of forty-four per cent iron. The West German firm Demag obtained the contract for the construction after an ardent dispute. Using imported coke—which forced its cost very high—this enterprise produced almost 500,000 tons in 1969. (In official circles, there was talk of doubling this production in 1972.) It was a prestige enterprise, since the price of this steel was higher than that which either of the two Germanies could have granted Egypt. But accession to independence does not come without such acts of assertions, not to mention the role of training school which such a modern enterprise could play in a country on the threshold of heavy industry.

More serious than the propagandistic aspect of this industrialization was the dependence that it entailed as a result of large foreign investments. One might well think that the establishment of state control over the economy would have allowed the *Raïs* to assure the financing of a large part of the industrial effort. From 1952 to 1965, the national investment in the area of industry doubled, whereas the public investment quadrupled. These are modest figures in the light of the immensity of the projects and the volume of production. In 1966, after the Second Five-Year Plan had been in operation for one year, Premier Ali Sabri confided to a foreign diplomat that the plan had been carried out 150 per cent in the services sector, that is, the swelling of the bureaucracy, but only 50 per cent in the production sector.

The result was an impressive public debt, which on the eve of the Six-Day War rose to more than 500 million pounds (6 billion francs). This was the equivalent of two years' worth of exports, at a rate of growth estimated by the international experts of the International Bank at about four per cent in 1967, for the last decade (the Five-Year Plan of 1965 fixed it at seven per cent).

But would not all these factors in the problem of Egyptian industrialization be changed by the use of the new energy provided by the High Dam? As soon as the Aswan turbines could furnish cheap and abundant electrical energy, would production not experience the "great thrust" announced in 1965 by Gamal Abdel Nasser?

The construction of the Sadd el-Ali was an admirable achievement. This dam, which stopped the Nile upstream from Aswan, created an artificial lake 600 kilometers long and containing 130 billion m^3 of water (15 times the capacity of Lake Annecy). An expected increase of arable Egyptian lands on the order of thirty per cent (allowing rapid development of the cultivation of rice, a decisive element in raising the standard of living and the nutritional balance of the Egyptian people), the furnishing of ten billion kilowatt-hours of energy, the production of nitrogenous fertilizers corresponding to the enormous needs of agriculture, growth of national revenue estimated at 234 billion—these are prodigious figures, and they were not the only products of a grand dream. A mass of stones and sand equal to twenty-seven times the pyramid of Cheops was thrown into the Nile to tame it: what Egyptian chief of state would not have been proud of this great work? Gamal Abdel Nasser had done it, and brought it to a successful conclusion. The constructions were being completed at the time of his death.

But the debt remained enormous and this giant instrument, whose vices had long been denounced—the evaporation of the water stored in the lake, the mud in the reservoir, the blocking of fertilizing silt at Aswan—would only be worth what the Raïs's successors would make of it. But this was not important; to undertake the construction and to conquer material obstacles and political adversaries took formidable courage. To do all this Nasser had risked the worst in 1956, and subjected Egypt to an indebtedness for which Moscow would make her pay in many ways. Only history, here as in other domains, shall be the judge.

But while awaiting this verdict, how can we not ascribe credit to Nasserism for the Aswan pyramid?

Planning, accelerated production, the recovery and development of the national fortune—these were the noble objectives
which this "socialism" envisioned but did not attain. But what
can we say of that other aspect of the Nasserian plan, the
transformation of society by the "resorption" of classes, set
forth in the speeches of 1962 and 1965?

If the major objective of the military system was solely
what was announced by three of the six principles of 1951,
that is, the destruction of feudalism, one may say that Nasser
accomplished his task. From the agrarian reform of 1952 to
that of 1961; from the Egyptianizing measures of 1956 to
the series of state control measures of June–July, and then of
November 1961; from the Five-Year Plan of 1960 to that
of 1965, one may say that a certain form of ownership and
exploitation was smashed and liquidated. There is no longer
in Egypt a landed aristocracy nor a monopolistic capitalism of
the Ahmed Abbud type. State capitalism—with occasional
grace by some cooperativist formula, half-socialist, half-popu-
list in inspiration—prevailed.

The problem is to find out whether this transfer replaced
the caste of pashas and beys with a new dominant class, that
of a state bourgeoisie which gave rise, according to a good
many Marxist analysts, to the Nasserian regime. Under the
impetus of the *Raïs,* did the state constitute itself as a supreme
entity, mediating class conflicts in order to avoid a revolutionary struggle which it frowned upon and which it attempted
to avert? Was it merely the secular arm of the triumphant
state bourgeoisie, which had become in its turn exploitive, a
Third Estate with Nasser as its Bonaparte?

The existence of this new class cannot be denied. It had
not only powerful economic foundations and means of action,
but even a style of life. It emanated perhaps from the army,
which in 1956 provided the essential levers of the economy
after having received its due share of the "machine room" of

the state apparatus; perhaps from that enormous, proliferating civil bureaucracy whose total strength was estimated at almost 1½ million people; or perhaps from those private or semi-private entrepreneurs who were widely stimulated after the 1956 eviction of foreign capital. In any case, a new social category was formed, and with it new styles, new awareness, new values and ambitions.

Although a product of the Nasserian enterprise, this class was looked on with the greatest mistrust by the *Raïs*. Witness the description he gave of it in a speech delivered in July 1961, made famous in a paraphrase by Mohammed Hassanein Heykal. According to President Nasser, everything would proceed from the nationalization measures of 1956, which made the state the principal entrepreneur, and from the Egyptianization measures, which would put private enterprise in the hands of local capitalists (the latter often serving as fronts for the old foreign ringleaders). It was then that the beneficiaries of the second operation would come together and form an alliance in order to obtain the best rate of profit from the principal entrepreneur, the state. On this basis was to be built the new bourgeoisie.

What the *Raïs* did not say, or what he said very discreetly, was that the alliance was not limited to the "new capitalists," and that the representatives of that "new entrepreneur," the state, expected to receive their share of the system (before the elimination or repression of the *nouveaux riches* in 1961). Thus the two partners of 1956 had dissolved into one: the new bourgeoisie.

In 1966 there occurred an almost tragic demonstration of this ascendancy of the state bourgeoisie over Nasserian "socialism." The *Raïs* wished to "create an example" after the assassination in the village of Kamshish of an intellectual of the Left, a native of the region named Salah Hussein. To put a halt to his revolutionary activities—propaganda, agitation, and appeal to the consciousness of the fellahin against the owners—it was said that the feudal interests of the region had had him eliminated by a hired killer. They were acquitted by a semimilitary tribunal.

Gamal Abdel Nasser wanted action and violently denounced the "counterrevolutionary bourgeoisie." But three weeks later, harassed by the higher ranks in the public sector, the president announced that a meeting with the leaders of the "socialist economy" had made possible "a new thrust to production." From exemplary justice he had moved on to necessary efficiency. It was a deeply significant confusion.

Could the new class and the firm control of the police permit the new statism to blossom into socialism? In a remarkable article in *Les Temps Modernes* in April 1963,[6] Maxime Rodinson, in search of reasoned hope, wrote:

> Under the shell of authoritarianism, and in a certain sense, thanks to it, forces are being forged and prepared which will not always accept its yoke. It is the destiny of progressive dictatorships to produce their own gravediggers. Among the Egyptian masses, thanks to the regime, an increasingly numerous stratum of increasingly varied social origins is acceding to culture. Among the values which it is learning, albeit protected by judicious restrictions, is that of liberty. And the latter, it is known, has the habit of disengaging itself from any matrix, and once laid bare, of offering man the most irresistible temptations.

This "shell of authoritarianism" was broken or cracked by nothing less than the painful fracture of the Six-Day War, four years later. At that time, under waves of violent pressure from the masses, there came about a still-unaccomplished attempt to disengage the living accomplishments of Nasserism from the old "matrix," and to lay them bare.

[6] "L'Egypte nassérienne au miroir marxiste."

PART SIX

Confronting Israel

24

---◦∞◦---

Colonel Abdel Nasser
and Captain Cohen

"At that time, I wondered why I nurtured this enthusiasm for a land which I had not yet seen; I heard only the echoes of my feelings. Afterward, I acquired a sort of understanding at the military school where I learned the history of Palestine in particular and of the region in general. . . . When the Palestinian crisis arose, I had the firm conviction that the combat in Palestine was not a combat on foreign soil, and that it was not at all a question of sentiment but of the duty of legitimate self-defense."

"In 1948, we became entangled in a war which was not ours, because of the British politics in the region, and because of the Arab leaders who collaborated with the British, thus betraying their peoples."

These two statements are by Gamal Abdel Nasser. The first is a passage from *Philosophy of Revolution*,[1] the second is reported by Yeruham Cohen, the Israeli officer who was said to have had long conversations with Lieutenant Colonel Abdel Nasser during the truce of autumn 1948.[2] Although there can be no doubt that a typical Syrian, Lebanese, or even Iraqi feels immediately receptive to anything concerning

---

[1] Gamal Abdel Nasser, *Philosophie de la révolution,* Cairo, 1954, p. 48.

[2] Yeruham Cohen, *Leor Hayom Ubamakhshah,* Tel Aviv, 1969, p. 201 (translation by J. Mandelstam).

Palestine, which many Arab nationalists see as a historical
part of Syria, the "Palestinian cause" was not really felt to be
an integral part of the "Egyptian cause" until the fairly recent
creation of the Arab League in 1945, and the appointment
of an Egyptian, Abderrahman Azzam Pasha, as secretary
general.

This charming personage contributed greatly to persuading
the rulers in Cairo that any settlement of the Palestinian question made without Egyptian participation must favor either
Zionist expansion or the seizure of Palestine by the Hashemite royal family. Formerly, the question of the Jews establish-
ing themselves between the Jordan River and the sea had
occupied a secondary place in the order of national emergen-
cies. It had certainly provoked reactions of anxiety, discontent,
and anger, but these sentiments began to take a bellicose turn
only with the overwhelming propaganda campaign waged by
the Muslim Brethren after 1945. This campaign received
behind-the-scenes encouragement from the palace and the
British, who saw a great many advantages in this unfurling of
emotions, and above all a useful diversion from the fundamental problems of Egypt. Even taking into account the burst
of racial hatred which was at the source of the attack on a
Cairo synagogue on November 2, 1945, anti-Semitism was
undoubtedly less virulent in Egypt than in most Catholic
countries.

The adoption of the partition plan by the United Nations
on November 29, 1947 (following the speech by Andrei
Gromyko on May 14, 1947, considered by international opinion to be a "second Balfour Declaration"), suddenly quickened
the anti-Zionist fever in those sectors of Egyptian opinion
where it was already rampant, and spread it to other milieux.
This was further aggravated by the fact that intrigues within
the League had welded Cairo policy to that of the Grand
Mufti of Jerusalem, Haj Amin el-Husseini, leader of the

intransigent Palestinian faction which appeared to be the only obstacle to the ambitions of the Emir Abdallah of Trans-jordan and the Baghdad Hashemites.

Consequently, the leading wing of Egyptian nationalism, which, though little influenced by the position of the U.S.S.R., had outlined the first elements of an anti-imperialist strategy, began to mobilize against the imminent consolidation of the Jewish state. Although part of the Egyptian Left followed Moscow's example, seeing both the ferment of progress and the menace of imperialism in the Jewish enterprise, the major-ity of young intellectuals and military men persisted in seeing there only the hand of Great Britain, attempting to consoli-date in the north a position contested on the Suez Canal.

Such considerations, as well as the belief—expressed in Nasser's pamphlet cited above—in a right to "legitimate de-fense" by the peoples of the area, led some Free Officers to a clearly hostile attitude toward the creation of the Hebrew state. Upon the announcement in New York of the adoption of the partition plan, Colonel Ahmed Abdel Aziz, one of the rare high-ranking officers respected by Gamal and his team, began to recruit volunteers. Nasser's intimate friend Kamaled-din Hussein left to join him in Palestine. But Captain Abdel Nasser hesitated. Though he went to offer his services to the Mufti, who rejected them, he recounts in his *Philosophy of Revolution* that he weighed his desire to participate in the struggle against the urgency of preparing for his exam at the officers training school. If the war was really vital for Egypt, these preoccupations seem curious in such a headstrong and ardent patriot.

Finally on May 16, 1948, he left, already a well-trained officer, designated by the command for the Negev front. But this episode can only be situated meaningfully if one notes to what extent Egypt's entry into the war appeared to be a sudden initiative taken only by the king. Ahmed Nari Pasha, a member of the Egyptian Defense Council, wrote five years later that this eminently responsible body was not consulted, nor was the question even raised when the council met on May 14, on the eve of Egypt's entry into the war.[3]

Gamal Abdel Nasser, promoted to the rank of lieutenant colonel upon entering the field, prepared for battle with the exaltation proper to any officer called to exercise the profession he has chosen and who does not yet know what war is really like. We have described the evolution of his state of mind during the year 1948, from his first contact with the reality of combat to his wound and eventual defeat.[4]

We are primarily concerned here with the glimpse of Zionism and of Israel which Gamal formed for himself in the course both of the battles—which revealed an authentic Israeli force, the Haganah, that behaved as a national army and not as the mercenary of a colonial power—and of his relations with various Jewish officers.

It was during the encirclement of the Fallouga pocket, where he was commanding the Sixth Battalion in October 1948, that Gamal Abdel Nasser had the opportunity to meet Captain Cohen, who had been designated by General Yigal Allon, the commander of the Negev front, to enter into negotiations with Colonel Taha, the commander of the besieged forces, with the intention of suspending hostilities. Abdel Nasser with Yeruham Cohen had been appointed to prepare a meeting between Allon and Taha. He pursued the dialogue during the truce which followed soon after. And it would seem he was considered the best "Israelist" of the army, for he was sent again a year later, after the Rhodes armistice, to attend to the burial of the Fallouga victims, which allowed him a new meeting with Yeruham Cohen.

These exchanges were sufficiently cordial to justify a subse-

3 Published by *La Bourse égyptienne,* July 25, 1953.
4 See Part Two, Chapter 7, "Adventure in Palestine."

quent exchange of gifts, at least from the Israeli to the Egyptian. Ten years later, in any case, President Abdel Nasser showed a visitor, with a satisfaction devoid of irony, a pen which his former Fallouga interlocutor had just sent him, and he spoke of him without malevolence in his various evocations of the Palestine war.

The description of the young Egyptian commander given by Captain Yeruham Cohen was frankly favorable:

I found in him a personal charm, a frankness, an obstinate patriotism. . . . He was interested in the social problems of his country. It was manifestly clear that he understood and approved of our struggle against the British. He was well acquainted with the combats of the Haganah and, on the basis of the Zionist struggle against the English, was making an effort at understanding the possibilities offered by a mobilization of the masses in a resistance movement. . . . Without doubt, he envied us.[5]

Was this a matter of a purely technical curiosity, a unique attempt to extort "recipes" from an enemy? Such an interpretation seems a bit ungenerous. In fact, the exchanges between Yeruham Cohen and Gamal Abdel Nasser rose to a political level and sometimes even took on a confidential tone. This is how the Israeli captain evoked Nasser's reaction when he spoke to him of the kibbutzim, agricultural development, and the social services of the Jewish Agency:

In the course of our conversations, it appeared to me that Nasser had wondered why this could not be done in Egypt, why the Egyptians should not profit from our scientific and social experiments in the domains of agriculture, industry, education and health. After I had told him of the difficulties and obstacles which we had to surmount in the era of British power, he became more and more persuaded of

[5] *Haaretz*, January 30, 1953 (translation by J. Mandelstam).

these possibilities. He engaged in comparisons of similar problems, and perhaps he found, in certain cases, correspondences or identities between the problems of the two nations.[6]

In any case, the Egyptian officer did not refrain, in these interviews with an adversary, from severely judging his own government, which, according to him, had allowed itself "to be led by the English into a war which was not its own. . . . They had pushed Egypt into a struggle against Israel in order to divert her from freeing the Suez Canal and the Sudan from British domination."[7]

The duality of Abdel Nasser's sentiments at the beginning of the campaign has been mentioned. It could only have become more acute in contact with men and events. This discovery of Israel was corroborated by intense severity toward the Arab Jordanian allies, and even to the Palestinians, and by an unreserved condemnation of the Egyptian leadership. Was Nasser tempted to recognize the cogency of the theses of most of his friends on the Left, on the artificiality of the war and the real content of the Jewish state? The fact is that what was for him a working hypothesis even before the war had become fact. Everything had to begin with a change in the Cairo regime. The leitmotif of his actions would be the phrase spoken by Colonel Ahmed Azziz to Salah Salem and Kamaleddin Hussein: "The real fight is in Egypt!"

And while at Rhodes, the Israeli and Egyptian officers separated after signing the armistice convention of February 24, 1949, saying, "Reunion in three months for the peace treaty." Gamal Abdel Nasser and the Free Officers simply buried the Israeli question for years.

In their clandestine literature—tracts and newspaper col-

[6] *Ibid.*

[7] Robert Aron, *Nouveaux Dossiers de l'histoire contemporaine,* Paris, 1971, p. 239.

laborations—the question hardly appeared, save as one of the quarrels with the palace, accused of having delivered "defective armaments" to the army engaged in Palestine. Certainly the question of the justice of the 1948 engagement was never raised, as in the conversation with Yeruham Cohen. The Palestinian theme remained very marginal.

When, at the beginning of 1952, "Kim" Roosevelt's men made contact with the Free Officers and probed their intentions, in order to discover which external adversary could consolidate and animate the Egyptian nationalism which the CIA wished to make into a bulwark against communism, they heard no mention of Israel. In an answer transmitted to Roosevelt, Nasser assured him that if the objective of his group was indeed revenge against the humiliations it had suffered, their rancor was directed first against "their own superior officers, then other Arabs, then the English, then the Israelis—in that order!"[8]

25

Prelude to Gaza

Of course, the wound of Palestine continued to fester in the defeated. The manifesto signed in the name of Mohammed Naguib and read by Anwar el-Sadat on the morning of July 23, 1952, the preface to the new regime, makes clear reference

[8] Miles Copeland, *The Game of Nations,* New York, 1969, p. 56.

to the war of 1948. In the second sentence, it recalled that the "dissolution" of the power which "affected the army itself" was "one of the causes of our defeat in Palestine." But at no moment was revenge spoken of; mention was made only of "defending Egypt."

One of the five committees then created by the junta to lay the foundations of a new foreign policy was entrusted with the mission of studying questions "relative to Palestine." But what was striking in the demonstrations of the new ruling group was their discretion on the subject of Israel.

From Mohammed Naguib, who, on a visit to Gaza on August 23, 1952, was satisfied to express good wishes for "the independence of Palestine," to Salah Salem, who declared to Pierre de Bethmann: "Israel? We are not seeking a quarrel with anyone—but let Israel not seek to exceed its boundaries,"[1] the climate at the beginning of the regime was truly one of non-aggression. And in May 1953, when John Foster Dulles was received—quite coldly—in Cairo, Cyprus radio, controlled by the English, pointed out that "Israel was not even mentioned during the interviews." Richard Crossman, the future labor minister and "notorious Zionist" who had come to Cairo at this time without much hope of being received by the young officers, recounts that after several days of waiting he was greeted with a lively cordiality by Nasser, who asked him to be his personal guest.

"At that time," recounts Crossman, "he judged that Israel ought not to distract him from the problems of Egypt, those of the social revolution. He was neither anti-Semitic nor even really pro-Arab until Bandung and the break with the West. It was only then that the chances of a rapid Nasser–Ben Gurion agreement seemed to me to decrease. . . ."[2]

On July 23, 1953, on the occasion of the first anniversary

[1] *Tribune des Nations,* March 13, 1953.
[2] *New Statesman,* October 10, 1970.

of the arms coup, Naguib and Salah Salem held a press conference before more than one hundred foreign journalists. Nasser, recovering from an appendectomy, attended in silence. One of us asked Naguib what the chances were for an agreement with the English. Salah Salem answered: "Egypt refuses the conditions, set by London: membership in a defense pact including Great Britain, with whom we must first settle our differences over Suez, and also Israel, with whom we are still at war from a technical point of view, because of occupied and contested territory."

This formulation was bizarre and ambiguous enough to allow many interpretations. Was it only a question of the Negev? Was this the only object of contestation between the two countries?

This reference to Israel was one of the rare occasions during the first two years of the new regime when the problem even arose. Never, or almost never, did the subject enter into our conversations either with Naguib, Salem, or Sadat or during the two or three times with Nasser before an interview in October 1954. Everything occurred as though the canal and its occupation by the English blocked all other perspectives—and as though Israel, as long as it were not mentioned, could pursue its far-off existence. Was this the "let us think of it always, speak of it never!" of Gambetta on the subject of Alsace-Lorraine? Witnesses to this stormy silence, we dared not break it to learn more.

In Israel, the Free Officers movement was greeted favorably. Since July 25, David Ben-Gurion had wished success to Mohammed Naguib, without forgetting, moreover, that Premier Aly Maher had had various contacts, from 1936 to 1942, with the leaders of the Jewish Agency. On August 18, the Israeli premier increased his overtures toward the "new" Egypt. Not a week went by that the Tel Aviv press, notably *Haaretz,* did not make allusion to the possibilities of peaceful settlement, sometimes alluding to Mahmud Fawzi, then Egyptian Ambassador to London, sometimes even to Mohammed Naguib, who apparently did recognize in private the existence of "secret contacts."

It is certain that at the end of 1952 discussions took place between official representatives of the two countries. But they were of brief duration. In an interview granted the day after the death of Gamal Abdel Nasser,[3] David Ben-Gurion declared: "Naguib was a good person. He was intelligent and gentle. Today more than ever, I think that we could have made peace with him. . . ." But whether it was because of one man or the other, nothing took shape during the eighteen months when the general exercised nominal power.

It was, nevertheless, at this time, on the occasion of the visit to Cairo by Ralph Bunche, assistant secretary general of the United Nations, that negotiations toward an exchange were begun: peace in return for a band of territory which would permit Egypt and Jordan to touch, with right of passage to Elath granted to the Israelis.[4]

But it was when Naguib was at the pinnacle of power, in May 1953, and on his personal initiative that the first step was taken to reopen the question of Egyptian "withdrawal" from the Palestinian affair: the creation of the "Voice of the Arabs," a radio station whose programs were to infuriate, often understandably, both the Israelis and colonial authorities, from Casablanca to Aden.

At the hour when Gamal Abdel Nasser—having signed the evacuation treaty with the British, and having openly taken on

---

[3] *Actualité,* October 1970, interview conducted by Philippe Granier-Raymond.

[4] Jean Mandelstam, "La Palestine dans la politique de Gamal Abdel Nasser, 1952–1955," doctoral dissertation, Paris, 1970, p. 137.

the responsibilities of power—was to inherit the Palestinian dossier and regard it in the light of his new freedom of action, how might one characterize the Palestinian policy of the new regime in relation to that of the old? Let us first note that during the first interview which Nasser granted us, the word "Israel" was not even pronounced. We spoke above all about North Africa and of the repercussions of that crisis, which was worsening then, on Franco-Egyptian relations.

In his dissertation devoted to the Palestinian policy of Nasser from 1952 to 1955, Jean Mandelstam characterized the officers' strategy with respect to their approach toward Israel in two words: "circumspect and rational."[5]

This was true. Until February 1955, when circumspection and reason would no longer have currency, for reasons in part unrelated to the *bikbashi,* the Nasserian policy was the same as that of the early days of the regime, with its oscillation between reserve and feverishness, moderation and obstinacy. During a visit to the University of Cairo at the beginning of 1954, we witnessed Naguib, Abdel Nasser, and Salah Salem received by actual jeering and the cry "give us arms for the canal and for Palestine. . . ." To which Salem retorted: "At your age, we too were demanding arms to throw us out!" This was a realistic, though unpopular, statement.

By pressuring the British to subscribe to an evacuation by a contract favorable to Cairo, did the Americans hope to acquire the right to make Gamal Abdel Nasser settle with Israel? This was undoubtedly so. But on this point hardly anyone listened to Jefferson Caffery and William Lakeland. Even supposing that he was persuaded of the merits of the Washington proposals, which remains to be proven, the Egyptian leader, who, for having signed the agreement with London, had just escaped a volley fired in Alexandria, was not very eager to plunge into a still more perilous negotia-

[5] *Ibid.,* p. 121.

tion. And yet the last quarter of 1954 did not end before certain interesting attempts had been made.

Israel had given a hostile reception to the Anglo-Egyptian treaty signed on July 27, 1954. This was not because it raised the military curtain which had separated the two war-ring bodies on the canal, but because it carried no clause relating to passage through the Suez Canal of Israeli vessels after the departure of the British "gendarmes."

At dawn on September 28, 1954, a cargo ship flying Israeli colors, the *Bat Galim,* appeared in the waters of Suez: this was a test intended to demonstrate the permanent violation by the Egyptians of the Constantinople Convention. The *Bat Galim* was stopped and examined. But did it then open fire on batteries lining the Suez? Egyptian authorities asserted it did, pointing to the death of two sailors, which an on-the-spot investigation did not enable us to verify (journalists do not always have good eyes . . .). In Cairo, Salah Salem spoke of "unspeakable aggression." But the Egyptian government agreed to receive an international committee of investigation, a gesture of goodwill which seemed, in the final analysis, to make the *Bat Galim* incident a less negative test than it had at first appeared.

It was at this point that two Labor Parliamentarians passed through Cairo: Richard Crossman, already familiar to Nasser, and Maurice Ohrbach, who had come to plead the cause of Jewish spies arrested some time earlier (although Aneurin Bevan told us that any attempt at a settlement between Egypt and Israel seemed to him premature). This was not the view of Crossman or Ohrbach. The latter especially took the oc-casion of his presence in Cairo to establish himself as an intermediary between Nasser and Moshe Sharett. Then pre-mier of Israel, Sharett was known in the Arab world for a plan to repatriate 100,000 refugees—the most courageous gesture ever made by a high, responsible Israeli officer.

These contacts were sanctioned, if not by written documents, at least by reports which were judged interesting by Sharett and his collaborators. An Israeli civil servant, himself involved in another series of contacts, told us earlier of the impression of happy surprise created in Jerusalem by the statements of "hope" and "sympathy" addressed to the premier of Israel by the head of the Egyptian government. Maurice Ohrbach made two trips between Cairo and Jerusalem. No one discouraged him. But other events distracted him from his mission.

At the same period, discussions of at least equal interest were occurring about the Johnston plan, named for the former American cinema magnate entrusted with gaining acceptance by the Israelis and Arabs of a plan for the utilization of the waters of the Jordan and Yarmuk rivers. This would allow a resettling of the Arab refugees to begin. These conversations had presented the Egyptian authorities, as well as the Jordanians, with an opportunity to accept the principle of cooperation on a long-term basis with Israel in sharing the essential water reserves of the region. When I asked the man who was then the director of Arab affairs, and who has now become foreign minister, General Mahmud Ryad, if these parleys had not assumed the value of a *de facto* recognition of the Jewish state, I obtained only an evasive response, but its reserve surprised me.

But the chance for a durable settlement was then lost; it was the Syrian government which caused it to fail. But Israel too must carry part of the responsibility for the failure, for in the course of these exchanges of views, the Tel Aviv government suddenly raised its demands relative to the distribution of the waters to be stored in Lake Tiberias.

Did any possibility of initiating negotiations remain? Alluding to the last Israeli test, to American hopes, to the British feelers, and to the new situation created by the treaty with

London, I put the question to the Egyptian head of state at the end of October 1954. His answer, which was communicated to me in writing, was not encouraging:

> The state of Israel incessantly creates difficulties for the UN observers in the accomplishment of their already arduous tasks. The last of these difficulties to date is the declaration made last week by the Jewish authorities that the observers would no longer be permitted to visit the sites of the frontier incidents. Could such a people really be enamored of peace? Is it possible to believe in such a state?
>
> Finally, the Arabs have a thousand times made known their clear position with regard to the Palestinian problem. They will never renounce it under the pressure of a power, whatever it might be, nor before a maneuver, whatever its scope.

Had all the bridges been burned? The pessimists had fine days ahead of them. On October 1, an Israeli spy ring had been discovered in Cairo, whose nominal authority, a certain "John Darling," was nowhere to be found. Twelve persons were arrested for "Zionist plots"; all were more or less accomplices in ridiculous acts, such as an attempted arson of the American Library of Alexandria, a gesture which probably had as its objective to sow discord between Cairo and Washington. The trial proceeded normally, in the presence of the French consul who had come to advise the principal defendant, Dr. Moussa Marzouk, a Jew of Tunisian origin who was then a French protégé.

Gamal Abdel Nasser declared very sincerely to Roger Baldwin, American president of the International League of the Rights of Man, and to Maurice Ohrbach, that there was no question in this case of the death sentence. On January 27, 1955, however, the death penalty was inflicted on Marzouk and on his accomplice, Samuel Azar. Further steps were taken.

Edgar Faure, then *président du Conseil,* with the chief rabbi of Cairo appealed to the clemency of the *bikbashi-*president. The effort was wasted: on February 1, Marzouk and Azar were legally assassinated in the courtyard of their prison.

This was a heinous gesture, when it was obvious to the head of the Cairo government, as to all observers, that this schoolboy plot in no way endangered the Egyptian state. (The gesture was, moreover, to give rise to the "Lavon affair," named for the Israeli defense minister who had attempted to prevent the special services from becoming involved in this lamentable operation, and had to retire to make way for Ben-Gurion.) It was claimed in the *bikbashi*'s entourage that, having had to hang six Muslim Brethren several weeks earlier to check an authentic and frightful terrorist plot, he could not reprieve the Jewish spies. In various Muslim countries where the hanging of the "brothers" had had a very deleterious effect, the hanging of the Zionists was awaited as a reparation.

Had Marzouk and Azar been the victims of a sordid deal? Many others were to pay as well.

Eight months earlier, the Cairo government had made a serious decision: authorization was given to the Gaza refugees to form commando groups to harass Israeli territory (a gesture which passed almost unnoticed, but which that most perceptive dean of French correspondents in Cairo, Gabriel Dardaud of Agence France-Presse, considered the beginning of a new Israeli-Arab war). On February 28, 1955, a sort of thunderclap struck us from that almost forgotten frontier: at Gaza, an Israeli commando team had just struck twice in one hour, leaving forty-six dead (thirty-seven Egyptian soldiers and nine Palestinian civilians).

General Burns, the head of the UN observers, immediately cabled to New York: "The Israeli army has attacked Gaza." Six days later, the Mixed Armistice Commission spoke of a "premeditated and organized attack committed by order of the Israeli authorities." Once more, as they had done against the Jordanians, in Nahalin, for example, Tel Aviv had recourse to the strategy of massive reprisals to put an end to harassments considered minor by neutral observers.

An investigation held at the site revealed that the violations of the armistice agreements, in the course of the preceding three months, were about even: forty-seven on the Israeli side, fifty-three on the Arab side.

"We acted to prevent war by cutting short the Arab provocations," an Israeli diplomat told us in the course of one of our trips to Paris. But the most authoritative of the neutral observers in Cairo observed that, in his opinion, "the Israeli attack was out of proportion to acts previously committed on either side, and opened a new era, that of wide-scale military operations in a zone which for a long time had only known a festering insecurity."[6]

26

Nasser Speaks

What was the reaction of Gamal Abdel Nasser, the man who had strung streamers across the streets of Cairo carrying the proud inscription: "Lift your head, comrade, the time of humiliation has passed!"

[6] Jean and Simonne Lacouture, *L'Egypte en mouvement,* Paris, 1956–1962, p. 221.

His initial reaction was silence. Nasser and Amer, thus challenged, had just discovered that almost three years after their accession to power, the Egyptian army was even more incapable than in 1948 of facing its neighbor to the northeast. Was Naguib right? For lack of an officers' "return to the barracks" which he had demanded a year earlier, Egypt again found herself unarmed.

The head of the Egyptian government thus accepted his "punishment" in silence. But he prepared a response which was broken down into four acts. The first was the sending to various capitals of arms purchasing missions, of which the most successful is known to have wound up in Prague, with all that followed. The second was his attempt in Bandung to have Israel condemned by the Third World. This attempt ended in only half-success, since Nasser's most influential ally in this matter, Chou En-lai, had preferred to deal tactfully with the irritability of the Indians and Burmese, although he did support a motion satisfactory to Nasser, the spokesman of the Arab world. The third reply of the *bikbashi*-president was the arming of new units of *fedayin* (the word then began to appear in the press); but the most curious of Nasser's reactions was the fourth.

General Burns, head of the UN observers, received an order from the United Nations to summon an Israeli-Arab conference to "avoid recurrence of the border incidents." Nasser suddenly decided, against all expectations, to be represented. And on June 5, he suggested a surprising proposal: the simultaneous retreat of both armed forces by one kilometer on each side from the line of demarcation. Was it a trick of war, given that an acceptance by Tel Aviv would have led the Israelis to evacuate several border kibbutzim, and since the *fedayin* would have been able to avoid this regulation? Who can tell?

Gamal Abdel Nasser's offer was refused, and the negotiations presided over by Burns were broken off in August, when a new battle occurred at Khan Yunis, and in which the responsibility was more evenly shared than at Gaza. To counter his new losses of several score casualties, the Egyptian commander sent into the Israeli territory a commando gang which killed eleven men. The result was an Israeli bombing raid on September 1, in which several score more Egyptian civilians were killed, and then Israel occupied the demilitarized zone of El-Auja and seized the post of Sabha, where the Egyptians left thirty-five dead.

A month after the brief visit which the Egyptian General Staff allowed us to make to Sabha in order to persuade us foreign observers of the brutality of the blows struck against Egypt, I was received by President Gamal Abdel Nasser. Several weeks earlier, John Foster Dulles and Anthony Eden had in turn launched new peace settlement plans. The second of these provoked marked reactions: Her Majesty's prime minister suggested a return to the partition plan of 1947—which would remove from Israel a third of the territory it then controlled.

Aside from the escalation of violence on the border which distressed all observers, the major event of the last three months had been the arms exchange concluded between Cairo and Prague. Certainly Washington was discontented and London anxious. But this operation had with one act established the prestige of the Egyptian leader, "beaten" in Gaza and Sabha, but finally recognized as a masterful player. Let us again listen to him answer the questions which we put to him at the end of the year 1955. This time, from the point of view of his relations with Israel, his internal politics, and the whole of his world strategy, was to be the turning point of the regime; it was the year when Nasserism was remodeled and projected outwards.

Do you estimate that your arms purchases have now made your strength equal to that of Israel?

Yes. When we receive the arms recently bought in Czechoslovakia (and in France) we shall consider that we have caught up with the Israelis in the arms race they began two years ago. The balance of forces will be realized between Israel and Egypt—and I mean Egypt, not the Arab states.

On the basis of the position of strength which you have now acquired, can you envision a negotiation for a peaceful settlement of the Palestinian question?

At first, this balance of forces should allow for the re-establishment of calm at the borders, for until now it was because Israel felt herself to be stronger that she unleashed hostile actions against us. Now that she knows she can no longer do this with impunity, we may hope for peace.

And after this?

In my estimation, the basis of negotiations proposed by Mr. Eden, the 1947 partition plan of the United Nations, is the best.

But do you not find that the fact that the Arabs rejected this plan in 1947 and waged war to prevent its application weakens their position should they now invoke it again?

It was not the Arabs who prevented the realization of the plan in 1947 and incited the Palestine conflict, but rather the British. It was they who had received an international mandate to administer and bring about the evolution of an Arab Palestine. Now from 1920 to 1947 they favored the expansion of Zionism and, when they withdrew in 1947, they left face to face on the lines of partition fixed by the United Nations, the Zionists, who were actively arming themselves, and the Arabs, who were simple, unarmed peasants. This was to offer all of Palestine to

Zionism, and it was against the factual violation of the spirit of partition that the Arab states took up arms in 1948.

It is now clear that the Israelis want to make peace on the lines of the armistice guaranteed by the declaration of the Big Three of 1950, and by you on the basis of 1947. Could one envision finding a middle term between these two objectives, for example by granting the Arabs a band of territory along the Gulf of Aqaba, which would permit communication between Jordan and Egypt, that is, the re-unification of the Arab world?

In fact, the reunification of the Arab world is indispensable. The present division is unnatural. We must re-establish our lost unity. In fact, I insist on repeating that we can only negotiate if two problems are solved: the refugees, and the borders. The expulsion of a million inhabitants from Palestine and their replacement by new inhabitants is a phenomenon without precedent in history. The Germans did not do this to you, nor did Genghis Khan in the countries he conquered. The refugees must be given the right to choose between returning to their homes or receiving proper indemnities.

But all would choose to return to their country. . . .

No. Because the condition of second-class citizenship which Arabs now experience in the state of Israel will not encourage them to return. Many would prefer to settle down in another Arab country with a good indemnity.

But if the vast majority desires to return, is it physically possible for such human masses to return to a state of a million and a half inhabitants?

Why not? I don't know whether it was Mr. Sharett or Mr. Ben-Gurion who declared several days ago that Israel was preparing to receive a million additional immigrants. In this case, does not the right of entry belong above all to the first occupants?

Don't you think that the Johnston plan could permit a resolution of the problem, if the refugees were reinstalled in Arab Palestine, that is, on their national soil?

The Johnston plan can only provide a subsidiary answer to the problem. We supported it to show our goodwill.

Sincerely, Mr. President, should one not believe that in the mind of all Arabs, Israel must sooner or later disappear as a state, or at least be reduced until it is only a kind of Jewish Vatican?

No. As for us, we demand only that this state not violate the rights of Arabs. We want these rights to be recognized.

Even at the price of peace in the Middle East, and even of all peace?

We wish for peace, here and in the world, you know this. But why must it always be the lot of the same small nations to sacrifice themselves to the general interest?

The man had matured since our last discussions, the year before. The assassination attempt at Alexandria; the hanging of the Muslim Brethren and of Marzouk; Gaza; Bandung; the arms . . . all had been profound experiences.

He was soon to be thirty-eight, his temples were graying, his slight paunch had grown really heavy. He had lost that country boy awkwardness in uniform which had made him resemble the trembling and serious character of *L'Ame retrouvée* (The Spirit Recaptured), a novel by Tewfik el-Hakim—for a long time among his bedside books. This was a public man who, in four years, had finished his apprenticeship in cynicism, had struggled a great deal, lied a great deal, and acquired a formidable mastery. He was preparing to be elected chief of state by 99.9 per cent of Egyptians: he already knew the figure, having lost his illusions.

His authority was redoubtable. He knew his dossiers, and had not only learned to lie but also to tell the truth (sometimes), which was more difficult. If his arguments were contestable, he lived in contestation. Each step, each word, each intonation by the man who wished to impose an independent Egypt upon the world, and himself upon Egypt, was strewn with ambushes, mines and counteroffensives. He now knew this, even while still skillfully practicing the art of dialectical complicity, which made him the mirror of his interlocutor, and his interlocutor a false victor caught in his nets of successive, if not simultaneous, sincerities. He beat himself unmercifully, a jouster beaten black and blue, ready to exploit his successes to the hilt, and to camouflage his disasters.

We no longer found, in these last days of 1955, the young man flaming with suppressed anger who said "no" to the masters of the game. We discovered the master of a game which was hardly any different. And he still had so much revenge to wreak.

27

Peace Feelers and Preventive War

At the moment when the dramatic year 1956 opened, a year which was to see yet another armed confrontation only eight years after the first, the arguments of Cairo and Tel Aviv remained widely separated, but not to the point of destroying all hope for long-term conversations. Egypt and Israel were separated, among other, even more profound causes, by the gulf of a war won by one country and lost by the other.

In 1948, Israel had increased by more than thirty per cent the lands allotted to her by the United Nations partition plan. When Eden spoke of a return to the borders of 1947, Ben-Gurion, in the name of ninety-nine per cent of the Israelis, countered: "There can be no question of redividing an inch of the land won with our blood!" As to the refugees, Sharett's suggestion to accept 100,000 in staggered waves seemed abandoned by those who had just regained power, headed by Moshe Dayan.

On the Egyptian side, there was scarcely any more talk of "throwing the Jews into the sea." But who really admitted the existence of the Hebrew state? Who, aside from certain leftist organizations (the Partisans of Peace, for example) had done so clearly and without reservation? Cairo put the question of the Negev first, appealing to the 1947 plan. This was an understatement. When Gamal Abdel Nasser spoke to us as he did of a lasting and recognized state—the border question aside—he was taking a risk and was careful not to let such an interview be reprinted in his own press. But he also knew very well that these statements committed him and meant that he was inclined to fight politically to reduce the Israeli problem rather than militarily to destroy it.

In fact, at this time, Nasser's "Palestinian policy" could not be better defined than by the formula "neither peace nor war." Each term of the option involved too many risks for him to assume before consolidating his military strength, his system of alliances, and the solidity of his regime. This does not mean that he was prohibited from preparing one or the other alternative in the long run. This zealot for Egyptian independence could not tolerate having one or the other path closed to him. Hence at the beginning of 1956 he undertook

several arms purchases at once, outfitted the *fedayin,* tightened
Arab alliances, and extended his political feelers toward Israel
at the same time.

Let us consider these political feelers. In the month of
June 1970, in his villa in Tel Aviv, crumbling under the
weight of memories, David Ben-Gurion, tossing his white
mane before the copy of Michelangelo's David which seemed
to keep watch over his aged sleep, spoke to us of Nasser. "A
statesman, yes. But too big a liar ..." And he evoked the
various attempts at negotiations begun from 1955 to 1970.
"The most interesting were those of January to April 1956.
A neutral intermediary made four trips between him and
me. ... But I have sworn not to say any more about it. All I
can add is that after the envoy's fourth visit to Cairo, Nasser
said to him: 'Let's stop these contacts now. If I go any further, I shall be killed. . . .' "

The death of Gamal Abdel Nasser must have made the old
Israeli leader feel that his oath weighed less heavily upon him.
Several days after the passing on of his adversary, he received
a reporter from *Actualité,* Philippe Ganier-Raymond, at the
Sdé-Boker Kibbutz. The visitor asked him at the outset if the
name of the intermediary of 1956 had not been Robert
Anderson, the former American secretary of the treasury and
then of defense, a personal friend of Eisenhower.[1] David Ben-
Gurion interjected: "It was you who said his name, not I!"

Then, feeling freer, he recounted how Robert Anderson,
improvising in the role of personal mediator, had first gone
to see the head of the Egyptian government:

"Nasser did not appear hostile to meeting with me. He
even said that it would be very useful and might lead to a
kind of arrangement. But immediately after, he made statements of such bad faith—I could not even report them today

[1] Who, ten years later, would attempt a repeat performance in Vietnam, in
a team with General Billotte.

to my mother if she were still alive—that when Anderson
came to Jerusalem, the first thing he said to me was: 'Nasser
is willing to meet you, but beware, he is a liar.' I said to him:
'Let us try all the same.' In fact, I was much more optimistic
than he. The negotiations lasted four months, until April
1956. Anderson came and went from Cairo to Jerusalem.
He reported Nasser's words to me and he reported my proposals to Nasser. In Cairo, he stayed in an average tourist
hotel. He met with Nasser only at night, in secret places,
never the same one twice.

"It was on the seventeenth or eighteenth of April, 1956,"
Ben-Gurion specified, "that the break came; Anderson spoke
of a non-aggression commitment between the two states. 'If I
give the order to cease fire, they will fire on me!' Yet in saying this, he was sincere, for the first time in four months of
negotiations! . . ."[2]

Other attempts at negotiations took place between the two
great leaders of Middle Eastern politics, sometimes through the
mediation of Tito (in 1955), sometimes through Richard
Crossman (in 1956), or through envoys who were even more
discreet. At the end of the interview already cited, the elderly
"B.G." confided to his visitor:

"Eight days before the death of Nasser, one of my friends
who was returning from Cairo told me, 'Nasser wants to meet
with you as quickly as possible.' And then Nasser died. It was
a pity, for, this time, I am sure that Nasser was not lying."

In fact, it is highly likely that Gamal Abdel Nasser had
never expected anything from the contacts with David Ben-
Gurion, whom he also considered a "liar" and an irreconcil-
able enemy. His relations with Ben-Gurion were always
different from those which he had maintained, indirectly of
course, with Moshe Sharett: with the one he had recourse only

---

2 *Actualité,* October 12, 1970.

to foreign intermediaries, with the other he agreed to use native Egyptians, independent of the Labor Parliamentarians of whom we have spoken. But let us recognize that, in the time of Sharett as in that of Ben-Gurion, peace was never very close.

It was at the very moment when the *Raïs* broke off negotiations with Anderson that United Nations Secretary General Dag Hammarskjöld arrived in Cairo, troubled by the deterioration of the situation indicated to him by General Burns. He also conferred at length with the two leaders. Restive as he was concerning all contact with press, he gave us the impression of leaving somewhat less disturbed. Neither of the two principal authorities seemed to him desirous of pushing the crisis to the point of armed conflict, in spite of appeals for revenge sent out by radio from Damascus, Amman, and Cairo by the unrestrained voice of Ahmed Said, and the threatening declarations with which General Dayan was quite unsparing.

On June 18, 1956, Ben-Gurion forced Sharett to resign, and resumed the leadership of the government. The plan for a preventive operation against Egypt, of which he had already spoken to his colleagues in November, was reintroduced as the order of the day. Moshe Dayan too was ready. Would the Suez Crisis be the opportunity? The nationalization of the company was greeted with a relative coolness in Tel Aviv. The Israelis were satisfied with noting the fever that was mounting in London and especially in Paris, where missions were multiplying. The cabinet of Bourgès-Maunoury, the French minister of defense, gave a warm welcome to Shimon Perès, confidant of David Ben-Gurion. And so the tripartite operation of the autumn began to simmer tranquilly.

Nasser, for his part, had gravely underestimated the risks, as we have seen. For him, as for the majority of observers at this period, the anger provoked by the nationalization of the Suez should only have amounted to a flare-up, the true crisis centers being situated on the Jordan River, where London had just lost Glubb and thus its control of the Jordanian army, and where incidents still more serious than those of Sinai were occurring, and on the Euphrates, where Iraq was preparing to complete her great "Fertile Crescent" design.

He did not see that while pretending to concentrate on the eastern front, Ben-Gurion and Dayan had decided to strike in the south. There, they were no longer pitted against the English, as they were on the Jordan or the Euphrates. In the south they were at least objective accomplices in one of London's secret hopes—the destruction or weakening of Nasser—and they were declared allies of the French, who had openly vowed to stamp out the "little Hitler of the Nile Valley."

Was it in fact at Sèvres, on October 23, 1956,[3] that the "secret agreement" which apparently sealed Abdel Nasser's fate was signed by Paris, London, and Tel Aviv? In any case, six days later Dayan's forces swept toward the canal—with French tanks and the air support of planes piloted by the French—followed by raids by French and English aviators and, on November 4, by the ephemeral parachute operation on Port Said. Gamal Abdel Nasser was saved by the intervention, tacitly coupled if not combined, of the two great powers.

Was a new era opening between the *Raïs* and Israel? Had the resounding success of Dayan's army convinced Nasser of a military superiority which it was not too late to match? Did the landing of Russian arms at Alexandria cause him to mistrust a new form of foreign influence? Would Eisenhower's decisive gesture in his favor render him more receptive to the mollifying suggestions of the Americans? Would the inertia of the Arab states during the crisis deter him from the Arab vocation which he had felt swelling within him?

None of these was to happen. Just as he was before the

[3] This fact is found in Maxime Rodinson's *Israël et le refus arabe*, Paris, 1968. It is a reliable source.

storm, so the *Raïs* remained afterward: his leitmotif continued to be "neither war nor peace." Of course Dayan's army
was formidable. Hence a United Nations defensive curtain
would be accepted. Was Dayan frightening enough for a political shift to be attempted? While awaiting this, the problem
would be "buried," as after 1952.

The United Nations succeeded, after months of efforts, negotiations, and pressures, in obtaining from Israel the evacuation of Sinai, where the blue helmets of the United Nations
would stand guard. Gathered around Dag Hammarskjöld, the
foreign ministers of Israel, Egypt, France, Great Britain, and
the United States agreed that the passage of Israeli ships
through the Strait of Tiran would be guaranteed by the Western powers. This promise was made by the ministers present
and not ratified by the Egyptian government, still less by the
Parliament, but it was authenticated and confirmed in letters
between Gamal Abdel Nasser and Dag Hammarskjöld.

On November 7, 1956, David Ben-Gurion exclaimed before
the *Knesseth:* "We have just founded the third Kingdom of
Israel!" But by actively participating in the Suez operation,
the aged founder of the kingdom had also made Gamal Abdel
Nasser the hero of a world. Henceforth, the Philistines had a
leader. Though Nasser stood apart from the real Palestinian
debate, his every gesture during the following years was heavy
with threats to the Jewish state—above all the Syrian *Anschluss*
of 1958.

Out of the adventure of autumn 1956, Abdel Nasser, in
spite of the defeat of his troops on the battlefield, had emerged
exalted—the symbol and spokesman of Arabism. By intervening, Paris and London had veiled Israel's real military superiority, and had involved Tel Aviv in an unhappy complicity.
However unfortunate the operation for the reputation of the

Jewish state, it revealed itself to be profitable for her from the strategic point of view: the Egyptians opened the Strait of Tiran, which commanded access to Elath, and accepted, although the Israelis had not, the installation on their soil of the blue helmets of the United Nations. This attitude is very revelatory of the state of military inferiority to which Nasser again found himself reduced. He preferred the humiliating shield of the United Nations to a confrontation with Moshe Dayan's army.

For ten years, the Egyptian chief of state barricaded himself behind the curtain of the United Nations in order to maintain the status quo of 1957. Egypt had chosen to "freeze" the Palestinian problem. More than ever, "neither peace nor war" was the rule in Cairo. After 1960, the enormous effort accomplished for the construction of the High Dam, with Soviet credit and staff, seemed to summarize the ambition of the regime. To invest so much in that work, and to erect so high above Egypt that fantastic reservoir which posed the threat of a biblical deluge over the valley of the Nile in case of conflict, was this not a permanent decision against war?[4]

These arguments can be challenged. But we have an interesting countertestimony, which we owe to some of the most intimate of Nasser's associates, the Syrian leaders who attempted to build the UAR with him from 1958 to 1961. The most violent denunciation of Gamal Abdel Nasser's Israel politics came not from Tel Aviv but from Damascus. It was Akram Hourani, leader of the *Baath,* the socialist party of the Arab resurrection, and former minister of the UAR, who published a pamphlet against Nasser in June 1962, which described him as an "ally of Zionism," and maintained that in

[4] At the same period, Shimon Perès declared to Simonne Lacouture in Tel Aviv: "What I wish for Israel is the state of non-war. Neither war nor peace." And David Ben-Gurion: "We need this psychological tension for the cohesion of our state."

innumerable conferences and ministerial meetings in Cairo, Nasser had been opposed to the suggestions of his Syrian colleagues that energetic measures be taken against Israel, notably in 1959, to prevent the diversion of the Jordan River.

In September 1961 Nasser witnessed the breakup of the UAR. The anti-Israel pressure from Damascus, having become external, took the form of a permanent outdoing of Nasser. But the Israel strategy of the *Raïs* was hardly modified by this. Each Arab conference—notably in 1964—saw the following scene take place: the Syrian delegation, often supported by the Iraqi, demanded a rapid move toward direct action against Israel. And Nasser would intervene: it is not yet time, the allies of Israel are too strong, let us organize ourselves, let us try to convince the world of our rights by improving our propaganda, and let us ask the richest among us—a glance toward the Saudis and Kuwaitis—to contribute to the common fund for the liberation of Palestine.

He spoke thus to Gilles Martinet: "War is not a solution, or if it is, it is the worst of solutions. . . ."[5] A little later, Habib Bourguiba made a long journey to the Near East. After lengthy conversations with Nasser in Cairo, he urged the Arabs to remember "the facts" and to fight a political battle on the theme of the UN partition plan. Simultaneously, the Egyptian chief of state made very similar declarations to *Réalités*—although he was prudently careful not to recall lost battles—declarations which could be considered a kind of recognition of the Jewish state.

Must one then consider the Nasser of the period 1957–67 a "pacifist" with regard to Israel? Must one believe that the May–June crisis took him completely aback, that he found himself launched in a conflict which did not concern him,

[5] *France-Observateur,* April 30, 1964.

forced to fight over a problem which in his mind was already practically resolved?

It was not so simple. Without mentioning the numerous statements which escaped from him when he confronted the Arab crowds, weaving around him a net of bellicosity in which he was eventually entrapped—the tribune in him outdoing the strategist—a significant declaration should be pointed out. This he made on May 23, 1967, before the television cameras of the BBC. To a question from a British newsman on the possibility of recognizing the Jewish state, Gamal Abdel Nasser answered: "A state? No. We cannot recognize that. A Jewish people, a nonpolitical community, yes. But not a state."

So many and such diverse statements were made. Let us not dwell upon the lies, nor the duplicity. Many Western statesmen—not to mention leaders of the socialist camp—could bow to Nasser in this matter. Let us try to limit ourselves to the facts, without forgetting that speeches can also be facts.

28

The Race to the Abyss

"The UAR will not let itself be pressured into the adventure of a war against Israel as long as all the Arab states are not unified." This voice, speaking in Cairo on December 17, 1963, was no Cassandra, no prophet, merely the voice of an anonymous editorialist on Cairo radio, a close collaborator of the

Raïs. His statement summarizes ten years of history, but it expresses a desire more than a reality.

Since three years before, the UAR had been drawn little by little toward the epicenter of the cyclone. In 1960, Kassem pleaded for the official recognition of the "Palestinian entity" and to this effect issued a passport and instituted a volunteer corps. In 1962 the Syrians required the activation of a military committee of the League. And in 1963, Ahmed Shukeiri, a Palestinian politician formerly in the pay of the Saudi Arabians, succeeded in having himself designated "official delegate from Palestine" to the Arab League committee, where he acquired a certain stature by stridently outbidding everyone else. The "Voice of the Arabs," unusually badly controlled by a government which knew so well how to impose its will in all other domains, seemed to express the views of Shukeing rather than those of Abdel Nasser.

Sensing the imminent arrival of the moment when he would be overwhelmed by all this, on January 13, 1964, the *Raïs* called a conference in Cairo of all the heads of the Arab states to discuss strategy which would forbid Israel from diverting the Jordan River for her own profit. These "Pan-Arabic games" were a superb spectacle such as had never been seen before. Nasser carried off his usual success: he bowed very low before the "Palestinian entity" and imposed the creation of a Unified Arab Command which, placed under the authority of an Egyptian general, would allow him better control over the turbulent Syrians and the Palestinian commandos, whose weight was beginning to be felt in Jordan.

This was a fine recovery operation which revealed Nasser in his best form. He was to have thirty months of relative tranquillity which his opponent in Jerusalem, Levi Eshkol, apparently the opposite of a hawk, did not begrudge him. This allowed the *Raïs* to give a somewhat more democratic form to his regime: a short-lived experiment in differentiation of power, with three heads of government (Ali Sabri, Zakaria Mohieddin, Sedky Soliman).

He tried to settle the Yemen business with the Saudi Arabians, to complete the work on the High Dam, and to repress implacably the new intrigues of the Muslim Brethren in 1965.

By autumn 1966, two Palestinian organizations had been in existence for a little more than a year, formed from the magma of the OPL[1] according to Shukeiri's blueprint. One, *Al-Saika,* was based in Syria, where it received the active help of the authorities; the other, *Al-Fatah,* was based in Jordan, where despite its differences with the government it developed rapidly. In February 1966, the leftist element of the *Baath,* that of Salah Jdid, supplanted the right wing of the same party and took power. Syrian activism was thus reinforced, causing an increase in the initiatives of the *Saika,* which urged the *Fatah* and its military branch, *Al-Assifa,* toward a perilous emulation.

Anger was mounting in Tel Aviv. In June, Eshkol attempted to persuade the ultras that the American guarantee was worth more than any reprisal. He was scarcely heard by the army, nor by the *Rafi* (Ben-Gurion's party) nor by the *Heruth* (that of Menahem Begin). On September 11, General Itzak Rabin, chief of the General Staff of the Israeli Army, declared: "The battles which Israel must wage against Syria as reprisals for the sabotage raids which she is suffering are aimed at the Syrian regime. Our objective is to suppress the cause of these raids. . . ." Did this mean the current government of Syria? Damascus became aroused and Salah Jdid persuaded Abdel Nasser, by unknown means, to pledge his guarantee.

A military aid pact was signed on November 4. Mohammed Heykal, spokesman for the *Raïs,* might well write that

[1] Organization of Palestinian Liberation, itself descended from the ANM (Arab Nationalist Movement).

the UAR was not obliged to intervene automatically in any Israeli reprisal raid against Syria. In fact, the UAR was already trapped. Nasser, alerted as he was by the federation of 1958–61 and by the union attempt of 1963 to the strange concept of responsibility held by most of the leaders of the *Baath,* let himself be convinced. Henceworth he would take upon himself the excesses of Damascus. On November 4, the Six-Day War really began.

Hardly more than a week was necessary to measure the risks of the situation: on November 13, three Israeli soldiers were killed at the approaches to the Syrian border. What would Israel do? Eshkol preferred not to test immediately the solidity of the Syro-Egyptian pact and chose to strike elsewhere. A raid was launched against the Jordanian village of Samou, leaving eighteen dead and 134 wounded. Hussein immediately complained that despite the attack the alleged leaders of Arabism remained silent. Nasser accepted this chastisement, champing at the bit. The Syrians, clearly, lost nothing by waiting: in an interview published by a Zionist journal published in France, Shimon Perès declared in January 1967, that "they too fully deserved a good lesson in turn."

The "lesson" was to come three months later: on April 6, a border incident provoked recourse on both sides to air power: six Syrian MIGs were shot down over Damascus. Again this time, the Egyptian United Arab Command was content to observe. The Damascus protestations took on an even greater violence than had those of Amman after the Samou affair. Was Gamal Abdel Nasser really that "friend of the Zionists" whom Akram Hourani had denounced?

But an incident which apparently concerned a totally different area was to arouse him from what was already considered his "torpor" and more effectively than these "classical" Israeli-Arab escalations. On April 21, 1967, the army seized power in Greece. One might observe with a smile that there was nothing in this to offend the ex-*bikbashi.* But Abdel Nasser immediately situated this coup in the perspective of Washington's Mediterranean strategy, in which the experts hardly concealed their anxiety, as much over the issue of the rise of leftism in Syria as over Soviet military penetration from Latakia to Alexandria. For the *Raïs,* the Pattakos operation was the beginning of an anti-Communist counteroffensive in the Mediterranean, of which the Syrians would be the first targets, and he the next.

This accounts for the dramatic character which events assumed for him after that date, and for the nervousness of which he gave so many signs. He ceased to interpret the Mideastern exchange of blows as the vicissitudes of a regional folklore which he believed he had learned to control, and rather saw it as a vast operation by the greatest power in the world, whose enmity he had incurred. He had already provoked other Western states, and had escaped unharmed. But Washington was not Paris. Blow upon blow, the threats multiplied. On May 8, the *Raïs* received a note from Damascus warning him that the Israeli General Staff was preparing an imminent attack against Syria. On the eleventh, a dispatch from the Associated Press reported that an Israeli official had spoken of an operation against Damascus. On the twelfth, *The New York Times* wrote: "Certain Israeli leaders have decided to strike Syria in order to end the wave of terrorism." On the same day the following declaration was attributed to General Rabin by a British newspaper: "As long as the government of Damascus is not overturned, no regime will feel secure in the Near East."

Fabrications? Poison? It does seem clear that between May 10 and 15 several Eastern European "sources" informed Cairo and Damascus that the Israelis had sent the following warning to Moscow: if the *Fath* raids continued, a "punitive action" would be undertaken against Syria. And the following was still clearer: *Tass* published a note on May 13 saying Moscow knew from a reliable source that an Israeli attack against Syria was predicted for May 17. Nothing could have been more precise.

The Arab world grew febrile. In Beirut, a conference of French ambassadors to the Near East, begun without any reference to the Palestinian problem, ended in a frenzy. Appeals for aid came from Charles Helou, the president of the Republic of Lebanon, as well as from Damascus. A high-ranking French diplomat spoke of "another Suez," but this time in an offended tone.

Had Israel, then, sought only to frighten the Syrians by calculated subterfuges? This was a poor calculation of the risks by a country which hardly knew any strategy but forward movement, and whose motor was better equipped than its brakes. It was also a poor estimation of Nasser's situation, given the blows struck against the Arabs in November and April which he had been obliged to leave unanswered, not to mention the state of mind in which the Greek operation had put him.

Levi Eshkol and his collaborators were not satisfied with raids and whispered threats. On May 15, the nineteenth anniversary of the founding of the state, a march was organized for the first time in Jerusalem. This was a challenge hurled at the United Nations, which still did not recognize the city as the capital of the Jewish state. On the eve of this event, Abdel Nasser had triggered a parallel operation, even more laden with consequences: several military columns were ostensibly crossing through Cairo, en route toward Sinai. Was this a strategic move or simply a bluff? The Cairo correspondent of Agence France-Presse, Jean-Pierre Joulin, wrote a pointed dispatch, well aware that anything even remotely concerned with strategy would be censored by the Egyptian authorities. He reasoned, if this troop movement is really serious, they'll stop my cable. Otherwise . . ." The dispatch went through. It was even reprinted in the principal Egyptian daily, *Al Ahram.*

But two days later, the *Raïs* adopted a much more serious measure which in fact opened a new phase in the race to the abyss. It had begun in November and—whatever his real intentions—every gesture seemed to sweep him forward more quickly. Before proceeding with the story of those "six days" which for Nasser lasted almost four years, from November 1966 to September 1970, I shall attempt to situate the two adversaries and to understand their intentions on the eve of the ultimate escalation.

The state of Israel had just entered its twentieth year. Since the triumph of 1956, her perspectives had grown darker. After the industrial and commercial "boom" of 1965, a crisis had appeared in 1966. This magnificently egalitarian society became stratified into classes, of which the profiteers were not the least in evidence. A tendency toward emigration intensified.[2] The national unity of the fifties had given way to factional struggles revealed on the military front by the Lavon affair, on the political front by the shattering of the Labor Party and the creation of Ben-Gurion's *Rafi,* and on the diplomatic front by the confrontations between two trends; the "moderates," Levi Eshkol and his minister of foreign affairs, Abba Eban, and the "radicals," grouped around Moshe Dayan and Shimon Perès, disciples of Ben-Gurion.

At the beginning of 1967, Israel was ill. She needed above all a demonstration of the sympathy and solidarity of the world, and especially of the Jews of the Diaspora. This did not mean that preventive war was an imperative of her politics. For Eshkol, as for Nasser, the wave of "events" would be

---

[2] It was said that a notice hung in the Tel Aviv airport: "The last to leave is requested to turn out the lights."

stronger than his real intentions. Charles Yost indicated this very clearly in an article for *Foreign Affairs:* "Neither of the two governments wanted war in the spring of 1967."

As for Nasser, we must repeat once again—because none of his deeds are understandable otherwise: he was a "man of re-action," a master of the counterattack, more skillful at deflect-ing or returning blows than at delivering them. He played defensively, as one would say of a boxer; "a good volleyer" as one would say of a tennis player.[3] In short, he would make a fire with the wood he was given. But this fire could become a conflagration.

The situation of Gamal Abdel Nasser was, in that month of May, at once tragic and exalting. Tragic, because the Egyptian treasury was on the edge of an abyss; because the United States for the first time was refusing to yield to Egypt's solici-tations; because the Yemen expedition was proving interminable; and because the last more or less sincere allies who re-mained, the Syrians, seemed more and more dedicated to a battle against Israel. And he was plagued by these two obses-sions: Egypt's swelling population growing at twice the rate of its productive capacity, and the development of Israel, which might destroy at any minute a territorial and judicial status quo which was, after all, absurd. Anyway on the one hand, the curse of a people dedicated to suicidal proliferation, and, on the other, the dynamism of a nation urged by its leaders to grow constantly by the immigration of every last one of its coreligionists.

But the *Raïs* also had some trump cards. The Soviet Union had never given him such vigorous testimonies of friendship as during Gromyko's last trip to Cairo. His Saudi rival had never suffered a setback comparable to his last trip to London, where, upon urging the British to form with him a united front against Nasser's move, in east and south Arabia, he received

---

[3] My ignorance of chess restrains me from making a comparison with this game, which would be the most appropriate for Nasser.

the answer that Great Britain did not wish to fight Nasser, but to negotiate with him.

Despite the importance of the Greek affair in his mind, the principal element of Nasser's situation was the Israeli-Arab conflict. It was not an advantageous one. The majestic vanishing act of January 1964 was no longer feasible. The problem was there and this time could not be buried. And after having failed in his attempt to settle the Yemen affair in 1965, here he was again, mercilessly implicated in the escalation begun in Damascus.

He then came under two different influences. First, there was Moscow, where he was frankly told that it was in his interest to maintain his prestige in the Arab world, and that the elimination of the Syrian government by force would be a serious defeat for him and for the U.S.S.R. as well. Hence the note from *Tass* and other bulletins passed on to Nasser. Second, there was the influence of an army clique, the most powerful of its kind because it belonged to the war minister, the ex-colonel Shams Badran, a creature of Abdel Hakim Amer who had since become the real "brains" of the marshal. The minister now manipulated the *mushir,* who no longer reflected Nasser's ideas but those of Badran. Unfortunately this former information officer had the temperament of a shady dealer, sparked by unlimited ambition.

Badran and Amer believed that the army, which was under their thumb, had grown very strong. The minister wanted to prove this to the *Raïs,* whose skepticism remained lively: Gamal, though a good staff officer, had never been very strong on the subject of national defense. Moreover, he mistrusted the army, and did everything to ensure that, although well equipped, it would remain a controllable force. How could one explain by pure folklore the strange assignment of specialists to unsuitable posts, tank men assigned to radar, while radarists, educated at great expense in the Soviet Union, were sent to the front. Apart from this mistrust, which is reminiscent of Stalin's before June 22, 1941, there was Gamal's endemic inability to see certain facts: on June 5, 1967, he required long hours in order finally to understand.

Whatever the situation may have been, his subordinate submitted an optimistic estimate of the military means at Egypt's disposal in May 1967. Must one infer that he desired, prepared, and launched an operation which could only lead to war? In a declaration made the following year in Washington, the victorious General Rabin (then ambassador to the United States) asserted that the *Raïs* had not wanted a military conflict and had believed that he could limit the affair to the diplomatic terrain. But this was not the opinion of another adversary of Nasser, Moshe Dayan. Speaking to us in June 1970 in Tel Aviv, he maintained that Nasser had probably wanted, at a certain moment, "to stop the projector" because the movie was taking an unfortunate turn. But, nonetheless, the screenplay and the production had been written and designed by him.

We shall side with the majority opinion of neutral observers: the *Raïs,* in our view, believed he was entering a great diplomatic *Kriegspiel* on May 15, 1967, which would allow him to resume control of the Arab world by obliterating the wounds of 1956 (the blue helmets and the obligatory opening of the Strait of Tiran to Israeli ships); once again he would become a major stake, disputed by Moscow and Washington. He well knew the rules of this game, which had profited him so much in the past—when his credit with Washington had been unlimited.

There exists a Nasserist version of the May 1967 affair available in the West. This was provided in an interview published by *Le Monde* on February 19, 1970:

"I did not want to begin a war in 1967, and the Israeli leaders know this perfectly well. It was not my intention to close the Gulf of Aqaba to Israeli ships. I had not asked Thant to withdraw the UN troops from Gaza and Sharm el-Sheikh, which commands the entrance to the Gulf, but only from a part of the frontier stretching from Rafah to Elath. However, the secretary general of the UN, on the advice of a high officer of the organization, an American, decided to recall all the blue helmets, thus placing me in the obligation of returning the Egyptian forces to Sharm el-Sheikh, and of setting up the blockade. Thus we fell into the trap set for us."

This defense testimony should be placed on the record. But one must mention that Nasser's responsibilities under the circumstances were crushing. Whatever his intentions may have been, he is open to heavy criticism for having chosen his allies, and understood his adversaries, very ineptly. As for his allies, one may ask why a man of the *Raïs*'s stature and experience burdened himself with a character like Shukeiri, allowing him, at his side, to become Israel's trump card? Why did he permit this unscrupulous demagogue to mime the most infamous threats and the most unrestrained challenges at the Jewish state, thereby encouraging the audacity of a people who, when menaced with genocide, had every right to draw its revolver?

But Nasser committed another equally serious error: he was not able to foresee the enemy's reactions. How, after fifteen years of troubled proximity, could he have expected that Israel would passively submit to the Tiran blockade? How could he have actually believed that Washington would be able to restrain Tel Aviv, unless he had once again swallowed the myth that the Jewish state was nothing but a "beachhead of American imperialism," a piece of nonsense which Lieutenant Colonel Abdel Nasser no longer believed even after the Sinai evaluation of 1957. Thus the *Raïs,* a real statesman, allowed himself to be seduced by the gobbledygook dispensed by his own radio!

.   .   .

On May 14, Nasser had paraded his infantry before the balconies of the big hotels of Cairo. It was still a game. Did Nasser believe the game could go on when, on May 16, he ordered his chief-of-staff, General Mohammed Fawzi, to demand that the Indian General Rikhye (commander of the UN units stationed since 1956 at the Sinai border) to withdraw his blue helmets so that he, Nasser, might act against Israel "in case an act of aggression should be committed against an Arab country"?

It was a strange step, which the *Raïs* well knew to be unacceptable. According to the terms set forth in letters exchanged between himself and Dag Hammarskjöld eleven years earlier, such a decision could only be made by the secretary general of the UN, at the request of the concerned government. Was Nasser still playing a game?

U Thant replied immediately, recalling certain conventions, also reminding Cairo that "international forces were not there to be spectators to a resumption of hostilities." A provisional withdrawal could result only in definitive and total withdrawal. The secretary general went on to consult the representatives of the seven nations which had placed their forces at the disposal of the UN.[4] Two of these diplomats declared themselves against the withdrawal. The other five were rather in favor, the most interested parties being the spokesmen for India and Yugoslavia, since the soldiers doing duty in the Sinai Peninsula at that moment belonged to these two nations.

On the evening of the seventeenth, U Thant informed Cairo that, if Cairo insisted, the withdrawal would be effected as soon as possible. The following day, the eighteenth, while General Fawzi's forces were mobilizing in the sectors occupied till then by the blue helmets, Mahmud Ryad, the Egyptian

[4] Brazil, Canada, Denmark, India, Norway, Sweden, and Yugoslavia.

foreign minister, informed the foreign embassies in Cairo that the "UN troops had finished their mission in the UAR."

Israel protested immediately: this operation could not occur without her consent. The secretary general then suggested that General Rikhye's units be installed in Israeli territory, an idea which Israel rejected, referring to the texts of 1956–57.

Let us pause for a moment over Nasser's decisions which, after the Ryad declaration, ceased to be a game and became a series of very risky threats. It is true that he could impart no credibility to a strategy of dissuading Israel from attacking Syria, except by removing the curtain which had assured the Hebrew state of a relatively peaceful Egyptian neighbor. Once the Blue Helmets were removed and the confrontation resumed, the threats from Cairo had to be taken seriously. But if it is true, as the Egyptian side has often maintained, that the *Raïs* wanted only the partial withdrawal of the curtain, thus creating a mere opening or "window" toward Israel, then one may well wonder what caused all that frenzy.

Once again that very responsible observer who attempted to play a beneficent role in the affair, the American ambassador to the UN Charles Yost, writes: "The UAR as well as the United Nations acted, as had Israel several days earlier, precipitously and with little diplomatic sense." But Yost pertinently added that "a little more thought on one side or the other would only with great difficulty have preserved the peace: for, on May 17, the crisis had reached such an intensity that both parties seemed launched in an uncontrollable race."

"Has Nasser gone mad?" This was the question asked by the head of a diplomatic mission in Cairo to the military attaché of his embassy when he learned, on May 22, that the *Raïs* had just decreed the blockade of the Strait of Tiran. Since the substitution of his forces for those of the UN at

Sharm el-Sheikh, which commanded the strait, one might
have suspected that this step was near. Yet the hastiness of
the decision intensified existing qualms. Suddenly the Soviets,
who, until May 22, had seemed to be urging Nasser to remain intransigent, began to play a more conciliatory role.
Similarly, Thant rushed to Cairo, although tardily indeed.
What he obtained however was not negligible: Nasser agreed,
while awaiting an amicable settlement, to let cargo vessels
pass through Elath if the maritime powers would pledge not
to transport any strategic products by means of them, and he
agreed to the nomination of a UN mediator to pass between
Cairo and Jerusalem.[5]

But Israel was not satisfied with these mitigations. For Levi
Eshkol, the blockade "violated international regulations in a
flagrant manner," and constituted an "aggression against
Israel." The formula of a *casus belli* was currently used in the
Israeli press and ruling circles. There was no doubt that, from
that day on, Tel Aviv was preparing to act. For his part,
President Johnson qualified the Egyptian gesture as "illegal
and possibly disastrous."

Where did Gamal Abdel Nasser stand in all of these oc-
currences? Everyone who met him in Cairo at that time mentioned his nervousness and the impression of distress revealed
by this grand master who had triumphed in so many close
chess matches. He seemed shaken by obstacles he had counted
on overcoming.

As for the UN, he had expected it to play the role of
paladin of the Third World. He thought that only with great
difficulty would he be able to extract from it the evacuation
of the Blue Helmets: yet this he obtained with no trouble at
all. The Tiran blockade might have provoked a reaction from
the United States as violent as that of the Franco-British to

[5] E. Rouleau *et al., Israël et les Arabes, le 3e combat,* Paris, 1967, p. 103.

Suez: but all he received was a reprimand. The crusade was transforming itself into a very hazardous steeplechase.

Why did he make so many rash moves? The Egyptian hawks had stepped up the pressure. Shams Badran, the war minister, had appointed new leaders for the front-line units: the minister's friends would be advantageously placed for the honors of victory.

The *Raïs* was reluctant to adopt this approach despite Marshal Amer's support. He wished to substitute hard-hitting diplomacy for outright bellicosity. This attempted changeover from the military to the political merely delayed the inevitable events for several days.

Abdel Nasser did not refrain, moreover, from furnishing credence to the war propaganda. On the twenty-third, while visiting an air base in the Sinai Peninsula, he declared to the officers: "Israel wants to fight? *Faddal!*" (Fine!) On the following day he received, at home, a delegation from the National Assembly, to whom he said: "Israel shall be destroyed." (This statement, which was not officially broadcast, naturally disturbed a French correspondent who learned of it through an eyewitness. He rushed to the minister of information, Mohammed Fayek, who tried to minimize these "mere words intended for domestic consumption.")

On May 25, Shams Badran left for Moscow, where he asked for new arms. To his great surprise, he was rudely rejected. Kosygin criticized the "regrettable errors" committed by the *Raïs:* the demonstration of force at Sinai, the Tiran blockade. The head of the Soviet government apparently also recommended that the petroleum necessary to Israel not be included in the list of strategic products blockaded, and the Soviet defense minister advised the gradual withdrawal of troops from Sinai.

On May 28, Gamal Abdel Nasser, the president of the United Arab Republic, held a press conference in Kubbeh

Palace before three hundred journalists from all over the
world. None of those who had known him and who saw him
that day will ever forget the changes worked in that steely
character by the crisis in which he was caught. This was no
longer nervousness, but feverishness. His ravaged face had
aged brusquely. His hands trembled as he lit up cigarette after
cigarette. Was it the feeling of the inexorable, the awareness
that nothing more could be done to "stop the movie projector"? This is not the whole answer.

Rereading today the text of those declarations, which were
then considered a new step in the escalation, one finds indications which were neglected in the immediate situation. One
of the best observers of Egyptian politics, Jean-Pierre Joulin,
told us that he had that day the impression that "never had
peace been nearer—and war too—in the Middle East." There
were, of course, statements such as: "If Israel wants to attack
us, we say to her *Ahlan wa Sahlan!* [Welcome!] . . . We
accept no coexistence with Israel, for the very existence of
that state is an act of aggression against the Arabs. . . ." But
there are also in the press conference of May 28 clear
references to the possibility of a total settlement of the
Palestinian question, and an invitation to revive the Egypto-
Israeli Armistice Commission. Upon leaving the Palace of
Kubbeh, reports Eric Rouleau, one of the most intimate
collaborators of the *Raïs* said to him: "Well, here we are at
the crossroads. If Israel consents to reopen the Palestinian
question, we shall have peace; otherwise, war is inevitable."[6]

If Nasser wanted on that day to open the door to peace, he
failed as utterly as he had failed in his efforts to restrain the
ultras of Cairo. No one had grasped his more specific allu-
sions, and the next day M. Balafrej, the highly competent
envoy and personal representative of the king of Morocco who

[6] *Le Monde,* December 28, 1967.

had come to contact Nasser on behalf of Hassan II, again declared that the conflict was "inevitable."

On May 30, a dramatic coup occurred, a new lead toward the abyss: King Hussein of Jordan landed in Cairo and signed a defense agreement with the *Raïs.*

Israel found herself caught in a vise: those in Eshkol's circle who still hesitated to begin a preventive operation were then convinced: the next day, Moshe Dayan and Menahem Begin entered the Jerusalem government. Who could still have hoped, on June 1, 1967, that peace had a chance? The Israeli statements became as hysterical as the Arab ones. While the Iraqi premier Aref was arranging "a rendezvous with our brothers in Tel Aviv," the Palestinian Shukeiri declared: "There will be practically no Jewish survivors," and the Syrian radio broadcast a song with the refrain, "Massacre them, bring back their severed heads!" Nasser himself said: "We are burning with desire to resume the battle."

There were, however, certain indications to the contrary. On May 31, the representative of the UAR to the United Nations spoke of a compromise formula for Tiran. Two days earlier, Cairo had welcomed Charles Yost, the head of the American delegation to the UN, who from May 29 to June 3 made one last desperate effort to avert war. To find a way out of the blockade, other than a line of international ships in the straits, as suggested by Dean Rusk, Yost obtained an agreement from Nasser that the Tiran litigation be taken before the International Court at the Hague. It was decided that Zakaria Mohieddin, vice president of the UAR, would leave on June 4 for Washington, and that his American counterpart, Hubert Humphrey, would return this visit to the UAR several days later. Charles Yost left Cairo assured that Israel would not now attack. Was Washington attempting to stifle the conflict with its sheer weight? On June 2, Nasser received an influential British MP, Christopher Mayhew, who asked him: "If they do not attack, will you leave them in peace?" to which Nasser replied "Yes.... We do not intend to attack Israel."

The *Raïs* installed himself on June 3 in a general staff bunker in Heliopolis, a suburb of Cairo, but he continued to resist the pressure of Abdel Hakim Amer and Shams Badran, who maintained that the first to strike would be the victor. It was at this point that his confidant Mohammed Heykal published an article in *Al Ahram* which can be summed up thus: Israel is going to attack from the air, we will have to hold up under the shock, but our counterattack will be victorious.

An odd atmosphere of peace was hovering over Egypt on June 4; a number of correspondents actually left Tel-Aviv. "Not this time . . ." Others flew out of Cairo, reassured by the rumors surrounding the visit of Charles Yost and the approaching exchanges between Washington and Cairo. That evening, while Marshal Sedky Mahmud, the chief of the Egyptian air forces, was relaxing far from the Red Sea front, one of his colleagues was marrying Mahmud's daughter. The entire general staff of Marshal Amer was there, feasting until dawn. But their return home, in the early morning, alarmed them: the Israeli air force, whose leaders had kept a vigil through the night, were opening fire. By five o'clock, nearly all the military airports of Egypt had been attacked, and in less than two hours, in successive waves, General Hod's air force had pinned down that of Marshal Sedky Mahmud. By mid-morning, June 5, the war was lost and Nasser learned of this disaster only six hours later, a fact which itself furnishes a good idea of the relations between himself and his coworkers!

For two days, personally directing the operations from his Heliopolis bunker, the former professor of tactics at the military academy refused to believe the worst. He tried to resume control, if not of the situation, at least of his own officers—such as the commander of the Sinai sector, General

Mortada, who, not obtaining—understandably—the air support which he had been demanding since the dawn of the fifth, had for all practical purposes become mutinous and refused to communicate with the general staff. Exasperated at having failed to push through their plans for an offensive, Amer and Badran refused all cooperation.

On the sixth, after the Jordanian forces had entered the war, Nasser attempted a ruse which showed how anxious he was to escape. His telephone conversation with King Hussein was recorded by the Israeli monitoring service:

Nasser: "Undoubtedly, my brother, you want to know what is happening on the front. The combats continue. Do you think we might implicate the United States? Or the United States and Great Britain?"

Hussein: "The United States and England . . ."

Nasser: "In fact, do the English have aircraft carriers in the region?"

Hussein: ". . ." (inaudible)

Nasser: ". . . We have had some problems at the beginning but we shall win, for God is with us. We shall say that the Americans and the English are attacking us from their aircraft carriers. . . . Do not abandon the struggle, my brother, our planes will strike the Israeli airports this very morning. . . ."

Hussein: "Thank you. Be in good health."[7]

This abracadabra dialogue, perhaps no more ridiculous than those exchanged, for example, between Wilhelm II and Franz Josef at the time of the Marne—says a great deal about the fantasies and myths in which the *Raïs* was enmeshed. This

[7] Julien Besançon, *Bazak,* Paris, 1967, p. 188.

total confusion between the true and the false, along with an epic triviality, cruelly caricatures the whole of his behavior during these weeks of the spring of 1967. The great political strategist seemed not to understand the relation between an act and its consequences, the fall of the hammer and the sound it makes. He had become an absurd hero.

On the seventh, Gamal Abdel Nasser, having ascertained that Moscow was not reacting—and with reason—to his accusations against Washington, left his bunker for the front. It was then, and only then, that he understood the full extent of the disaster: routed and fleeing units, pursued by the enemy air force.

On the evening of the eighth, Egyptian opinion, which had been deceived for more than four days, learned that the "UAR has accepted the cease-fire." This was a crushing blow. Obviously, the first reaction was hostile to the *Raïs.* "Out with that incompetent . . ." said the people in the street in the early morning of June 9. In the leader's own circle, reactions were varied. The military, at least those who were directly under Amer and Shams Badran, counseled him to leave. They judged that it was he who had led the country to defeat by allowing Israel to attack first. Others, notably the leaders of the Arab Socialist Union and all those who had ties with the Soviet Union, recommended that he stay on; and certain others, who spoke of resuming the struggle in a popular form, in Upper Egypt if necessary, thought that the *Raïs* should at least remain as its symbol.

A restricted council of the Arab Socialist Union, to which he summoned his oldest friends, was held on the afternoon of the ninth. Nasser declared: "Since Zakaria Mohieddin had advised another course, and thinks that a compromise is necessary, let him be my successor: he has my blessing." Was he entirely sincere? Was he hoping for, and preparing for behind

the scenes,[8] a reversal of popular sentiment in his favor?
Speaking six months later with Emmanuel d'Astier, he compared his gesture in June with an earlier "false exit": "In
1954, I calculated, I maneuvered. This time, in June, I was
exasperated . . ."[9]

But now, at the bottom of the abyss, the greatest hour of
Nasserism had come, the true rite of the leader, the night of
legitimacy.

"We listened to Nasser on television," Eric Rouleau recounted.

His features were drawn, his face tortured. He seemed
thunderstruck. With a hesitant, jolting diction he read his
text, stammering over the words; Nasser, the great democratic leader. His voice was choked as he announced that
he was retiring from political life.

Then, from the twelfth floor of our building, we heard
a great rumbling which swelled, muffled and threatening
like an approaching storm. But the weather was magnificent. So we went out on the balcony and, from all sides,
we saw people come out of their houses like ants, and
heads appear at the windows. We went down. It was twi-
light and the city was half plunged in the darkness of the
blackout. The people made up an extraordinary spectacle,
running up from everywhere, crying out, weeping in pa-
jamas, barefoot, the women in nightdresses, children too,
all gripped by an unbearable suffering, wailing: "Nasser,

[8] The demonstrations of June 9 were according to all the evidence provoked
by the supporters of the *Raïs,* for they began even before he announced his
departure, which he did only at the end of his speech.

But that manipulation was triggered only by a largely spontaneous movement. It has also been observed that to cut the demonstrations short, men of
the military—adversaries of the *Raïs*—set off an air raid alarm and fire from
DCA's (anti-aircraft weapons) which aimed at frightening the crowd—and did
not succeed.

[9] Conversation with E. d'Astier, *L'Evénement,* November 1967.

Nasser, don't leave us, we need you." This was the great, rumbling stormlike noise we had heard. . . .

. . . Three great waves broke over Cairo. Spontaneously, people were crying: "To the American Embassy, we must burn it, it was the Americans who incited Nasser's departure." At no moment were slogans shouted against Israel. One heard, "No Zakaria, no imperialism, no sterling, no dollars."

A second wave rushed toward the National Assembly, for the radio had announced that the deputies were gathering there in order to decide whether or not they would accept Nasser's resignation. Around the building, tens of thousands of people were crying "Nasser, Nasser," and each time that a deputy prepared to enter, he was taken by the collar and threatened: "If you do not vote for Nasser, we will kill you when you come out." And he would protest: "Of course I will vote for Nasser."

The third wave consisted of nearly a half million people massed along the length of the eight-kilometer route which leads from the center of Cairo to the presidential villa of Manshiet el-Bakri. They slept all night on the road, blocking the exits from the villa in order to keep watch over Nasser and to ensure that in the morning he would go to the National Assembly to withdraw his resignation. . . ."[10]

These cries, this weeping over the departure of a vanquished man, as clearly responsible for disaster as any leader had ever been, a man who had badly miscalculated the risks and badly prepared the country and its army, who had issued a challenge without being prepared to see it taken up, who had threatened a country stronger and better organized and equipped than his own—this grief was surely the apotheosis of the special rapport between this leader and the masses, a rapport of personification and incorporation.

[10] Rouleau *et al.*, *Israël et les Arabes, le 3e combat*, pp. 135–7.

It was not wisdom that they expected from the chief, but physical presence, warm and fleshly. He seemed all the more real now that he was obviously at fault and unhappy. Neither Napoleon III, nor Wilhelm II, nor Hitler had known this collusive, demanding intimacy, this leveling, voracious pressure. I and the people? The people and I? It was Nasser-Egypt humiliated, suffering, united until the end of the trial.

Another event occurred expressive of this mutual possession: several hours after Nasser's farewells, and while the parliament was preparing to debate, the vice president of the chamber entered a post office, announced himself, and gave the clerk a cable congratulating the new president, Zakaria Mohieddin. At that point this cog in the bureaucratic wheel straightened up and refused to send the telegram, which he described as "treasonous." The official called a policeman to have the rebellious clerk arrested. But the *shawish* in his turn objected to the order.

The defeated man maintained his charisma despite his resignation, despite the transferral of power to a comrade. And this happened in a land of exemplary obedience, highly inclined to submit to the changing decrees of history. And it happened in favor of a defeated man, a man who seemed to belong only to the past. Here, above all, Nasser's leadership, on the day after his failure, gave evidence of strange powers.

29

The Twelve Hundred Days

On June 10, Gamal Abdel Nasser withdrew his resignation and again assumed his burden. The Israeli army had not crossed the canal, but was encamped on a fifth of Egyptian territory, controlling at once a bank of the canal (thereby canceling the benefits of the 1956 operation); the entire petroleum production of the Sinai Peninsula, that is, two-thirds of that of Egypt in 1967; and one of the most popular tourist regions. From Port Said, Ismailia, and Suez, hundreds of thousands of refugees were surging toward Cairo, the delta, and the Nile Valley, all of them already overpopulated. A broken, maddened, divided country had called him back and was looking to him as the authority which could rescue it. What could he do? How could he manage in the face of such a disaster?

Gamal Abdel Nasser was no longer the man of the *Putsch* of July 23, 1952, but of the plebiscite of June 9, 1967. He was no longer the officer who had seized power one day by daring ruses. He now called himself the instrument of the people; but he acted as a solitary strongman. He was now a leader called forth and trusted by the masses, who felt this strongly enough to forbid the officers who had disagreed with Amer and Badran on June 9 and 10 to proclaim themselves for him. He wanted to avoid the atmosphere of a "pronunciamiento." If he was recalled, it must be by the people alone.

This feeling would henceforth modify his relations with the
army. Despite his desire to keep his distance from it, even to
the point of caring for it as poorly as any chief of state ever
did, he was tied to it by the past, by custom, and by implicit
interests. Now he had all but severed these ties. In this way
he hoped to settle scores with the officers directly responsible
for the catastrophe, and also to forge a new national and
international Palestine strategy without continual consultation
with the military.

If he had accounts to settle, the summer of 1967 was the
time for a "purge." Members of the small Jewish community
were attacked, a group now composed only of paupers or of
citizens sufficiently patriotic and unsympathetic to Zionism to
have risked staying in a country at war with Israel, and which
now sought to take revenge. Five hundred were thrown into
prison.

But the principal target was the army general staff. Nasser
was aware of his own responsibility, and it was crushing. But
he also knew that activists such as Amer and Badran had led
him further than he had wished and he knew this from information supplied by the second most powerful man in Egypt,
Salah Nasr, the head of the *mukhabarat* and director of the
henchmen of the Intelligence Service. He now staged an
operation in two phases against two types of officials.

The day after the defeat, Abdel Hakim Amer was installed
in his large luxurious villa at Giza, which contrasted strikingly
with the simplicity of Gamal's home. These two men, who
had been linked by a friendship of twenty-five years, were now
irrevocably alienated. The "Robinson" of the military academy, who was called Abdu by Nasser's family at home, had
vainly counseled the *Raïs* to begin hostilities at the end of
May, and had then encouraged him to resign on June 9. Amer
did not forgive him for having chosen Mohieddin and not
himself—he was the regime's number two man—nor for his

refusal to attack, thus condemning "his" army and "his" air force to disaster.

It was an embittered Amer who cloistered himself in his villa with Shams Badran on June 10, guarded by three hundred praetorians of the special forces. The Giza villa became a Fort Chabrol. Pamphlets were printed there denouncing the conduct of the *Raïs* and suggesting rapprochement with the West, since the Russians had not been able to support their Arab friends, and demanding a "return to democracy." A fraction of the army was certainly in favor of these ideas. But how far did the *mushir* wish to go?

To make a clean breast of the matter, Gamal sent an ambassador, Mohammed Heykal, who entered the fortress and invited Amer to meet with Nasser. At first the marshal refused, but after ten days of hesitation he finally accepted.

The dinner took place at Gamal's home, in Manshiet el-Bakri, in the presence of the five vice-presidents (or Free Officers of the Council of the Revolution of 1952 who remained at their posts). During the meal, the *Raïs* had the villa of Abdel Hakim Amer surrounded. Then, upon leaving the table Amer was informed: "You are under arrest!" General Fawzi had just surrounded the marshal's residence, where Shams Badran had been pressured into yielding on pain of seeing the building "reduced to cinders." It was a defeated Amer whom Zakaria Mohieddin escorted home, to what was no longer a fortress but again a mere villa. He remained under surveillance. But the operation awakened protest in the army, where Amer had a lively personal popularity, and where many thought that he had been right and that Gamal, by his lack of action, had condemned the Egyptian forces to catastrophe.

Then the *Raïs* decided to go further and to forsake the "corporate" framework. Until now, everything had taken place in the shadows. Practically no rumors had escaped about these coming and goings, these dragnets. Now, since the officer corps was grumbling, Nasser would bring the debate to the public square where he knew himself to be stronger (especially since June 9). The press blared headlines denouncing the army "plot," and revealing (insofar as the public was still unaware of it) the "dealings" of the general staff and the defense minister, and the "complicity" between Amer and Badran. Now Nasser sent his two most important military leaders, Mohammed Fawzi and Abdel Moneim Ryad, to seize the *mushir.*

The arrest was another dramatic scene: "How do you dare, you who are not Free Officers, to lay a hand on me, Gamal's closest companion!" And Amer attempted to kill himself. He was taken to the hospital, where antidotes were administered, and then to a rest home near the Pyramids, where he was guarded by troops.

But how was he guarded? He succeeded in procuring poison, apparently through the intervention of Salah Nasr, chief of the *mukhabarat.* In despair over the slanderous press campaign being waged against him, he committed suicide.[1] Nasser, who slept during this period with a revolver within reach, was astounded. He, Nasser, was the man most responsible for the June debacle, who had set himself up as a judge. He, Nasser, had driven his dearest friend to suicide. He declared to a Western ambassador: "This was even more cruel for me than the defeat."

The liquidation of the bosses of the political police was accomplished in an even more fantastic style, if that were possible, which recalled the "night of the long knives" of the Third Reich, without its pederastic overtones. In the middle of the night, surrounded by his bodyguards and twenty offi-

[1] We do not accept, even as a hypothesis, the rumor that Amer was liquidated, except insofar as the furnishing of the poison and the cruel press campaign helped drive him to suicide.

cers, Gamal Abdel Nasser burst into the offices of the *mukhabarat,* the domain of the most feared man in Egypt, Salah Nasr, and ordered him to turn over his "confidential files." Having complied, and not without difficulty, Colonel Nasr and his collaborators were arrested. Simultaneously, the police raided scores of member secret servicemen, who were immediately imprisoned. The regular police had orders to open fire on anyone who attempted resistance.

These purges, or liquidations, paved the way for show trials that attracted world attention. There was the trial of Shams Badran, in which the former minister haughtily and boldly defended himself, step by step, before being condemned to life imprisonment; there was that of Salah Nasr, in which the former "master of the secrets" disclosed certain shady aspects of the regime, published by *Al Ahram* with a rawness unknown for almost twenty years. The president of the tribunal, Hussein el-Shafei, an old comrade of the *Raïs,* asked in a severe tone: "Did you procure women for the officers and the *mushir?*"

Salah Nasr: "Of course, how could I refuse the *mushir* anything?"

Shafei: "But what kind of women?"

Salah Nasr: "Your wife, for example!"

Shafei: "Clear the court!"

But the Egyptian people were not satisfied with the mere settling of such sordid accounts. Yes, they had given a reprieve to Gamal—but henceforth they also wanted a voice in the national deliberations. In the meetings of the Arab Socialist Union the tone changed—likewise in the streets and public places. Visiting Egypt in November 1967, I was struck by the new freedom of speech: from the most humble servant to Khaled Mohieddin, an old comrade who had always held a somewhat special status, no one was restricted any longer in criticizing the regime, or even the *Raïs* himself. The army had been brought to justice in the person of several of its leaders, as had the secret police. But this was only the beginning.

There were other forces at work, however, during this period of reprieve. There was not only the social weight of an incurably bureaucratic and pyramidal system, but also the fact that the regime, ruined by defeat and the occupation (which cost the country two hundred million pounds annually), was kept afloat by the gold of Saudi Arabia and Kuwait. There are forms of help which weigh heavily, and create unpleasant involvements.

Gamal Abdel Nasser himself, though struck by the disaster and aware of his errors, nevertheless did not succeed in learning a lesson from them. On July 23, 1967, he showed a humility suited to the occasion. "Whatever the faults of others may be, my responsibility in the defeat is total.... The Egyptian public has given me more than I ever dreamed possible. Its reaction of the ninth and tenth of June is more than I deserve. I no longer claim to be the leader of my people. At the very most I would wish to be the expression of one phase of its struggle."

But before the year was over, he had recovered not his pride but a kind of assurance. The man who had been miraculously healed in June had found courage again. He had certainly been resuscitated by the people, but not to the point where he was willing to place himself again in its hands.... These twelve hundred days are like the Napoleonic one hundred days; a Benjamin Constant was missing, however.

But the year 1968 was not to end without abruptly calling him to account. On two occasions, in February and then in

November, the old popular coalition of workers and students which sometimes recaptured the tone of its predecessors of 1946 demanded its right to democracy.

At the origin of the movement of February 1968 was the condemnation of the air force generals by the military tribunal. Public opinion accused the generals not only of inefficiency and negligence, but also of treason: the few years of imprisonment inflicted upon them seemed to many an act of complicity by the tribunal. An uprising gathered strength, from Helwan to Shubrah (working-class neighborhoods of Cairo), punctuated by two slogans: "No leniency for the traitors!" and "No socialism without freedom!" Several thousand demonstrators besieged the National Assembly and the newspaper *Al Ahram,* directed by Mohammed Heykal, a confidant of the *Raïs.* Finally they occupied the polytechnical college for three days. Pamphlets were circulated in March, demanding "a free parliament endowed with true democratic substance," and denouncing "the void in the domestic political organization of the country, the sterility of the Arab Socialist Union . . . and the insufficient correction of errors committed."

Nasser made certain sacrifices to save the situation: he was not afraid of a retrial for the generals already condemned. On August 25 and 29, the penalties inflicted on the generals were heavily increased. Then, in September, the *Raïs* enjoined the congress of the Arab Socialist Union "not to form the central committee from people devoted to the chief of state, but to regroup all the people and unify it within this framework." He also announced "the liberation of the creative forces of trade-unionism" pending "sincere elections" to remodel the central committee and the executive committee of the ASU, followed by a constitutional review.

Were the elections really "sincere"? Those in the Arab Socialist Union were not; but they involved the promotion of a large number of new personalities who merely used, in speaking to the militants, a language somewhat less rigid and empty than the traditional bureaucrats of the ASU. This did not fail to impress the best foreign observers: "The decision-making power in the United Arab Republic ceases to belong to a single individual—a truly revolutionary fact which signifies the end of personal power."[2]

But the *Raïs* had taken care to keep in the background certain personalities—some Communists, among others—who could have been able to compose a real opposition. He was willing to use them, but not to see them elected. Nasser said this openly to Lutfi el-Kholi, who had come to complain to him about the defeat of his comrades.

On November 20, at Mansurah, a city in the delta which had been a long-time bastion of the Wafd, and where an institution of secondary education had for some time shown an openly rebellious spirit, demonstrations broke out in favor of more liberties. Peasants soon joined the students. The fever spread to Alexandria, kindled in the meantime by an Israeli raid on Nag-Hammadi which had, once again, produced no reaction from the government.

In the *Raïs*'s native city, young people and proletariats demonstrated to cries of "Freedom!", "Down with Sharawi Gomaa!" (the minister of the interior and leader of the ASU), and even "Resign, Nasser!" The last slogan is emphasized by the authors of *La Lutte des classes en Egypte,* who add that it was now "for the first time since 1955 a mass expression of anti-Nasser feeling."[3]

The crowd bore on toward the government club, the place of recreation and retreat of the city governor. Soon the movement reached Cairo, where the demonstrators clamored slogans demanding liberty and mocking the reforms. The uprising lasted three days. It demonstrated that the regime

[2] Pierre Rondot, *Le Monde Diplomatique,* April 1969.
[3] Mahmud Hussein, Paris, 1969, 1971, p. 318.

had not really been able to measure up to the expectation of the crowds, who were hoping for liberalization and not a tactical reform at the summit. It also revealed the weakness of the repressive apparatus of Nasserism which, perhaps cautioned by the leader, hardly dared intervene.

While the system, thankful for the reprieve of its leader on June 9, 1967, attempted to find new wind and to channel astutely these popular pressures, the most pressing problem, that of territorial occupation and relations with Israel, returned to the surface.

The last three years of Nasser's regime, the "twelve hundred days of Gamal," were dominated not only by gropings towards democratization. They were also obsessed by the urgency of a solution. The slogan "neither peace nor war," which had shielded the *Raïs* for so long, could no longer be repeated. It was necessary to make a choice. And, just as Nasser had glimpsed but not initiated a shift toward democracy, now, exhausted by the ordeal, he was slowly to find his way toward peace.

30

The Way Toward Peace

The plebiscite of June 9, 1967, was at once that of Pétain and that of de Gaulle. It was that of the father-protector hastily liquidating the disaster, and that of the patriotic leader refusing to confirm it. By denouncing the choice of Zakaria Mo-

hieddin and by asking Nasser back, the crowd had revealed its
dream: continuity was in direct opposition to the facts. If
Gamal stayed on, it was because he had not really been defeated, because they, the people, had not really been defeated.
But the people had also opted for the maintenance of an old
Nasserist strategy which was by now worn very thin; the
"neither peace nor war" formula which had inspired fifteen
years of rule, one month of politico-diplomatic maneuvers
and, when the moment of truth finally came, six days of utter
defeat.

But the plebiscite was neither entirely Petain nor entirely
de Gaulle. This June 9 was not followed by a June 18 or a
Montoire. Gamal Abdel Nasser accepted the cease-fire which
acknowledged the defeat without upsetting the state. He did
not go further, to meet with Eshkol or Moshe Dayan. He also
refrained from any more extreme strategy, for example the
"popular war" recommended by several of his friends on the
Left. This was not only because he profoundly mistrusted the
people, and especially the people in arms, but also because
he judged that the strategic conditions for such a combat were
not favorable. We find here again certain of the determining
elements in Egyptian history: the countryside was inconsistent
with revolt or guerrilla warfare.

Receiving the Italian Communist leader Giancarlo Pajetta
during the summer, Nasser answered a question about possibly having to resort to a maquis: "Look at Egypt. . . ." He
placed his hand flatly on the table. "Where could you plant
or buttress a resistance? . . ." And to another visitor, who asked
him the same question, he retorted: "You have seen the
Egyptians? When the Israeli war planes fly over our cities,
what do they do: they go out to have a look . . . you see!"

Everything suggests that as early as June 1967 the *Raïs*
could foresee no solution other than a negotiated settlement.
But he set three fundamental provisos. The first: negotiation

must not involve any *preliminary recognition* of the state of Israel, this recognition being for Nasser an essential barter element, a master trump. This negotiation could not therefore be "direct," as the Israelis demanded. All he possessed was what Maxime Rodinson has so aptly called "the Arab refusal." But this refusal was monumental and he would exchange it for anything short of all he wanted.

The second condition was the total evacuation of Egyptian territory. Concerning the other geopolitical aspects of the debate, even the Palestinian national rights and their territorial holdings, the *Raïs* fluctuated from one month to the next. But not, however, on the territorial integrity of Egypt— though it was understood that Gaza was a special case.

The third condition was that the parleys not begin before the re-establishment of a certain balance of forces, and, if possible, of prestige. In 1968, the son-in-law of the *Raïs* and one of his advisers on Palestinian affairs, Hatem Sadek, in Paris was still maintaining that no political solution could intervene before a "victory." Was this to be on the canal, in the Sinai Peninsula, or elsewhere? No specifics were offered; the "victory" would perhaps be merely a Russian arms shipment. But Egypt would talk only when she was back on her feet.

Three months after the defeat, the Arab chiefs of state met in Khartoum. The Egyptian *Raïs* had just liquidated, with the least possible cost, the Yemen affair. He had checked the hidden army revolt. He had resumed his old stature despite everything, and he still dominated the Arab debate. Of that conference in September 1967, foreign visitors, for the most part, remember above all the famous "three no's": "no" to peace, "no" to negotiation, "no" to the recognition of Israel. However, some observers had from the beginning noted that the Cairo leader was preparing a long-term switch by writing the formula "political solution" into the final resolution. Others went even further: in *Le Monde,* Eric Rouleau emphasized that the resolution adopted "certainly eliminates 'reconciliation' (*al-sulh*), but in no way eliminates 'peace' (*al-salam*) from the present wording, which would consist in 'eradicating the consequences of aggression.' It therefore permits Egypt to offer Israel an end to the state of belligerency, security, and a *de facto* recognition of her (pre–June 5) boundaries in exchange for the evacuation of the occupied territories."

President Nasser returned from Khartoum with much vagueness in his diplomatic prospects—as he had in fact wished—and much precision in his financial prospects. The wealthy states, Saudi Arabia, Kuwait, and Libya, assured him that they would cover the two hundred million pounds (over five hundred sixty million dollars) which the Sinai occupation and the blockade of the canal had cost him. He would now be able to run Egypt economically and perhaps even maneuver toward his "political solution."

Six weeks after the Khartoum conference, the British delegate to the United Nations, Lord Caradon, drafted a resolution which was adopted by the Security Council. Called "the resolution of November 22," or in UN circles "two four two," since it bore the figure 242, it recommended essentially the following: (1) the withdrawal by Israel from the territories occupied during the conflict; (2) the end of a state of war and the recognition of the sovereignty and territorial integrity of all states in the region; and (3) a guarantee of the freedom of navigation in all waterways and a fair settling of the refugee problem.

The text was admirably balanced, and can be summarized as follows: peace in exchange for the occupied territories. It would have constituted the best possible basis for a "political solution" had it not entailed one serious inadequacy and one rather conspicuous diplomatic trap.

The inadequacy concerned the Palestinian problem which was here presented merely as a matter of "refugees," whereas it had been clear for more than a year that the Palestinian community had ceased to be a pathetic object for international charity and had become a central topic in Near Eastern politics. (It had been the moot point of the Syro-Israeli escalation, and hence of the war.) The trap was the subtle drafting by Lord Caradon of part (1) which, in the English version, spoke of the evacuation "of occupied territories" and not "of *the* occupied territories." This would allow the Israelis to insist that they remain in certain regions already under their control.

Now the other official versions, Russian as well as Spanish and French, were grammatically precise on the demand imposed on Israel. Certainly the preamble to the resolution stated in every language that "all acquisition of territory by force is inadmissible"; and it was true that Lord Caradon himself had specified that he was concerned with the entirety of occupied territories. But the imprecision remained, and perhaps Lord Caradon thus furnished a new proof of his lucidity and talent, for without that fluid margin, the Israelis would certainly have refused the begrudging and conditional adherence which they did grant, little by little, to the "242."

Nasser did not trouble himself unduly over these semantic quibbles. Finding in the text, though in a somewhat confused form, what was also in his mind (the exchange of land for peace), he adhered to it in the tone of one who is willing to condescend to contribute to world peace, though not without indicating that it was all quite insufficient. But he finally adhered officially to the English text, of which an essential stipulation implied recognition of and security for "all states in the region," that is, of Israel. And he agreed to receive the mediator appointed by the United Nations, the Swedish diplomat Gunnar Jarring.

The situation on the front was tense at this moment. The canal separated the combatants, but did not prevent commandos from crossing it. On the preceding October 21, missiles fired from the Egyptian shore had sunk the Israeli destroyer *Elath*. Was this on the express order of the *Raïs*? An interesting event may be recalled here, which occurred during a conversation between Nasser and Emmanuel d'Astier.[1] During this interview Nasser received a dispatch announcing the destruction of the *Elath*. A secretary handed him a written note: "The President read it; his face betrayed nothing. I asked him: 'Good or bad news?' His head lowered, he smiled constrainedly, 'It's not bad.[2] There has been a naval battle in the waters of Port Said. An Israeli destroyer has been sunk.' And immediately he moved on to other subjects."

It seemed that the operation had surprised him. Was it an overstepping of orders by the first-line units? The role of the Soviets in these circumstances remained unclear. Perhaps this was the famous "victory" preliminary to any opening of negotiations. Yet it was a victory which cost him the Suez refinery, destroyed by Israeli reprisals.

One must bear in mind various factors which limited the *Raïs's* freedom of movement. Allusion has already been made to the weight of the Egyptian masses, whom he tried to contain but who revealed themselves, from Helwan to Mansurah, to be generally unfavorable to a negotiation (which does not mean that the masses, in their depths, were not in favor of a political solution). It should be recalled, moreover, that even if the *Raïs* had resumed control of the defense ministry and

[1] *L'Evénement,* November 1967.
[2] The English words used in the conversation, as Astier was to mention to us, were "rather good."

the general staff, the fighting units kept alive the theme of revenge. This was symbolized by a leader of great value, General Abdel Moneim Ryad who, before he was killed on the canal in 1969 during an artillery duel, had acquired an immense popularity almost eclipsing Nasser's. His funeral in Cairo was the occasion of national mourning which stupefied observers.

During this period, addressing a Western ambassador, the *Raïs* declared: "Help me, or else I shall soon be unable to answer for either the army or the Palestinians." As for the Palestinians, Nasser's situation was very different from that of Hussein. In Cairo, he had control of them. The PLO had a radio station at its disposal until June 1970 and used it within a setting of supervised "liberty."

Nasser was very much aware both of the rights of the Palestinians and also of the terrible embarrassment which these rights were for him, insofar as they prohibited the signing of a comfortable separate peace. He also knew the prestige which this struggle had brought to Arafat, and Arafat's friends and rivals, especially among the young. He could not watch without anguish the rising star of a man who might sooner or later become what he had been from 1956 to 1967. His attitude toward them would thereafter be one of total ambiguity, oscillating between a premeditated forgetfulness and a paternal support.

In February 1961, the *Raïs* even accepted a contact which, if it had become known, would have drawn the wrath of the *Fath* and the PFLP upon his head. Two personalities of the west bank came to see him, with the consent of Israeli authorities, to ask for his endorsement in the creation of an organization which would represent Palestinian interests. He did not discourage them, but refused all the same to answer the message from Tel Aviv presented by the two travelers.

As for his relations with the Soviets, they also fluctuated,

within the framework, naturally, of a more or less unconditional alliance. Although reserved and even critical on the
subject of Nasser's strategy in May 1967, scathing on the
subject of the conduct of the operations and the behavior
of the Egyptian command (especially the air force), the
Soviets on the whole assumed their responsibilities as protectors, aware that they could no longer let their Arab friends
be beaten without suffering an irreparable moral and strategic
defeat.

Had they not, by means of the war, installed themselves in
force on the canal, after having assumed key positions in
Egyptian industry and production? Had they not, in fact,
acquired a position comparable to that of the British in the
preceding period? Hence they made a gigantic effort—which
is estimated for 1967–70, in military deliveries alone, at six
billion francs, not counting some ten thousand "experts"
charged with servicing the missiles, maintaining the machinery,
and educating the Egyptian staff and combatants.

What goal could they have had other than making sure
that their protégés would not be crushed? During a conversation in Cairo in November 1967, Serge Vinogradov, then
ambassador from the U.S.S.R., told us: "But why do you think
I am here, if not to help make peace?" On the whole, the
statement seems borne out by the facts. From the point of
view of the Israeli leaders, the enormous Soviet effort permitted Gamal Abdel Nasser not to negotiate with them (i.e.,
to capitulate). From the Egyptian viewpoint, the argument
is reversed: this massive Soviet aid put the *Raïs* in a position
from which he *could* envision a settlement, but on the only
basis upon which he could act, that of military equilibrium.

Let us re-examine the chain of events leading to prenegotia-
tion contacts of July 1970. Toward the end of 1968, Nasser

was harassed both by Israeli raids within his territory and by popular demonstrations which tended to present him as a tyrant and a "capitulator," as well as by the rising prestige of the Palestinian leaders.

In March 1969 he launched what he called the "war of attrition," declaring that the cease-fire of 1967 no longer had any meaning. He officially denounced it on July 23 of the same year. This resumption of the conflict brought on terrible blows from the Israeli air force: from June 1969 to June 1970, these raids cost Egypt an average of forty casualties per day, and involved particularly cruel episodes such as the bombardment of Abu Zaabal in the Cairo area, which left more than eighty civilians dead.

He turned to his Soviet allies. In June 1969, shortly after the launching of the "war of attrition," Andrei Gromyko returned to Cairo for discussions which were to play a key role in the continuation of the debate. This was due less to the novelty of the proposals made by the chief of Soviet diplomacy than to the reassurances he offered: his move was not that of a Russian diplomat, but that of the representative of the most formidable combination of powers imaginable—an American-Soviet consortium.

This was the origin of a common plan, in which the United States renounced its plea for the bilateral negotiations demanded by Israel, and agreed that the envisioned agreement need not exactly be a peace treaty. For their part, the Soviets renounced their demand for a preliminary Israeli withdrawal back to the borders of June 5, 1967, and accepted that the total settlement be staggered and gradual. Instead of a general peace treaty, the negotiators would limit themselves to several "non-war" agreements.

Gromyko pressed Nasser: "By signing, you will recover your lost territories concluding a real peace agreement with

Israel. You will preserve your future while eliminating the after-effects of your past."[3]

Nasser was not yet ready to accept this face-saving "contractual agreement." He did not feel strong enough to unleash a cascade of "separate peaces"; he continued to demand thoroughgoing agreement without capitulation. General Fawzi declared: "If you sign, I can no longer answer for the army." But the *Raïs* was shaken by Gromyko's offer. This complicity between Washington and Moscow seemed decisive. Everything depended on it; he would have to turn it to his best advantage.

The *Raïs* was thus in a fair way to drop his old strategy vis-à-vis the big powers. It was not exactly a question of a forced contract, but it was similar. There remained the Arab states and organizations. The king of Morocco invited the chiefs of state to a "liberation conference" for the last week of December in Rabat. For the *Raïs,* who attended almost against his will, the objective was less to obtain an increase in aid from his partners than to regain his freedom.

As for an increase in aid, Houari Boumedienne offered important military support in the name of Algeria, but in a tone pierced by skepticism; for the Algerian president, it was clear that Nasser was seeking only a political solution, and he made his opinion evident with an irony that embittered the Egyptian leader. The "wealthy" chiefs of state who had been aiding Cairo since Khartoum refused on their part to increase their subsidies greatly. Faysal spoke only of a surplus of ten million dollars. Then, towards noon on December 24, a dramatic coup occurred which surprised only those who had not closely observed the steps of the Egyptian *Raïs* and had not attempted to discover his ulterior motives.

[3] Josette Alia in *Le Nouvel Observateur,* June 15, 1969.

Gamal Abdel Nasser requested the floor:

"My brothers, the problem of this conference, which seems to have been forgotten, was that of the total mobilization of Arab potential, with a view to liberating the occupied territories.

"I realize that what is being promised is far from answering our present needs summed up in the report of General Mohammed Fawzi. Yes or no: does the Arab summit approve these proposals? Yes or no: does it wish to take steps to enforce them? If these delays continue, I judge that it would be better to close our discussions. It would be an act of courage to inform Arab opinion that we are not able to reach an understanding. They will then draw the inevitable conclusions."

Then, without waiting for the slightest reaction, Nasser rose and left in great haste, fearing that someone might detain him by grabbing his coattails. To the Libyan leader Khadafi who had dashed forward to catch him, he violently flung: "Many are those who rejoice in the occupation of our territories by Israel."

Having seized the very first pretext, the *Raïs* believed himself "liberated from the Arabs." Had he recovered his autonomy of action? The Palestinians remained; they had to be handled more tactfully. He conversed with Yasser Arafat:

Nasser: "I have always been, and I remain, of the opinion that the conclusion of a political settlement would preserve us from incalculable catastrophes. . . ."

Arafat: "Why not seriously envision the coordination of the struggle on every level, in particular that of the Arab armies and the Palestinian guerrilla?"

Nasser: "That is a question to be examined later. But in inaugurating a strict austere regime we would risk, by creating discontent in the Egyptian ranks, playing the enemy's game, for his first objective remains to overthrow Nasser."[4]

At the beginning of 1970, the serious raids by Moshe Dayan's air force worsened and multiplied. According to all evidence, the government of Golda Meir—who on Levi Eshkol's death in 1969, succeeded him and substituted combative rigidity for circumspect obstinacy—was attempting to eliminate Nasser by trampling him down. The *Raïs* was aware of this. He felt the weariness grow among his people. If one is to believe a member of his entourage, he was overwhelmed by the destruction that was accumulating.

On January 22, 1970, the day following an Israeli raid on the small island of Shadwan, he left secretly for Moscow, where he remained two weeks, undergoing medical examinations and talking with Leonid Brezhnev and Alexei Kosygin. Did he tell them—as one of the best observers of Nasserism has reported—"I shall drop everything, unless you help me"? The fact is that immediately following this trip, SAM 3 missiles, which were to play an important role in the summer of 1970, were delivered to Egypt.

This new gesture from Moscow seemed to comfort him and restore his understanding. On February 16, 1970, receiving a special envoy from *Le Monde,* Eric Rouleau, he made the most positive and promising declaration for peace ever pronounced in the Arab world. It is astounding that the Jerusalem government paid so little attention to it.

According to the *Raïs,* there was no reason not to make peace with Israel if the Palestinian refugees obtained the right to choose between repatriation in Israel and compensation, in conformity with the 1948 resolution by the General Assembly of the United Nations.

"Since the war of 1967," he added, "another problem has

[4] Simon Malley in *Africasia,* January 1970.

been added: that of the occupation of the Arab territories. The resolution of the Security Council voted on November 22, 1967, provides a solution to these two problems, while offering Israel guarantees concerning her right to a sovereign existence, security and peace, as well as freedom of passage for her ships through the Gulf of Aqaba and the Suez Canal."

The journalist asked him if he was ready to enter direct negotiations and to sign a peace treaty.

"The resolution of November 22, 1967, did not provide for such a procedure," replied Abdel Nasser. "Mr. Gunnar Jarring, the representative of Mr. Thant, is charged with drawing up a document sealing our agreement, while our signature will be guaranteed by the Security Council."

"Most Israelis," Rouleau objected, "are persuaded that this refusal is in reality dictated by your wish to destroy their state."

"Such a conviction is absurd. In fact a peace treaty could easily be violated on the day after its signing. World opinion must know that we cannot negotiate with the Israelis as long as they occupy twenty per cent of Egyptian territory, seventy per cent of Jordan and fifteen per cent of Syria. Negotiations under these conditions would lead not to peace, but to an unconditional surrender. The French who refused to deal with the occupant during the Second World War are in a good position to understand us. I do not wish to be the Pétain of Egypt."

"Supposing that the Israelis agree to evacuate all the territory conquered in June 1967, and to grant the optional right of repatriation to the Palestinian refugees; would you then consent to conclude a peace analogous to the one which obtained, for example, between France and Germany?"

"If the Israelis conform to the solution which I recommend, there would be no further litigation to separate us."

"Would you go so far some day as to establish economic and diplomatic relations?"

"I repeat, there would be no further problems between us and the Israelis. Of course, total normalization will be reached only by stages. It is not in fact reasonable to believe that we would succeed in eliminating with one sweep of the pen the bitterness accumulated during twenty years of war."

This was the first time the *Raïs* went so far, speaking of a true "peace" as well as of the possibility of normal diplomatic relations with the Hebrew state. The announcement at the end of March 1970 of a trip to Cairo by Nahum Goldmann was situated in this very interesting perspective. The president of the Jewish World Council was held in low esteem by the Israeli authorities (Golda Meir detested him as much as Ben-Gurion did), but he was an important Zionist figure and his prestige was great in the United States. The interview had been prepared, with the help of Tito, by an Egyptian personality of the Left, the former Free Officer Ahmed Hamrush, who had been a link between Nasser and the Communists around 1950. But Nahum Goldmann's relations with the Americans were so good that Washington agreed wholeheartedly to this new step.

Golda Meir and her government forbade Dr. Goldmann to go to Cairo. This was an obvious mistake, which weakened the moral position of Israel, and, within the country itself, strengthened the party of peace. This last development did not leave the Egyptian *Raïs* indifferent. Several of his colleagues have told us how he had been intrigued for months by the appearance of a "peace party" in Israel.[5] By making known that he would receive Nahum Goldmann, perhaps he wanted above all to weaken Golda Meir's position by undermining her political foundations, and by uniting with a rival

[5] He was said to be an admirer of a book by Uri Avnery, *Israel Without Zionism.*

against her. But it seems that Nasser's objectives were wider
—he wanted at once to begin at least a semi-official dialogue,
to improve his "trade image" in the United States, and also
to show that he distinguished between Judaism and Israel.
However, in brief, the attempt misfired.

But the idea of peace was pursuing its course. At the same
period, during a luncheon at the UAR Embassy in Paris, I
interrogated an Egyptian diplomat on the reasons for the
nomination of Mohammed Heykal to the ministry of national
orientation. Why had this promotion been granted a man
who was already the second most powerful Egyptian after the
Raïs? "To prepare public opinion, a prestigious man is
needed. . . ."

"Prepare public opinion for what?"

"For peace, of course. . . ."

Was the idea already so open? One of the best experts on
Near Eastern politics, with whom we left the Embassy, then
told us:

"If Nasser were only the *Raïs,* peace would already be
made. As an Egyptian, he has chosen. But he is also the
zaim[6] of the Arabs. . . . To agree to make peace with Israel
is to renounce the Arab 'crown.' Is he ready for this?"

Several weeks later, in June, I was in Israel: with the exception of several figures who had long taken for granted
the idea of a costly but necessary peace, great skepticism still
reigned concerning Nasser and his intentions. Neither the
interview in *Le Monde* nor the speech of May 1—in which,
obviously finding Soviet influence to be a bit heavy-handed,
Nasser had extended his hand to the United States—found
any favor in the eyes of the experts and authorities in Tel
Aviv. Golda Meir especially spoke of the *Raïs* in a harsh
and desolate tone, interrupting her sentences with long sighs.

---

[6] *Raïs* means leader. *Zaim* means inspirer.

"You who know him, why do you not persuade him to meet us?" Moshe Dayan appeared better informed. He thought on June 10, 1970, that Nasser's option for peace was already made, and that only the price remained to be determined (which, in his mind, would take time). More than the maneuvers of the *Raïs,* he mistrusted those of Washington.

Two weeks later, William Rogers, the U.S. secretary of state, presented his "plan"—a revival of the "242" resolution of the United Nations, paired with a ninety-day ceasefire and a resumption of the mission of Gunnar Jarring, the Swedish diplomat already charged in 1968 with helping the two camps. The plan received a frankly unfavorable welcome in Israel. More months passed, and the return of the occupied territories, implicit in the Rogers plan as well as in the resolution of Lord Caradon, grew painful to Tel Aviv.

On June 29, 1970, President Nasser left Cairo once again for Moscow. He was to make one of his longest stays there —until July 17. It would be easy to lose oneself, as usual, in conjectures over the tenor of the two discussions which he held with his hosts. But the meaning of this trip was soon clear: six days after his return, delivering his annual speech for the eighteenth anniversary of the coup of July 23, 1952, he declared his acceptance of the Rogers plan. Whatever his ulterior motives, he had just taken, vis-à-vis his own people and that of the Arab world, a risky choice: the choice of peace.

Many questions have been asked about the influence of the trip to the U.S.S.R. on his decision, and also about the reasons why the *Raïs* chose this particular moment to set out, apparently for good, on the road to a "political solution."

The first explanation which circulated portrayed a reticent Nasser convinced by the Soviets to limit his risks and finally play the card of negotiation. This seemed all the more likely in that the Rogers plan was in fact a mixed Soviet-American project, elaborated in the course of the six preceding months by two men, American Undersecretary of State Joseph Sisco, and Soviet Ambassador to Washington Anatol Dobrynin. Thus it was not an American operation, but rather a settlement plan in which the two big powers had taken a joint initiative. Under these conditions, how could he oppose it?

But, in the entourage of the Egyptian president, it has since then been asserted that it was Nasser who convinced the Soviets of the urgency of a settlement, for all sorts of reasons peculiar to Egypt, many too obvious to be repeated, but also for a special reason, relative to the entire Near East: the rise of the Palestinian influence.

If hostilities did not cease in the near future, the *Raïs* estimated, the revolutionary Palestinian groups, such as those of Yasser Arafat and especially Naief Hawatmeh and Georges Habbash, would assume a considerable moral and strategic importance. Let us not forget that the month of June 1970 was also that of the great breakthrough for the *fedayin,* in which it was plausible for them to seize power in Amman —although they declined to do so, that they might keep a Hashemite shield against Israel. As much for the Soviets as for the Nasserists, the risk of an outbreak on the Left was great. Only peace could arrest such a development.

These were not, however, the arguments which the *Raïs* developed before his friends of the Arab Socialist Union, whose central committee demanded to hear him on the day after the speech of July 23. There, he attempted to justify his decision before an audience more undecided than hostile.[7]

This first argument concerned procedure: the Rogers plan differs only in details from Resolution 242 of the UN, which Egypt had already accepted. The second argument was stra-

[7] Cf. "Nasser's New Strategy," by Ammon Kapeliouk, *New Outlook,* September 1970.

tegic: by accepting the plan before Israel, Egypt would put
Israel in a detestable position before world opinion. The third
argument concerned the rub of the problem: if Egypt could
recover her territories and those of the Palestinians without
fighting and suffering new losses, how could she hesitate?
The fourth argument was opportunistic: Egypt is told that
she has changed by accepting an American text—Egypt, the
great adversary of imperialism! But it is not Egypt which has
changed, it is the United States!

And the *Raïs* added to his speech three more cynical arguments, which, it was said, derided the hearts of listeners still
obsessed by the old slogans: first, that the decision of July
23 had the effect of interrupting all American arms shipments to Israel; next, that the Israelis were completely dis-
oriented, as proved by the Begin declaration, according to
which "the Rogers plan contains the seeds of the destruction
of Israel"; finally, that the Cairo gesture had already provoked a serious crisis of confidence between Israel and the
United States.

Thus, Gamal Abdel Nasser accepted, and rendered acceptable to his country, the Rogers plan. Two weeks later, after
Mrs. Meir had agreed to dissolve her cabinet in order to join
with the Soviet-American plan, the cease-fire was put into
effect for ninety days on either side of the canal, in two
"frozen" zones of fifty kilometers each: as of August 5, the
two adversaries were to abstain from all military activity, and
especially from reinforcing their positions. Were the wheels
of peace finally in gear?

This was both true and untrue. It was true in that all
those who talked to Gamal Abdel Nasser at this time, and
who had a good knowledge of the man and his history, acquired the conviction that the *Raïs* really wanted to find a
solution. He seemed persuaded that the common desire of the
United States and the Soviet Union to put an end to the

Near Eastern conflict opened a way for him to be the great regional eminence.

It was also true in that Nasser had made a fundamental choice awaited by many friends of Egypt—and of Nasser himself—between the Nile Valley and the Arab world. Not that he had decided to turn his back on the Arabism which had so captivated him and cost him so much, but that he saw opening before him perspectives of that other, African Arabism, which the two Libyan and Sudanese revolutions were offering him. Whereas from the northeast he received only rebuffs and harsh blows, to the south and west two neighboring countries, both African and Arab in culture and both in favor of Nasserist "socialism," were making a proposal of friendship. One brought water, and that unity of the Nile Valley which was a major objective of Egyptian politics; the other brought petroleum, that is, reserves of currency. No reconversion could have been more tempting. Egyptian opinion favored it. The old revolutionary song of 1919, "*Biladi, biladi . . .*" (My country, oh my country), by the national musician Sayed Darwich, returned to many lips: it was a new call for an "Egyptian Egypt."

Let us quote in this connection a passage from Eric Rouleau's study: "This emotional withdrawal into the valley of the Nile, this will to re-establish as quickly as possible the integrity of the national soil, nourished a conciliatory current. Now one often hears: 'Let them return Sinai to us, and all our problems will be solved.' "[8]

Was this an irreversible shift toward peace? Perhaps not, because of the resistance which had become evident as much in Israel as among the Palestinians. The rulers of Jerusalem remained the same, and they had for more than twenty years refused to take into account peace factors in the Arab world,

[8] *Le Monde,* April 9, 1970.

convinced that only intransigence, the demand for preliminary diplomatic recognition, and a few "good lessons" could
bring any Arab leader to the conference table. It was not
from Golda Meir, the very symbol of this prudence—although the leader of the Tel Aviv government had nonetheless had the courage to prefer the dissolution of her cabinet
to a rejection of the Rogers plan—that a conversion could
be expected.

There was another major obstacle. The Palestinians refused to allow a settlement which, without neglecting them
entirely, would stop short of admitting their national rights
in principle and would continue to treat them as refugees. In
his interview of February 16 in *Le Monde,* Gamal Abdel
Nasser asserted that his prestige would allow him to overcome this resistance, as well as that within his own army.
But was he considering all the factors, including the growth
of that Palestinian force which had been so long forgotten,
and which he had treated as a means rather than as an end
in a settlement? Had he taken the measure of Palestinian
anger, and of the echo which it awakened throughout the
Arab world, as far as the west bank?

A third obstacle arose between the public decision made
by the *Raïs* on July 23, 1970, and actual peace. This was
his own voracity, not always easy to distinguish from that of
his Soviet allies. The demon which impels certain rulers always to seek a little more gain or "profit" incited the Soviet-
Egyptians, after the cease-fire of August 7, to place their
missile launching sites nearer the canal. These were the famous Sam 3's, obtained by Nasser six months earlier from
Moscow. When the Israelis protested, Cairo spokesmen replied with several rather phlegmatic arguments. They asserted that it was purely a question of defensive armaments,
and that these new emplacements did not alter the relationship of forces unless Israel wished to attack.

Although the Israelis were not above all reproach, since they proceeded forthwith to reinforce the "Bar Lev line," everyone agreed that the Cairo authorities had placed themselves in an unfortunate moral position. They could not, so long as the status quo was not re-established on the border, prevent the Israeli government from suspending on September 6 the conversations conducted by Mr. Jarring.

It was in this climate of mutual bitterness and violent recriminations that the peace machinery began to slip out of gear. The most serious crisis which had yet pitted Hussein against the Palestinians broke out in Jordan. The king of Jordan had also accepted the Rogers plan, thus aggravating the hatred which the Palestinian organizations had sworn against him. At the beginning of the second half of September, he was pushed into a desperate position by the incessant demands of *Al-Fatah* and the PFLP—which had just defied international opinion by diverting several commercial airplanes and holding fifty innocent travelers as hostages. Taking advantage of the anti-Palestinian climate, and egged on by his supporters, Hussein unleashed against the *fedayin* an operation of unspeakable ferocity which all too soon became genocide: soldiers were buried alive, refugee camps were destroyed by bombs, and villages by napalm.

The horror of this campaign was accentuated by the fact that it was begun immediately after a visit to Cairo by the Jordanian king, who appeared as an arm of the Arab leaders and a policeman of the international community, charged with protecting not only his own crown, but the peaceful continuation of commercial air flights. He became a guardian of liberty, allowing Nasser and his interlocutors to make peace without further consideration of the Palestinians.

On September 25, King Hussein and Yasser Arafat, leader of *Al-Fatah,* met in Cairo under the aegis of the *Raïs.* They were attempting to find, if not a solution to the crisis, at least a way to put an end to the massacre. In this they succeeded: and the international press published a photo in which could be seen, hand in hand, the man who had just massacred some twenty thousand of his compatriots, and the head of the very organizations which he was trying to crush. Behind them, his arms around their shoulders, was the Egyptian *Raïs,* who had passed from the role of leader of the Near Eastern revolution to that of magnanimous mediator.

The romantic, unflinching student, the austere *bikbashi,* the Arab *zaim* who made sparks with every word, the Egyptian *Raïs* feared by the West and adored by the Soviet Union, was succeeded by a graying and stooped figure, benevolent and eager for compromise. Was the change definitive? There was no more time for Gamal Abdel Nasser to invent a new avatar.

PART SEVEN

The
Chess Player

31

September 28

On September 28, at around 6:15 P.M., all efforts at cardiac resuscitation were abandoned as Gamal Abdel Nasser, president of the United Arab Republic, died of a cardiac arrest.

Doctor el-Sawi, the *Raïs*'s private physician, began to weep. Tahia, the president's wife, rushed into the room and, bending over the body of her husband, seized his hand and kissed it.

Several very close colleagues had gathered at the bedside of the dying man: Sami Sharaf, Mohammed Hassanein Heykal, General Mohammed Fawzi, Mahmud Fawzi, Vice-President Anwar el-Sadat, and Minister of the Interior Sharawi Gomaa. They had been notified when the heart attack had taken a tragic turn. Some were silently weeping, others prayed.

When the doctors announced that they had given up all hope, the visitors withdrew to confer in the next room and make their very first decisions. Tahia Abdel Nasser detained Mohammed Heykal for an instant: "I want nothing. I never wanted anything in my life but him. He was not a president to me, he was my husband. My only wish is to be buried at his side."

A council of Nasser's colleagues convened in the house of Manshiet el-Bakri and appointed Anwar el-Sadat, vice-presi-

dent of the republic, to break the news to his fellow citizens
—just as he had informed them of the *coup de force* of July
23, 1952. Radio and television programs were soon interrupted, and verses from the Koran replaced the usual broad-
casts. People wondered what was happening; some had a
presentiment of the painful news. As soon as Sadat made the
announcement, a popular explosion occurred which echoed
that of June 9, 1967, and prefigured that which was to break
forth on October 1. All Cairo was in the street, forming an
immense concert of lyric compassion. And the cry began to
rise over the city: "You live, O Abu Khaled!"

Gamal Abdel Nasser had suffered for more than ten years
from diabetes, an illness which requires a lot of rest. Yet he
worked from twelve to fourteen hours a day. On two occasions,
in 1968 and 1969, he had considered retiring from office. During the autumn of 1968, suffering cruelly from arterioscle-
rosis of the right leg, he spoke of his intentions for the first
time to his friend Heykal.

Nasser had just completed a three-week cure at a resort in
Georgia and was convalescing in Alexandria. "We were both
seated on the beach," recounted Mr. Heykal in *Al Ahram,*
"when Nasser looked at me and said: 'I am seriously thinking about a question which I would like to discuss with you.
If the pain does not lessen, how can I continue my work?
In that case, I would resign.' " Heykal attempted to dissuade
the president and advised him to organize his work more
effectively. Gamal, according to his confidant, replied: " 'How
can I accomplish my task when I am so tired? It is not fair
to the people. Only one thing prevents me from resigning: I
am afraid that my gesture would be interpreted in the Arab
world as a sign that I despaired of the chances of victory.' "
The two men agreed that they must count on a possible cure.

But coronary complications intervened, provoking an initial heart attack in September 1969. The Egyptian chief of

state again considered retiring. He confided to Heykal, who had once again counseled him to lighten his work load: "Don't you realize that is impossible? Every delegation that comes to Egypt wants to meet me. On every occasion I must appear in public. Besides, I must personally decide all questions concerning the war. . . ."[1]

In the course of a visit which he made to the Soviet Union in July 1970, Gamal Abdel Nasser spent two weeks in a nursing home. The Russian doctors advised him to work less. But as soon as he returned to Cairo he resumed his habitual rhythm of activity.

Then the feverish month of September 1970 arrived, with the Jordanian crisis, the dramatic visits of King Hussein and Yasser Arafat, and finally the pan-Arab conference of September 22. On Sunday the twenty-seventh, in the morning, friends who noticed the deep circles under Nasser's eyes and the weariness of his step as he climbed the stairways urged him to rest. "Men, women, and children are dying in Jordan," he replied. "We are engaged in a race against death. . . ."

At ten o'clock in the evening, after the signing of the agreement between Hussein and Arafat (where the famous photograph which has fixed his image as a peacemaker was taken), Nasser left the Hilton, feeling extremely tired. On Monday morning, constrained by an absurd protocol, he made it his duty to say farewell to the chiefs of state who had been his guests for a week.

At 10:30, he telephoned Mr. Heykal to ask about the latest developments in the Jordanian situation. He ended the conversation thus: "I feel extremely tired, and unable to stand on my feet." Heykal answered: "It is time you took a vacation," and suggested that he spend several days in Alexandria. "I must greet the Emir of Kuwait," said the *Raïs;* "then I

[1] Heykal in *Al Ahram,* October 9, 1970.

shall go home to sleep. . . . I want to sleep a long sleep . . . I want to sleep and sleep."

After a brief rest at Manshiet el-Bakri, he left at 12:15 for the Cairo airport. While greeting the Emir of Kuwait he felt, he said, sharp pains.

Upon returning home, he asked his wife if she had eaten lunch. "I was waiting for you," said Tahia. He sighed as he entered his room. "I don't think I could eat a thing." She followed him uneasily and watched him undress. She then called his private physician, Dr. el-Sawi, who examined him rapidly and called in two specialists. They diagnosed a severe heart attack due to a coronary thrombosis.

The doctors, wrote Heykal, increased the oxygen insufflations, electric shock, and cardiac massage, but to no avail —the president was expiring. At 6:15 P.M., all hope was abandoned. His death occurred on September 28—the ninth anniversary of the break-up of the UAR, and the third anniversary of the death of Abdel Hakim Amer, two of the cruelest dates in the life of Gamal Abdel Nasser.

32

Seven Names to Make a Man

Nasser had lived slightly more than thirty years of his life buried in the anonymity of the masses; five years of semi-clandestine existence, both before and after his rise to power; and fifteen years of intensely public life, burned by projectors and the eagerness of the people. At which moment should one seize and fix the image of this many-faceted figure, whom each year, each battle, each disaster only revived?

One cannot forget the orphan of 1927, the ardent schoolboy of 1934, the wounded student, the contemplative cadet, the defeated soldier of 1948. And why should one leave in shadow the schemer of Cairo, the camouflaged leader of 1952, the harsh dictator of 1954, the exalted tribune of Suez? Should one confine oneself to the triumphant *zaim* of Damascus, to the man overwhelmed by the events of 1967, or to the self-transcended mediator of the final days?

It is impossible to freeze an image in this frenetic film. As a point of departure, let us take the names and nicknames which defined him and shaped him, each in its turn. This might be one way to place him in relation to himself and others without too greatly impoverishing his meaning, for each of his names reflects the opinion of others.

"Gamal Abdel Nasser": destiny gave him a name which resounds in every language with a striking virile force, whether or not the two harsh, rasping syllables of the family name are isolated from the rest. In Arabic, these first sonorous syllables signify "Beauty, servant of the maker of victory." "*Nasr*" means victory; *Nasser,* the maker of victory, one of the titles by which "Allah, the All-powerful, the Merciful" is addressed. Thus Nasser was from the beginning designated by beauty, faith, and victory.

But this name which unfurled like a flag, for history and its trials, was hoisted only intermittently. For those close to him, for the crowd, for rumor and legend, for his enemies, for the friendly or hostile press, he bore in turn seven names which, when brought together, reconstruct the whole person just as the fragments of painted brick discovered in the Karnak peristyle have become once again people of the nineteenth dynasty.

He was Gamal first, for his mother Sett Fahima, for his uncle Khalil, and for Hassan el-Nachar, his first school friend; and later as well for his comrades in the *Putsch,* for the audience in Alexandria, and for the fervent crowd.

"Jimmy"[1] was the nickname given to him by Abdel Hakim Amer, and the one which certain cadets and later certain officers, such as his brother Leissy and his very close friends, used. This is not to mention his interlocutors at the American Embassy whom he called "Steve" and "Dave" and who called him "Jimmy" in return, as did certain students somewhat later in denouncing him as the "accomplice of the Americans."

For the foreign press, he was then the *bikbashi* (a title of Turkish origin which means "leader of thousands"). They were amused by the dissonance between this serious figure with lowered eyes, with the air of a permanent conspirator, and the pretty, facetious Turkish title which might have belonged to a hero of Voltaire or Gobineau.

The demonstrators of the streets of Cairo, irritated by the treaty signed with the British, had chosen to make him "Ibn el-Bustag," son of the postman. This was derisive perhaps, but it was also a good sociological observation. His was a revolution of the lesser ranks, of petty bourgeois on their way to becoming members of the grande bourgeoisie.

But soon he became the *Raïs,* the president, the "boss," to quote the excellent title of a fine book by Robert St. John.[2] This name expressed in a simple form, at once familiar and threatening, the authority of the man of the constitution of 1956, of the nationalization of Suez, of the negotiations with the great powers. But he was not the *Raïs* only for outsiders or those abroad. One of his American biographers points out

[1] Inspired, at the start, by the "non-Egyptian" Arabic pronunciation of his name, "Djemal."

[2] Robert St. John, *The Boss,* New York, 1960.

that in his closest entourage he was so called: "Is the boss here?"

But outside Egypt, at the height of his glory, and in times of crisis, he remained simply "Nasser." To Guy Mollet and to those in Tel Aviv the name suggested convenient comparisons with a far crueler dictator and furnished journalists with a simple word for their headlines, and the Arab crowd with that marvelous verbal hashish: "Nasser, Nasser! . . ." This formula, chanted for hours and with emphasis on the "a" and the final "r" could already induce a feeling of victory. Besides this, there were "Nasserism" and the "Nasserites." In short, it was a good insignia.

But the "*Raïs*" and "Nasser," and even the sumptuous "Gamal Abdel Nasser" were to blend and form one final name, that which the crowd at the funeral cried louder than any other: "Abu Khaled" (father of Khaled). Thus the tradition which reduced the father to the role of progenitor of his eldest son, as well as reducing the son to the role of simple offspring (Ibn el-Bustagi) had made of this already somewhat fabulous personage the father of an unknown young man of twenty called Khaled. It was a way of ensuring that all the descendants resemble the primal father, that figure who alone could promise security at the very hour when it might be lacking.

The single word "stature" sums him up. There are tall, strong, fat or heavy men. He was exactly what is called a man of great stature: six feet tall and two hundred eleven pounds in his last years. When he rose before the microphone, he reminded one of a statue from the Cairo museum, in heavy, high-relief granite.

Nasser always seemed to dominate the groups in which he found himself, whether at the UN or in Belgrade, Damascus, or Alexandria. The influence he exerted over men like Hussein or Arafat, whom he dominated with his sheer bulk, was in part due to that stature, on which he knew how to play with magnanimity. And what force there was in the handshake of this champion preparing for combat!

His face had more charm in life than it appeared to have in photos or films. True, it was a hard face, with a forehead narrowed by astrakhan locks, and dark eyes shot through with a greenish light—gazelle-eyes for some, tiger-eyes for others—eyes so close together that they seemed to pinch his nose, which stood out like a post, and to bear deep inside some troubling obsession. His complexion was the color of the Nile at flood, very "Upper Egypt," and imparted true nobility to his heavy face with its formidable jaws, the jaws of a meat-eater, though he hardly ate any, preferring a peasant diet of beans, rice, and cheese.

Perhaps this was the face of a wild animal at rest. Yet it was lit by a slightly nervous, but very communicative smile. The source of his charm was a metallic voice which, resounding in public, became ingratiating in conversation, and a glance which though it could be imperious, even cruel, most often conveyed a very Egyptian sort of languor, velvety and a bit embarrassed. To be unaware of a certain seductive power which we would call "Latin," the power of a "magnet"—the word is his[3]—which emanated from his somewhat feline body, is to understand nothing of a career founded as much on the charm of the tête-à-tête as on the enchantment of the common people and daring strategic moves.

He worked very hard. To a visitor who asked him in 1968 what he had learned in fifteen years of political life, he answered simply: "Not to go to bed at two o'clock in the morning any more." He devoted from twelve to fourteen hours a day to his work, though in a much less irregular man-

---

[3] We have quoted his interview with J. Benoist-Méchin. He then used the English word "magnet." In Arabic, the word *magnatis* has a somewhat farcical, vulgar side, at once "charming" and "sorcerer."

ner in his last years than in 1952–3. At that time it was customary for him to seek admittance around midnight to the office of a Free Officer (who would rarely be there alone, but surrounded more usually by a squad of secretaries, solicitors, and friends). Since the installation of his office in the Kubbeh Palace, he divided his work between Farouk's former palace and his house at Manshiet el-Bakri, where he spent mornings reading the "intelligence syntheses" drawn up by his services (formerly Amin Shaker, then Ali Sabri, and finally Sami Sharaf, who led a team of more than fifty specialists). At the palace he received visitors for many hours, and asked many questions. But he preferred to be interviewed himself in his drawing room at Manshiet el-Bakri.

The presidential offices had been installed for several years in the enormous palace at Heliopolis where so many kings had been born. It had become a kind of factory, with Agdelmagid Farid, secretary-general of the presidency, as its director. Here one could find Nasser's old friends, grown somewhat remote but still in their niches, and entrusted with "special" missions of supervision, cross-checking, and intelligence. Among these was Abdelkader Hatem, who had formerly succeeded Salah Salem at the head of the propaganda service and in 1959 had played the role of the regime's ideologue.

Cyrus Sulzberger of *The New York Times* received this answer when he asked the *Raïs* in early March 1969 whether he had any "dreams for twenty-five years hence": "I have no personal dream. I have no personal life. I have nothing personal. . . ."

Several months earlier, Emmanuel d'Astier had sought to acquire even more information. He asked about Nasser's parents and his childhood; he could only extract a few fragments of confidential statements: "For an Arab, that is a difficult question. . . . Yes, my grandfather was a peasant . . . I do

not remember my mother . . . we were a very large family"
(and he counted on his fingers to find the number).

His attitude in this matter was and remained that of a
middle-class Egyptian. His wife Tahia led a discreet but un-
concealed life. Her position was similar to that of many
Egyptian wives. A Westerner often met these women escorted by their husbands in public places, but if he invited
the couple to dinner, the wife would invariably be too tired
or hampered by her children to come along. But we have
seen that Tahia did appear at his side at certain receptions;
she was an attentive hostess for the friends and visitors whom
the *Raïs* wished to honor personally.

And when d'Astier saw fit to ask him "And what about
women?", he received this answer, which reflected some in-
voluntary humor, perhaps, but which was very revealing:
"Read what we say about it in our charter. I believe in complete equality. . . . My daughter Hoda works in the presidency: I wanted it that way!" To another interlocutor he was
to say proudly: "My second daughter was rejected in an examination. Are we not forming an egalitarian society?" It
was true that he could not be reproached with nepotism, or
with familial exhibitionism. Photos of Nasser with his children appeared from time to time, but it could not be said
that this family of five daughters and sons in a way burdened
the Egyptian people.

Gamal was nonetheless proud of his children. When he
received Richard Crossman in 1955, he led him, before serving dinner in the kitchen, into the adjoining room where two
little girls were sleeping. Crossman expressly noted this attitude which was not, however, typically Egyptian. Nasser
never made any plan for his sons, repeating that it was for
them to choose their own future. There was nothing he loved
so well as to spend two or three days with his family on official property—that of the prime ministers—at the Cataracts

twenty kilometers from Cairo, where there were flowers and tennis courts.

This good father was not a very affectionate son. He did not love his father, a post office employee whom he reproached with having been an unkind husband and having remarried too soon after the death of Fahima. Relations between Gamal and Abdel Nasser Hussein were often stormy. The *Raïs* hated to see his father's photograph in the newspapers and he sometimes remarked on this to an editor-in-chief, who had thought he would please him by publishing it. "I do not want, for my father or my brothers, any publicity which might corrupt them. I want them to live like ordinary citizens."

Gamal nevertheless had his brother Leissy assigned to a responsible post as head of the Liberation Assembly for the city of Alexandria. He did not have reason to congratulate himself on this stretching of his principles, and he eventually had Leissy placed under house arrest as a penalty for a too whimsical management of his affairs. Another brother, Shawki, acquired a dubious reputation by translating into Arabic the *Protocols of the Elders of Zion*. The last, Ezz el-Arab, seems to have had no political existence.

Nasser was typically Egyptian in his natural sentimentality. He was often guided by old attachments in making decisions. Nevertheless, he drove one of his best friends to suicide and two others into exile. One of his companions of July 1952, Colonel Yussef Saddiq, said several years later in Geneva: "What I don't like about him is that he doesn't know how to cry. . . . Yes, for example, after the war in Palestine, we all cried except for him. . . ."

Was there really nothing personal in his life? He enjoyed various recreations, games, sports, and the pursuit of culture. Above all he loved the game of chess, to which he devoted long hours in the company of Abdel Hakim Amer, under the critical eye of Mohammed Heykal. "A political game," d'Astier pointed out to him in November 1967. "Yes, and that is why I no longer play it: I have other games, now. . . ." After the estrangement of Marshal Amer after the great crisis of 1967, it seems that he did not in fact substitute for Amer another privileged partner.

He had one other passion: movies, which he was not content merely to watch, but which he made himself, edited, and showed to his family. And he played tennis, in spite of his heavy frame, and ping-pong, at which he was quite adept.

Nasser read a great deal; books less than magazines, and magazines less than newspapers. *Al Ahram,* of course, two or three American dailies, the best British weeklies, and often the Beirut *Jarida* took up three or four hours of his day.

He was passionately interested in journalism. After seeing him over and over haunting the press bed of the *Misri,* the *Akher Sa'a,* or the *Rose el-Youssef,* putting his hand on the brush-proof and voraciously rereading the proof itself, Abdel Hakim Amer said to him one evening in 1954: "You should have been a newspaperman. . . ." It was no accident that his best friend in his last years, Mohammed Heykal, was himself a journalist, and that the "civilian" to whom he was the most attached at the beginning of the revolution was the editor-in-chief of *Al-Misri,* Ahmed Aboul Fath. Surely one of the *Raïs*'s regrets was not to have been talented as a writer himself. But he knew better than to hold it against Heykal for being indispensable to him in this area.

Art does not seem to have played a large role in his life. The furniture and paintings one glimpsed in his home did not suggest that he took much interest in them. Like many Egyptians of his generation and milieu, he was rather late in discovering Pharaonic art, which had for a long time been considered by the Muslims and middle classes to be irreverent and pagan. (Nowadays schoolchildren are taken on trips to Sakkarah.) In 1954, when the admirable "solar boats" of Guizah were uncovered, he insisted on visiting the works. He was observed emerging from the excavation more astonished than delighted. But he was touched, because it had been Egyptians who had done these things. They had been neither Arabs nor Muslims, but they had been worthy. Why had he not been told about them sooner?

He was more sensitive to music, and above all to the music of his country and the song-poems which made Umm Kalsum the only person born in Egypt whose glory could eclipse his own, after that of Mustafa Nahas. Nothing touched the hearts of Egyptians, and many other Arabs, more than that silken, melismatic voice, which would slip away and become lifted again in immense modulation, its tender outbursts interrupted by melodious sighs. Gamal was infatuated with her song; early on in the regime, he would never miss one of her Thursday evening concerts, which often lasted five or six hours.

But he also loved other music. It has been pointed out that several days before the *coup d'état* of 1952 he made the decision to act on July 22 while listening to a recording of *Scheherazade,* significantly a Russian work on an Oriental theme.

Was Nasser an authoritarian, a born dictator, unable to tolerate contradiction, reducing everything around him to a *tabula rasa?* This description lacks subtlety. Gamal Abdel Nasser, a son of the Saïd, was a naturally passionate and intolerant man. He was capable of a great violence and his calm was more restraint than serenity.

Let us not even try to imagine his reaction to the caprices of one of his sons, a mistake by his secretary, or an oversight of his wife's. Let us observe instead the reflexes of this man,

who wished, and knew, how to control himself before foreigners. In the course of our discussions in November 1955, I
pointed out to him that what he was demanding of Palestine
might endanger world peace. Before giving his very judicious
answer that it was always the small nations who were required to be watchful of the peace of others, he showed a
glance and gesture of anger, very brief but very revealing.
Three years later, Benoist-Méchin contrasted one of his
declarations on Egyptian non-intervention in Algeria with the
opinion of "certain newspapers." The retort burst forth:
"When one is speaking with a chief of state, one does not
weigh his word against newspaper articles!" But he quickly
resumed control of himself.

What was striking in these conversations was not so much
his reactions, which were sometimes harsh, but the fact that
the foreign interlocutor always had the impression that he
could go as far as he liked with him. An American diplomat
even pointed out that almost all the journalists whom he had
accompanied to the *Raïs* afterward remarked: "Did you hear
what I dared to say to him?" He himself asked many questions in the most sincere and modest tone, thus inviting boldness. How candid his look could be, only to become suddenly
fiery.

This man, so self-possessed, so charming to almost all his
visitors, also hanged a certain number of leaders of the Muslim Brethren, sent to the gallows two Zionist spies guilty of
mere peccadilloes, allowed his jailers to beat to death several
Communist leaders and militants, caused or permitted political adversaries to be tortured, drove his best friend to suicide.
In his name thousands of more or less active opponents
suffered in a half dozen concentration camps, not to mention
the five hundred baffled Jews whom he imprisoned on the
day after the disaster of June 1967.

Was Nasser cruel? With the exception of his former

friend Ahmed Aboul Fath, his adversaries almost never maintained this. He was capable of terrible reactions, and capable also of taking pleasure in sadistic revenge, or of holding a vicious threat over a friend. He had an indescribable way of looking at a colleague or a minister, and saying, "You really ought to stay at home for a few days," but he was not bloodthirsty. This does not mean that the tortures which blemish his regime's record were due solely to the initiative of Salah Nasr or Zakaria Mohieddin, any more than the defeat of 1967 was entirely due to the errors of Abdel Hakim Amer, Sedky Mahmud, or Shams Badran. The immense power at his disposal, the meticulous control he exercised over the entire machinery of state, and even over the whole of public life and a good many private lives, made him the man truly responsible for what occurred in Egypt from April 1954 to September 1970. This can be qualified only by the fact that his passionate concern for detail often blinded him to the total situation.

He was not cruel, then, but crafty, undone by cunning as others are by vice, and unshakably mistrustful. It is not possible to undertake functions such as his, constantly menaced from inside and out, without surrounding oneself with extreme precautions and constantly keeping in mind the idea which he confided to Cyrus Sulzberger: "I shall tell you something which I have drawn from my own experience: at the summit, there is a perpetual struggle for power." From this conviction, and from the certitude which he had, especially after the crisis of March 1954, that no one but himself could carry on the enterprise begun in 1952, he derived a system of interlocking security measures of an improbable and costly complexity.

The army had been the source and the first base of his power. But it had almost abandoned him in 1954, and threatened to constitute a force equal to his own. Hence the almost pathological care with which he endowed it as an heir, while keeping watch over it like Bartholo. The *mushir* Amer was assigned to "pamper" it, but all around the services kept a close eye on its activities, constantly reshaping its general staff, dismembering its units, and paralyzing the whole. The means of surveillance contributed to immobilizing the army in June 1967: troops were prohibited from approaching to within twenty kilometers of the cities, and gasoline was rationed, thus assuring the impotence of the army's best unit, that of General Shazli. Nasser's mistrust was clearly ruinous. In fact, Nasser's regime was not supported by the army, but rather by the army's special services, the *mukhabarat*. With the exception of Heykal and Amer, all those who really counted in Nasser's political life came from there, from Zakaria Mohieddin to Ali Sabri, from Shams Badran to Sharawi Gomaa, from Sami Sharaf to Amin el-Hewidi. The *mukhabarat* was the major power, active in the university, in the working-class neighborhoods, in Damascus, Geneva, Beirut, and Algiers—everywhere except Israel, where it was rather quickly neutralized. But since it was advisable that the *mukhabarat* not be too powerful, it dealt through two other networks, the *mabahes el-Ama*—the political police—and the specialized services of the presidential office.

Over this pyramid of intelligence services, sometimes complementary but more often contradictory, reigned the *Raïs,* drunk with suspicion and power. Who would not have grown somewhat eccentric in this climate of conspiracies against conspiracies, in this atmosphere of a permanent plot against oneself? The strangest fact of all was that during the biggest crisis this formidable manipulator of records and rumors let himself be fooled like a child by the information provided by the Soviet and Syrian services. Had he suddenly forgotten the virtues of careful verification and the poisonous power of misinformation?

Here one penetrates to the center of Nasser's intellectual system, a superb edifice built upon a deep fault: the inability to distinguish true from false. This great political figure, who confounded so many adversaries and survived the worst disasters, suffered from an indescribable illness, half Arab folklore and half personal character. He found it extremely difficult to distinguish—in his own words, in those of others, and even in the realm of facts—the real from the imaginary.

We have a perfect snapshot of him in his telephone conversation of June 6, 1957, with King Hussein. First he imagined that the disaster could be attributed to the Anglo-Americans, thus recreating the scenario of the Franco-English intervention of 1956. But he needed only several seconds more really to believe it and to become indignant. The same thing happened when he gave his "word as a soldier" to Christian Pineau that no NLF commando had been brought into Egypt, or when he assured Roger Baldwin that some jailed Jewish spies were not risking capital punishment, or when he asserted before Edouard Sablier that the French diplomats arrested in 1961 were guilty. "He's a liar," said Ben-Gurion, but this is far from certain. Was this simply a confused desire to believe or not to believe? An astonishing power of imagination and suggestion, or autosuggestion, since by dint of thinking of oneself in the third person one ends by taking one's fancies seriously? Or merely a strange aptitude for reconstructing facts and dreams?

Let us not forget that, of all the men to whom modern Egypt owes her sorrowful but real renaissance, Nasser chose as hero the feckless, ill-starred Ahmed Arabi, and as mentor an ineffectual mandarin, Mustafa Kamel. He did not choose the two real pioneers, the builder, Mohammed Ali, and the liberator, Saad Zaghloul. We must also remember that he was the one for whom nothing resembled victory so much as a defeat, and who arrived at the most perfect confusion of the two in history. But after so many magical substitutions and conjuring tricks, after mocking historical facts so gloriously, how could he possibly believe in them? For him history would always remain that dangerous *Putsch* of the night of July 22, 1952, whose every tragicomic episode and error served him; it would always remain the drama of the Suez, whose every catastrophe turned to his advantage. Hence it was difficult for him to know whom or what to believe.

Of course he believed in God, the "maker of victory" for whom he was named, at once the "all-powerful" and the "merciful." He was a good Sunni Muslim, hence optimistic, and certain that faith armed with a bit of virtue was sufficient to guarantee success and good fortune. But he was also a modern Muslim. In *The Boss,* Robert St. John attributes to him this curious statement: "When I was young, I did not want to be a Muslim because my father was one. . . . Since 1947, I do believe in something at the bottom of my heart. . . . But I think that all religions are fundamentally the same. . . ."[4] In 1954, he spoke to us of the Koran as a book unsuited to the institution of political action, and whose precepts should be considered in a cautiously critical spirit.

When Emmanuel d'Astier asked him: "What does God mean to you? Is He the language and the laws of the Koran?" he answered: "No longer. For me, He means saying: because He accepts it, I do this. Because He rejects it, I do not do that. . . ." This intimacy with God was perhaps arrogant, but in any case such interiorization was hardly banal in such a ritualistic milieu. It permitted this "Muslim by race" (as Péguy spoke of a Christian by race) to adopt a relatively secular strategy.

4 St. John, *The Boss,* New York, p. 229.

Legend, gossip, even the tone in which Nasser's name is often pronounced would have us believe him a racist, but this is incorrect. We shall not discuss at length the Shamuels of "lentil alley" who were the neighbors of his youth, nor shall we linger over his friendly relations as a young man with a young Jewish artist named Lydia who drew his portrait when he was seventeen. We have already sufficiently emphasized his cordial rapport with Yeruham Cohen. It is more interesting to consider the admiration he conceived for the two young Zionists who assassinated Lord Moyne, British minister to the Near East, in 1944. This act and the subsequent hanging of the two young men haunted him for a long time, and he spoke of it to his own people. "Here were men ready to die for their cause, who hold up an example to us. . . ." Was it this example which led him to terrorism himself, and which still exalted him when he fired on Hussein Sirry Amer in January 1952? We may be sure that Zionism, its followers and the exploits of all kinds accomplished in its name, had marked him even before his meeting with Captain Cohen.

Perhaps one must recognize in him a fascinating phenomenon, the "Zionist in reverse" described by Ibrahim Farhi in a brilliant evocation delivered over Radio Luxembourg on the day after the *Raïs*'s death. On the other hand, one ought perhaps to believe that he never yielded to the temptation to confuse Jews and Israelis, as in that rather glib declaration made in February 1969. "The Jews are our cousins. Moses was born in Egypt. The Israelis say that we are anti-Semitic, which is absurd. We are Semites ourselves and we consider the Jews of our country to be Egyptians."[5]

In March of 1953 we saw him, along with Naguib, coming out of a synagogue where they had been to greet their

[5] Interview with Cyrus Sulzberger.

fellow citizens who were Jewish. But fifteen years later he
sent hundreds of terrified artisans to jail merely because they
happened to pray in the same language as the pilots who
were flying sorties with impunity over Cairo. And, in the
meantime, no one ever heard of a Jew, however eminent or
apt for service to the nation, being named to a public office,
to a university position, or to the national bank or the
national labor union. Whoever knows Egypt knows the
patriotism of most of its Jews, which is strong enough to have
survived frequent exile, and the estrangement of a large part
of its population from Israel. In noting this one must add that
discrimination is naturally very different in a country hard-
pressed by Moshe Dayan's armored divisions from what it is
elsewhere.

Nasser, hardly affected by racism, was also very little interested in the outside world. Some might object that he read
avidly the commentaries in the Anglo-Saxon press. But his
interest was that of a strategist who wished to understand the
criticisms and gambits of an adversary, as a chess player might
try to guess the next move of his opponent. During his
"American period" he was very much taken in by the statements and confidences of the spokesmen of Washington.
"When I came to power, I was in favor of the Americans. I
speak English. I read their magazines. I admired their dreams
and their technical accomplishments. I thought that there
could be nothing better than 'the American way of life,' and
I believed naïvely in their anticolonialism." Such were his
words to Benoist-Méchin in 1958.

He never did give up a certain admiration for the British.
And no sooner did one of them show him sympathy, be it the
ambassador Sir Harold Beeley, or an MP such as Richard
Crossman, than he would overcome his highly political Anglo-
phobia and display the respect of a reader of Liddell Hart, of

a sportsman, of a peasant's grandson who knew what Willcox and Scott-Moncrieff had done for Egyptian agriculture.

And what of the Russians? He seemed to maintain a healthy relationship with them, on a nation-to-nation basis, although it was punctuated by crises such as the Iraqi revolution, the 1967 disaster, and perhaps also the strain of early 1970. But there were none of the lasting complexes which plagued his relations with the Western powers. In addition to this he saw the arrival or the return of many qualified men from Moscow: Daniel Solod and Serge Vinogradov, Dimitri Shepilov and Alexei Kosygin. Their arms were never so full of gifts, and their demands were never so disdainful, as to arouse his suspicion, or even his anger.

He did not know much about France. On the one hand he spoke of 1789, but on the other he said that, if he had wanted to save Farouk from being executed, it was in memory of Louis XVI. On another occasion he spoke favorably of de Gaulle, but Nasser was probably relieved that his name evoked too intense a reaction in Paris to allow him to visit there: he sent Abdel Hakim Amer in his place in 1965. "Gay Paris" seemed to him even more damnable than the nightclubs of Cairo and Beirut. He leafed through *Paris-Match,* but less often than *Time* or *Life.* He learned to read French very late in the game, and then only with difficulty, but he wanted it included in his children's education. And while he was extremely pleased to receive Sartre in 1967 and was interested in the final efforts of Gaullist diplomacy with respect to the Arab world, France seemed always very far away.

This ardent nationalist did have some foreign friends, however. It is hard to talk of friendship with Tito, but one can certainly say that their relations were cordial and even trusting, given the fact that the two men had roughly the same

diffident characteristics. The best of relations also prevailed
with the Yugoslavian ambassador in Cairo, Marko Nikezic,
and with the consul, Faiek Dizdarevic, the son-in-law of
André Philip and the brother of Belgrade's first ambassador
to Algiers, a very good friend of Ben Bella. In fact, if Nasser
really did have a good foreign friend it was the ambassador
whom Ben Bella himself had sent, Lakhdar Brahimi, who was
as pure as amber and more apt than anyone to keep the peace
between these two "sacred monsters." Brahimi also proved
up to the task of straightening out relations between the
Raïs and Houari Boumedienne after the ouster of Ahmed Ben
Bella, and again after the 1967 disaster.

By and large his friends must be sought within Egypt, though
he had none who were not such in a political way. In this
sense he was like Charles de Gaulle, who also cared little to
preserve for himself a "parallel domain" peopled with walking companions, card partners, or just plain friends.

Gamal's friends and his political allies were the same, but
two men seem to have managed the politico-affective role
which was the closest anyone ever came to being a friend of
the *Raïs*. These were Abdel Hakim Amer and Mohammed
Hassanein Heykal. The former was, next to Hassan el-Nashar,
who died at twenty-five, his best friend from 1938 to 1967.
The latter was the most faithful confidant of his years of
rule, from 1953, when they worked on the *Philosophy of
Revolution* together, until the very last hours.

Abdel Hakim Amer, the onetime "Robinson," was called
"Abdu" at home. Nasser's last son bears his name, though
after 1967 he was called only "Hakim." There is a family
tie here, and no other man alive shared Gamal's life to this
extent. In 1960, on the death of the Sheikh Ali Amer, the
field marshal's father, Nasser himself went to the village of

Minieh to represent the son whose duties to the nation had called him away to Syria. To those who displayed surprise, he replied, "I regarded the Sheikh as my own father."

Official relations between Gamal and "Abdu" no doubt changed after 1967, for the field marshal, though right in disagreeing with his friend and leader, had nonetheless become the symbol of his greatest error. But their friendship remained close and honors continued to be bestowed on the *mushir*. The president could not help growing irritated, however, with the increasingly fatuous and free life style of his friend, if only because it was so different from his own.

Tales about Amer's women and hashish were making the rounds. Was "Abdu" still upright? At any rate he kept bad company, Shams Badran for instance, whose influence worked against the *Raïs*.

When the break-up came, it was not as agonizing as it would have been ten years earlier. But it was reportedly quite trying even so, and, when d'Astier asked him somewhat indiscreetly how it had been, Nasser, who had been talking quite freely until then, cut him off rudely saying, "I do not want to answer that question!"

Mohammed Hassanein Heykal was not a very old friend of Nasser; the latter apparently noticed him when Heykal was working as a reporter in Palestine for the weekly *Akher Sa'a*. At that time Gamal's favorite journalist was Ahmed Aboul Fath. Shortly before his falling out with the latter, who was in fact Saroit Okasha's brother-in-law, he became friends with Heykal. The occasion was Nasser's request that Heykal republish in pamphlet form, and also effectively rewrite, Gamal's memoirs of the Palestine war, which had originally appeared in Heykal's newspaper. The journalist persuaded the *bikbashi* to make them into a book in which he could present himself more fully. Thus was born the *Philosophy of the Revolution,* an odd collection of ordinary memories and numerous digressions. What was Heykal's part in this work? Another journalist, asking Heykal if he had read the book, received the following answer: "In a word, dear friend, I wrote it."

From then on Heykal was an intimate adviser, a man for delicate missions, for editing difficult material. Abdel Hakim Amer was certainly different from Gamal in his gaiety, openness, and flexibility. But what about Heykal? He was a jovial manager, squat, yet supple, somewhat American in his matter-of-fact style, but at the same time very Egyptian. He was very typical of the new breed of men, strong in business, sure of themselves, sometimes living it up a bit and yet capable of being real taskmasters.

The "new class" which we have often mentioned was well spoken for by this daring master builder, who made *Al Ahram* into the best news outfit in Egypt and led it on to what is now almost its one-hundredth year of publication. Without government censorship he could perhaps have made it into a great international paper, but censorship denied him the liberty without which information is not worth the paper it's printed on. He was an intelligent, active man, with a keen sense of how to communicate to his readers. For ten years his Friday articles were the barometer of—if not an active force in— Egyptian government policy. It was known that he usually wrote them after a long session with the *Raïs.*

One question arises: how was it that this intimate confidant, personal friend, and valuable professional did not have, in the final analysis, more influence on the *Raïs?* How can it be that this man, bound to the Americans by so many things—primarily, it appears, by his convictions—could have been the spokesman for a policy which has led Egypt, after eighteen years of struggle for independence, into a unilateral alliance with Moscow? Was Gamal that unshakable? Was the force of circumstances irresistible? Did Egyptian independence inevitably lead in this direction? Perhaps Mohammed Hassanein Heykal was in fact much less pro-American than legend would have it. After all, one cannot forget that he was the man who opened the gates of information to the recently liberated Communists, even if they were only the doors of *Al Ahram.*

What future has this man, this active reflection of the departed leader? We can wager that he will not be satisfied merely to write the best book on Gamal Abdel Nasser, a biography which will also be an autobiography. . . .

Who, after these men, was closest to Nasser? Certainly Sami Sharaf, a political adviser for more than ten years, the first man to appear, each morning, at Manshiet el-Bakri along with Gamal's private secretary Mohammed Ahmed. Square-set, wooden-faced, taciturn, Sami Sharaf is typical of those old intelligence officers who formed the very foundation of the Nasserian state. He had been associated, as much as Nasser's two personal friends, in all the crises and important decisions. He probably gave Nasser the firmest support in the 1967 disaster. His influence had become considerable, especially after the elimination of Salah Nasr, the relative estrangement of Ali Sabri, and the complete estrangement of Zakaria Mohieddin, the other "lords of the secrets." His true influence was gauged on the day when he pushed through his cousin, General Fawzi, as minister of defense.

A man has reappeared, in the course of recent years, whose importance is reflected in his rapid promotion since Nasser's death: Mahmud Fawzi, the diplomat *par excellence,* the man whom the *Raïs* constantly consulted. Fawzi manages to maintain the honeyed sweetness of a smile which seems ready for some eternal kiss, along with the inherent coarseness of the Cairo government, that encampment of soldiers in civilian clothes. In Fawzi, Nasser again chose a man very different from himself, a bourgeois brought up in the English manner, whose refined conversation is garnished with polite silences. He turned naturally toward the West—without, for all that, favoring it. There is no doubt that Fawzi played an important part in the decision of the final months, and that he is a symbol, within the new regime, of the option for realism and peace.[6]

Ali Sabri was certainly Gamal's closest collaborator: he had been head of the cabinet from 1954 to 1957, minister of presidential affairs until 1962, president of the executive council until 1964, and finally premier from 1964 to 1965. As secretary of the Arab Socialist Union and contact man with the Soviets, he was a sort of leftist "ideologue," Moscow's man with the *Raïs*. In fact, in 1952 he was Gamal's go-between with the CIA and the American Embassy, and we have quoted above several of his statements, from 1954 to 1962, which hardly lead us to picture him with a knife between his teeth. His supposed leftist stand probably comes from two sources: first, Nasser, precisely because he believed Sabri to be impervious to the temptations of communism, appointed him more than once as his intermediary with the Soviets; second, because Sabri's two sworn adversaries, Heykal and Zakaria Mohieddin, had a reputation for being pro-Western. This prudent, intelligent man of state files and documents, who made little noise at a low volume, seems rather far away from Leninism, and rather less socialistic than certain other companions of the *Raïs*. Possibly he believed that a Soviet alliance was an absolute necessity and acted accordingly. But it is unlikely that he took such extreme

---

[6] As consul-general of Egypt in Jerusalem, thirty years ago, he had the opportunity of knowing the leaders of the Jewish Agency, with David Ben-Gurion at their head.

initiatives—except to block the way against a joint operation of Heykal and Mohieddin.

Of all the officials whom Gamal Abdel Nasser attracted to the center of power, Zakaria is probably the closest to a real statesman. Most people who lived in Egypt in 1965–6, when he was premier, say that the country seemed to them to be governed somewhat better than usual. Was he the only conspirator of July who could really tell right from wrong, and distinguish between fact and fiction? For a long time he was the "number one cop in Egypt," and consequently he retained a slightly sinister aura. It appears that the *Raïs* never considered him to be a friend, as he did his cousin Khaled: he was mistrustful of the man. Yet it was Zakaria whom he named as heir in the disaster of June 9, 1967. Was this done simply to eliminate him? To say so would be to attribute to Nasser far more Machiavellianism than could be believed.

In setting him up as the proponent of "another" political position, the *Raïs* helped to surround Zakaria with a myth, the myth—or mission—of a pro-Western alternative. More "managerial" than actually pro-American, Zakaria certainly supported the state capitalism which Nasser had imposed in promoting both Soviet-style statism and Yugoslav collectivism. The figure of Mohieddin suggests a kind of Kosygin of the Nile Valley, where Lenins are fewer and further between than in Moscow.

If Gamal had three friends, the third was definitely Khaled, Zakaria's cousin, a heart-warming, smiling progressive who, full of jovial audacity, could disarm the *Raïs* with his candor. The young major from the armored infantry did just that, for example in 1954, when he backed the Naguibist coup against Nasser. His only punishment was exile to Switzerland.

When he returned, a couple of years later, just in time for the Suez crisis, he took up his seat again in the council. When

Nasser came in everybody rose except for Khaled. "Well," said Khaled, "nobody told me. Everybody stands up now, when you enter?" They both laughed. Khaled alone continued to smoke in front of Nasser, though others refrained out of deference. Khaled's role was always a bit special; he never lost his frankness, but he also never reached the heights that his long involvement, loyalty, courage, and generosity might have made accessible to him. He had to content himself with being a representative to peace movements. He was esteemed and protected, but also held back.

Among the other Free Officers, for many years the closest to the *Raïs* was Saroit Okasha, whose sensitivity to the needs of the state and whose simplicity and culture were held in high esteem by Nasser. But he suffered from the outset because of his bourgeois origins and later even more so from the "treachery" of his brother-in-law, Ahmed Aboul Fath, the friend who became an enemy. Still later he was to be criticized for remaining on friendly terms with Salah Nasr, one of the scapegoats of 1967. So this controversial man had to be content with the respectable job of minister of culture, which gave him the chance to work with UNESCO in coordinating the project to save Abu Simbel. He also played an important part in the reopening of relations with France in 1958 and in the early peace feelers in the Near East.

Anwar el-Sadat, the unexpected heir, after having been one of Nasser's early "Mankabad" friends, and the herald of the coup of 1952, was involved in so many endeavors, plans, crises, and defeats that he became one of the intimate circle. It was he whom Nasser designated as first vice president, and thus the intermediary, in December of 1969, to the Rabat Conference, where so many sinister plots were rumored to be underway. The *Raïs* often made fun of Sadat, whom he called the *bikbashi sah* (colonel yes-yes) because of his excessive docility. "If he would only vary the way in which he agrees,

instead of always saying *sah,* I would feel a lot better," Nasser
would joke. But from "sah!" to "sah!" the ubiquitous Anwar
turned out to be Nasser's successor. The *Raïs's* handyman, he
learned to do just about everything. He was not the first man
to grow into a position of responsibility.

What other influential companions were there? At the end
of the "reign" the four most important were (along with
Heykal, Fawzi, and Sami Sharaf), Sharawi Gomaa, the boss of
the Arab Socialist Union and Minister of the Interior, an
intelligence officer and vigorous administrator who defined
himself frankly as "one hundred per cent Nasserist." Next
came General Sadek, (yet another) former chief of special
services who was promoted to chief of staff after having taken
the initiative in declaring a state of emergency following an
Israeli commando raid in 1968, while Nasser, the only one
qualified to make such a proclamation, was absent. Finally
came Abdelmagid Farid, the secretary general of the Assembly,
and Amin el-Hewidi, who both came up through intelligence service.

Such was, and is, with the exception of Abdel Hakim Amer,
the Nasserist brain-trust. Such were those whom one might
have called the "king's men." Not very picturesque, these
men had a plain style which camouflaged much brutality, and
a professional comradeship which concealed many treacheries.
Nasser did not know how to create institutions; neither did
he know how to gather about him a strong governmental
team. Like de Gaulle, the best he could manage was a kind of
trusteeship of power.

Yet, considering the society from which he emerged, the
obstacles which he overcame, the personnel available to him,
one is compelled to give a fairly high rating to the man of
the Suez and Aswan, of the Sinai, of Yemen, and of Abu-
Zaabal (his concentration camp). In the words of a CIA
agent who had dealings with him between 1952 and 1954

(quoted by Joachim Joesten): "The problem with Nasser is that he has no vices. We can neither buy nor blackmail him. We hate this guy's guts, but we can't touch him: he's too clean. . . ."[7]

33

Waiting for an Ordinary Man

"He dissolved like a grain of salt in water . . . ," says Abdu, the Cairene man-in-the-street who knows that the only thing which doesn't pass away is the face of the Eternal. Already the posters which, bearing his square, virile, stirring face, bore witness to Nasser's own obsequies, yellow and wither on the walls of Cairo. Most shop windows still display his portrait wreathed in black. But already a shift has taken place: the great ship has left port and reached the open sea, into a mist of memories where history will seek to locate him. The time for posters has passed, the time for statues is yet to come.

In the meantime, Egypt lives on in a kind of interim period, she who felt plunged into the void on the twentieth of September, 1970. A strongman's orphan, she finds more than a few reasons to be happy. Travelers confirm this: a certain weight has been lifted; one does not exactly breathe easily but at least more normally. The time for the average man,

[7] *Nasser*, London, 1960. Quoted by Maxime Rodinson in *Le Monde*, September 30, 1970.

whoever he might be, was in sight, the man of the "*bikbashi sah*" ready with the right word at the right time. Would it be a long time? Undoubtedly. There would be regrets and nostalgia which would magnify the *Raïs* out of proportion. In the meantime, let us try to look at his heritage in its proper perspective and to survey the acres of farmland which, in eighteen years, had grown out of acres of desert.

Was he really the first true Egyptian to lead Egypt since the Pharaohs? Yes, in a sense. Because he was not Albanian like Mohammed Ali nor a son of the landed bourgeoisie like Arabi, Zaghloul, or Nahas? Perhaps. But especially because, culturally, by origin and by custom, by faith, by his nearest acquaintances and by his failings, he was a common man.

He was exceptional in energy and in talent, but banal, very banal, in many characteristic traits of behavior. Were Zaghloul and Nahas not as authentic as he? Yes—but they were removed from the masses by knowledge of foreign import laws, by marriage or habitat, by personal relations, by restaurants which they frequented, by books which they read, and visits which they had made—Versailles, London, Vichy, Baden.

Nasser was not so set apart. A lover of *ful* and of the voice of Umm Kalsum, fond of interspersing his statements with Saïdi locutions and ponderous peasant sayings, he gave Egypt back to herself, for better or for worse. He was abusive, overwhelming, adventurous, violent, and extravagant, but he was completely Egyptian even in his wildest hours of pan-Arab fantasies. He was Egyptian.

Did Nasser break with the past? Or did he come to grips with it, learn how to inherit, to perpetuate, and to digest it? In fact, Gamal Abdel Nasser will be said to be, much more than it had been believed, an inheritor. Though he did not give them due credit, his vision and his deeds follow, on the whole, the two great men who resurrected Egypt, Mohammed

Ali and Saad Zaghloul, the baptizer and the liberator.[1] He would not otherwise have had, from the first, the formidable continuity and implacable assurance of his views, nor his limitless cynicism which reduced everything to expediency. Only a foreign adventurer, a soldier of fortune ashore on another continent in the pay of the Anglo-Turks, could have forced Egypt to comply with his laws, forced the Egyptians to assent to his views. What were they, if not the raw material of his greatness?

Nasser could not adopt this attitude—he was the son of a fellah, a man of the twentieth century. But though he also strapped Egypt on the operation table, he made of her, not a strong giant, as the great viceroy had done, but a military cooperative. The shock treatment of Mohammed Ali had, in the first instance, substituted state feudalism for clan feudalism. Nasser undertook to break the agrarian capitalists and the moneyed aristocracy. To whose benefit? A third estate? Or was it to the benefit of those whom we must already call "the people"?

Relying less on the nation as a whole than on elites, Saad Zaghloul had undertaken to liberate Egypt in 1919. More narrow at the outset, Nasser's base broadened until it surpassed that of the Saadian revolution. Perhaps this resulted from the change of life which the system of the *Raïs* brought to a large segment of the peasant masses and especially to mill- and factory-workers who became economically consolidated and politically advanced, however harsh the regimentation of the trade unions.

By comparison with Zaghloul, Nasser lacked a certain human quality. A great popular leader has to be true while sublimating the truth, as a great work of art does to reality—for example, the Sheikh el-Balad in the Cairo Museum. Saad

---

[1] In his November 9 speech at Al-Azhar, he nonetheless likened himself to Mohammed Ali in saying that the British had wanted to "re-create Navarino."

Zaghloul was authentic. He shone with his own light—he did not merely reflect the light of others. He taught and attracted followers. Paternalism? The muscled fraternalism of the *Raïs* did not have the same human flavor. He was more picturesque, more ostentatiously truthful, but he had less cultural value. A leveling populism replaced real popular action.

It was no accident that Gamal Abdel Nasser, whom so many factors set apart from Mohammed Ali and so many others likened to Zaghloul, still understood the former better than the latter. But it was not by chance either that he led his movement of 1952 under the aegis of Arabi Pasha, that humiliated officer, frustrated landowner, bewildered leader and evanescent strategist, rather than under that of Mohammed Ali or Saad.

His targets were sometimes unclear, like an escaping prey in the gunsight of a nervous hunter, but the basic objective was clear: to be independent. But must we give Nasser his due for realizing what Zaghloul had only partially initiated? In taking up the aims, and some of the procedures, of the Wafd, and in adopting a strategy as rich in ruses and in "stages" as that of his enemy Bourguiba, the Egyptian leader uprooted the British occupier in less than four years, not only its military power but its financial grip as well. In 1956 Egypt was independent. But what about in 1970?

The parallel between the British occupation and the Soviet presence does not hold up for long. On this point let us again consider the words of the *Raïs*. Speaking to William Attwood of *Look* magazine[2] in March of 1968, Nasser refused to entertain a comparison of the two foreign presences. "The British imposed their advisers on us by means of a treaty. But after the Sinai, I asked the Soviets to send us

[2] Also former U.S. ambassador to Guinea.

officers to train our men. It was I who decided to have them come and it is I who shall decide when they will leave."

This eventual decision will not depend solely on the successors of Gamal but on many factors: the strategic situation in the Near East, on the one hand, and international opinion and the world position of the U.S.S.R. on the other. It will also depend on the resolution of a debt currently estimated at a billion dollars (for weapons alone), a debt which Moscow will not seek to recover by the same means as would the old European capitalism, but which will nonetheless be a burden. And, finally, the decision will depend on a political and cultural presence which has become considerable.

Until a half century ago, and even more recently, the culture of the ruling classes of Egypt was distinctly "imported." But one cannot speak today of a "Marxist colonization," as one once spoke of the eclectic and aesthetic alienation of the old Europeanized elites. The Marxist organizations are rooted in the Egyptian reality, and indeed their analyses and programs are marked—except in the case of occasional followers of Lukacs or Bettelheim—by a solidity which we shall call pyramidal in order to make clear its authenticity.

It is not simply because almost everything interesting which was written about Egypt at the end of Nasser's reign has been more or less inspired by social realism and dialectical materialism that one must inveigh against the new cultural domestication. The concentration camps were, for those who survived them, tough schools of truth and initiative. But what needs to be pointed out is both the conformism which is being created, and the repression and the harassment of nearly all the non-Marxist sector which Mohammed Hassanein Heykal has not taken under his explicit protection— these have diminished Egypt. One cannot sum up the situation simply by saying that quantity had been substituted for quality in the national priorities, that the doctrinaires have ousted

the snobs. But much of Egypt's charm and beauty, now labeled reactionary, has evaporated or been driven out. This will go down on the record against the *Raïs*.

More Egypt for more Egyptians: such could be the cultural definition of Nasserism, which, in its last year, saw four million children in school and a hundred thousand students at the university. But apart from some breakthroughs in critical spirit, such as the period from 1961–2, when the discussion and development of the charter was taking place, intellectual formulas and police control too often turned this new Egyptian Egypt into an amputated Egypt, an Egypt stunted by chauvinism and dogmatism which either exiled or silenced its own elites.

Who could deny the material benefits which accrued to Egypt, later the UAR, by eighteen years of Nasserism? We have mentioned the Sadd el-Ali, the High Dam of Aswan, one of the keystones of the regime, which followed the example set by Mohammed Ali (who himself was the builder of the first great dam, near Cairo). How can one weigh Nasserism without adding to the scale the prodigious mass of the "Sadd," its agricultural benefits (an increase of one-third the amount of arable land), and its contribution to industry (an estimated increase of twelve per cent during 1968–9 in heavy industry driven by the dam). Of course one must consider the drawbacks of the project, the silting, the retension of alluvium, the evaporation, the risk which the great volume of water held back by the dam has imposed on the thirty million Egyptians living below it. And one must admit that the High Dam is not "the" solution, because there is no single solution in a country whose own peculiar problems as well as those inherited from years of foreign exploitation and inertia swarm like unwanted children. But the inevitable conclusion is that, without the High Dam, Egypt would have succumbed to the asphyxia or the apoplexy of overpopulation.

Based on Aswan, industrialization has become *the* great national project—Gamal Abdel Nasser never failed to emphasize this. The fourfold increase of industrial production in eighteen years, the tripling of the effective working population, the doubling of exports was of tremendous value to the independence of the country, to the modernization of its institutions, and to its cultural development. But it was not an effective response to Egypt's most persistent challenge: her soaring population.

When Gamal Abdel Nasser took power in 1952, Egypt counted some twenty-three million inhabitants. When he disappeared she had to feed thirty-three million. In the meantime the cultivated area was expanded by nearly a million hectares and agricultural production increased. But was this increase as large as forty-five per cent, as recent official figures show? If so, it is very hard to explain the rise in wheat imports, which doubled between 1955 and 1965. Moreover, studies undertaken and precisely analyzed by René Dumont do not confirm this high figure.

In short, like other collectivized agricultural areas (with the exception of China and North Vietnam), Nasser's Egypt stagnated, especially in cotton production, which increased only from eight to ten million gantars[3] in twenty years. But new areas devoted to rice production (more than 500,000 feddans[4] in ten years) liberated Egyptian agriculture from the old, speculative monoculture which experts have so long criticized.

The problem of subsistence and standards of living cannot be reduced to a simple relationship between the amount of

[3] A *gantar* equals approximately one hundred pounds.
[4] A *feddan* is about the size of an acre.

cultivated land and the growth of the population (an average of 2.9 per cent over the last few years). Many other factors play a part. If it is true that Egypt had a million industrial workers, as the *Raïs* asserted, in 1969, then the unemployment problem was moving toward a partial solution. But industrialization and urbanization have not wiped out rural unemployment, or rather "non-employment," be it seasonal or no. Nasser pointed this out in 1965 in a sharp criticism of the staff of the Arab Socialist Union, whom he found to be very ill-informed on the problem.

Why should a high birth rate, even one which is alarmingly high, be regarded only as a calamity? All vital growth is of value. But the critical period in which this country finds itself makes it necessary for corrective measures to be sought out. The Nasserist system was not afraid to advance birth control (which Islam tolerates more easily than either Christianity or Judaism) as a solution: over a thousand family-planning centers were opened. Did the thirty-three million Egyptians of 1970 live better than the twenty-three million of 1952? We must avoid the official statistics, which show for example an increase of three hundred per cent in the GNP over eighteen years and a two hundred ten per cent increase in per capita income. It would need clever bookkeepers indeed to provide such good news to the Egyptian people. But a simple maintenance of the old standard of living, given the ten million new consumers, and in improvement in social and sanitary services in the villages, which all had running water by 1970, is a good enough record. It was made possible by some fairly radical shifts in incomes and consumption—the bleeding of the aristocracy and the bourgeoisie—and by partially halting the monopolization of profits by the "new class."

An honorable result, especially if one considers the comical expansion of public services (1,700,000 civil employees in 1967), the awesome burden of the military (twenty-four per cent of the budget),[5] and the enormous expenditures for propaganda, the special services and repressive organizations, and the High Dam. The most recent assessments of the public debt are agonizingly high—more than two billion dollars. Grandeur is costly. We may wager that in a few years, when the accounts are drawn up, the costs of the mission of agents of the *mukhabarat* (the intelligence service) in Beirut and Baghdad will be found to have been greater than those of the High Dam.

"During the period of transition from capitalism to socialism, the bureaucracy will attempt by any possible means to take a disproportionate share of power in order to control production and to dominate social relations. It will try to monopolize these functions, and, in this way, to restore capitalism." It was Gamal Abdel Nasser himself who spoke these words in 1964, at the time when, having freed and apparently "rehabilitated" the best Marxist cadres, he was forming government organizations to safeguard the prescriptions of the charter. Self-criticism? Prophecy? "Socialism according to the charter" was to be kept in line by these measures.

Yet Nasser refused, at least until March 1969, to give the citizens any great measure of control and initiative and, in fact, trusted the bureaucracy alone. Nasser could sniff out the real intentions of bureaucrats as only a peasant could, a peasant who had suffered for four thousand years under the *nabut* (cudgel) of the village sheikh. Yet because he always favored the state above feudal clans, and the government staff above the producers themselves, Nasser wasted most of the

---

[5] This does not include expenditures assigned to what the Egyptian government calls the "balance of structures"—the maintenance of public order, which mobilizes many organizations, and costs the state almost as much as the military.

opportunities afforded by socialism. He instead imposed on the men of the Nile Valley a type of collectivism which, for better or for worse, adapted to the traditional "hydraulic system" the authoritarian formulas of the Soviet Union instead of Yugoslav-type cooperativism which gives greater freedom for worker initiative.

"There is no socialism without freedom!" cried the demonstrators of Helwan and Alexandria in February and November of 1968. To which Nasser replied *in petto* that there was no socialism either without constraints. The besieged and hungry Egypt of the 1950s was not the best laboratory for "socialism with freedom," which perhaps is not only a dream.

It was a sloppy, ill-tempered stab at socialism, improvised by a patriotic but economically and democratically uncultured statesman, and by men temporarily hauled out of jail to furnish him with ideas. The real question, in the last analysis, is this: did all this bungling really blaze the way to a collective improvement, or did it merely create a caricature of socialism too grotesque not to offend large segments of public opinion—and not only that of the privileged classes both old and new.

One can ask the same question about Arabism and more generally of all the strategies which involved Egypt in matters beyond her borders. It is significant that during Nasser's funeral the people of Cairo addressed the same agonizing question to both Hussein and Arafat: "What have you done to him?" It was a global denunciation of those politics beyond the Nile Valley which had forced Egypt and her leader to undertake too great a number of extenuating responsibilities. Only a few days before, when he still worked side by side with the chief of state, Mohammed Heykal had written in *Al Ahram:* "The UAR does not want to be the devoted executor of a foreign policy led by insolvent bankers and irresponsible gamblers. . . ." Heykal's anti-Arab apostrophe was even more virulent than that of the mourners of October first.

Does this signal a great withdrawal into the valley of the Nile, the abandonment of Arabism, the denial of the loftiest hours of Nasserism? Even before the Palestine quarrel had grown into inter-Arab genocide, one of the last foreign visitors to Gamal Abdel Nasser had suggested the possibility of such a withdrawal. And the *Raïs* answered laconically: "That is the question. . . ."

Everything points to it: the Syrian disaster of 1961, the fiasco of 1967, the excesses of Baghdad and the disappointments of Yemen. It will not require great daring for Nasser's successors to back out of Arabism. They will have only to read the history of the past fifteen years, and to consider the consequences of the ideas put forward since 1964 by the founder of the UAR. Like de Gaulle's successors, who must initiate the switch from a strategy of "each his own guide" and that of a more united Europe, they will have only to take a long, hard look in the mirror.

Yet consider these words of the man who, by creating the United Arab Republic and by supporting it almost beyond any apparent reason, had wiped the name of Egypt from the map. Emmanuel d'Astier once pointed out to him that "the 'UAR' does not mean much to us. But if you say 'Egypt' . . ."

" 'Egypt' means the Bible, it means the very essence of all religions," said Nasser. "I love the word 'Egypt.' "

All religions? This Muslim who was in personal touch with God, whom he saw as a kind of arbiter of good and evil rather than as a divine supervisor, did a great deal to secularize his country. It is not by chance that his most difficult battles were those with the Muslim Brethren, and that his most cruel measures were those he applied to them. For Nasser the earth and the sky did not meet. It was a matter of rendering unto God that which was God's and unto the *Raïs* that which was Caesar's.

One might say that Kemal Ataturk went much further, since he struck down even more furiously his own Muslim revival of 1922–3. But Ataturk's entire intent was different. This atheist had founded his state on the destruction of "the other power," that of the mosque. To do this he had to challenge its very principles. The divines of Egypt, long domesticated by power and modernized by thinkers like Mustafa Abdel-Razek, had not the same ubiquity of those who had resuscitated the Caliphat of Istanbul. Secular power could not be derived simply from crushing them.

Given the fact that the Muslim Brethren posed as great a threat to these Muslim doctors as did the chief of state, they preferred to ally themselves with the latter. This resulted in a conflict marked by bitter infighting, aborted attacks, and tactical retreats, which ultimately turned to the benefit of the *Raïs.*

Possibly Nasser was unable to go as far in this direction as Habib Bourguiba. A priest, the Reverend Father Henri Ayrout, one of the guiding forces behind the Christian schools of Upper Egypt, one of which, at Assiout, had been attended by Gamal's father Abdel Nasser Hussein, asked the *Raïs* about the Tunisian's achievement. "I would like to do what Bourguiba has done. But do not forget that the obstacles which he had to overcome in Tunisia were much less solid than those which I have to confront here, in the heart of Islam, at the very gate of Al-Azhar. . . ."

One might wish that Nasser had used some of the same circumspection with which he approached this question on other matters. But the virtuous "servant of the dispenser of victories" was in this respect a very modern man. One could sum up his careful and well-disguised efforts to secularize his country in much the same way that one analyst of Bonaparte's Muslim politics expressed the Corsican's thought. "It is not a matter of modernizing Islam but of Islamicizing modernity." A handsome cynicism, not very Nasserist in form, but nicely descriptive of the strategy of the UAR's founder.

In 1953, in his pamphlet-manifesto, he projected the future of Egypt into three circles, the Arab, the Islamic, and the African. The circle of his most daring and disastrous enterprises was the Arab. He never seemed to care much about the Islamic. There are many pompous lines in the *Philosophy of the Revolution* about the pilgrimage to Mecca and its political significance, and the relations which the *Raïs* maintained with the largest Muslim countries, Pakistan, Indonesia, Saudi Arabia, Iran, and Afghanistan. But he did not have a tenth of the interest in any of these countries that he had in Yugoslavia, with the possible exception of Arabia, and that was in order to thrash it. In the arguments between Karachi and New Delhi he almost always supported the Hindu state. His relations with Indonesia worsened after the defeat of Sukarno by more pious men. And the fate of the Soviet Muslims seemed to interest him only when he was in need of blackmail for the rare crises between Moscow and Cairo.

What about the African circle? I saw him at Addis-Ababa, at Accra, at Casablanca. He delivered his anti-imperialist, neutralist performance with great conviction. But the passion of the man of Suez and of the balcony in Damascus, of Aswan and even of Belgrade was not there. He was undoubtedly African, anticolonial, and aware of Continental solidarity. However, he was not "pro," but "con." Did he not choose to remain aloof from it, leaving it to Ben Bella, Nkrumah, and Nyerere? He was interested in Nigeria in 1954, having discovered, he told us with great surprise, that this country of thirty-five million souls contained an Islamic majority. He even got worked up over the Congo crisis, but rather in the same manner that he later gave his attention to events in Greece, that is to say, in order to condemn "gigantic imperialist maneuvers."

The geopolitical configuration made up of the UAR and the progressive nations of Libya and the Sudan formed by 1970 the real base of his power. But neither in Khartoum nor in Tripoli did he actively assist in the overthrow of the former regimes. And even when Mohammed Heykal went to Libya, on the day after the military coup, he met with all the men whom the *Raïs* thought important except Khadafi. When the young leader from Tripoli arrived in Cairo three days later offering to enter into a Syrian-type union—which could have been more fruitful and, on the surface, less dangerous—he received a friendly refusal. Khadafi asked for advice on how to organize single-party syndicalism at home, but was told that the experience of the UAR could not necessarily be considered a useful model. Was it Nasser's wish that Africa be the land of reason?

Had he had the time, the Egyptian *Raïs* would probably have had his African period. But the withdrawal from the Arab world, which he worked on so patiently from the January 1964 conference to its crystallization following 1967, would certainly have contributed to the introversion of Nasser's activity. The establishment of what the Arab world came to call a few months before his death "the Brezhnev-Nasser doctrine" came first and foremost. This was no matter of the right to police the socialist bloc which Nikita Khrushchev's successor had officially assumed. Nasser had been known to do this, a great deal of it even, in matters concerning "fellow states," both actual and assumed.

This Egypto-Soviet "doctrine," which seems to have been the subject of an exchange of notes between the two leaders following their meetings in January of 1970, can be summed up in the following way: the best way to build socialism is not by subversive activity and vociferous propaganda but by building the state. The definition of an effective staff is one which carries out productive work, development, and the training of personnel and of youth. It is less a question of how "red" it is than strong it is, how effective, how realistic. This doctrine approaches Kemalism, however indirectly, in a number of ways. It turns away from Chinese-type leftism, from the kind of revolutionary dynamism which Nasser had found tempting in 1961 and at the time of the Third World Conference in Cairo, and which he continued to favor until, during the quarrel at the Afro-Asian Conference in Algiers, he decided to go along with Moscow rather than Peking.

Would the "long march" of Gamal Abdel Nasser have passed through Soviet revisionism and returned to the political strategy of the *bikbashi* of 1954? Though later concerned more with efficiency than with doctrine, more with order than with justice, more with productivity than with ideology, the recurrent theme of his entire career was always service first and foremost to the Egyptian state. This theme had variations for populism, socialism, Arabism, and even internationalism.

His last months saw the *Raïs* increasingly called upon by his allies and by the vicissitudes of history to "come home" in order to strengthen it and to make it more sound. The temptation was urgent. The crowd at the funeral did not reach out to Gamal Abdel Nasser merely to assert its claim on the leader who had presented himself as its very incarnation. They buried him in their Egyptian earth, his earth. Born of Egypt, to Egypt he returned.

The circle closed, but what did it contain? The coup of July 23, Bandung, Suez, Damascus, Algeria, the laws of 1961 and of 1969 are history. But what are the results, the fruits of Nasserism, that risky voyage upon the high sea of years?

Was it only a great adventure? Was it only a failed revolution? Was it only a heroic transition from the reign of the clown-king to that of the average man, performing out the day-to-day routine as a delegate of banality? Was this all that really happened between the first Black Saturday to the sumptuous funeral of October 1, 1970?

The adventuresome Arabism, the quasi-socialism, the state itself may not survive those eighteen years, but Egypt will always have a sense of dignity, a spirit of modernism, and a consciousness of universality.

"Raise up your head, my brother, the days of humiliation have passed." These words were repeated for months in the streets of downtown Cairo, which were occupied for so long by the khawagas, foreigners by origin, sympathy, and customs. It was 1953, a time when, if one is to believe Robert St. John, Cairenes would turn to their friends and say: "This Nasser's got guts! He must have a little Turkish blood in his veins."

The reconstruction of the outward appearance of Egyptian dignity did not take place without setbacks. It was not exactly dignified to colonize Syria, nor to shout oneself hoarse against Israel. It was even less so to evade the consequences of an unfortunate conflict. But such are the fortunes of a responsible people: every free people has its Sedan, its Yorktown, its Caporetto.

Gamal was not, despite his name, a "dispenser of victories." It has been pointed out all too often that, quite the contrary, he spent his life dispensing disasters. If he was a political chess player he was often in check. But he made fun of the game as one makes fun of an adversary—ridiculing him, denying his existence in order to catch him off guard. This technique would have been only that of a febrile conjuror if it had not a means of regaining dignity. To deny defeat is also to permit continuity. Was it madness? Perhaps it was, but a people imprisoned in its valley, ruled from abroad, and internally sapped by hunger has little indeed if it has not the right to a little madness. This is the meaning of the Alexandria speech. It is Nasser's unique contribution.

But his challenge was neither maniacal nor suicidal. It was essential that the Egyptians remain standing—not struck down like Arabi or muzzled like Zaghloul. It was necessary that they grasp the instruments of control without being controlled by them. And this was what he did so decisively in Suez; the canal was taken over, controlled, enlarged, rehabilitated, it was "an Egyptian canal in the hands of the Egyptians" as the crowd was told in Alexandria on July 26, 1956.

It is less Nasser who was responsible for eleven years of good and fruitful management—interrupted by the follies of 1967—than Mahmud Yunis, the chief of the "corsair commandos" of the July 26 nationalization, who became the genial director and self-confident heir to the best engineers in the Western world. But even this demonstration of the ability of Egyptian staffs to manage imported technology was made possible by Gamal Abdel Nasser.

"Raise up your head, my brother, the days of technical ineptitude are over!"—the days when this people existed only to be guides to the Pyramids, makers of water jugs, Nubian porters, and water-carriers. Abdu and Mohsen and Hassan had at last entered the industrial era.

But was it necessary, in order for the new technology to achieve full value and meaning, that the man who gave it a miraculous character disappear? Despite a history of managers and engineers from Talaat Harb to Ismail Sedky and from Ahmed Abbud to Ali Shamsi, technical success still seemed a trick of the great sorcerer, of the *magnatis*. After Gamal's disappearance, Nasserian modernity would fit into Egyptian history more naturally.

Would post-Nasserism resemble the shrinking of the Nile, the retreat of the river to its bed? Would it mean a return to provincialism, the end of mighty aspirations? What Nasser discovered, during his long effort, is that interventionism is not universalism, and that incessant plotting against other powers does not constitute a revolution. But he also showed that there can be no revolutionary undertaking, no liberation effort, no self-mastery even, without the participation of others.

Gamal Abdel Nasser did not establish socialism in his country; he did not make his syndicalism viable; and he did not grant the average Egyptian his true liberation—because there can be no socialism in one country alone, no syndicalism which relies on the power of the state, no true liberation within the boundaries of a single nation. But his failures point, perhaps more clearly than his successes, to the road ahead. His nationalism, which struggled so hard for self-affirmation, discovered, if not for itself, at least for others, and for its successors, the liberating strength of solidarity, or, to quote Jacques Berque, "the unity of man through resentment."[6]

This excessive power in the Arab world, in the Near East, and especially in Egypt, obscured his creative contribution. Now that he was gone, they appeared. His openly tyrannical manner gave way at last to his liberating force. The national movement which he had seized control of could expand once more.

One month after the death of the *Raïs,* the leader of the new government in Cairo, Mahmud Fawzi, declared to Nasser's closest confidant, Mohammed Hassanein Heykal: "We must expend a great deal of energy on domestic problems in order for foreign relations to improve. I have spent my entire

[6] *Le Nouvel Observateur,* October 12, 1970.

life in this thought: the foreign reflects the domestic." And the former minister of the *Raïs,* openly longing for what was referred to in Italy twenty years ago as *"l'uomo qualunque"* —an ordinary man—defined his own concept of power: "It is necessary to review the relationship between the individual and the state," he said, "because a people which does not participate ends up a spectator."[7] Was this a shot in the dark or an echo of his longings? Was it a longing for a new, more ordinary leader, whoever he might be, or simply for the restoration of dignity to the Egyptian electorate?

Thus the heritage of Gamal Abdel Nasser takes on a shape approximating ordinary reality, more interiorized, more workaday. The leader who, in Ibrahim Farhi's words, "being unable to solve the problems of Egypt, chose to incarnate them," gave way to ordinary men who, being unable to incarnate them, will have to try, with the example of his successes and the lesson of his failures, to solve them.

[7] *Le Monde,* November 7, 1970.

BIBLIOGRAPHY

AND

INDEX

Bibliography

Abdel Malek, Anwar: *Egypte, société militaire*. Paris, 1962.
——: *La Pensée politique arabe contemporaine*. Paris, 1970.
Aboul Fath, Ahmed: *L'Affaire Nasser*. Paris, 1961.
Ammar, Hamed: *Growing Up in an Egyptian Village*. Oxford, n.d.
Aron, Robert: *Nouveaux Dossiers de l'histoire contemporaine*. Paris, 1971.
Ayrout, Henri Habib: *Fellah d'Egypte*. Alexandria, 1953.
Barawi, Rached: *The Military Coup in Egypt*. Cairo, 1952.
Benoist-Méchin, Jacques: *Un Printemps arabe*. Paris, 1963.
Berger, Morroe: *Bureaucracy and Society in Modern Egypt*. Princeton, N.J., 1957.
Berque, Jacques: *Les Arabes d'hier à demain*. Paris, 1960.
——: *L'Egypte, impérialisme et révolution*. Paris, 1967.
Besançon, Julien: *Bazak*. Paris, 1967.
Beeri, Eliezer: *Army Officers in Arab Politics and Society*. New York, 1970.
Copeland, Miles: *The Game of Nations*. New York, 1969.
Cromer, Lord: *Modern Egypt*, 2 vols. London, 1908.
Eden, Anthony: *Mémoires*. Paris, 1960.
Estier, Claude: *L'Egypte en révolution*. Paris, 1965.
Finer, S. E.: *The Man on Horseback: The Role of the Military in Politics*. London, 1962.
Fromont, Pierre: *L'Agriculture égyptienne et ses problèmes*. Paris, 1955.
Gibb, H. A. R.: *Les Tendances modernes de l'Islam*. Paris, 1949.

Glubb, John Bagot: *A Soldier with the Arabs.* London, 1957.

Greitly, Ali: *The Structure of Modern Industry in Egypt.* Cairo, 1947.

Haim, Sylvia G.: *Arab Nationalism, an Anthology.* New York, 1964.

Hamon, Léo: *Le Rôle extra-militaire de l'armée dans le Tiers Monde,* an anthology. Paris, 1965.

Henein, Georges: "Inventaire contre le désespoir," in *Etudes méditerranéennes.* Paris, 1957.

Heyworth-Dunne, J.: *Religious and Political Trends in Modern Egypt.* Washington, D.C., 1950.

Hourani, Albert: *Arabic Thought in the Liberal Age.* London, 1962.

Huntington, Samuel P.: *Changing Patterns of Military Politics.* Glencoe, Ill., 1962.

Hurewitz, J. C.: *Middle-East Politics, the Military Dimension.* New York, 1969.

Hussein, Mahmud, *La Lutte des classes en Egypte de 1945 à 1968.* Paris, 1969, 1971.

Issawi, Charles: *Egypt in Revolution.* London, 1963.

Joesten, Joachim: *Nasser, the Rise to Power.* London, 1960.

Kerr, Malcolm: *The Arab Cold War, 1958–1964.* London, 1965.

Kocheri, Afaf: "Socialisme et pouvoir en Egypte," doctoral dissertation. Paris, 1967.

Lacoste, Yves: *Ibn Khaldoun: Naissance de l'histoire—passé du Tiers-Monde.* Paris, 1966.

Lacouture, Jean: *Quatre Hommes et leurs peuples* (thèse de troisième cycle). Paris, 1969.

Lacouture, Jean and Simonne: *L'Egypte en mouvement.* Paris, 1956–1962.

Lacouture, Simonne: *Egypte,* in Petite Planète series. Paris, 1962–69.

———: "Le Gel de la culture en Egypte," *Esprit,* April 1969.

Laqueur, Walter Z.: *Communism and Nationalism in the Middle-East.* London, 1956.

———: *The Soviet Union and the Middle-East.* London, 1959.

Lerner, Daniel: *The Passing of Traditional Society.* Glencoe, Ill., 1958.

Little, Tom: *Egypt.* London, 1958.

Lloyd, Lord: *Egypt Since Cromer.* London, 1929.

Makarius, Raoul: *La Jeunesse intellectuelle d'Egypte au lendemain de la deuxième guerre mondiale.* Paris, 1960.

Mandelstam, Jean: *"La Palestine dans la politique de Gamal Abdel Nasser, 1952–1955,"* doctoral dissertation. Paris, 1970.

Mansfield, Peter: *Nasser's Egypt.* Harmondsworth, Eng., 1967.

————: *Nasser.* Harmondsworth, Eng., 1970.

Marei, Sayed: *La Réforme agraire.* Cairo, 1955.

Naguib, Mohammed: *Egypt's Destiny.* London, 1955.

Nasser, Gamal Abdel: *La Philosophie de la révolution.* Cairo, 1954.

————: *Recueils de discours.* Cairo, n.d.

Rodinson, Maxime: *Islam et capitalisme.* Paris, 1966.

————: *Israël et le refus arabe.* Paris, 1968.

Riad, Hassan: *L'Egypte nassérienne.* Paris, 1964.

Rouleau, E., J.-F. Held, and J. and S. Lacouture: *Israël et les Arabes, le 3e combat.* Paris, 1967.

Russel Pasha (Sir Th. W.): *Egyptian Service, 1902–1946.* London, 1949.

Saab, Edouard: *La Syrie ou la révolution dans la rancoeur.* Paris, 1968.

Saab, Gabriel: *The Egyptian Agrarian Reform, 1952–1962.* London, 1967.

Sadat, Anwar el-: *Revolt on the Nile.* London and Paris, 1957.

Safran, Nadav: *Egypt in Search of Political Community.* Cambridge, Mass., 1961.

St. John, Robert: *The Boss.* New York, 1960.

Trevelyan, Sir Humphrey: *The Middle-East in Revolution.* London, 1970.

————: *Conversation from Cairo to Baghdad.* London, 1970.

Vailland, Roger: *Choses vues en Egypte, août 1952.* Paris, 1952.

Vatikiotis, P. J.: *The Egyptian Army in Politics.* Bloomington, Ind., 1961.

Vaucher, Georges: *Gamal Abdel Nasser et son équipe,* 2 vols. Paris, 1959.

Weit, Erwin: *Ostblock Intern.* Hamburg, 1970.

Wheelock, Keith: *Nasser's New Egypt.* New York, 1960.

Wynn, Wilton: *Nasser of Egypt.* New York, 1959.

Index

INDEX

Hart, Liddell, 50, 366; *Foch,* 43;
*The History of the War of 1914–
1918,* 43
Hassan, Abdel Fattah, 80
Hassan II, King of Morocco, 143,
307, 331
Hatem, Abdelkader, 355
Hawatmeh, Naief, 338
Haydar, Gen. Mohammed, 71, 81,
93, 101, 104, 136
Hekki, Hekki Ismail, 198
Helou, Charles, 296
Helou, Ferjallah, 248
Henderson, Loy, 191
Hewidi, Amin el-, 362, 375
Heykal, Hussein, 127
Heykal, Mohammed Hassanein, 83–4
and *n.,* 87–8, 144, 197, 214, 235,
257, 293, 308, 316, 320, 336,
347, 348–50, 358, 362, 368,
369–71, 372–3, 375, 380, 385–6,
389, 393
Hilali, Naguib el-, 29, 91, 92, 97
Hilmi, Abbas, 3, 217
Hilmi, Yussef, 229
Hoare, Sir Samuel, 30, 33
Hod, General, 308
Hourani, Akram, 289, 294
Humphrey, Hubert, 307
Husri, Sati el-, 182, 183
Hussein, King of Jordan, 140, 143,
165, 294, 307, 309, 328, 342–3,
349, 353, 363, 385
Hussein, Adel, 24
Hussein, Ahmed, 31–2, 35, 55, 58,
72, 83, 87
Hussein, Ahmed, 165
Hussein, Attia, 24
Hussein, Kamaleddin, 57, 66, 68,
69, 72, 95, 98, 109 *n.,* 241, 243,
263, 266
Hussein, Mahmud, 84 and *n.,* 239,
250–1
Hussein, Salah, 257
Hussein, Taha, 16, 183
Hussein, Tewfik, 54
Husseini, Haj Amin el-, 59, 262–3

Ibn Khaldun, *Ibn Khaldoun: Nas-
sance de l'histoire passé du Tiers-
Monde,* 11 and *n.*
Ibrahim, Hassan, 47, 69, 77 and *n.,*
95, 109 *n.*
Ibrahim, Zaghloul, 23
Ibrahim Pasha, 182, 186
Ikasha, Saroit, 65
Illah, Prince Abdul, 192
India, 175, 209, 277, 302, 388
Indonesia, 159, 388
International Bank, 163–4, 228,
232, 254
International Convention of Con-
stantinople, 171, 272
Iran, 154, 189, 388
Iraq, 192, 193, 197, 198, 205, 224,
261, 287; and Baghdad Pact, 153,
155; revolt in, 200–2, 226, 227,
248; Communists of, 201, 248;
and Israel, 290, 307
Islam, 12, 189–90, 215, 238, 383,
387–8
Ismail, the Khedive, 8, 164
Ismail, Hafez, 41 *n.*
Ismailia, Egypt, 67, 79, 81, 169,
170, 173, 314
Israel, 122, 124, 158, 164, 175,
187, 188–9, 192, 249, 263, 267–
315, 322–42, 391; and Zionism,
59, 264, 265, 274–5, 279–80,
289, 294, 335, 360, 365; and
Palestine War, 60–7, 263–6, 283;
Haganah of, 63, 66, 264, 265;
raids of, 156, 179–80, 275–6,
278, 279, 294, 308, 321, 327,
330, 333; and nationalization of
Suez Canal, 167, 172, 175 *n.,* 177,
181, 286; and Six-Day War, 205,
294, 308–10; and Syria, 273,
290, 292–4, 295–6, 298, 299,
303, 307, 334; raids against,
275–6, 278, 294; and peace
negotiations, 284–6, 288, 296,
303, 323–8, 330, 333–6, 339,
341, 342; and return of territory
occupied by, 288, 314, 324–6,